Ornaments and Other Ambiguous Artifacts from Franchthi

Excavations at Franchthi Cave, Greece

FASCICLE 15

Ornaments and Other Ambiguous Artifacts from Franchthi

VOLUME I
The Palaeolithic and the Mesolithic

CATHERINE PERLÈS

With an Appendix by André C. Colonese

INDIANA UNIVERSITY PRESS

This book is a publication of

Indiana University Press
Office of Scholarly Publishing
Herman B Wells Library 350
1320 East 10th Street
Bloomington, Indiana 47405 USA

iupress.indiana.edu

Manufactured in the United States of America

Cataloging information is available from the Library of Congress.

ISBN 978-0-253-03184-6 (pbk.)
ISBN 978-0-253-03185-3 (web PDF)
ISBN 978-0-253-03488-5 (print PDF)

1 2 3 4 5 23 22 21 20 19 18

CONTENTS

ORNAMENTS AND ORNAMENTAL SHELLS OF THE MESOLITHIC

APPENDICES

TABLES

In the Text

In the Appendices

FIGURES

In the Text

In the Appendices

PLATES

PROLOGUE

This book is devoted to the study of small artifacts that archaeologists commonly label 'ornaments'. In the case of the Palaeolithic and Mesolithic assemblages from Franchthi, this interpretation is supported by the discovery of similar perforated shells, belonging to the same species, in several Upper Palaeolithic and Mesolithic burials elsewhere in Europe. Perforated shells were strung together as bracelets and necklaces, and adorned various garments such as cloaks, jackets, headdresses and loincloths.

Palaeolithic and Mesolithic human burials do not all yield ornaments, but their presence in burials does not come as a surprise: perforated shells are the earliest 'ornaments' known in Prehistory and were in use long before the Upper Palaeolithic. This last period witnessed an extraordinary increase in the variety, frequency and number of ornaments, testifying to both the taste for personal adornment of Upper Palaeolithic hunter-gatherers and the importance of symbolic systems of communication. In this context, it seems logical that some at least of the deceased would have been buried with their personal ornaments or embroidered garments.

However, Upper Palaeolithic ornaments are mostly known from non-funerary contexts: residential camps, aggregation sites or, more rarely, hunting camps. The large number of publications devoted to these ancient ornaments reflects their sheer abundance and the keen interest they have piqued among prehistoric archaeologists. We therefore know in detail how they were manufactured, how, as valuables, they were traded over very long distances, how they have been used to define ethno-linguistic groups, and how they may have functioned as systems of communication. There is one question, however, that to my knowledge has rarely been addressed: why should we find ornaments in great quantities at sites or within occupational levels without human burials, other than to please the specialists in prehistoric ornaments?

Obviously, every bracelet or necklace, whether prehistoric or modern, can break, and even if one seeks to recover the beads, some are bound to be lost. Finding the odd bead or pendant in a residential site can thus be easily explained as an accidental loss. How do we account, however, for ornament assemblages of hundreds of specimens, including many that are unperforated? Why were they left behind, even at sites located hundreds of kilometres from the their original sources? The answer certainly varies from site to site, and I make no pretence of having solved this general problem. However, in the case of Franchthi, behind the formally articulated research questions that have guided fieldwork and analyses, this nagging question has always been in my mind and was perhaps the main problem I wished to understand.

PREFACE

The Franchthi ornament assemblages have had a rather chaotic history. When the site was still being excavated, between 1967 and 1979, T. W. Jacobsen, director of the Franchthi project, entrusted their study to Peg Schaeffer. She mostly focussed on the Neolithic *Cerastoderma glaucum* bead production, but did not publish her results (Schaeffer, manuscript on file). In parallel, Judith Shackleton, in the course of her study of marine molluscan remains from Franchthi, recorded shell ornaments and devoted a short chapter of her monograph to the 'Non-Utilitarian Use of Marine Shells at Franchthi Cave' (Shackleton J. 1988). She also provided a list of all catalogued specimens, dating mostly to the Neolithic. A few years later, Michele A. Miller prepared a PhD dissertation on the ornaments from Franchthi and Sitagroi, which she submitted at Boston University (Miller 1997). T. W. Jacobsen offered her the responsibility for the final publication of the Franchthi ornaments, as one of the fascicles of the "Excavations at Franchthi Cave" series, published by Indiana University Press. The text and tables of this thorough work were completed many years ago, but the book lacked illustrations and was never published.

Years passed, and the 'Franchthi board' entrusted me to prepare a final synthesis of the Franchthi excavations. As I was working on the Mesolithic, I became perplexed by Shackleton's observation that many Mesolithic *Cyclope neritea* shells were perforated, and by her suggestion they may have been used as ornaments after having been eaten (Shackleton J. 1988: 39). I had no idea what a *Cyclope* looked like, but, as a French student of Claude Lévi-Strauss, I had retained that 'what is good to be eaten is not good to be thought about, and what is good to be thought about is not good to be eaten'. This was very different from what Lévi-Strauss actually wrote[1], but my misinterpretation was fruitful: it led me to wonder about Shackleton's interpretation, and to feel the need for further investigation. I thus decided to go back to the Franchthi storerooms at Nafplion, and to take a personal look at these *Cyclope neritea*. My first meeting with the snails—both the archaeological ones stored in bags and live ones from smelly lagoons—took place in 2005. I quickly became convinced that *Cyclope neritea* could not be eaten—in particular because the snails are too small—and that they had instead been exclusively used as ornaments. I realized on the same occasion that other Mesolithic shell ornaments deserved to be studied in more detail: the bags of shells contained numerous perforated dove shells (*Columbella rustica*), which had been mentioned as an ornamental species by Shackleton, but with no description or counts of perforated specimens. The situation was similar for *Antalis* (= *Dentalium*) sp., or tusk shells, which were far more numerous in Mesolithic levels than the monograph suggested. It was clear that this exceptionally large assemblage deserved more than brief mentions in a volume mostly devoted to shellfish. K. D. Vitelli, who had by then taken the responsibility for the Franchthi project, suggested that I write an article, which I agreed to do. The next summer, while working on Mesolithic shell assemblages, I suddenly wondered whether similar ornaments had not been overlooked in the Palaeolithic. Preliminary tests revealed the presence of numerous unrecorded Palaeolithic shell ornaments, even in the lowermost excavated deposits dating to the very beginning of the Upper Palaeolithic, when no shellfish were collected.

I had not by then envisioned that Neolithic perforated shells were also awaiting study in the shell bags: I believed at the time that all the Neolithic ornaments had been catalogued, including the hundreds of *Cerastoderma glaucum* beads, blanks and preforms studied by P. Schaeffer and M.

Miller. However, the massive quantities of Palaeolithic and Mesolithic ornaments that we retrieved, mixed with land snails and shellfish, eventually led me to check Neolithic shell bags. Hundreds of ornamental shells again came to light, and this radically changed the perception of the Franchthi Neolithic ornament assemblages, considered until then to be dominated by geometric beads and pendants.

At this stage, it became obvious that the study and publication of the Franchthi ornaments would be a major undertaking, even if one could rely on M. Miller's analysis of the catalogued specimens. It could not be a single scholar's project, but required funding and the constitution of a working team. I was not a specialist in ornaments, and M. Miller was no longer free for field studies. I thus asked Marian Vanhaeren, (CNRS, UMR PACEA) already well known for her expertise on Palaeolithic ornaments, to collaborate and share responsibility for the project. Sandrine Bonnardin (University of Nice) joined the team a few years later as a specialist in Neolithic ornaments. She was in charge of the high-magnification studies and the documentation of manufacturing and wear traces, which M. Miller could not implement when working for her dissertation.

We were helped by several colleagues and doctoral students, who spent days and weeks sorting the bags of shells and recording the ornamental specimens: Patrick Pion (University Paris Ouest), who took charge of the dove shells and *Cerastoderma* bead production, Julien Beck (University of Geneva), who specialised in questioning all our assumptions—including the fact of calling what we studied 'ornaments', André Colonese (University of York) who checked our molluscan identifications and identified all the micromolluscs from the smaller sieves, Séverin Ménard (Université Paris Ouest), who, together with his father, devised ingenious systems to take macrophotographs, Arnaud Contentin (presently Secretary of the École Française d'Athènes), Arnaud Blin (Conservateur du Patrimoine), and Mercedes Maya-Pion (Inrap).

The publication of the Franchthi ornaments was originally conceived as a single fascicle in the 'Franchthi Excavations' series. However, the analysis of the Palaeolithic and Mesolithic collections, and of our rich reference collections, were, by themselves long enough to be published as a single volume, without the further delays that the inclusion of the Neolithic would have entailed. In addition, the Palaeolithic and Mesolithic assemblages, mostly composed of perforated shells, are entirely different from the varied Neolithic assemblages, which comprise a great many geometric beads and pendants made from stone, clay and shell. The latter require a completely different analytical approach from the Palaeolithic and Mesolithic perforated shells, making the division into two volumes scientifically legitimate.

While fieldwork was a collective enterprise, this first volume ended up being written by a single author. Marian Vanhaeren had completed considerable work on the Palaeolithic and Mesolithic assemblages: she instituted the systematic scanning of the finds, removed the backgrounds on countless scans, and, above all, took hundreds of macro-photographs to document manufacturing and use-wear traces. Writing this volume should have been a joint venture, if Marian hadn't been too taken up by other commitments. It is nevertheless very much the result of our collaboration: I have made ample use of the many graphic documents she had provided, not only to illustrate the volume, but, more fundamentally, as analytical tools. Patrick Pion, who was also to collaborate on the sections devoted to dove shells, was promoted to a demanding and time-consuming position before he could participate in the publication. Patrick and Marian only fully withdrew from the project when the manuscript was well advanced, hence the plural used in most chapters. I decided to retain this plural as a testimony to the collective discussions we all had during fieldwork, or back in Nanterre with Patrick. Nevertheless, I bear entire responsibility for the interpretations and hypotheses developed here, and none of my colleagues can be considered responsible for my intellectual vagaries.

Like any other long-term project, the project "35,000 years of personal ornaments at Franchthi" owes a lot to several friends, colleagues and institutions and it is a pleasure to acknowledge their support. From 2006 to 2010, fieldwork was funded by grants from the INSTAP, for which I am especially grateful, and by a four-year grant from the French Agence Nationale de la Recherche (ANR-06-Blan-0273). Study facilities were provided in the storage building of the 4th Ephorate of Prehistoric and Classical Antiquities of the Greek Ministry of Culture, the Leonardo. We are especially grateful to have been given, until recently, free access to the Franchthi storerooms: this project could simply not have been undertaken and completed otherwise. Reorganization of the storerooms was made possible by a generous grant from the E. A. Schrader Endowment at Indiana University, which was critical for the completion of the project. The American School of Classical Studies in Athens efficiently handled the working permits and export permits, while its Director, Prof. J. Wright, did his best to facilitate our work.

I, and I would say the Franchthi project as a whole, are deeply indebted to Hélène Valladas (CNRS and CEA, LSCE/IPSL) and to Katerina Douka (Research Laboratory for Archaeology and the History of Art, University of Oxford). Both kindly decided to include some Franchthi samples in their 14C research programs. They provided the first AMS dates for Franchthi, in several cases of high scientific importance. Similarly, Ina Reiche and Katarina Lange (CNRS, C2RMF) devoted many weeks analysing blackened experimental and archaeological *Cyclope neritea* to determine the origin and conditions of the change in colour. Evi Pardala-Theodorou of The Goulandris Museum of Natural History kindly came to Nafplion several times to help with some problematic shell identifications and her husband George Theodorou opened up lively discussions on the origins of the shells and snails found in the Franchthi archaeological deposits.

Very special thanks to Karen D. Vitelli, responsible for the Franchthi project, who did not hesitate (or maybe she did?) to entrust the responsibility for the publication of ornaments to a lithic specialist. Special thanks also to Fotis Ifantidis, who removed the background of countless *Cyclope* and *Columbella* scans. Not only did he not complain, he even pretended he enjoyed doing this! Solange Rigaud kindly accepted to review the manuscript and opened up, in her discussion, exciting prospects that we shall both try to follow. Thank you also to Julie Devaux, who took responsibility for the laying-out of the manuscript, and did not hesitate to send me back to my computer for what she considered as sloppy illustrations!

I also want to express my deep gratitude to my collaborators, who did not always understand why they should spend endless hours scanning and measuring quasi-identical shells, which were not even all perforated. I can assure them, now that I have worked on these documents, that their work was not in vain and that it proved to be extremely useful and informative. Finally, a big thanks to our friends the Zotos brothers, who managed to keep us smiling and happy even during some rather tense episodes!

NOTES

1   "Les espèces [totémiques] ne sont pas choisies parce que "bonnes à manger" mais parce que "bonnes à penser" (Lévi-Strauss 1962: 128).

CHAPTER ONE

Goals and Methods

What Do We Study? An Ambiguous and Probably Heterogeneous Set of Artifacts

The title of this volume includes the term 'ornament', and I have already used it without restriction, as though it posed no problem and as though ornaments, as we commonly understand them, could easily be defined in an archaeological context. However, when applied to prehistoric artifacts, the term is laden with ambiguity. As a consequence, what we should include in our study and how we ought to call the material we were studying has been much debated among our team. The term 'ornament' (in French 'ornement' or 'parure') presents the disadvantage of being already interpretative. It presupposes a function—to adorn—while the category of artifacts that archaeologists usually group under this generic term is notoriously polysemic. It potentially includes not only ornaments *sensu stricto*, but also talismans, amulets, prophylactic and ritual objects, valuables to be exchanged, etc. (Vanhaeren 2010: 7-17; Vanhaeren & d'Errico 2011). In addition, beyond their aesthetic role, ornaments are also, or perhaps primarily, means of conveying information on gender, social status, age-sets and life cycles (Sciama & Eicher 1998). To add to the difficulty, ornaments are not restricted to the human body or human garments, but are often displayed on valuable—and sometimes not so valuable—objects. As stated by Vialou (1981: 393) when discussing the 'ornaments' from Kitsos Cave (Attica), "le matériel de parure de la grotte de Kitsos n'échappe pas à l'indétermination de la notion de parure. (...) Le matériel archéologique accumulé au cours des fouilles et décrit comme éléments de parure est hétérogène: les objets de parure ne ressortissant pas d'une preoccupation unique comme la fabrication d'outils, se réfèrent à des idées, à des pulsions, à des sentiments difficilement classifiables et souvent même indécelables".

To avoid implicit preconceived interpretations, an alternative to the use of the term 'ornaments' is the use of more descriptive terms, such as 'beads' or 'pendants'. These terms are relatively well defined, and they apply easily to entirely manufactured artifacts. They do not, *per se*, presuppose a specific function or meaning. Even then, however, some ambiguity remains. 'Shell beads' or 'shell pendants' are often used indiscriminately for beads and pendants manufactured from shell, and for entire shells only modified by perforation (e.g. Bar-Yosef Mayer 2013). In addition, these terms specifically refer to finished artifacts, while our study encompasses the whole production and use *chaîne opératoire*, and includes raw materials, unperforated shells, unfinished artifacts and finished artifacts that do not answer the definition of beads and pendants. In order to designate the whole assemblage under study, a more inclusive term is therefore required.

In the end, I retained the term 'ornament' for lack of a better option. It is not used in the interpretative sense, referring to artifacts that were necessarily 'ornamental', but as *an archaeological category* that encompasses many small, often perforated objects not known to have any other utilitarian function (Laporte 2009: 450). The term ornament allows us to take into consideration 'ornamental shell species' as a whole, and not just perforated specimens. Contrary to the French 'parure', it presents the additional advantage of not being restricted to (human) personal ornaments, but can also refer to the ornamentation of garments and objects.

However, neither this large and rather vague definition of 'ornaments' as a whole, nor the more specific definition of 'ornamental shells species', eliminate all problems. There remains a number of pieces or groups of pieces whose status—ornament, tool, container, ritual object, aesthetic item, etc., is uncertain. The problem is especially acute for the Neolithic assemblages, but we shall meet it also for some Palaeolithic and Mesolithic artifacts, despite the presence of a perforation[1]. Symmetrically, ornaments are not always perforated: the Mesolithic carp teeth attached to garments with glue and tendons from Vlasac in Serbia (Cristiani & Borić 2012; Cristiani *et al.* 2014a) and Hohlenstein-Stadel in Germany (Rigaud *et al.* 2014a) were neither perforated nor grooved. Not all ornaments are recognisable as such in a prehistoric context. For instance, the Neolithic assemblages from Franchthi contain a number of unperforated, finely crafted artifacts, not known to have any utilitarian function, such as *Spondylus* discs or rods. Should these be considered as 'ornaments', even within a broad and generous definition? The absence of documented adorned Palaeolithic, Mesolithic and Neolithic burials in Greece adds to the difficulty: unlike what can be done in other regions with richly adorned burials, we cannot refer to burials from the same cultural contexts to ascertain the use of what we tend or wish to consider as ornaments.

I thus chose to include in our study not only the small perforated beads and pendants that fit the archaeological definition of 'ornaments', but also a number of artifacts that may or may not fit this definition, but deserve to be discussed. All together, they represent an exceptionally rich collection of more than 12,000 specimens, which, even if their emic meaning remains uncertain, offers to the scientist extremely rich research perspectives.

A Resolutely Diachronic Perspective

When Marian Vanhaeren and I designed this project, we had only a very vague—and vastly underestimated—idea of the quantity and variety of ornaments that were awaiting us in the 'Leonardo's' storerooms of the Napfplion Archaeological Museum. On the other hand, we had a clear idea of the scientific issues we wanted to address, and how to address them.

Ornaments are well known as a hallmark of fully modern behaviour and as a non-verbal means of communication (Bar-Yosef Mayer *et al.* 2009; d'Errico & Vanhaeren 2009; d'Errico *et al.* 2005; Kuhn 2014; Kuhn *et al.* 2001; Kuhn & Stiner 2006, 2007; Stiner 2014; Vanhaeren 2005; Vanhaeren *et al.* 2013; Zilhão 2007). They are used simultaneously to indicate status differentiation within a group—in terms of age, gender, hierarchy, social role, power—and as symbols of the group's identity vis-à-vis neighbouring communities (e.g., Kuhn *et al.* 2001; Sciama & Eicher 1998; Vanhaeren 2010; Vanhaeren & d'Errico 2005; Wiessner 1982). Because of their social value, beads and pendants are also often exchanged over long distances (Godelier 1996; Marshall 1998; Taborin 1993, 2003), and the geographic distribution of exogenous ornaments is a good witness to social interaction networks.

Most previous studies relating to Palaeolithic and Mesolithic ornaments focussed on one or several of these aspects, and, logically, from mainly synchronic approaches: production of the ornaments (Cristiani & Borić 2012; Cristiani *et al.* 2014a, 2014b; Taborin 1993; White 1993, 2004, 2007), identification of interaction networks (Bar-Yosef Mayer 1997; Cristiani & Borić 2012; Komšo & Vukosavljević 2011; Rähle 1978; Whallon 2006), identification of cultural or linguistic groups (Newell *et al.* 1990; Rigaud 2011; Rigaud *et al.* 2014a; Rigaud *et al.* 2015; Taborin 2003, 2004; Vanhaeren & d'Errico 2006), and investigation of social differentiation (O'Shea & Zvelebil 1984; Vanhaeren & d'Errico 2005; White 1999).

Less attention had been paid to the long-term transformations of ornament assemblages, either from a general perspective (Taborin 1993) or from specific contexts. When this project was initiated, the few publications concerning ornaments from long archaeological sequences were mostly descriptive. Problems such as the relationship between environmental transformations and the choice of ornaments, the relationship between the design, production and use of ornaments and changing socioeconomic systems, or the relationship between the composition of the human groups and the nature of the ornaments, largely remained to be investigated. More recent synthetic approaches have, since then, shed light on some of these questions (Bar-Yosef Mayer 2010, 2014; Colonese *et al.* 2010; Rigaud 2011; Stiner 2014). New and important diachronic sequences have also been published with more comprehensive perspectives: Üçağızlı in Eastern Turkey (Stiner 2003; Stiner *et al.* 2013), Klissoura Cave 1 in Greece (Stiner 2010), Vela Spila in Croatia (Cristiani *et al.* 2014b).

None of these sites, however, provides a sequence spanning from the beginning of the Upper Palaeolithic to the end of the Mesolithic, much less to the Neolithic. Franchthi thus offered a unique opportunity to study transformations in ornament assemblages over more than 30 millennia, in a well-documented context that witnessed important environmental and economic transformations. Indeed, behind the deceptive permanence of the cave, many changes took place in its status, in the composition of the groups visiting or inhabiting it, in how they exploited the immediate environment and how they produced their tools and hunting equipment (Perlès 2010, 2016a). It thus seemed logical to expect concomitant transformations in the ornaments, pertaining to the choice of types, the procurement strategies, the organization of production and the techniques utilised. How ornament assemblages were transformed through time and how these transformations related to environmental and socioeconomic changes was thus the initial focus of our research project.

The Multiple Facets of Palaeolithic and Mesolithic Shells Ornaments

Preliminary investigation into Palaeolithic and Mesolithic ornament assemblages from Franchthi had shown that perforated shells were largely predominant. Franchthi being a coastal site where shellfish was exploited, a clear distinction had to be made between shellfish and ornamental shells. We shall follow here Stiner and colleagues' definition:

> "The term 'ornamental shell' is used in this study to distinguish one broad category of mollusc shells from two others, namely the residues of edible shellfish consumed at the site and the remains of land snails that were native to the cave. Because ornaments are items of technology, their definition must be sufficiently inclusive to permit both the exploration of production stages and consideration of the raw materials transported to the site. Classifying a shell specimen as ornamental thus acknowledges the potential presence of un-worked material at the site, which may have been rejected, cached, or forgotten. We stipulate, however, that unaltered specimens may be considered 'ornamental' material only if they were collected and transported deliberately by humans and fall within a type that was used exclusively for ornament-making and never as food." (Stiner *et al.* 2013: 383).

Albeit less elaborate than geometric beads or pendants[2], perforated shells present the particular interest of being at the interface between several ontological spheres: biological and environmental, technical and symbolic. The biological and technical spheres in particular entail many potential factors of variability that must be taken into account before concluding in favour of 'cultural' or 'symbolic' changes in ornament assemblages. We thus considered it essential to approach these shells primarily as natural species on the one hand, and as artifacts on the other.

Ornamental Shells as Natural Species

Three aspects of shells as biological species may induce variations that are relevant from a diachronic perspective: the relative availability of different shell species should vary according to climatically-induced environmental transformations, the shells are expected to reflect the natural morphometric and colour variability of all living populations, and the conditions of collection—location, ease, techniques—vary according to the taxon.

Climatically induced transformations affect water temperatures and the conditions of growth of marine molluscs, while the correlated changes in sea level modify the morphology of the coast and the habitats of the molluscs. We shall only allude to the first aspect here since we lack data on temperature requirements of the different taxa represented at Franchthi. In contrast, we can rely on the pioneering investigations of the palaeomorphology of Koildaha bay to reconstruct coastal paleoenvironments at different periods of the past, to estimate the potential availability of various shell taxa and compare the potential to the actual spectrum represented in the archaeological assemblages (Chap. 2 and 9).

The two other aspects, morphometric variability and differences in the ease of collection, directly refer to the molluscs as living populations. This led us to build up large systematic reference collections from the Argolid. An anonymous reviewer of an article in which I mentioned the constitution of reference collections for *Cyclope neritea/pellucida*, *Columbella rustica* and *Antalis* sp. (Perlès 2016) caustically questioned what he called a 'fashion', since museum collections were readily available. Without even mentioning the fact that museum collections are not optimal for experimental reproduction of the ornaments, there are many questions that museum collections cannot answer. Because the conditions of collection are rarely specified, the internal variability in shape, dimensions and colours that can be expected in an homogenous population cannot be documented. Likewise, it is impossible to assess whether these parameters remain stable from year to year when the molluscs are collected live, or from beach to beach in the case of species collected dead in thanatocoenoses. These potential factors of variability had to be controlled to evaluate the significance of dimensional variations within archaeological assemblages, and the potential choice of specimens by the bead-manufacturers.

Similarly, depending on the natural habitat of the various shell species, their collection is bound to differ in terms of time, energy and technique: museum collections do not tell us how easy or difficult it is to collect a given species. Does it require special skill or equipment? What is the average hourly rate of collection? Does it vary among individual collectors? What is the proportion of naturally perforated specimens that can be directly used as ornaments? Are age classes stable from collection locus to collection locus, or do they vary? Answering these questions is indispensable in order to envision who could have collected the various ornamental species, how it could have been done, and how valuable the collected specimens could have been depending on the time and energy devoted to their collection.

Although contemporary environmental conditions are different from those of the prehistoric past, our reference collections, which are presented in detail in Appendix 3, have proved to be an invaluable source of insights, and will be exploited throughout the present work.

Ornaments as Artifacts

As a specialist in lithic technology, I could not and did not want to forget that ornaments are also artifacts, just as chipped stone tools or bone tools are. After all, their 'symbolic value' is only an inference, whereas their 'artifactuality' is an indisputable fact. This technological approach will again be developed here along three complementary lines of investigation: by considering the production of ornaments as, (a) the outcome of different technical manufacturing and use sequences, (b) as technical productions influenced by the composition of the producer/user group and, (c) as one among several technical and economic activities.

As with any other artifact, we thus had to reconstruct the entire *chaîne opératoire* for each category of ornament, from procurement to discard, and bring to light diachronic variation in the design, the selection of individual specimens, the techniques of perforation and, when possible, in the way ornaments were used and combined. Ultimately, this would allow us to define specific ornament traditions, defined by the transmission, from generation to generation, of particular conceptions of ornaments—in the choice and association of types—and particular ways of producing and using them (White 1993). How these traditions were locally expressed at any given time, however, may have been influenced by the organisation of production—individual, collective or specialised—and by the composition of the groups that visited or inhabited the cave. Differences in the composition of the human groups are strongly suspected, in particular between the early and late Upper Palaeolithic phases and we need to take them into account when interpreting variation in ornament assemblages.

Ornament production must also be contextualised as one among many activities that took place at and around the site. It is essential to investigate how the production of ornaments was embedded—or not—into other daily tasks, such as stone or bone tool production, but also into economic activities such as fishing and the gathering of plants and shellfish (Stiner *et al.* 2013). This can be approached by comparing the density of ornaments, here calculated in relation to the volume of sediment excavated, with the density of the other categories of remains. We shall thus be able to appreciate, in particular, the relationship between the collection of ornamental species and the exploitation of other marine resources, fish and shellfish. More broadly, we shall try to determine whether the rate of production and discard of ornaments was directly related to the intensity of the other activities in each occupation phase, or whether it followed its own, independent rhythm.

Ornaments as Symbolic Units

This last alternative leads us back to ornaments as a particular kind of artifact that, as a non-verbal means of communications, functions primarily in a symbolic sphere. Many ethnographic examples show that individual perforated shells, beads or pendants may be heavily loaded with social and symbolic value (Clark 1991; Godelier 1996; Malinowski 1922; Pétrequin & Pétrequin 2006; Sciama & Eicher 1998; Trubitt 2003). Such 'ornaments' are actually much more than adornment items, and are especially valued and carefully curated. This may be the case for some of the Palaeolithic and Mesolithic ornaments at Franchthi, such as the ibex tooth or the perforated pebbles. Even the more abundant shell ornaments may have carried various symbolic meanings, referring to the sea, to fertility or to the human body. I have to admit, nevertheless, that I have never been at ease with discussing the potential symbolic meaning(s) of specific prehistoric artifacts, and will not attempt to explore these aspects here.

In addition, *functioning* in a symbolic sphere does not necessarily imply *being* a symbol or carrying a symbolic value. Different social or ethnic meanings will be transmitted by the choice of the basic ornamental elements, the beads and pendants, by their association, and by their combination (Dubin 1987; Formoso 2013; Kuhn 2014; Stiner 2014; Turgeon 2004; Wiessner 1984). These basic elements do not necessarily carry more symbolic connotation, *per se,* than do individual beads in one's everyday jewellery. Consequently, we cannot *presume* that the individual *Cyclope neritea* or *Columbella rustica* studied here was anything more to their bearers than pretty shells, even if the final composition they were a part of conveyed information on sex, age, status or group affiliation. The sheer abundance of ornamental shells in the Palaeolithic and Mesolithic levels at Franchthi, which largely exceeded 10,000 specimens, undoubtedly supports this view. In turn, the unique size of the ornament assemblage required implementing specific sampling and study strategies.

Sampling Strategies: Storage Conditions and Recovery Procedures

Since the pioneering works of Newell (1990), Taborin (1993), Laporte (1994) and White (1989, 1993), the study of Palaeolithic, Mesolithic and Neolithic ornaments has witnessed considerable analytical and theoretical advances (e.g. Bonnardin 2009; Cristiani *et al.* 2014b; d'Errico & Vanhaeren 2002; d'Errico *et al.* 1993, 2005; Laporte 2009; Rigaud 2011; Vanhaeren 2005, 2010; Vanhaeren & d'Errico 2001, 2003, 2005; White 2007; Zilhão 2006, 2007). Our own work is anchored in these new developments, but the emphasis on a long diachronic perspective combined with the richness of the assemblage necessitated adapted sampling strategies.

During the excavations, ornaments and ornamental shell species were recorded and stored in three different ways. In the early years of the project, geometric beads and pendants, as well as some perforated shells and shell bead blanks, were individually catalogued and kept with the 'Franchthi Varia', or 'FV' catalogued pieces. Beads and pendants continued to be individually catalogued, but when the rich Mesolithic levels were reached, only a few tusk shells continued to be catalogued. J. Shackleton set aside the rest of the tusk shells (*Antalis* sp. *[= Dentalium])* and, together with an assortment of worked and unworked shells, stored them in a different storeroom (*apotheke*). S. Payne also isolated tiny apical fragments of *Antalis* sp. from the < 5 mm and < 2.8 mm samples of residues, and placed them in well-labelled containers.

The vast majority of perforated shells, however, mostly *Columbella rustica* and *Cyclope neritea*, were left in the original excavation unit bags of shells, or sometimes of mixed snails and shell. Perforated shells had sometimes been placed in a smaller bag within the larger unit bag, but our wish to also study unperforated shells meant that unit bags had to be completely re-sorted. This usually resulted in finding specimens or fragments that had escaped the initial sorting, which explains why our figures do not correspond with those published by J. Shackleton (1988). The quantity of material retrieved from the shell/snail bags varied, but amounted sometimes to dozens or even hundreds of specimens. It thus quickly became clear that the process was too time-consuming to be completed for each Palaeolithic and Mesolithic excavation unit from every trench, and that sampling strategies were required. To devise these strategies, we took into account two factors: the sieving procedures implemented, which varied as the excavations went on, and the precision of the chronostratigraphic attributions.

Evolving Sieving Procedures

During the eight years of excavation (Jacobsen & Farrand 1987), more and more efficient sieves were progressively introduced (Diamant 1979; Payne 1983). Trench G was the first trench excavated down to Mesolithic levels, at a time (1967) when the site was only being 'tested'. It remains unclear whether the sediment went unsieved or whether a throw-screen with a ca. 1.5 cm mesh was used. The following season, in 1968, two dry-shaker sieves were introduced under the guidance of S. Payne (Diamant 1979): the 'Agora' sieve with three stacked sieves of increasingly fine mesh (2.7 cm., 1 cm. and 0.7 cm), and the 'McBurney' shaker with half-inch (ca. 12 mm), quarter-inch (ca. 6 mm) and eighth-inch (ca. 3 mm) meshes. At the end of the 1968 season only the McBurney shaker was used, albeit sometimes without the smallest mesh (Payne ms. on file: 3). Trench G1 was excavated that year, mostly with the McBurney shaker. In particular, excavation units G1 61 – 67, around and under the well-preserved Mesolithic human burial, were sieved through the 3 mm mesh. In 1969 all the sediment was dry-sieved with the McBurney shaker to the smallest mesh, and the finds directly sorted in the trays (Palaeolithic and Mesolithic deposits from H1). In parallel, S. Payne conducted experiments in manual water separation on selected excavation units. Thus, the Mesolithic sediments from H1A were in part dry-sieved, in part water-sieved, but the water-sieving residues were unfortunately lost. Water-sieves of 'Asvan' type were finally introduced in the middle of the 1971 season and used when excavating the Palaeolithic and Mesolithic levels in trenches FAS, FAN and H1B. After the 'flot' was scooped out, the residues from the sieves were collected together in a nylon mesh of ca. 1-1.5 mm. They were rinsed in fresh water and allowed to dry, then stored by size (>10 mm, > 5 mm, >2.8 mm and >1.8 mm). All > 10 mm and > 5 mm residues were sorted during the following seasons by categories of remain, on a table with small paintbrushes. S. Payne ultimately sorted also small subsamples of the < 5 mm and < 2.8 mm residues while he was looking for microfaunal remains.

Reviewing the evolution of recovery methods immediately raises the question of how changes in mesh size and technique (wet vs. dry sieve) affected the number and types of ornaments recovered. Comparison of the number of ornaments recovered from dry-sieved H1A and water-sieved H1B, two adjacent trenches, demonstrate important numerical differences that can be attributed to sieving procedures. Water-sieved trenches were thus clearly a first priority in the design of our sampling strategies. However, even within water-sieved sequences, differences in the grade of residues that were actually sorted introduce a bias into the samples. For instance, the majority of *Antalis* sp. were recovered in the < 5 mm and < 2.8 mm subsamples of the Upper Palaeolithic levels, while they are rare or absent in excavation units sorted only to the 5 mm sieve. Since this bias does not affect to the same extent the ornamental species with a rounder shape, it must be taken into account when studying variation in the proportions of the different ornament types (Chap. 4 and 7).

A Contrasted Chronostratigraphic Precision

Given the very large quantity of material to be studied, none of the specialists that participated in the Franchthi project was able to study all the material from all the excavated trenches. Each specialist selected a variable number of trenches, mostly focussing on the most complete and, preferably, water-sieved sequences. As a consequence, several of the trenches excavated during the first seasons have remained unpublished, and the available information, mainly deriving from the excavators' observations in the excavation notebooks, is insufficient to assign specific sequences of units to a given chronocultural phase. For instance, we know that pre-Neolithic deposits were excavated in trenches H, H1, H2A, B/E Balk, G and G1, but, for lack of contextual information, I was unable to assign the ornaments to a precise Palaeolithic or Mesolithic phase. The material from these trenches will be discussed when needed, in particular for trench G1, but will not otherwise be included in the analyses.

Our work is thus based on four trenches: H1A and the adjacent trench H1B, FAS and the adjacent trench FAN (Jacobsen & Farrand 2007: plate 2). We studied the entirety of three of these four trenches, H1A, H1B and FAS, resorting all the shell bags. H1A and H1B cover the Upper Palaeolithic, the Lower and Upper Mesolithic, but deep recent disturbances reached down into the Final Mesolithic. FAS covers the Upper Palaeolithic and the three phases of the Mesolithic, but a long erosional hiatus has removed substantial amounts of the Upper Palaeolithic deposits. Despite the gaps in each sequence, these three trenches alone already yielded thousands of ornaments and ornamental shells. Consequently we only partially studied, as a control, the Lower and Upper Mesolithic from FAN, and concentrated on the Final Mesolithic, which is best represented in this trench.

Methods of Study

The structuring principle of our approach lies in a reconstruction of the *chaîne opératoire*, i.e. the manufacturing, use and discard sequences of each category of ornaments in order to bring to light specific economic, technical and aesthetic choices. This requires taking into account the procurement of raw materials, their workability, the microscopic traces left during the manufacturing of the ornaments, as well as the deformations and traces left by use (Bonnardin 2009; White 2007).

Identification of Species and Definition of Ornament Types

Most shell species had already been identified by J. Shackleton in the course of her study of marine molluscan remains from Franchthi (Shackleton J. 1988). Additional identifications during our field study were based on "*Shells from the Greek seas*" (Delamotte & Vardala-Theodorou 2001) and "*Conchiglie del Mediterraneo*" (Doneddu & Trainito 2005), and checked when necessary by E. Vardala-Theodorou and A. Colonese. Colonese also undertook the sorting of the < 5 mm and < 2.8 mm Palaeolithic and Mesolithic residue samples, and identified all the micromolluscs to genus or species level (Appendix 2). Compared with Shackleton's, the taxonomic terminology of the shell taxa has been updated, and we follow here the recommendations from CLEMAM (Taxonomic Database on European Marine Mollusca. http://www.somali.asso.fr/clemam/index.php?lang_=en).

Perforated shells overwhelmingly dominate the Palaeolithic and Mesolithic ornament assemblages at Franchthi. In all cases, perforation constitutes the only technical action on these ornaments, but the technique of perforation and final appearance of the ornament varies according to the species or genus. Perforated shells were thus first classified according to the natural taxon, while the rare non-shell ornaments were classified under a standard terminology also based on the raw material (i.e. 'perforated tooth', 'perforated pebble', 'bone bead'). For the Palaeolithic and the Mesolithic, a naturalistic classification *stricto sensu*[3] was directly used to define the ornament types and their chronological distribution.

Observations and Recording

The archaeological database comprises the rare Palaeolithic and Mesolithic catalogued ornaments, and all uncatalogued perforated and unperforated specimens belonging to what we defined as ornamental shell species. Every item from the reference trenches was digitized at a resolution of 1200 dpi with Epson Perfection 4490 photoscanners on one or two faces, and measured with a digital calliper. Each perforated shell was examined from a technological perspective, and a subsample was submitted to traceological analysis under a magnification ranging from x20 to x40. Palaeolithic and Mesolithic perforated shells from trench H1B were examined under a Wild M3C microscope equipped with a Coolpix 995 digital camera. A few other ornaments were examined under a Perfex Science binocular microscope S 0650M1 equipped with a digital camera Motic Image Plus 2.0.

Ornaments and ornamental shells were recorded individually on Excel sheets. Details were noted on their archaeological context, taxonomic identification, state of preservation, measurements, manufacturing traces, location and extent of use-wear traces.

Phasing the Ornament Assemblages

After the initial two years of exploration, the cave and the Neolithic open-air settlement called 'Paralia' were excavated by 'excavation units' (henceforth 'units'), which aimed at following lateral or vertical changes in the sediment (Farrand 2000: 25; Jacobsen & Farrand 1987). Thus, "successive units may be either vertically or laterally contiguous, and they may encompass the entire area of the trench or only a small, circumscribed area within the trench, such as a pit or a hearth" (Farrand 2000: 25).

More than 200 units were sometimes excavated in a single trench, each unit a few centimetres deep and comprising a variable number of ornaments and ornamental shells[4]. Besides the small size of many samples from individual units, spatial variation in the distribution of ornaments introduces a second factor of random variation. In order to rely on representative assemblages and to define ornament phases, we therefore needed to group the material recovered in different trenches from contemporaneous sequences of units.

I have used as a chronostratigraphic base for the Palaeolithic and Mesolithic the Franchthi General Phasing (FGP) devised for the final synthesis of the Franchthi excavations (see Perlès & Vanhaeren 2010; Perlès 2013; Perlès *et al.* 2013). The successive phases of the FGP will henceforth be noted with a capital (e.g. Phase 4, Phase 9). This chronostratigraphic framework takes into consideration all available data: sediments (Farrand 2000), macro- and micro-mammals (Payne 1975, 1982; Stiner & Munro 2011), marine molluscs (Shackleton J. 1988), land snails (Whitney-Desautels in prep.), fish bones (Rose in prep.), carbonised seeds (Hansen 1991) and chipped stone tools (Perlès 1987, 1990). In the Upper Palaeolithic, changes in environmental, economic and artifactual data closely follow sedimentological changes and lithostratigraphic strata, so that the successive FGP phases could be easily distinguished. In the Mesolithic, by contrast, there were clear discrepancies between Farrand's lithostratigraphic phasing and all other data (Perlès *et al.* 2013). After discussion with Farrand, correlation among trenches and occupational phases were re-established so as to take into account environmental, economic and artifactual data.

The FGP phases are well defined, except for the inevitable cross cutting that occurred between two strata. They correspond to discrete periods of occupation, often characterised by a different status of the site and different subsistence strategies. Each phase is separated from the following one by an erosional or occupational hiatus, as indicated by ^{14}C dates and the abrupt artifactual changes. The FGP phases (Table 1.1) thus constitute a reliable base for the study of the ornaments. The chronostratigraphic framework presented in Table 1.1 allows us to establish correlations among the different trenches and to group sequences of units for different trenches, therefore limiting the problems of random variations within small samples. Broad ornament phases (Franchthi Ornament Phase, or FOP) can then be defined according to the presence or absence of specific taxa and ornament types[5] in each FGP phase. A more refined diachronic approach obviously requires taking into consideration quantitative variations within ornament phases: this will be explored in the following chapters. In the meanwhile, the simple projection of Palaeolithic and Mesolithic ornament types against the Franchthi General Phasing (Table 1.2) is revealing. Despite its very synthetic character, this table immediately contradicts our initial working-model: there is no one-to-one correspondence between the Franchthi General Phasing and the distribution of ornament types. In particular, similar associations of ornament types are found in in several successive FGP phases. This implies that the changes in the mode of occupation of the site, in the subsistence activities and technical production that were the basis of the Franchthi General Phases, are not systematically reflected in the ornament assemblages.

Secondly, despite a total duration of about 30 millennia from the early Upper Palaeolithic to the Final Mesolithic, the range of ornament types remains very restricted. This overall homogeneity, with the same three taxa always predominating, is all the more striking since, as mentioned above, there are many potential factors of variability. This immediately raises several important questions: is this continuity linked to a persistent lack of local resources? It is specific to Franchthi? Does it imply that these assemblages, which comprise shell taxa widely used around the Mediterranean, have no cultural value (Stiner 2014)? Or, to the contrary, does it reflect an unexpected cultural continuity between and within the Upper Palaeolithic and the Mesolithic?

Oddly enough in a study concerning ornaments, I had not initially envisioned the question of cultural continuity/discontinuity as a major theme of our research. Confrontation with the data has rendered it a prominent issue in the discussions that will follow, and led me to change the focus of the whole study, from change to permanence.

Phase	Lithostrati-graphy	Dates cal. BC	Units, trench H1A	Units, trench H1B	Units, trench FAS	Units, trench FAN	Attribution
0	P	Ca. 39,000 - 38,600 BC and earlier		215, 214	227-223		? Undiagnostic scarce chipped stone industry.
1	Q, Base of R	Ca. 38,5000 - 34,000 BC		213 - 208	222-217		Aurignacian, hunting halts, unfrequent occupations.
2	R	Ca. 26,500 – 26,000 BC	220-212 (211)	207-181	216-209		Gravettoïd, Hunting halts unfrequent occupations.
3	S1	Undated	210-205	180-173 (172-171)			Gravettoïd, Hunting halts unfrequent occupations.
4	S2	Ca. 12,300-12,000 BC	(204) 203-190	170-162			Late Epigravettian denser occupation, base camp.
5	T1 T2 T3	Ca. 11,200-10,900 BC	189-176 (175)	(161), 160-155, (154)			Late Epigravettian, dense snail middens, diversified fauna.
6	U/V	Ca. 10,600 – 10,400 BC for the basis	174-167	153-151	(207), 206-203 (202), 201-199		Final Epigravettian, less intense occupations, fewer remains.
7	W1, W2 (FAS and FAN only)	Ca. 8,600 – 8,300 BC	(166) 165-122	150-122	(198-196) 195-174	230-197	Lower Mesolithic. Cave used as a burial place. Abundant remains, land snail middens.
8	W2 (FAS and FAN only)	Ca. 8,000-7,600 BC	(119), 117-100	115-104	169-155	191-186 (185) 184-175,	Upper Mesolithic. Importance of fishing, including tuna.
9	W3, X1 (FAS and FAN only)	Ca. 7,050 – 6,750 BC	Mixed	Mixed	(154) 153 (152) 151-149	174-173, 171-169, 167-164	Final Mesolithic, sparse occupations.

Table 1.1: General phasing of Franchthi Cave Palaeolithic and Mesolithic occupations. Interphases and subphases are not indicated on the table. Details of units are given only for the reference trenches in the cave. Units in parentheses show some mixing between two phases.

Franchthi general phasing	Franchthi ornament phase	*Homalopoma sanguineum*	*Cyclope neritea/pellucida*	*Antalis sp.*	*Columbella rustica*	Perforated tooth	*Glycymeris glycymeris*	Bird bone bead	Perforated pebbles	*Conus mediterraneus*
0	**1**	(X)	X	X	(X)					
1	**1**	X	X	X	(X)					
2	**1**	(X)	X	X	X			(X)		
3	**1**	(X)	X	X						
4	**2**			(X)		(X)				
5	**3**		X	X	X		X			
6	**3**		X	X	X		(X)			
7	**4**		X	X	X		(X)	X?	X	
8	**4**		X	X	X					
9	**4**		X		X					(X)

Table 1.2: Distribution of Palaeolithic and Mesolithic ornament types according to the Franchthi General Phasing. Bold marks indicate the dominant types in each phase, parentheses indicate fewer than five specimens.

NOTES

1 For instance, the perforated *Glycymeris* sp. from the Upper Palaeolithic, the perforated *Cerastoderma glaucum* from the Neolithic, or the wild boars tusks of the Final Neolithic.
2 They are « low modification ornaments », according to Heckel 2015.
3 Every artifact can be assigned to one class, and to one class only.
4 Detailed lists of excavation units and their ornament assemblage are given in Appendix 1.
5 The significance of absences must actually be assessed case by case with statistical tests, in order to eliminate random variations in small samples, in particular for rare ornament types.

ORNAMENTS AND ORNAMENTAL
SPECIES OF THE PALAEOLITHIC

Upper Palaeolithic ornaments from Franchthi belong to two distinct chronological periods separated by a long temporal hiatus (Table 1.1). The early Upper Palaeolithic (Franchthi General Phasing, Phases 0 to 3), ranges from ca. 39,000 to ca. 25,000 cal BC. Phase 4, dated to ca. 12,300 – 12,000 cal BC is almost devoid of ornaments. The late Upper Palaeolithic (Phases 5 to 6), ranges from ca. 11,200 to ca. 10,400 cal BC.

The spectrum of ornament types is narrow. Palaeolithic ornament assemblages at Franchthi comprise almost exclusively perforated shells. A perforated tooth and a bone bead are the only exceptions. Two stone beads were also found in the Palaeolithic levels but we consider them intrusive. Among the ornamental shell species, *Cyclope* sp. appears to be predominant, followed by *Antalis* sp., *Columbella rustica* and *Homalopoma sanguineum*. Given different recovery biases for each taxon, *Antalis* sp. segments may have been actually more numerous than *Cyclope* sp.

CHAPTER TWO

Environmental Data: Past Shorelines and Potential Resources

During the Palaeolithic, the present-day Koiladha bay (Fig. 2.1) was a coastal plain whose shape and size changed according to Late Pleistocene eustatic variations of the sea level. Submerged shorelines were identified during surveys by high-resolution marine seismic reflection profiling, while a sidescan sonar was used to ascertain the nature of the sea floor (van Andel & Lianos 1983, 1984)[1]. This allowed van Andel and Lianos to reconstruct past shorelines at different periods that they dated between 18,000 uncal BP and the present. In turn, Shackleton and van Andel (1986) estimated the marine resources that would have been available to the Franchthi inhabitants at each period, according to the substrate (Shackleton & van Andel 1986; Shackleton 1988).

The maps of the bay were drawn from observed submerged shorelines (van Andel 1987, figs. 13-17, 21), with approximate dates based on their depths projected onto a general post-glacial sea level rise curve (Shackleton 1988, figs 9-13). These dates must now be adjusted according to more recent curve(s) of late Pleistocene / Holocene sea level rise, as van Andel himself advocated after the publication of Fairbanks' new curve (Fairbanks 1989; van Andel 1990). Lambeck (1996) further refined the reconstitution of sea level rise for the Aegean in general, and the Argolic Gulf in particular, by using a more complex model of eustasy and glacio-hydro isostasy integrated with topographic data in tectonically stable areas. We will rely here on the curves published by Lambeck to re-date the maps and shorelines at different depths[2].

Three of the detailed shore maps correspond to the Upper Palaeolithic. The deepest one, at – 120 m, corresponds to the Late Glacial Maximum (LMG). It is of little use to us since no deposits from this period have been excavated. The next shoreline identified is at about – 73 m (Fig. 2.2). Given the numerous climatic fluctuations and oscillations of the sea level before the LMG, the – 73 m shoreline could de dated roughly to 40,000, 38,000, 33,000, 25,000 and 11,000 uncal BP (Lambeck 1996, fig. 3). The last three dates, which correspond to ca. 35,500, 28,000 and 11,000 cal BC, correspond to Franchthi Phase 1 (Aurignacian), Franchthi Phase 2 (Gravettoid), and Franchthi Phase 5 (late Epigravettian).

During these three phases, the coastal plain was reduced to less than half its maximum extension during the LMG. The distance from the cave to the shore was about 3.8 km, i.e. of easy reach in less than an hour. According to the reconstructed shoreline, diversified habitats could be exploited: the central portion consisted of long beaches interrupted by lagoons and marshes, with rocky shores to the north and the south (Shackleton & van Andel 1986: 139). Although Shackleton and van Andel only mention *Cerastoderma glaucum* and *Bittium reticulatum*, there is no reason not to expect also *Cyclope neritea* and/or *C. pellucida* in the marshes where the 'Franchthi river' joined the coast and brought fresh water. The bivalves *Donax trunculus* and *Donacella cornea* would have been found on the sandy beaches, a good location also to find shells

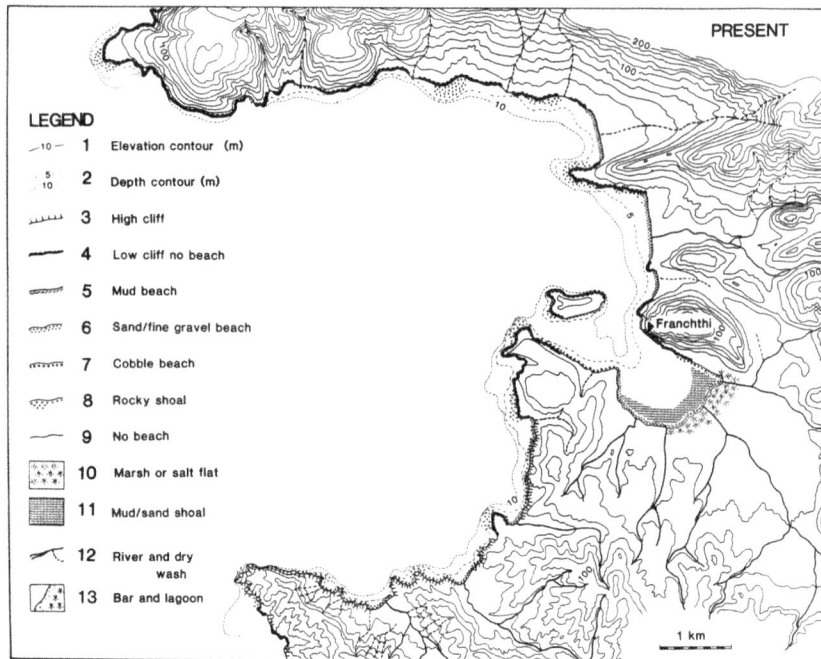

Fig. 2.1: Shore habitats of the present-day Franchthi embayment and legend of the following maps (after van Andel 1987).

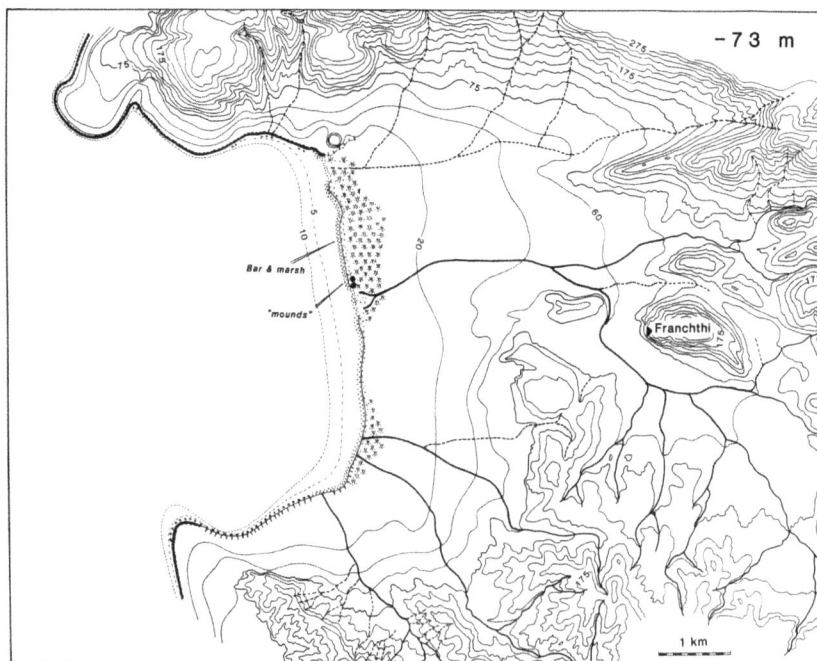

Fig. 2.2: Shore habitats of the Franchthi embayment at ca. 42,000, 35,500, 28,000 and 11,000 cal BC (after van Andel 1987, dates corrected after Lambeck 1996). Elevation contours in metres a.s.l. at that time.

of *Antalis* sp. rejected by the waves. *Columbella rustica* could be expected on the rocky shores on each side of the bay, alongside the edible trochids and limpets mentioned by Shackleton and van Andel. The variety of habitats inferred within one or two hours walk from the cave suggests that a wide range of edible and ornamental species, the latter comparable to those found at Klissoura Cave 1 in the Argolid (Stiner 2010), would have been available during Phases 1 and 2. Despite the relative proximity of the coast, however, edible marine molluscs were not collected or not brought back to the cave, and a restricted range of ornamental species are the only evidence of an exploitation of the littoral.

No map corresponds to our Phase 3 (undated, probably around 24,000 – 25,000 cal BC) and to the much later Phase 4 (ca. 12,250 cal BC). While we can expect the coast in Phase 3 to be roughly similar to that of the preceding Phase 2, the landscape must have been different during Phase 4, with a sea level at ca. – 90/100 m, an enlarged coastal plain and a distance from the cave to the sea of approximately 5 km. Paradoxically, this is precisely the time when the first evidence for small scale fishing, mostly of Sparids such as sea breams, appears in the record (Rose, in prep.; Stiner & Munro 2011).

The sea level again reached – 73 m during Phase 5, with a distance to the sea and palaeo-environments comparable to those of Phases 1 and 2. Consequently, the presence of abundant fish remains and the first evidence of shellfish collecting, mostly of *Patella* sp. and *Cerithium vulgatum* (Rose in prep.; Shackleton J. 1988), cannot be attributed solely to the greater proximity of the coast or to the reduction of the coastal plain. It also reflects different economic strategies during the Early and the Late Upper Palaeolithic (Stiner & Munro 2011).

The third shoreline, at – 54/53 m, would in turn correspond to 30,000 uncal BP, a period when the cave was either not occupied or the corresponding deposits eroded, and to ca. 10,100 uncal BP or 9,700 cal BC, probably contemporaneous with the end of Phase 6 (Fig. 2.3). It shows very different coastal environments, the rapid rise of the sea level having left no time for significant coastal deposition (Shackleton & van Andel 1986: 139). The beaches, now about 3 km from the cave, would have been mainly cobbles, beneath high cliffs, with rocky shores on both ends of the bay. Molluscan assemblages should, in theory, be composed mainly of trochids (*Phorcus* sp. (= *Monodonta* = *Osilinus* sp.), *Gibbula* sp. and limpets (*Patella* sp.), with *Cerithium vulgatum* and *Hexaplex trunculus* immediately off-shore. However, the presence of abundant *Cyclope neritea* collected live in Phase 6 demonstrates that open marshes also were present nearby.

The variety of habitats within one to two hours walk from the cave during most phases would thus suggest that a wide range of edible and ornamental species should have been available. Thomas (1987), however, strongly questioned the validity of the habitats reconstructed by van Andel and Shackleton and, consequently, the determination of potentially available species. He argues in particular that the substrate does not suffice to reconstruct past coastal ecology and molluscan habitats. His criticisms are well founded, but they do not, in my opinion, invalidate the variety of microenvironments linked to a contrasted palaeotopography, nor do they invalidate the notion of a marked selectivity in the exploitation of shellfish[3] (Shackleton & van Andel 1986; Shackleton J. 1988).

Ornamental shell species were exploited over a much longer period of time than shellfish[4.] They too reveal a striking selectivity, all the more significant that the choice of species remains surprisingly stable despite constant environmental variations.

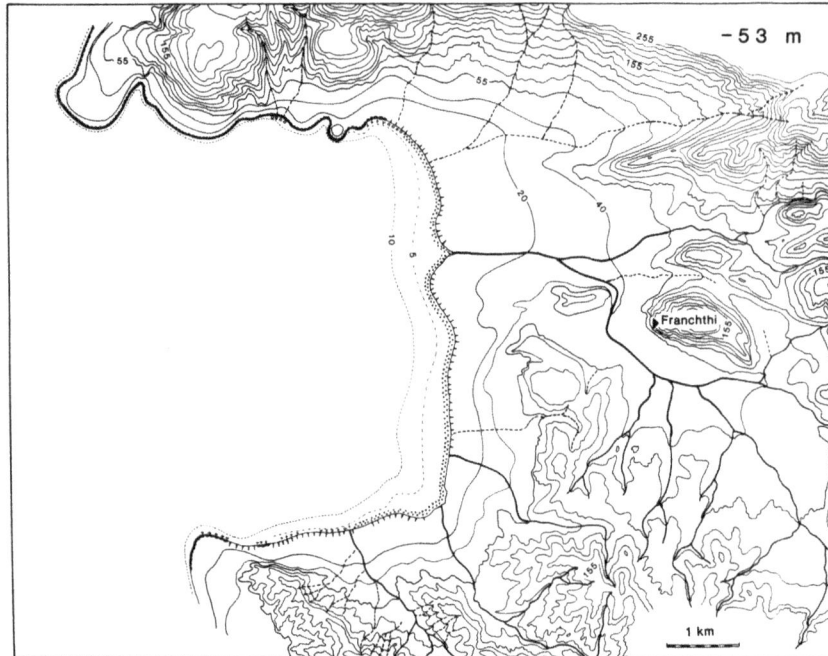

Fig. 2.3: Shores of the Franchthi embayment at ca. 34,000 and ca. 9,700 cal BC (after van Andel 1987, dates corrected after Lambeck 1996). Elevation contours in metres a.s.l. at that time.

NOTES

1   New underwater surveys of the bay have been undertaken since 2014 under the direction of J. Beck (University of Geneva), Despina Koutsoumpa (Ephoreia of underwater archaeology) and Dimitris Sakellariou (Hellenic Center for Marine Research). The results are not available at the time of writing.

2   Before 10,000 BP uncal, we used the Paros curve (fig. 3) with a correction of – 2 m for hydro-isostatic effect, as indicated on Lambeck (1996), figs. 4a and 4b.

3   Which, as he notes himself, is an « unexceptional conclusion » (Thomas 1987 : 236).

4   Shellfish were only exploited, or at least brought back to the cave, from Phase 5 onwards.

CHAPTER THREE

The Exploitation of Cyclope neritea *and* Cyclope pellucida

The genus *Cyclope* presently comprises two species of small necrophagous gastropods, *C. neritea* (L. 1758) and *C. pellucida* (Risso 1826), characterised by a dull brown upper convex surface and a shiny, ivory flat base (Fig. 3.1 and Appendix 3.1). Both species live in the quiet brackish waters of coastal lagoons or salt marshes, sometimes together. Both were widely used as ornaments by prehistoric groups around the Mediterranean basin, as necklaces, headdresses, breast plastrons, loincloths, and bracelets (Taborin 1993, 2004). *Cyclope* sp. are present at Franchthi in the earliest excavated levels, below the tephra deposit dated to ca. 39,000 BP and throughout all Palaeolithic phases.

Fig. 3.1: Modern Cyclope sp. *collected in Nafplion. Photograph C.P.*

Taphonomic Issues and Representativeness of the Sample

The sample analyzed comprises all the *Cyclope* sp. and fragments recovered directly in the trench and in the > 5 mm residues. With rare exceptions, we found and sorted all trench and > 5 mm shell bags from the Palaeolithic levels. Conversely, S. Payne sorted only subsamples of the < 5 and < 2.8 mm residue, where we found identifiable fragments of base, columella and apices of *Cyclope* sp. These amount to 9% of all *Cyclope* sp. in FAS, but only to 0.8% in H1B[1] where a number of small shell residue bags are missing. Since the samples of < 5 mm residues ranged from 1/8th to 1/32th of the total volume, the actual number of Cyclopes[2] actually present in Palaeolithic deposits was higher than indicated in the available counts.

In addition, some specimens may have completely disappeared through chemical attack in the most ancient Upper Palaeolithic levels, where the state of preservation is very poor. Until the very last Upper Palaeolithic levels, in Phase 6 (Table 3.1), a large majority of the shells show various degrees of typical chemical alteration (Vanhaeren 2010: 52). In Phases 0 and 1 in particular, many specimens are reduced to the columella and apex. It is thus impossible to determine whether they were perforated or not (Plates 3.1 to 3.7).

As a consequence, the sample studied only represents a fraction of the initial sample, and may not be representative for the earlier phases, in particular for the rate of perforation. The figures presented are minimal figures.

Phase	Altered	Non altered	Undetermined	N
0	100*	0	0	16
1	92.3	7.7	0	52
2	87.1	85.2	0	95
3	80	0	20*	5
5	92	5.8	2.4	188
6.a	80.6	14	5.3	149
6.b	31.6	64.2	5.1	98

Table 3.1: Altered and non-altered Cyclope *sp. by phase, in percentages. Interphase 5/6 has been grouped with Phase 5. *The total number is very small and percentages are unreliable. Phase 6 has been subdivided because of marked differences in the state of preservation.*

Agent of Accumulation

Given the distance from the sea and the elevation of the cave, direct marine deposition of the *Cyclope* sp. can be ruled out. We found no references of predatory birds eating *Cyclope*, but the possibility should be considered (Claassen 1998: 71-73). Here again, however, the distance to the intertidal zone and the presence of intact individuals eliminates this possibility (Rigaud *et al.* 2014b: 671-2). The shells are also light enough (mean weight of 0.4 g) to be moved by saltation by the wind (Cameron *et al.* 1990), but the archaeological specimens do not display the characteristic effects of wind erosion (Rick 2002) and it is unlikely they could have moved ca. 3 km or more on plant-covered ground. An anthropic deposition of the Cyclopes, either as food or as ornaments, is the only satisfactory option.

Cyclope sp.: An Exclusively Ornamental Taxon

In the original publication on marine molluscs from Franchthi, J. Shackleton defined her second malacological zone, which roughly corresponds to the Mesolithic, as the "*Cyclope neritea* Zone". She based this definition on the abundance of *Cyclope neritea*, which she considered primarily a food resource (Shackleton J. 1988: 39). She noted the high proportion of perforated specimens but considered their use as ornaments as secondary to their dietary use. In the same volume, to the contrary, M. Deith and N. J. Shackleton stated that *Cyclope neritea* was a purely ornamental species, collected dead on beaches (Deith & Shackleton 1988: 135). Reese (1990) quickly criticised the hypothesis of consumption of *C. neritea* and pointed out that there is no record of Cyclopes being eaten by man. It is indeed difficult to try and eat the flesh of the *Cyclope neritea*[3], which breaks when pulled out of the shell after boiling. In addition, the caloric input would be negligible: the total weight of the dried flesh of 130 *C. neritea* barely reached 1.8 grams. Alternately, our Greek hosts in Nafplion stated that they could be used as bait, but we were not able to verify this. In any case, the presence of *Cyclope* sp. in levels where no fishing is recorded, the very large quantities in the Mesolithic, the anthropic perforations as well as frequent use-wear traces make their systematic use as bait highly unlikely. *Cyclope neritea* can be considered as an ornamental species at Franchthi, as in all other prehistoric sites where it has been found. However, there is a distinct possibility that not only *C. neritea*, but also *C. pellucida* as well as a fossil species, were used as ornaments.

Characterisation and Taxonomic Identification

Without the original shell colours and no possibility of DNA analyses, the only criterion we can use to discriminate the different species of *Cyclope* sp. is the dimensions of adult specimens. Since we have shown high correlations between the maximum length, width and height of live snails (Appendix 3.1), the maximum diameter only will be examined.

For the Palaeolithic as a whole, 56.5 % only of the adult Cyclopes, of a total of 572 specimens, are sufficiently well preserved for the measure to be meaningful. The maximum diameter of all Palaeolithic adult specimens shows a Gaussian distribution centered around 0.9-0.99 cm. However, this normal distribution is entirely spurious. When the early Upper Palaeolithic phases (Phases 0 to 3 included) are distinguished from the late Upper Palaeolithic phases (Phases 5 and 6)[4], the distributions are clearly distinct (Fig. 3.2). The total number of measurable specimens is unfortunately low in the earlier phases (n = 32) because of poor conditions of preservation, but the contrast vis-a-vis the later phases is marked: the mode and larger values are outside the range of the richer and much better preserved sample from Phases 5 and 6 (n = 231)[5].

Contrary to modern samples and to later assemblages, the range of sizes in the early Upper Palaeolithic is extended and does not display the regular Gaussian distribution of a single, homogenous population (Appendix 3.1). Although the distribution may be biased by the small size of the sample, this suggests the presence of two, if not three different species. The mode, between 0.7 and 0.8 cm, and the mean (0.85, s.d. = 0.21) are well below the values for adult *C. neritea* in all of our modern collections, and smaller than in Phases 5 and 6. It corresponds better to the present-day values for *C. pellucida*. If this is the case, some at least of the larger specimens, between 0.9 and 1.1 cm, may belong to the larger *C. neritea*. Finally, the rare specimens over 1.3 cm, well outside the range of modern *Cyclope neritea* (Fig. 3.3), could indicate the presence of Pliocene fossil specimens (cf. *Cyclope migliorinii* Bevilaqua 1928), although very large specimens are also noted in ornament assemblages from Epirus (Kotjabopoulou & Adams 2004, note 3).

Phase	Mean maximum diameter	Standard-deviation	Number
0-3	0.85	0.21	32
5	1.03	0.12	98
6	0.97	0.12	133

Table 3.2: Mean maximum diameter of measured adult Upper Palaeolithic Cyclope *sp., in cm. Phases 0-3 have been grouped because of the small size of the samples.*

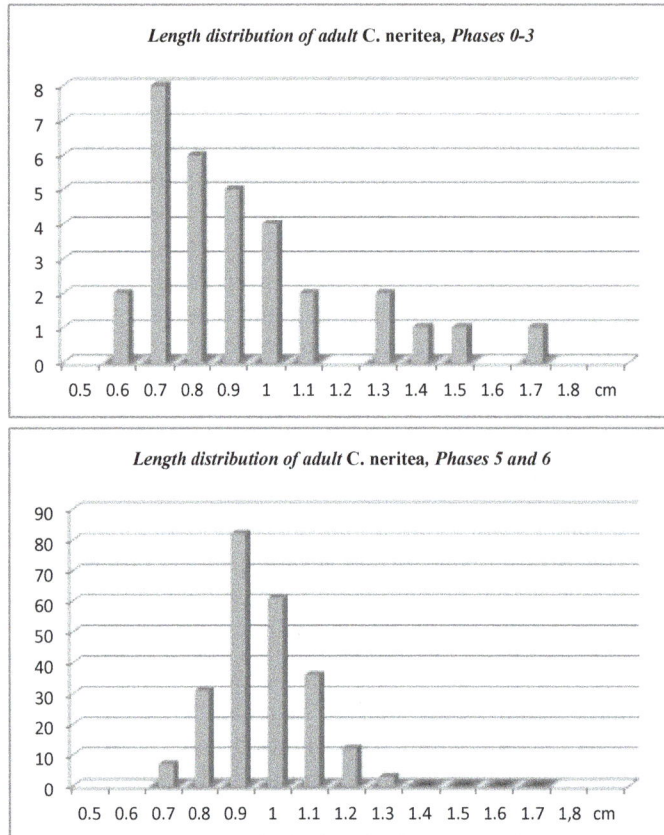

Fig. 3.2: Maximum diameter of adult Cyclope sp. in the early Upper Palaeolithic phases (top) and late Upper Palaeolithic phases (bottom).

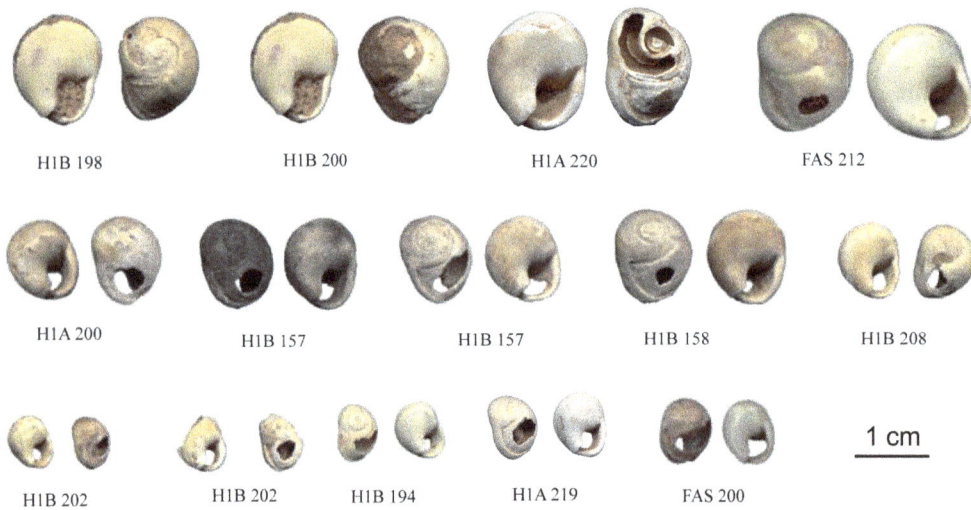

Fig. 3.3: The three characteristic dimensional groups of Cyclope sp. from Palaeolithic levels. CAD M. Vanhaeren and C. P..

In the later Palaeolithic phases, the length distribution is very different: it is nearly Gaussian and centered around 0.9 to 0.99 cm. The smallest classes (0.6 – 0.79 cm), which constituted 51% of the sample in the earlier phases, have dropped down to 5%. The large, potentially fossil, specimens are no longer present and the mean maximum diameter has increased to 0.98 cm, with a small standard deviation (s.d. = 0.12). However, statistically significant differences appear when each phase is considered separately (Fig. 3.4).

The Cyclopes from Phase 6 have a smaller mean than in Phase 5[6], but a more Gaussian distribution. There are thus important dimensional variations throughout the Upper Palaeolithic. The mode of the small adults in the earlier phases is comparable to that of the Final Upper Palaeolithic burials of La Madeleine (France) and the Children's Cave at Grimaldi (Italy), while the mode observed in the later periods is nearer to that of modern collections of *Cyclope neritea* (Vanhaeren 2010: 259)[7]. Several factors could potentially account for these dimensional variations. Over-exploitation could only be invoked for the decrease in size and range in Phase 6 (Álvarez-Fernández *et al.* 2011; Hunt *et al.* 2011 and refs. therein) but it is unlikely considering the low rate of collection.

Climatic variation is another potential factor (Álvarez-Fernández *et al.* 2011; Bailey & Craighead 2003). However, according to the $\delta^{18}O$ in core GISP 2, water temperatures would have been slightly warmer on average in Phases 5 and 6 (ca. 11,000 – 10,500 cal BC) than during our Phase 2[8] (ca. 26,000 – 24,000 cal BC). An increase in size when water temperatures increase would run contrary to the trends observed with other gastropod species (Álvarez-Fernández *et al.* 2011; Teske *et al.* 2007). It is thus unlikely that growth conditions explain the differences in size between the early and late Upper Palaeolithic phases.

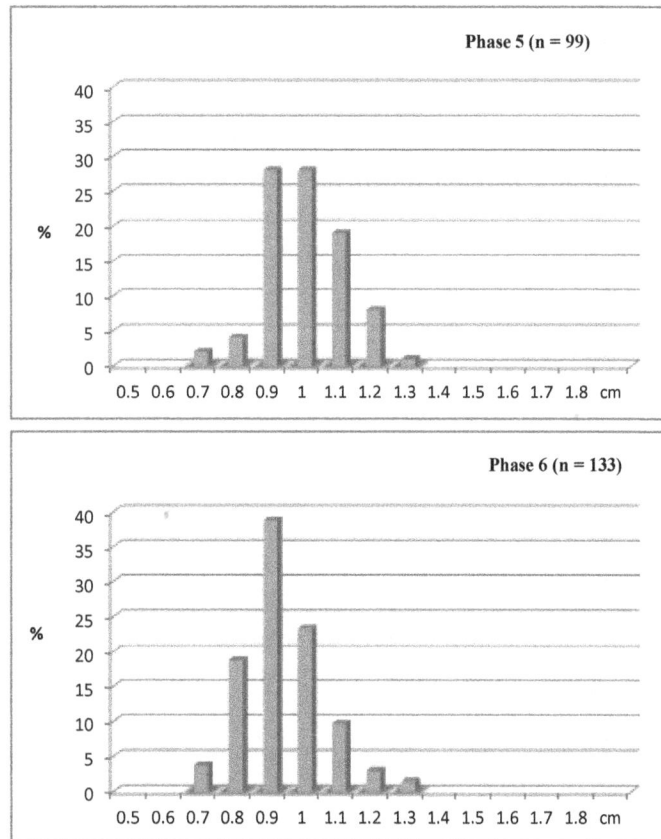

Fig. 3.4: Distribution of maximum diameters of adult Cyclope sp. *in the late Upper Palaeolithic phases.*

A third possibility is a shift in the main species collected. Besides the very large specimens, which may be fossils, the small size of most *Cyclope* sp. in the earlier phases may reflect a predominance of the smaller *C. pellucida*, which is characterised nowadays by a mean diameter of 0.8 cm (*Forum Natura Mediterraneo* 2009) or by a range of 0.5 to 0.8 cm (Parenzan 1970, quoted in Vanhaeren 2010). To the contrary, *C. neritea* would predominate in the later phases, albeit it would be of a smaller average size than our modern collections (Appendix 3.1). A mix of the two populations, in different proportions, would explain why the range of sizes clearly exceeds that observed in modern populations of *C. neritea*, except in Phase 6, which seems to correspond to a homogeneous population of rather small *C. neritea*.

We did not find indications about the environmental requirements of *C. pellucida*, which might explain why the dominant species would have shifted in time. One can find the two species together (Simon-Bouhet 2006) and a mix of *C. neritea* and *C. pellucida* has been suggested in other Upper Palaeolithic sites around the Mediterranean (Adam *et al.* 1997; Martini 2007). Thus, whether or not we are dealing with a single, highly variable population, or with two populations, the most parsimonious hypothesis is that all *Cyclope* sp. were collected together, in the same location(s).

Collecting Dead or Live Cyclopes?

A striking feature of our assemblages is the presence of a variable but sometimes high proportion of unperforated juveniles (Table 3.3). These proportions must be taken cautiously considering the high number of badly preserved specimens, but they suggest that the proportion of juveniles was especially high in the early phases, where it can reach a third of the determined specimens. The juveniles, characterised by the absence of an outer lip, are too brittle to be used as ornaments and were always rejected unperforated. Their high proportions in the early assemblages may thus indicate a deficit in adults, which would have been taken away after perforation. However our own collections show that the rate of juveniles can be quite variable from year to year (Appendix 3.1), so that we cannot rule out either natural variation in the populations.

The presence of juveniles also indicates that the Cyclopes deposited in the cave are not—at least not only—the remnants of broken necklaces or ornamented garments, but that they were collected on nearby shores, either in thanatocoenoses or under water, and brought back to the cave in order to be worked.

Phase	Adults	Juveniles	Undetermined	Total
0	4	2	10	16
1	15	7	30	52
2	45 *47%*	17 *19%*	33 *35%*	95 *100%*
3	1	0	4	5
4	0	0	0	0
5	133 *71%*	4 *2.1%*	51 *27.1%*	188 *100%*
6	155 *62.7%*	21 *8.7%*	71 *28.7%*	149 *100%*

Table 3.3: Proportion of adults and juvenile Cyclope *sp. per phase.*

Shells collected on beaches in thanatocoenoses show characteristic pitting and abrasion induced by the action of the sand and waves (Stiner 1999; Stiner *et al.* 2013), which none of the well-preserved specimens display. In addition, the brittle shell of *C. neritea* and *C. pellucida* preserve poorly in thanatocoenoses, and it is nowadays difficult and very time consuming to find intact specimens on Argolid beaches. The Palaeolithic groups may thus have collected live Cyclopes under water, as suggested by the size distribution that corresponds to a live population. This would explain the presence of juveniles: in the muddy environments favored by *C. neritea* and *C. pellucida*, collection is virtually 'blind', done mostly by touch, and it is impossible to distinguish adults from juveniles (Appendix 3.1). Despite the absence of visibility[9], our own experience shows that collecting live Cyclopes by poking into the mud is far more efficient than looking for dead specimens on beaches. It requires no special skill or instrument other than a container, and can be practiced by both adults and children.

The collection of Cyclopes may have taken place during hunting expeditions that brought the groups near the shores, or it may have constituted an end in itself. One thing is certain: it was not embedded in the exploitation of other intertidal resources. In the early Upper Palaeolithic phases, neither edible marine molluscs nor fish were consumed. In the later Upper Palaeolithic phases, some marine molluscs, in particular *Patella* sp., *Cerithium vulgatum* and *Phorcus turbinatus* were gathered and eaten, but they live in rocky coastal environments, not in lagoons. Collecting *Cyclope* was thus the primary purpose of the exploitation of nearby lagoons.

Selection of Specimens and Production of Ornaments

Once collected, all Cyclopes were brought back in bulk to the cave, without sorting the juveniles and the adults. To get rid of the flesh of the live snails, they had to be boiled, dried or buried in the earth, but there is no indication of the precise procedure that was followed.

In the later Upper Palaeolithic phases, 18 to 26 % of the Cyclopes are dark grey or black (Table 3.4). Analyses performed at the Centre de Recherches des Musées de France have shown that the change of colour was due to heating under reducing conditions (Lange *et al.* 2007, 2008).

Phase	Non heated			Heated			Not recorded	Total
	Adults	Juveniles	Undetermined	Adults	Juveniles	Undetermined		
0	5	4	2	0	0	0	5	16
1	15	6	28	0	1	2	2	52
2	44 48%	16 17.5%	30 32%	1 1.1%	1 1.1%	0 0%	2 2.2%	92 100%
3	1	0	5	0	0	0	0	6
4	0	0	0	0	0	0	0	0
5	99 52,6%	2 1%	37 20%	33 17.5%	2 1%	15 8%	0 0%	188 100%
6	132 53,4%	18 7,3%	50 20,2%	23 9,3%	3 1,2%	18 7,3%	3 1,2%	247 100%

Table 3.4: Proportion of burnt adults and juveniles Cyclope *sp. by phase.*

We do not consider, however, that heat-treatment was intended to remove the flesh: to turn the shell black without destroying it, it has to be exposed to a high temperature over several hours, well protected within a bundle of leaves and earth from direct contact with the glowing embers (Perlès & Vanhaeren 2010). There was no need to follow this lengthy procedure if the goal was simply to remove the flesh and use the shell as a bead with its original colours. Nor can accidental burning, which certainly took place, be the sole explanation: there is no correlation between the rate of burnt *Cyclope* sp. and the rate of burnt land snails or edible marine molluscs, and the proportion of burnt *Cyclope* sp. is systematically higher than that of animal bones (Perlès & Vanhaeren 2010, tables 1 and 2).

Heat-treatment thus appears to have been an intrinsic step in the preparation of ornaments during phases 5 and 6, designed to alter the coloration of the shell and produce a 'black-and-white' contrast between treated and non-treated specimens. Curiously, this heat-treatment was applied indiscriminately to adults and juveniles. The proportion of burnt adults and juveniles is identical, despite the fact that juveniles were not subsequently perforated. This could possibly have avoided a double process of sorting, first to remove the juveniles, then to remove the specimens that cracked during the heat-treatment.

If the juveniles were systematically rejected, a quarter to a third of the adults were also either rejected or lost (Table 3.5). The rate of perforated adults is comparable to the overall rate of perforated gastropods at Riparo Mochi in Italy and Üçağızlı Cave I in Turkey, also by the sea (Stiner 1999, 2014; Stiner *et al.* 2013). However, the proximity to the shore is not the predominant factor explaining why so many Cyclopes were left unperforated: in the Late Epigravettian of Riparo Tagliente, far from the sea, only one third of the *Cyclope* sp. were perforated (Cilli & Gurioli 2007). The accumulation of stocks of raw material—perhaps also for exchange?—appears to have been a common practice. Some specimens may have also been glued to garments or artifacts rather than perforated and threaded.

Phase	Perforated	Non perforated	Undetermined	Total adults
0	0	1	4	5
1	3	4	8	15
2	13	8	23	44
3	1	0	0	1
4	0	0	0	0
5	93 *m = 1.02; sd = 0.11*	21 *m = 1.05; sd = 0.1*	33	33
6.1	49 *m = 1; sd = 0.13*	12 *m = 1.06; sd = 0.11*	18	18
6.2	58 *m = 0.94; sd = 0.1*	18 *m = 0.94; sd = 0.05*	0	76

Table 3.5: Mean and standard deviation of maximum diameter (m, s.d.) for measurable perforated and non-perforated adult Cyclope *sp. by phase.*

In the earlier phases, the state of preservation is too poor to test for size differences between perforated and non-perforated adult specimens, but perforated specimens cover the whole range of dimensions, from the smallest to the 'giants'. In the later phases, when preservation is better, it can also be shown that the diameter was not a criterion of selection: the mean appears to be slightly larger for the non-perforated specimens (Table 3.5), but the differences are not statistically significant[10]. Other possibilities may account for the presence of these non-perforated specimens: they may have been rejected because of their colour, they may have been kept as stock, or simply lost. Whatever the case, the only criterion of selection that can be brought to light in our assemblages is that of adults versus juveniles.

The perforation was then easily done with a small wooden stick or a bone splinter and required no specific skill (Appendix 3.1). Judging from the better-preserved specimens, in the earlier phases the tool was simply inserted in the opening, pressed on the shell, and eventually slightly twisted to enlarge the hole (Fig. 3.5, left, Fig. 3.6). In Phases 5 and 6, larger perforations show that the tool was subsequently removed and reinserted from the outside, to enlarge them by pressing the tool against the edge of the perforation (Fig. 3.5, centre, Fig. 3.6). More rarely, the whole upper part of the body is missing, as with the '*appliqués*' that were sewn on the back of garments in two Mesolithic burials at Vlasac (Cristiani & Borić 2012). The removal of the upper whorls can be intentional, but it can also be due to taphonomic processes, in particular decalcification (Vanhaeren 2010: 52). The latter cannot be ruled out at Franchthi, but a few well-preserved specimens with well-developed use-wear (Fig. 3.5, right) show that this mode of perforation was occasionally, albeit rarely, practiced in the Palaeolithic of Franchthi.

H1A 175

FAS 200

1 cm

Fig. 3.5: Different types of perforation in the Upper Palaeolithic. From left to right: initial perforation, simple perforation, enlarged perforation and removal of upper whorls. The first two can be done without removing the tool from the shell's opening. The last two require reinserting the tool from the outside.

Perforating Cyclopes is easy, but requires some attention: the lip can easily be broken, and some perforated and broken Cyclopes probably broke during perforation rather than during use (Table 3.6). Many of the broken specimens, however, show intense use-wear on the dorsal and ventral faces (Fig. 3.7) and had been worn for a long time before they broke. The overall rate of perforated Cyclopes with a broken lip appears rather high in comparison with the late Epigravettian assemblage of Riparo Tagliente, the only one for which we found data. At Riparo Tagliente, ca. 16% of the perforated *Cyclope* sp. were broken at the lip (Cilli & Gurioli 2007), less than half the overall rate at Franchthi.

Successfully perforated Cyclopes could then be threaded or sewn onto a garment. Cyclopes were used in various combinations during the Upper Palaeolithic. In the Children's Cave of Grimaldi, the two children appear to have worn loincloths made of 14 – 15 threads of *Cyclope* sp. tightly strung together in pairs to create a herringbone pattern (Vanhaeren 2010: 260-263). At nearby Barma Grande, an adult and two adolescents wore *Cyclope neritea* headdresses ornamented with deer canines, and one also had a necklace comprising *Cyclope* sp. The young woman from the Cavillon wore a sort of hood ornamented with more than 200 Cyclopes as well as a leg bracelet of the same shells (Taborin 2004: 175-177). Further East in Liguria, at Arene Candide, an adolescent was buried with a hood, a breastplate, arm and leg bracelets, all ornamented with *Cyclope* sp., *Luria* sp., deer canines and ivory pendants (Pettitt *et al.* 2003; Taborin 2004: 177). Different modes of perforation possibly corresponded to these different modes of attachment, but this aspect does not seem to have been the subject of detailed examination.

Heavily Worn Beads in a Production Centre?

Phase	Perforated	Perforated, lip broken	Total
0	0	0	0
1	1	2	3
2	11	2	13
3	1	0	1
4	0	0	0
5	56	26	82
6	62	48	110
Total	131 (62.6%)	78 (37.3%)	209

Table 3.6: Intact perforated Cyclope *sp. and perforated specimens with a broken lip. The table only includes non-ambiguous specimens. Interphase 5/6 has been grouped with Phase 6.*

At Franchthi, the majority of perforated Cyclopes show more or less developed wear around the perforation and sometimes also on the ventral face. The asymmetry of the wear on simple perforations, which concentrates on the labial (outer) part of the perforation (Fig. 3.9), confirms that we are dealing with use-wear and not with soil abrasion or chemical dissolution. This is further demonstrated by the pronounced deformations and furrows on ventral faces created by the tension of the thread (Fig. 3.10). The absence of use-wear on the rear of the perforation indicates that the beads were strung with a tight knot around the lip. An arrangement of the shells in a 'herringbone pattern', as mentioned above, would correspond well with this distribution of wear traces. Enlarged perforations tend to show a different pattern, with wear extending all around the periphery (Fig. 3.9). A double knot can be envisioned, suggesting these beads were not strung but sewn on a garment.

The presence of a large proportion of worn Cyclopes may appear surprising at a site where they were collected and transformed into beads. It demonstrates that Franchthi was not only a production site for beads to be taken away, but also a place where ornaments and adorned garments were recycled, with worn or broken elements replaced by new ones, and, possibly also, new embroidered garments manufactured. Many freshly perforated beads must have left the site, in quantities that we shall never really comprehend.

Phase 1   *Phase 2*

H1B 208   FAS 212   H1A 219   H1B 204   H1B 203

Phase 3

1 cm

H1B 174   H1B 202   H1B 201   H1B 194

Phase 5

H1A 179   H1A 178   H1A 175   H1B 160

H1B 156

H1B 155

Phase 6

H1A 174   H1A 173   H1A 170

FAS 200

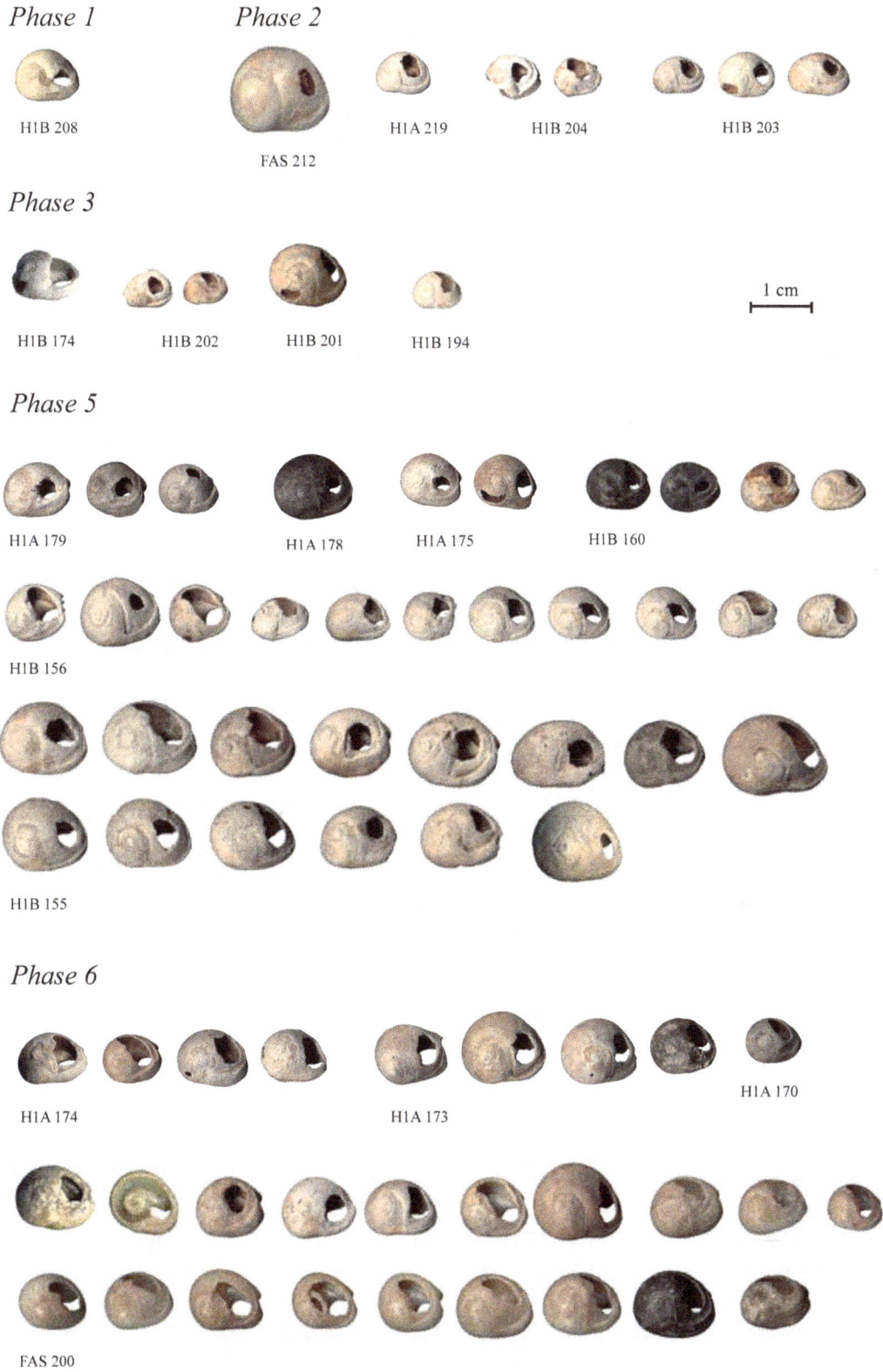

Fig. 3.6: Sample of (relatively) well-preserved Palaeolithic Cyclope *sp.*

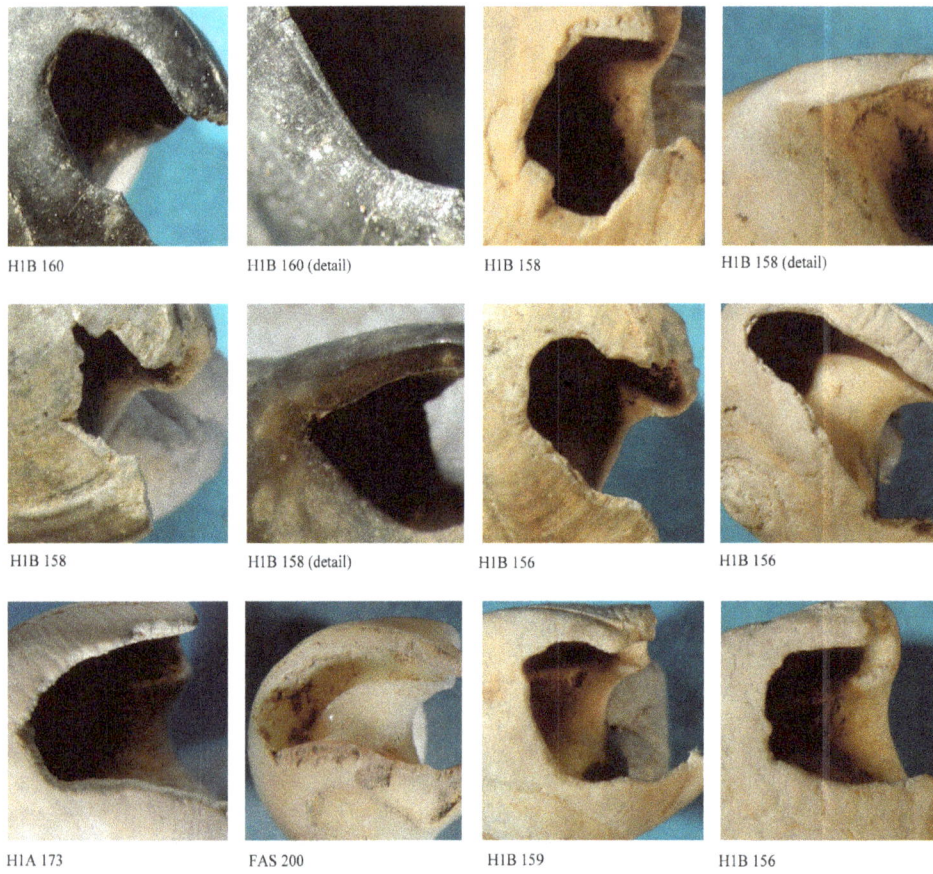

H1B 160　　　　　H1B 160 (detail)　　　　　H1B 158　　　　　H1B 158 (detail)

H1B 158　　　　　H1B 158 (detail)　　　　　H1B 156　　　　　H1B 156

H1A 173　　　　　FAS 200　　　　　H1B 159　　　　　H1B 156

Fig. 3.7: Perforated Cyclope *sp. with broken lip and use-wear on the dorsal and ventral faces.*

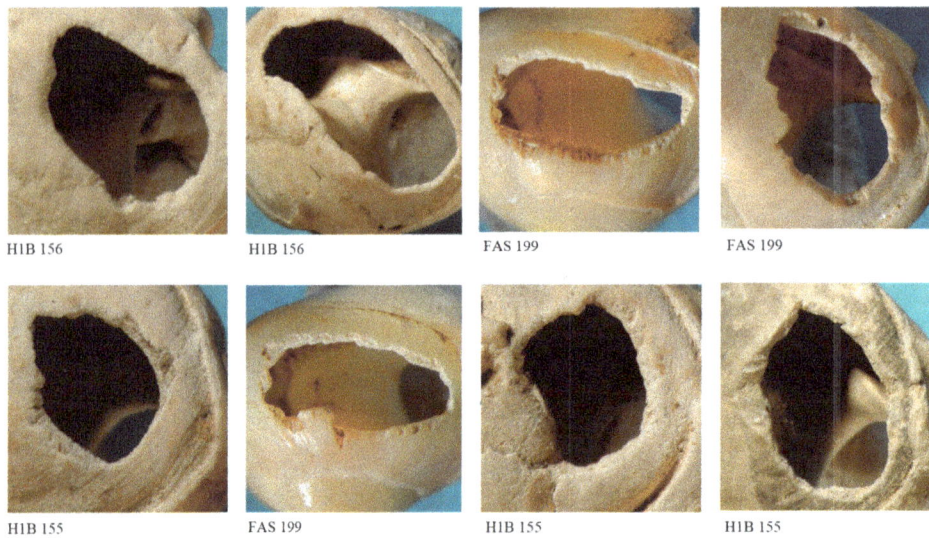

H1B 156　　　　　H1B 156　　　　　FAS 199　　　　　FAS 199

H1B 155　　　　　FAS 199　　　　　H1B 155　　　　　H1B 155

Fig. 3.8: Perforated Cyclope *sp. showing no or limited use-wear. No scale. Photographs M. Vanhaeren.*

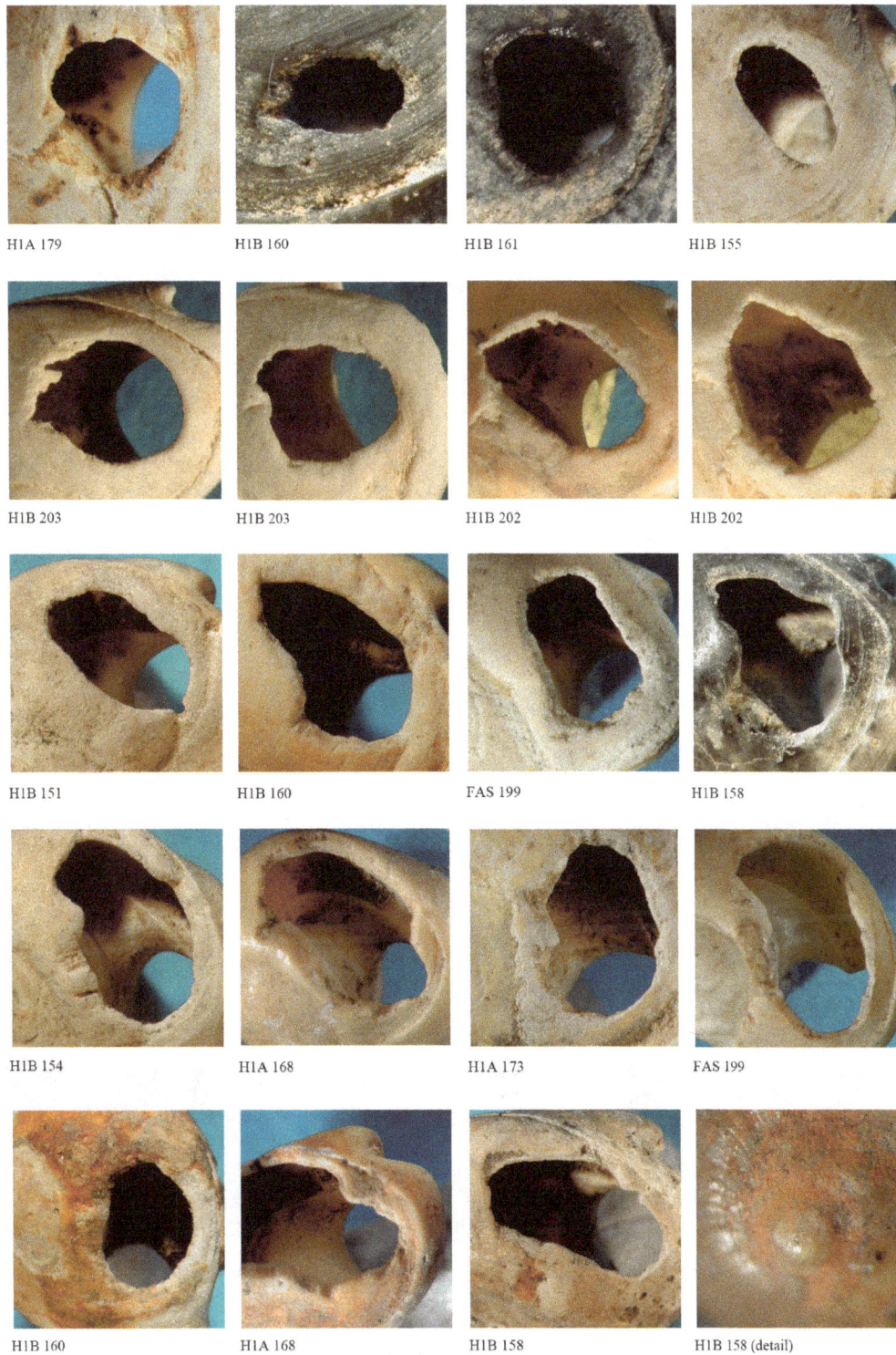

H1A 179   H1B 160   H1B 161   H1B 155

H1B 203   H1B 203   H1B 202   H1B 202

H1B 151   H1B 160   FAS 199   H1B 158

H1B 154   H1A 168   H1A 173   FAS 199

H1B 160   H1A 168   H1B 158   H1B 158 (detail)

Fig. 3.9: Use-wear on the perforation of Cyclope *sp. The use is especially developed on the labial part of the perforation. Shells on the last row show traces of pigment. No scale. Photographs M. Vanhaeren.*

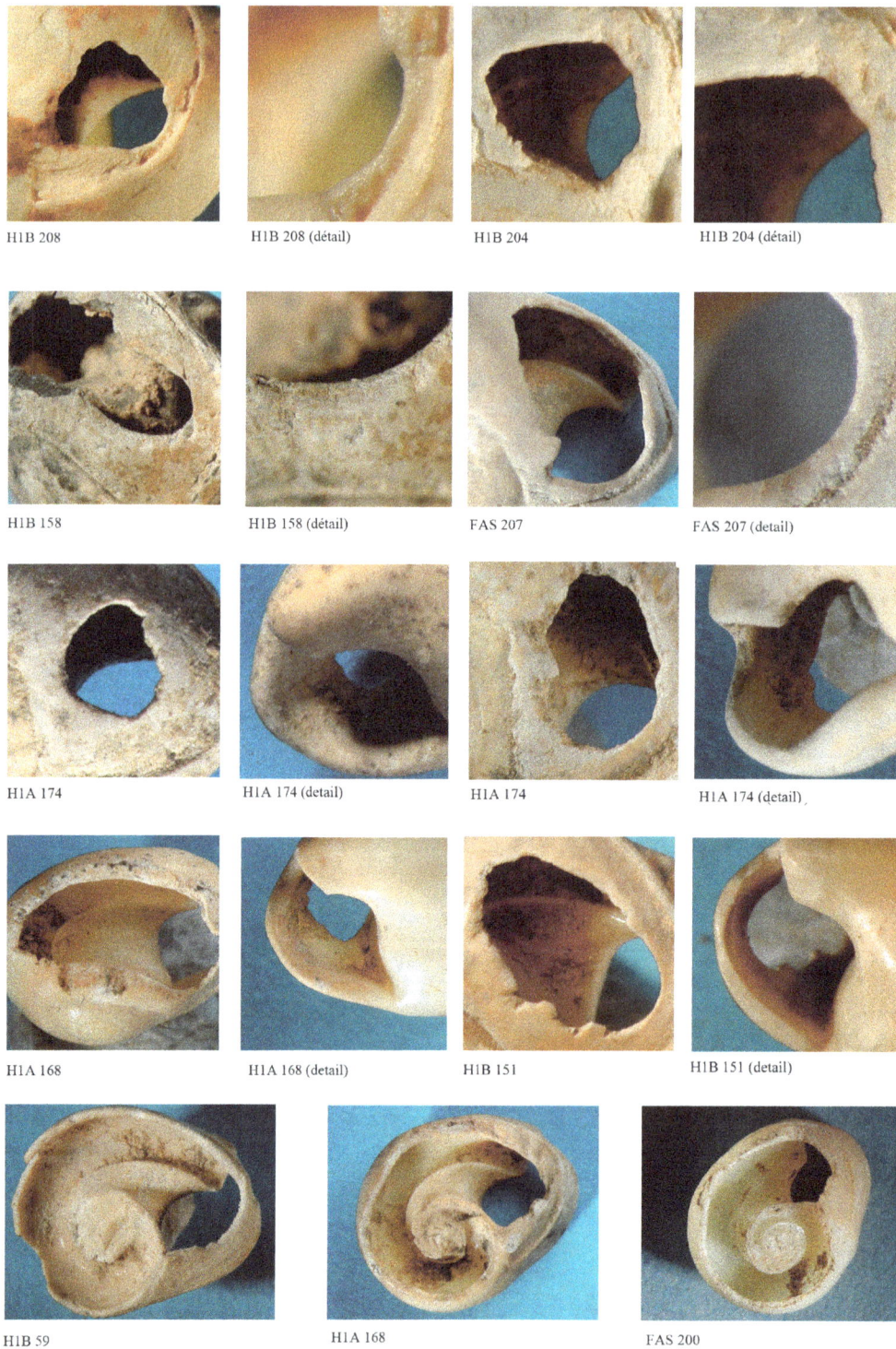

H1B 208   H1B 208 (détail)   H1B 204   H1B 204 (détail)

H1B 158   H1B 158 (détail)   FAS 207   FAS 207 (detail)

H1A 174   H1A 174 (detail)   H1A 174   H1A 174 (detail)

H1A 168   H1A 168 (detail)   H1B 151   H1B 151 (detail)

H1B 59   H1A 168   FAS 200

Fig. 3.10: Detail of use-wear and thread deformations on Cyclope *sp. First two rows: detail of wear on the labial part of the perforation. Bottom two rows: details of deformations and furrow created by the thread on the ventral face. No scale. Photographs M. Vanhaeren.*

NOTES

1   The smaller residues from trench H1A have not been sorted.
2   Because these poor snails no longer interest anyone, they have received no vernacular name in French or in English. To avoid the repetition of the cumbersome '*Cyclope* sp.' or '*Cyclope neritea/pellucida*', we shall henceforth nickname them 'Cyclopes'.
3   It would be even more difficult with the smaller *Cyclope pellucida.*
4   There are no *Cyclope* sp. in Phase 4.
5   The difference in means is not statistically significant but this might be due to the small size of the sample from Phases 0-3. To the contrary, the difference in class distribution is highly significant (χ^2=74, df = 8, p > 0.01).
6   The difference between the mean diameter in Phases 5 and 6 is statistically significant. T = 3.35, n1 = 98, n2 = 133, p < .01.
7   A very large dimensional range among *Cyclope* sp. was also observed in the Upper Palaeolithic ornament assemblages from Klithi and Boïla in Epirus (respectively 0.65 to 1.51 cm and 0.78 to 1.7 cm) but the mode(s) is not specified (Kotjabopoulou & Adams 2004: 44, 46). The range is smaller at Kastritsa (1.0 to 1.45 cm), with rather large dimensions compared with Franchthi (*idem*: 41).
8   The majority of the Cyclopes from the early phases come from Phase 2.
9   It actually varies depending on the time of the collecting. See Appendix 3.1..
10   For Phase 5, *t* = 0.98, p = 0.32; for Phase 6 : *t* = 1.39, p = 0.167. Neither is significant at p < 0.05.

PLATES

Plates 3.1 – 3.2: Palaeolithic Cyclope *sp. from trench FAS.*

Plates 3.3 – 3.4: Palaeolithic Cyclope *sp. from trench H1A.*

Plates 3.5 – 3.7: Palaeolithic Cyclope *sp. from trench H1B.*

FAS

223

223 (cont.)

222   221   220

219   218   217

217 (cont.)   216

215   214

212

209   208   207

203

1 cm

FAS (cont.)

200

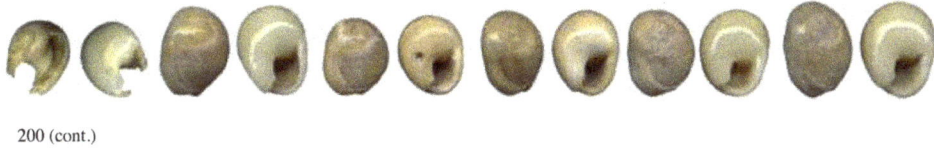

200 (cont.)

200 (cont.)

200 (cont.)

200 (cont.)

200 (cont.)

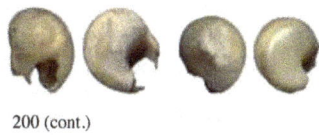

1 cm

200 (cont.)   199

199 (cont.)

H1A

220   219   218   211

179

179 (cont.)

178   175

174

174 (cont.)

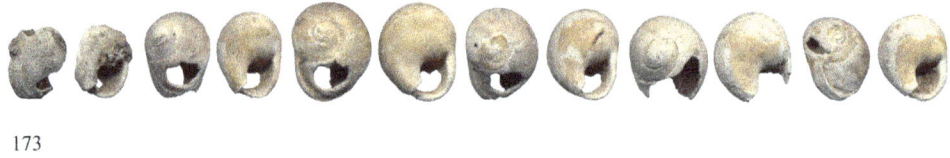

173

173 (cont.)

173 (cont.)   172

1 cm

H1A (cont.)

171   170   169

169 (cont.)

168

168 (cont.)

168 (cont.)

168 (cont.)

167

167 (cont.)

167 (cont.)

1 cm

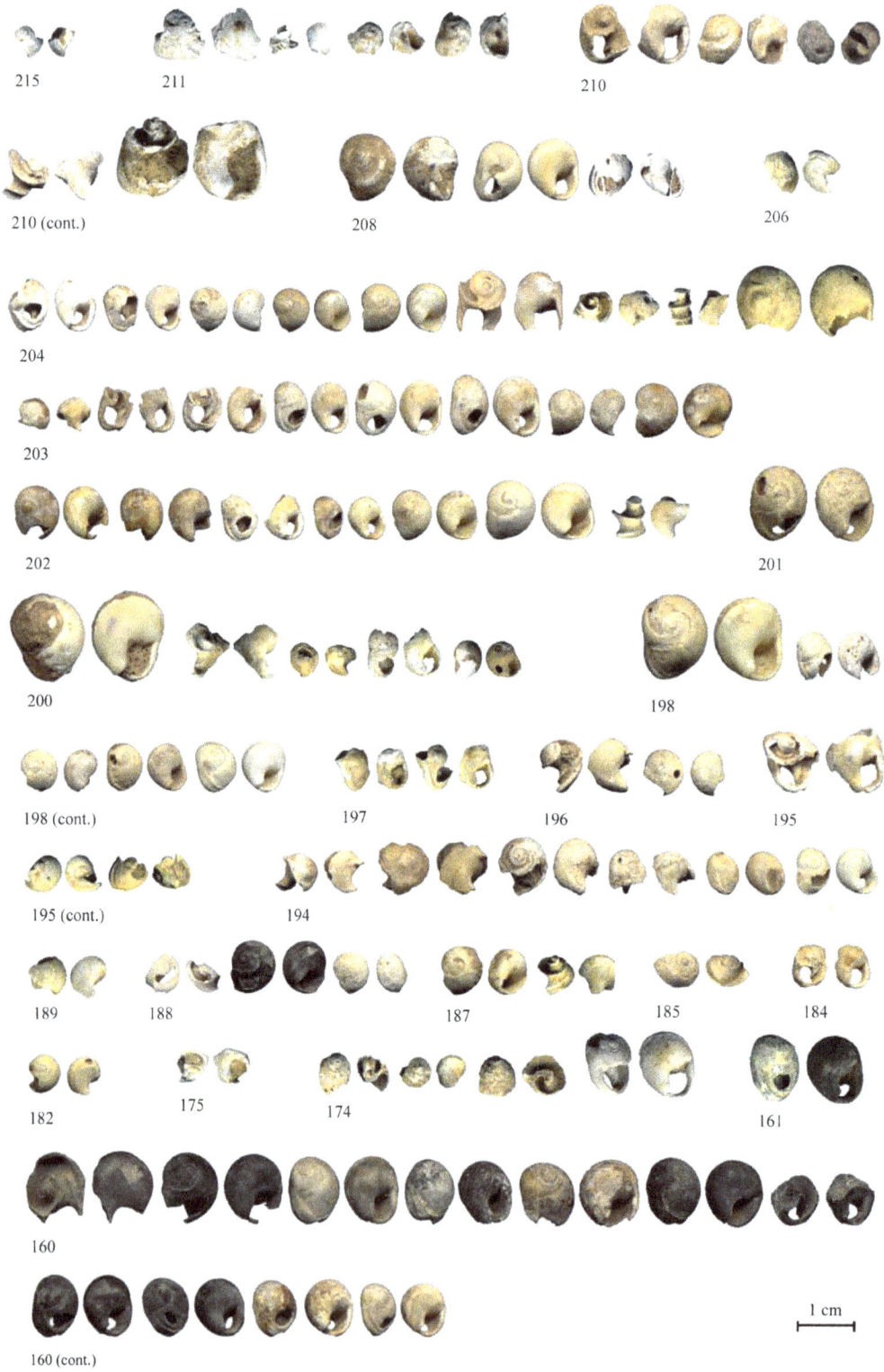

H1B

215   211   210

210 (cont.)   208   206

204

203

202   201

200   198

198 (cont.)   197   196   195

195 (cont.)   194

189   188   187   185   184

182   175   174   161

160

1 cm

160 (cont.)

H1B (cont.)

H1B 159

HIB 159 (cont.)   H1B 158

H1B 158 (cont.)

H1B 158 (cont.)

H1B 158 (cont.-   H1B 157

H1B 157 (cont.)

H1B 157 (cont.)

1 cm

H1B 157 (cont.)   H1B 156

H1B 156 (cont.)

H1B 156 (cont.)

H1B 156 (cont.)

H1B 156 (cont.)

H1B (cont.)

H1B 156 (cont.)

H1B 156 (cont.)

H1B 155

H1B 155 (cont.)

H1B 155 (cont.)

H1B 155 (cont.)

H1B 155 (cont.)

H1B 155 (cont.)

H1B 154   H1B 153

H1B 151

H1B 151 (cont.)

1 cm

CHAPTER FOUR

A Problematic Ornament Type: Antalis *sp., the Tusk Shell*

The genus *Antalis* is better known as *Dentalium,* its former denomination, or tusk shell in English. The shell is a long hollow tube with a large extremity—the anterior extremity—and a very narrow one—the posterior extremity. These scaphopods are a frequent component of prehistoric ornament assemblages (Bar-Yosef Mayer 2008; Taborin 1993, 2004). They are difficult to find alive as they usually live at depths where dredges are needed, with most of the shell buried and only the narrow posterior opening protruding. Tusk shells are thus usually collected in thanatocoenoses, where they are found in variable quantities according to the beach, waves and current. The size of the segments varies according to the nature of the beach, with larger segments on sandy beaches and smaller segments on gravelly beaches (Appendix 3.3). They are present both in the Atlantic and the Mediterranean; the quasi absence of tides in the Mediterranean Sea probably explains why our rates of collection appear to have been lower than on the Atlantic coast (*idem*).

Segments of *Antalis* sp. are present at Franchthi in the earliest excavated levels, below the tephra deposit dated to ca. 39,000 BP (Farrand 2000). They are consistently represented throughout the Palaeolithic sequence. In absolute numbers, *Antalis* sp. segments are less numerous than *Cyclope* sp. However, a higher proportion of the Palaeolithic *Antalis* (ca. 75%) were retrieved in residues from the < 5 mm sieves. Since S. Payne sorted only a fraction of these residues, tusk shells could actually have been substantially more numerous than Cyclopes.

Taxonomy

The Franchthi Palaeolithic assemblages comprise smooth tusk shells, finely ribbed tusk shells, and thick-ribbed specimens with different numbers and patterns of ribs. The smooth surface of some specimens, however, seems to be the result of the peeling off of the outer layer rather than an original feature (see Fig.4.1, n° 8).

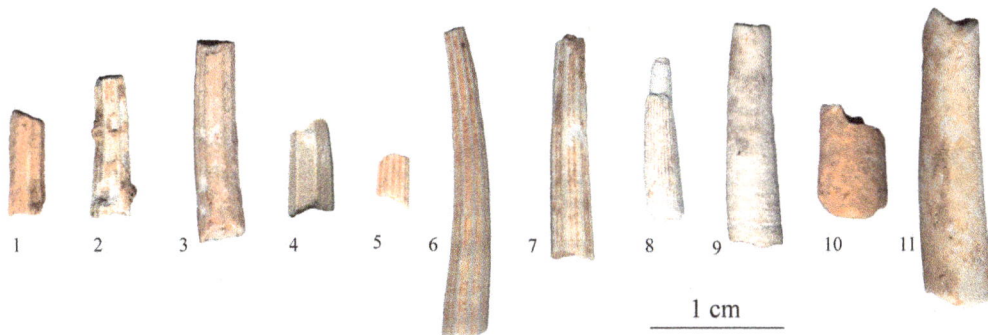

Fig. 4.1: Different types of Antalis *sp. from the Palaeolithic levels. CAD M. Vanhaeren.*

Several species are undoubtedly present, but the different species of *Dentaliidae* are notoriously difficult to differentiate (Kurzawska *et al.* 2013). Delamotte & Vardala-Theodorou (2001) list seven species of *Dentalium* (= *Antalis*) and one species of *Fustiaria* in present-day Greek waters. In addition to these, fossil specimens may also be present in our archaeological series. For lack of reference collections, we have not attempted to make specific identifications. Thick-ribbed tusk shells, comparable to *A. inaequicostata* largely predominate, but they may actually group several species. Smooth or finely ribbed tusk shells, comparable to *A. vulgaris,* constitute a small minority (less than 10%), probably artificially inflated by peeled-off specimens. The marked predominance of thick-ribbed tusk shells is in total contrast with our reference collections, which comprise exclusively the smooth *Antalis* cf. *vulgaris.* The cause of this discrepancy is unknown.

The Palaeolithic *Antalis* sp.: A Partial Recovery

J. Shackleton, in the course of her study of the marine molluscs, had set aside most of the tusk shells from the > 5mm residues. We found very few when re-sorting the shell bags. However, a large majority of the *Antalis* sp. segments—76.5 % for the three trenches—was recovered in the < 5 mm and < 2.8 mm residues (Table 4.1). These residues were sorted by S. Payne in fractions of 1/4th to 1/32th of their total volume, and the *Antalis* sp. segments were set aside. If the < 5 mm and < 2.8 mm residues had been entirely sorted, the number of small and medium-sized tusk shell fragments would have been considerably higher.

Trench	R ≥ 5 mm	R < 5 mm
H1A	13	51
H1B	19	63
FAS	22	50
Total	51 (23.6 %)	165 (76,4%)

Table 4.1: Number of Antalis *sp. found in residues from the ≥ 5 mm sieves and < 5 mm sieves.*

From Large to Tiny: Dimensional Variation

As a consequence of these recovery procedures, the longer and wider segments of *Antalis* sp., which were mostly recovered in the > 5 mm residues—entirely sorted—are slightly overrepresented in the following graphs compared with the smaller specimens. Since this bias affects less than a quarter of the total sample, I have preferred not to try and compensate for it by artificially multiplying the smaller samples by the fraction of the residues actually sorted.

Sharp dimensional contrasts can be visually perceived when looking at the entire Palaeolithic assemblage (Plate 4.1). However, the distributions of length and maximum diameter are continuous and no distinct classes can be established (Fig. 4.2).

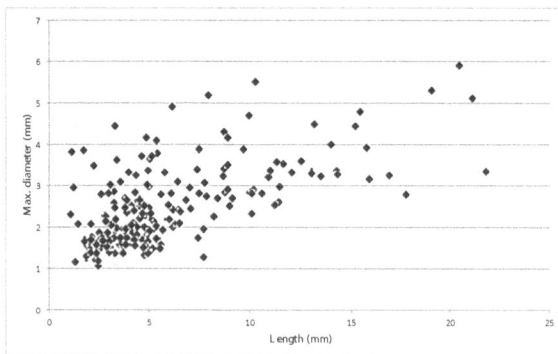

Fig. 4.2: Length and maximum diameter of Palaeolithic Antalis *sp. segments.*

FAS

227 226 225 224 223 222 221 220 219

218 217 216 215 214 213 212 210 209 208 206 205 204 203 202 199

H1A

220 219 218 217 216 215

213 212 211 210 209 208 191 186 185 183 182 178 175 174 169 168

H1B

215 210 209 207 206 205 204 203 202

200 *FV 418* 191 *FV 406-409* 188 *FV 404-405* 185 *FV 416* 182 181 175

FV 415 *FV 386*

158 157 155 154 151

1 cm

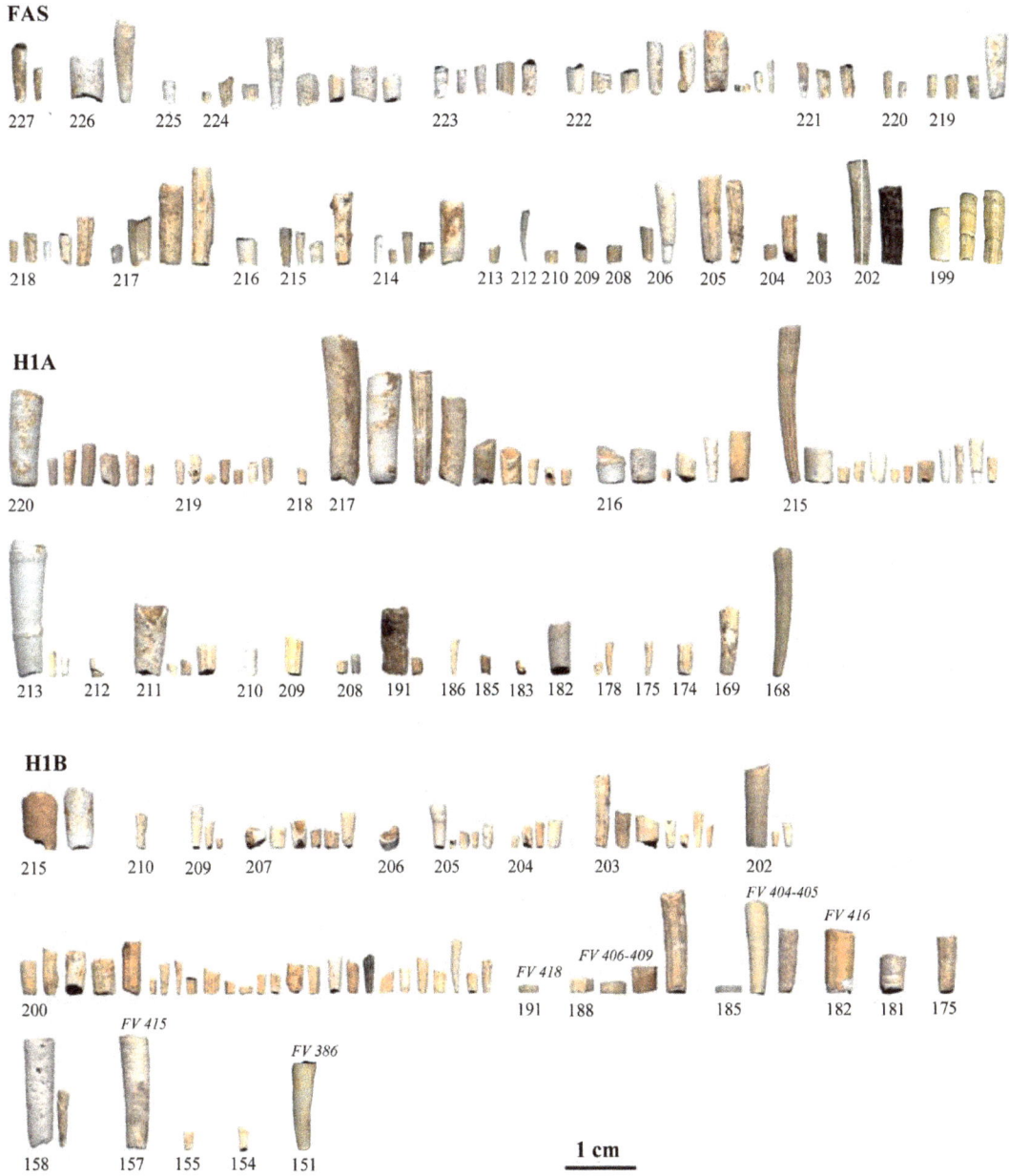

Plate 4.1: Palaeolithic Antalis *sp. Some of the smaller posterior segments are missing on the plate. CAD M. Vanhaeren and C.P.*

If we examine each parameter separately, the structure of the assemblage becomes clearer. The length distribution (Fig. 4.3) clearly shows the predominance of tiny segments, ranging from 1 mm to 6 mm[1], and a sharp drop between 6 and 7 mm. At the other end of the spectrum, very few segments exceed 15 mm, a small value compared with our reference collections. The very small size of Palaeolithic *Antalis* sp. segments at Franchthi is unusual compared with other Palaeolithic assemblages (Vanhaeren 2010). It is comparable, on the other hand, to the dimensions of Late Natufian assemblages (Bar-Yosef Mayer 2008, figs. 1 and 2) but the latter seems to correspond to segments of a larger diameter.

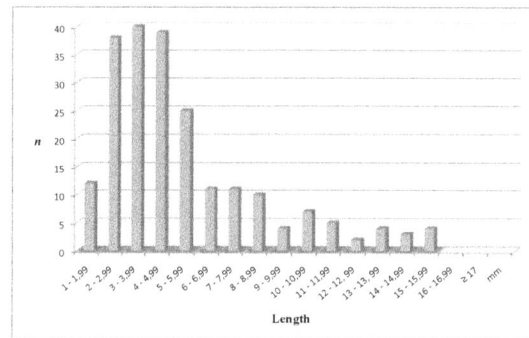

Fig. 4.3: Length of Palaeolithic Antalis *sp. segments.*

The distribution of maximum diameters (Fig. 4.4) shows a marked peak of very small diameters, between 1.5 and 1.75 mm, followed by a flat distribution up to 3 mm and a gradual decrease up to 5 mm. Among the larger specimens, a few are larger than any we have collected (d > 4.25 mm). This could be due to the difference in species represented, but it could also correspond to a few fossil specimens. Despite important differences in absolute numbers[2], the range of dimensional classes is comparable in the early and late Upper Palaeolithic phases (Table 4.2). The slight proportional increase of the larger segments to the detriment of the smaller ones in the later phases is not statistically significant. The distribution of minimum diameters (Fig. 4.4) is closer to a normal distribution, but confirms the predominance of narrow posterior segments.

Altogether, an unusually high proportion of short, and especially very narrow posterior segments characterises the Palaeolithic assemblages from Franchthi. This raises the question of the origin and significance of these small segments, some of which are too narrow to be threaded.

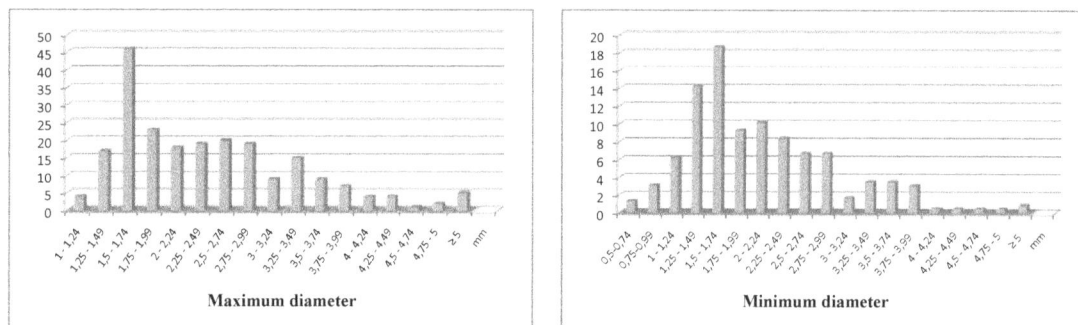

Fig. 4.4: Maximum (anterior) and minimum (posterior) diameters of Antalis *sp. segments.*

Maximum diameter	1- 2mm	2 - 2.99 mm	> 3mm	Total
Phases 0-3	78 (42.4 %)	65 (35.3 %)	41 (22.3 %)	184
Phases 4-6	12 (40 %)	9 (30 %)	9 (30%)	30
Total	90	74	50	214

Table 4.2: Distribution by class of maximum diameter of Antalis *sp. segments.*

One or More Agents of Deposition?

It could be tempting to think that medium and large shells correspond to the familiar tubular *Antalis* sp. beads, while the smallest segments were bead production debris resulting from snapping off the narrow posterior extremity. The dense cluster of very small segments (L < 6 mm, D. max < 2 mm) comprises 41% of the total assemblage. These segments are similar to the segments (one to three per shell) we obtained when snapping off the posterior extremity of complete *Antalis*—in this case *Antalis* cf. *vulgare*—so that the shell could be threaded[3]. Theoretically, if one supposes that a fair proportion of the tusk shells were collected with an intact posterior extremity, the proportion of manufacturing debris to beads would appear realistic. However, many of our *Antalis* sp. segments show characteristic wave and sand erosion of the extremities, and were collected already broken. In addition, it should be recalled that ca. 75% of the *Antalis* sp. were recovered in subsamples within the < 5 mm residues. If the residues had been entirely sorted, the total number of small and medium-sized segments would have been considerably higher. For instance, on a sample of H1B units for which the rate of sampling is available (H1B 214 –202), the 30 *Antalis* sp. from the < 5 mm residues would amount to 560 specimens if multiplied by the rate of sampling[4]. The complete sorting of the residues would thus have inflated the proportion of small posterior segments in relation to the larger specimens recovered in the > 5 mm sieves. Consequently, the hypothesis that all the *Antalis* sp. segments correspond to beads and manufacturing debris would imply (a) that most tusk shells were picked up intact on beaches, which does not appear to be the case (b) that the production of beads was very intense, and (c) that the ornaments were mostly composed of unusually small beads for a Palaeolithic context.

We must thus consider alternative interpretations. The smaller *Antalis* sp. segments are indeed especially abundant in Phases 0 – 2, which are also rich in micromolluscs, 3 – 5 mm long on average, and where J. Shackleton identified a large proportion of *Bittium* sp. (Shackleton J. 1988). A. Colonese's detailed identification to the genus or the species of all the available FAS and H1B samples, from the < 5 mm and < 2.8 mm residues confirmed that the genus *Bittium* (including *B. latreilli* and *B. reticulatum*) was best represented among the marine shells (n = 208), followed by *Rissoa* sp. and Higromiidae (Appendix 2). The same deposits are also extremely rich in tiny uncarbonised Boraginaceae seeds (*Alkanna* sp, *Anchusa* sp., *Lithodora* (*Lithospermum*) *arvense*), preserved thanks to their high silica content (Hansen 1991).

Both the seeds and the micromolluscs (Fig. 4. 5) are considered as natural deposits. The smaller segments of *Antalis* sp., which are comparable in size and weight to the *Bittium* and other micromolluscs, could thus be part of this naturally deposited molluscan assemblage. The larger ones, to the contrary, would have been intentionally picked up on the beaches and brought back to the cave. The close correspondence between the distribution of medium and large segments (L > 6 mm, D. max > 2.25 mm) from Franchthi and handpicked tusk shells from Kouverta beach (Appendix 3.3) would seem to support this dual origin (Figs. 4.6 and 4.7).

Fig. 4.5: Pebbles, cf. Bittium *sp. (centre), and Boraginaceae seeds (right) from the < 2.8 mm residues of H1B 212. Photograph M. Vanhaeren.*

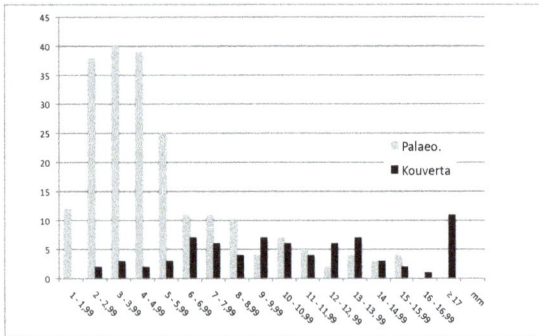

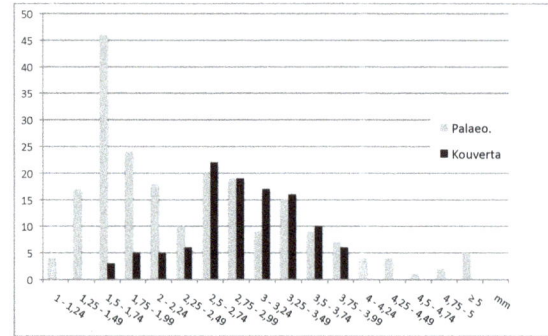

Figs. 4.6 and 4.7: Length and maximum diameter of Antalis *sp. segments from Palaeolithic levels at Franchthi and Kouverta beach (Argolid).*

To test whether the *Antalis* sp. segments could be, at least in part, natural deposits, we calculated the Pearson's coefficients of correlation between *Antalis* sp. segments, *Bittium* sp. and Boraginaceae seeds on all the series of units where figures were available for the three categories of remains. In theory, null or negative correlations should indicate that *Antalis* sp., *Bittium* sp. and Boraginaceae seeds were deposited by different agents. Positive correlations would be more ambiguous, since they might reflect either similar deposition processes or simply the presence of especially rich units where all categories accumulated in abundance. To test the alternative hypothesis of an anthropic deposition, we also calculated the correlation coefficients with the stone microflakes in the same < 5 mm residues (Table 4.3).

These calculations reveal no correlation in the three trenches between *Antalis* sp. and microflakes, no correlation between *Antalis* sp. and Boraginaceae seeds in H1A, and between *Bittium* sp. and Boraginaceae in FAS. In all other cases, moderately positive correlations were obtained. However, when the graphs are plotted, the correlations appear mostly based on very few

Trench	Antalis sp./ Bittium sp.	Antalis sp./ Boraginaceae seeds	Bittium sp./ Boraginaceae seeds	Antalis sp./ microflakes
H1A 220-168	na	- 0.026 (not sign.)	na	na
H1B 215-202	0.56 (sign. at p < 0.05)	0.53 (sign. at p < 0.05)	0.56 (sign. at p < 0.05)	0.1
FAS 227-199	0.51 (sign. at p < 0.01)	0.5 (sign. at p < 0.01)	0.29 (not sign.)	- 0.18

Table 4.3: Pearson's coefficients of correlation between Antalis *sp. segments,* Bittium *sp., Boraginaceae seeds and microflakes from the < 5 mm residues.*

units and therefore weaker than suggested by the coefficient. In particular, the positive correlations between Boraginaceae seeds on the one hand, *Bittium* sp. and *Antalis* sp. on the other hand, are based on two or three units only (Fig. 4.8). In FAS for instance, the removal of the single unit FAS 223, from a total of 28 units, leads to a drop of the correlation coefficient between *Antalis* sp. and Boraginaceae from 0.5 to 0.18 (not significant). Similarly, the significant correlation between these two categories in H1B is based on two units only out of 15, and falls at 0.15 when they are removed. It can thus be assumed that the seeds were deposited independently from the shells, possibly washed down with the sediment or brought in by rodents and birds, as suggested by Hansen (1991: 101).

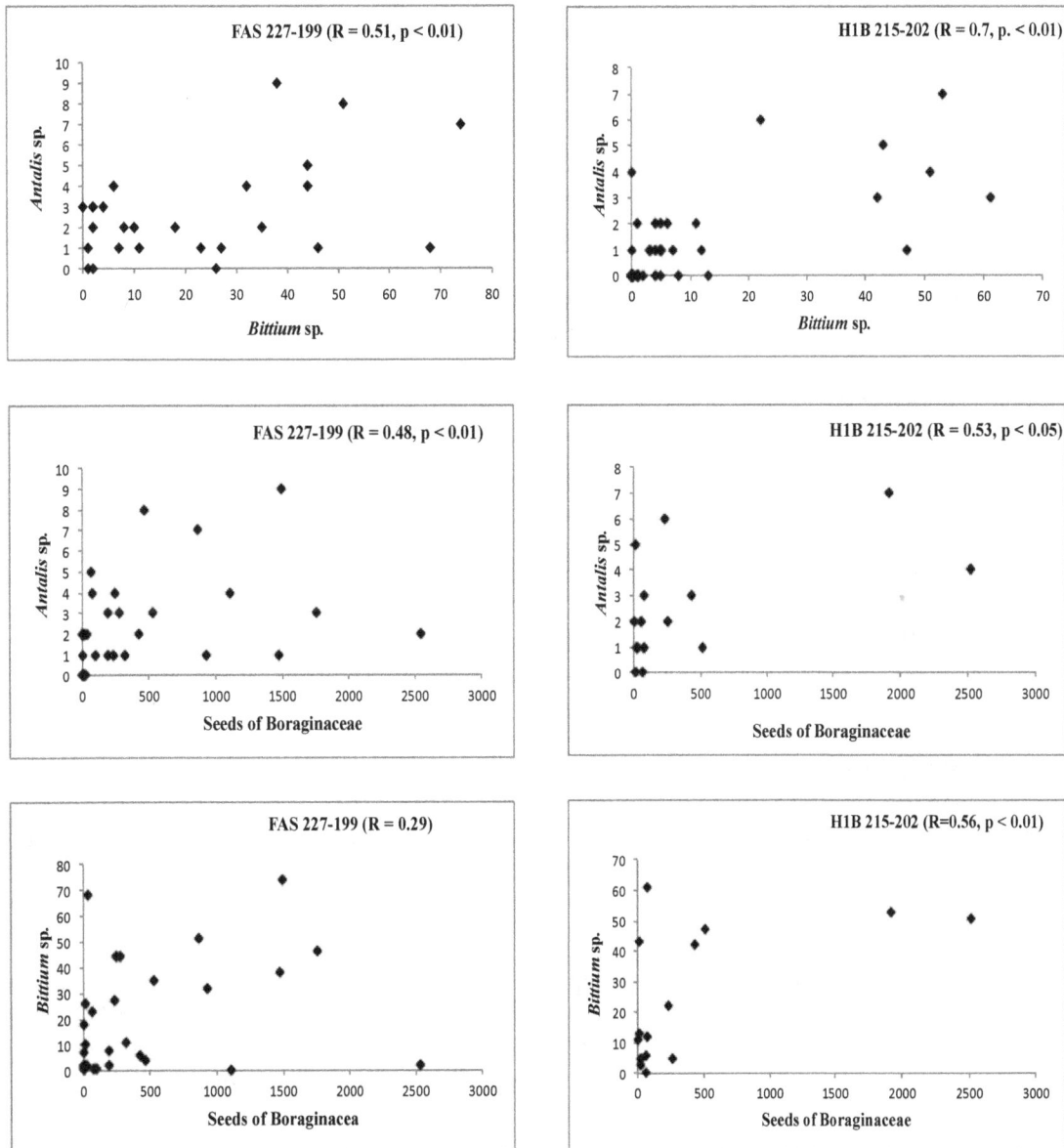

Fig. 4.8: Graphs of correlation between Antalis *sp. segments,* Bittium *sp. and uncarbonised seeds of Boraginaceae in FAS and H1B (data on* Bittium *sp. are not available for H1A).*

The correlations between *Antalis* sp. and *Bittium* sp. appears somewhat stronger, although in both FAS and H1B they are based on a minority of units, but not necessarily the units with the largest volume of sediment. Though not decisive, these moderately high correlations contrast with the complete absence of correlation between *Antalis* sp. segments and retouch microflakes, the only component of assuredly anthropic origin in the < 5 mm residues. Under these conditions, it is difficult to reject the hypothesis that some at least of the *Antalis* sp. segments belong to the micromolluscan assemblage.

Farrand (2000: 56) notes that the excavators identified deposits of marine sand with "bits of marine shells" in Stratum R, which encompasses our Phases 1 and 2, rich in small tusk shell segments. He considers that the "exotic sand component of these loams can be attributed, in part, to human agency (...) walking back and forth across the coastal plain" but that "there is also the possibility, even the likelihood, that some of the fine-grained sand grains may have been blown in by the wind sweeping across the Gulf of Argos and the wide coastal plain" (*idem*: 93-94). J. Shackleton (1988: 65) also favored the hypothesis of wind-blown micromolluscs. Small scale, homemade experiments[5] make us doubt they could have been transported in suspension. They are easily displaced by saltation but a distance of 3.5 km—the distance from the sea to the site during Phases 1, 2 and 5—seems very long over a steppe-covered slope. In other coastal Palaeolithic settlements where *Bittium* sp. was recovered in large quantities, other hypotheses have been suggested. Stiner (1999) envisioned an introduction with sea sponges at Riparo Mochi (Italy), or with driftwood or algae (Kuhn & Stiner 1998). At Le Lazaret (France) and Grotta della Serratura (Italy) *Bittium* sp. is considered to have been brought in with seaweeds used as beddings[6] (Barrière 1969; Colonese & Wilkens 2005). Zilhão and his colleagues (2010) attribute the accidental introduction of a few inedible species at Cueva de los Aviones (Spain) to the packaging of edible marine molluscs in seeweeds soaked in water so as to prevent rapid decay. Other than wind, various human activities could thus be responsible for the introduction of the *Bittium* sp. and other micromolluscs, including *Antalis* sp. segments.

However, three other observations complicate the discussion and cast doubts on a systematic association between *Antalis* sp. and *Bittium* sp. First, *Bittium* sp. are still present in the < 5 mm Mesolithic residues, but small *Antalis* segments (D max < 2.2 mm) are extremely rare and the correlation between *Bittium* and *Antalis* in H1B Mesolithic units[7] is null (Pearson's r = 0.02). This demonstrates that the introduction of *Bittium* does not necessarily entail that of small *Antalis* segments. Second, *Antalis* sp. segments are especially abundant in Phase 0 (Stratum P), the only phase where they supersede *Cyclope* sp. in numbers. This had initially seemed in favor of a natural introduction, since human occupations are sparse during this phase. However, Phase 0, whose lithic assemblage is undiagnostic, should correspond chronologically to the 'Uluzzian' of Klissoura Cave 1, also in the Argolid: both strata directly underlie a tephra layer attributed to the Campanian Ignimbrite (Farrand 2000: 56; Koumouzelis 2010: 11). Significantly, at Klissoura Cave 1, *Antalis* sp. is especially abundant in this Uluzzian phase (Stiner 2010, table 4 p. 292). More generally, Zilhão (2007) clearly considers *Antalis* sp. as the most characteristic ornamental species for the Uluzzian, based on evidence from the Italian Grotta del Cavallo[8].

Third, very small segments of *Antalis* sp. used as beads were recovered at Kastritsa cave, located on the shore of the Ioannina lake, some 115 km away from the Late Glacial Maximum shore. In particular, two large *Antalis* sp. beads respectively contained one and two narrower segments, which would have been inserted as a result of stringing (Kotjabopoulou & Adams 2004: 41). Altogether, the tubular *Antalis* sp. segments from Kastritsa ranged in length from 6 to 20 mm, from 2 to 4 mm in maximum diameter and 1.5 to 3 mm in minimum (posterior) diameter.

The evidence from Kastritsa, where anthropic deposition is indisputable, show that tusk shell segments as short 6 mm in length and as narrow as 1.5 mm in minimum diameter were part of the ornament assemblage[9]. The Late Pleistocene Natufian Grave XIII from Hayonim Cave (Israel) confirms the use of very small apical segments in prehistoric ornaments (Kurzawska *et al.* 2013: Fig. 3)[10]. Thus, while it would be unreasonable to assume that no small *Antalis* sp. segments were naturally included in the micromolluscan assemblage at Franchthi[11], there are also converging lines of evidence to suggest that a majority may well have been small beads. We shall henceforth retain 1.5 mm as the minimum diameter for tusk shell bead*s* in subsequent counts, in order to avoid artificially inflating the number of ornaments. Indeed, narrower segments[12] may be bead manufacturing debris or unintentional deposits, but not threaded beads.

Tusk Shells as Beads

High magnification examination of all *Antalis* sp. segments was implemented on the H1B sample, to look for both traces of manufacturing and use. The poor state of preservation of our Palaeolithic *Antalis*, showing a mix of wave abrasion and chemical attacks (Fig. 4.9), rendered, however, traceological studies difficult and limited in scope.

Vanhaeren (2010: 45-50) has shown that it was difficult to differentiate natural breakage from intentional fragmentation of the *Antalis*, unless the shells had been sawn with a stone tool. Unfortunately, no trace of sawing has been identified on our sample. There are, however, converging indices of the use of *Antalis* sp. as beads. While a majority of the smaller segments display uneven breaks at one or both extremities (Fig. 4.10), a majority of the larger specimens (D ≥ 2.5- 3 mm) show straight fractures. Several specimens are also characterised by a marked contrast between the worn and rounded anterior (i.e. large) extremity, and the straight and unworn posterior (i.e. small) extremity, comparable to experimentally snapped and grounded *Antalis* beads (Fig. 4.11: A –C). This would correspond to the intentional removing of the thinner extremity, so as to thread the bead more easily. The reverse combination is also documented (Fig. 4.13:4), suggesting an intentional reduction of the size of the bead. There are some instances, in addition, of medium or large diameter segments with irregular breakage at both extremities (Fig. 4.12:A), either pre- or post-depositional. Other large *Antalis* segments display, as would be expected, well worn and rounded extremities, directly comparable to our beach-collected specimens (Fig. 4.12:B).

Important beach polish is also characteristic of the five small *Antalis* 'roundels', which can be produced naturally when two shells get nested one inside the other one (Vanhaeren 2010: fig. 11). The very good state of preservation of several of these roundels (e.g. Fig. 4.12:C-D) contrasts with that of many longer segments, possibly because they were cut towards the thicker, anterior, part of the shell. Rare traces of ochre have also been observed (Fig. 4.13 and possibly Fig. 4.12:C). Three *Antalis* sp. roundels were also uncovered at Kastritsa and one at Klithi. All are wide compared with the tubular segments of *Antalis*; this suggests they did not break off accidentally, but were intentionally picked up to serve as beads (Kotjabopoulou & Adams 2004). At Franchthi, they also concentrate within the largest values, around 3.8 mm diameter and the well-polished faces confirm they were intentionally collected as such.

H1B 200   H1B 175   H1B 175

Fig. 4.9: Wave abrasion and chemical attack on Antalis *sp. (not to scale). Photographs M. Vanhaeren.*

Fig. 4.10: Morphology of the extremities of small Antalis *sp. segments, all from H1B 200. Note the predominance of irregular fractures. Not to scale. Length of the segments between 2.5 and 5 mm. Photographs M. Vanhaeren.*

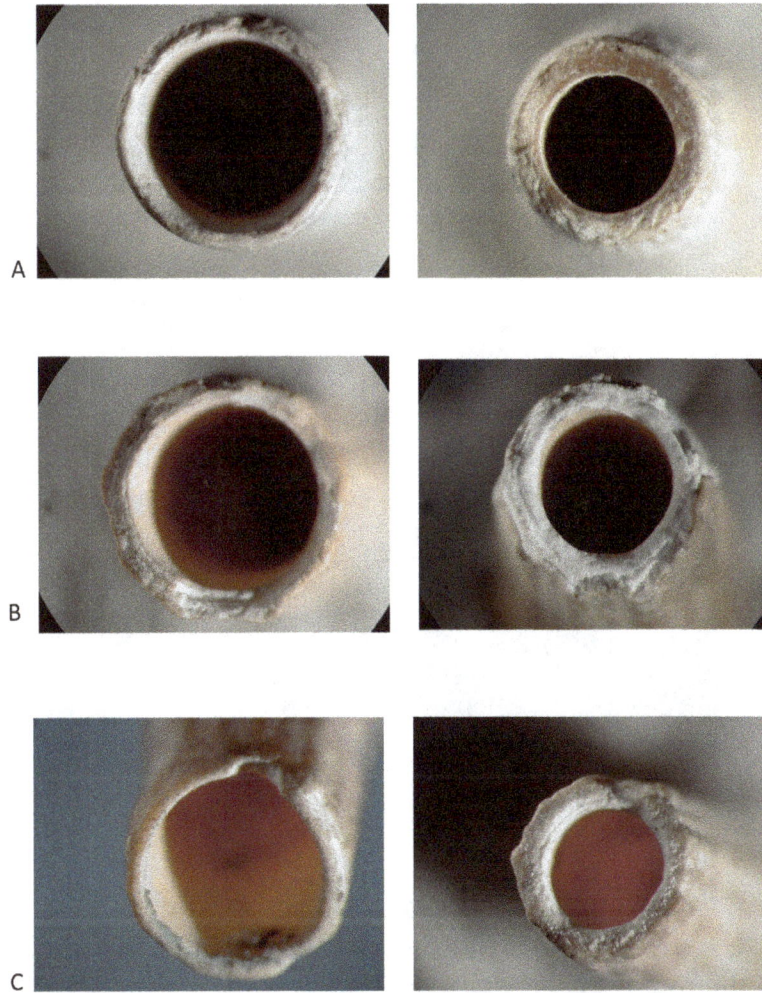

Fig. 4.11: Anterior and posterior extremities. A: H1B 157. L = 15.7 mm, D max = 3.94 m, D min = 2.84 mm. B: H1B 182 (FV 416) L = 8.87 mm, D max = 4.15 mm, D min = 3.57 mm. C: H1B 188 (FV 406), L = 14.27 mm, D max = 3.36, D min = 2.85 mm. Photographs M. Vanhaeren.

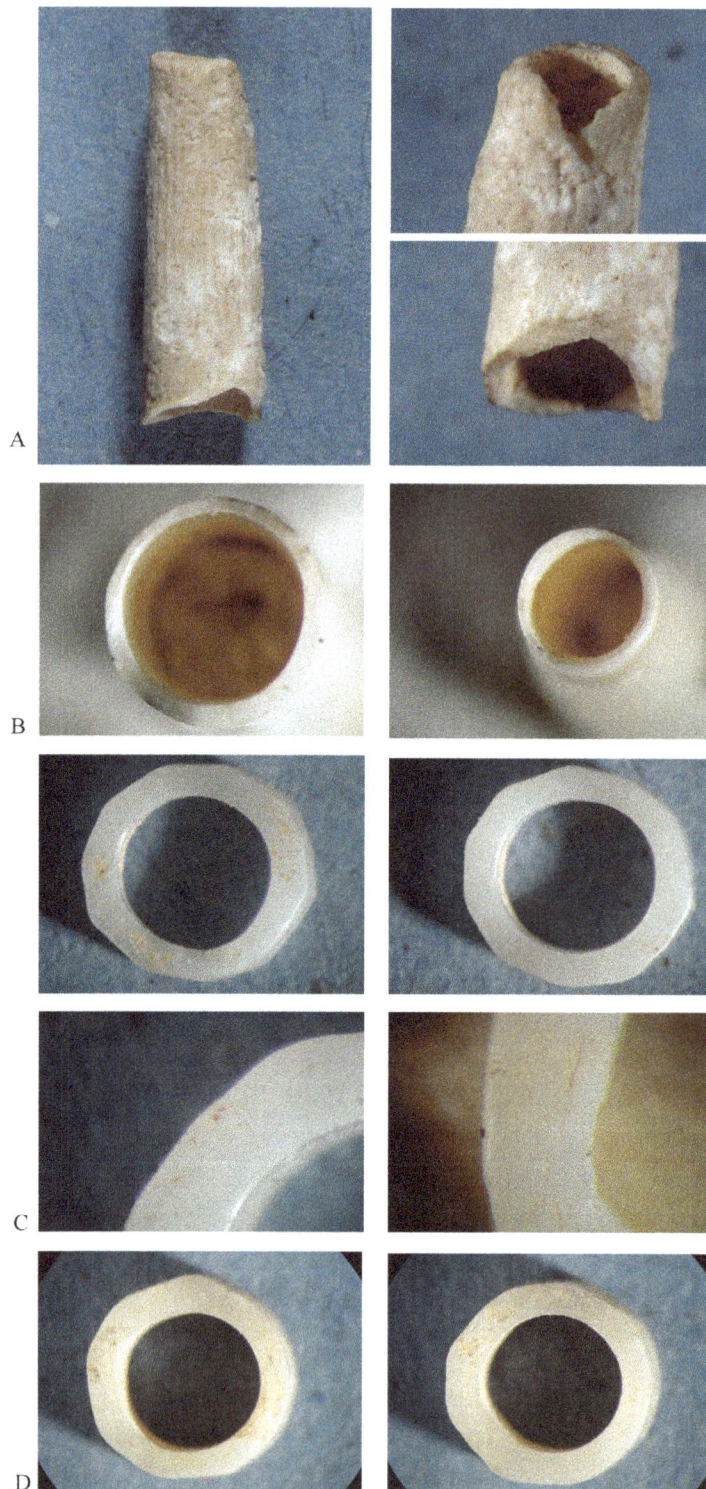

Fig. 4.12: Anterior and posterior extremities. A: H1B 157. L = 15.7 mm, D max = 3.94 mm, D min = 2.84 mm. B: H1B 182 (FV 416) L = 8.87 mm, D max = 4.15 mm, D min = 3.57 mm. C: H1B 188 (FV 406), L = 14.27 mm, D max = 3.36, D min = 2.85 mm. D. H1B 188 (FV 408), L = 1,7 mm, D max = 3.85 mm, D min = 3.84 mm. Photographs M. Vanhaeren.

Fig. 4.13: Top: H1B 158. Antalis sp. segment with one slightly worn and one straight fracture, bearing traces of ochre. L = 7.85 mm, D max = 2.75 mm, D min = 2.29 mm. Bottom: FAS 199. Antalis sp. segment with traces of ochre (L = 10.58, D max = 2.82, D min = 2.24 Photographs M. Vanhaeren.

NOTES

1. Because of the very small size of many segments, we shall give here the dimensions in mm, not in cm.
2. *Antalis* sp. specimens remain more abundant in early UP phases even when the numbers are standardized to take into account the variations in the volume of sediment excavated (see *infra*, Chap. 7)
3. It is possible to thread an *Antalis* shell with double horse hair, for instance, down to about 1.5 mm in minimum diameter. Any other kind of thread, such as vegetal fibers or tendons, would require larger apertures.
4. However, such a simple arithmetic multiplication does not take into account random variations on small samples and provides highly unreliable figures.
5. With hair driers and electric fans.
6. *Bittium reticulatum* lives and feeds in seaweeds (Borja 2008).
7. HIB is the only trench for which we have detailed counts of the micromolluscs in the Mesolithic.
8. Even though Álvarez-Fernández and Jöris (2008) question their actual use as suspended ornaments.
9. Bar-Yosef Mayer (1989: 171) mentions even smaller beads, 1 mm wide, from a Kebarian *Dentalium* workshop at Urkan-e-Rub IIa in the lower Jordan valley.
10. There are also many short segments, but we do not know whether they represent individual beads or broken fragments of longer beads.
11. As seemingly confirmed by the moderate correlation between the number of *Antalis* sp. segments and *Bittium* sp.
12. 22 % of the total *Antalis* assemblage fall under 6 mm in length and 1.5 mm in minimal diameter.

CHAPTER FIVE

Columbella rustica, *Rare but Heavily Worn Dove Shell Beads*

Columbella rustica (Linné 1758), or dove shell, is a small Mediterranean gastropod of ovoid shape with a pointed apex. It is brightly coloured from almost white to beige, orange or brown, and ornamented with patterns of dots and zigzag lines (Appendix 3.2). It lives on rocks at depths from 0.10 to 30 metres. It is variously claimed to be omnivorous (Delamotte & Vardala-Theodorou 2001), carnivorous (Milišić 1991, 2007 quoted in Komšo & Vukosavljević 2011) or herbivorous (http://mglebrusc.free.fr/textes/la%20mer/Faune/columbella.html).

Columbella rustica is not known by man, but was widely used as an ornamental species around the Mediterranean in prehistoric times. In the Western Mediterranean dove shells are rare in the Upper Palaeolithic and characteristic of Mesolithic ornament assemblages (Álvarez-Fernández 2010). On the contrary, it is well represented in the Initial and early Upper Palaeolithic levels in the Levant (Kuhn *et al.* 2001), and in the Uluzzian and Aurignacian levels from Klissoura Cave 1 (Stiner 2010). At Franchthi, it is much less abundant than *Cyclope* sp. and *Antalis* sp., with only 44 specimens that concentrate in the later Upper Palaeolithic phases (Phases 5 and 6). Given the very different environmental requirements of *Cyclope* and *Columbella*, they could not have been collected together: each taxon had to be searched for at different points along the coast.

A Fair Representativeness of the Sample

The sample analyzed comprises all the intact *C. rustica* and identified fragments from the > 5 mm residues. André Colonese recovered only seven fragments in the shell samples from the < 5 mm residues. Since these samples correspond to 1/4th to 1/32th of the total of the sediments, the actual number must have been higher. However, these specimens are too fragmentary to be informative and sorting of all residues would not have added relevant data.

The shell of *C. rustica* is much more compact that the shell of *Cyclope* sp. and the overall state of preservation is better, despite superficial chemical attacks and frequent breakage along the sutures of the spire or on the dorsal face of the last whorl. Intact dove shells are indeed the exception rather than the rule (Table 5.1), but most specimens with a broken apex—loss of the first, sometimes second whorl—were probably collected as such on the beach and can be considered 'archaeologically intact' (see Appendix 3.2, Table A3.6). More severe breakage took place after the dove shells were used as beads: many lost their base or last whorl after they had been perforated and worn, as indicated by use-wear on the preserved edges of the perforation (Fig. 5.1). The shell being rather solid, this high rate of breakage should be attributed to taphonomic processes after partial decalcification rather than to use: in the Mesolithic, when the state of preservation is better, the rate of breakage is much lower.

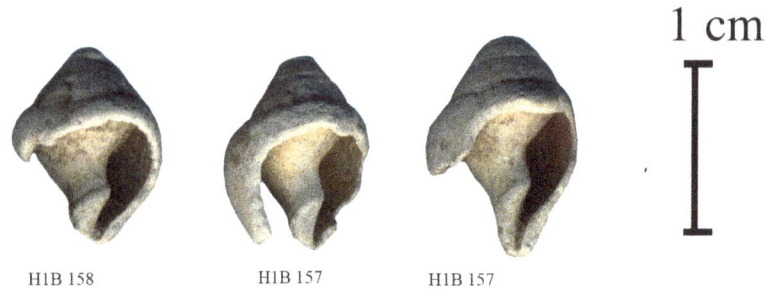

1 cm

H1B 158   H1B 157   H1B 157

Fig. 5.1: Examples of perforated and broken C. rustica.

Intact		Broken apex		Broken base		Spire (with part of the last whorl)			Fragment
Perforated	*Non perforated*	*Perforated*	*Non perforated*	*Perforated*	*Non perforated*	*Perforated*	*Non perforated*	*Undetermined*	*Undetermined*
6	2	9	0	4	3	3	0	3	14

Table 5.1: State of preservation of the Palaeolithic C. rustica.

Despite these chemical attacks, it seems unlikely that specimens could have entirely dissolved. Thus, aside from the small fragments from the unsorted < 5 mm residues, the sample can be considered representative and the very unbalanced distribution between the early Upper Palaeolithic phases (Phases 1-3), with only one perforated *Columbella*, and the latest Palaeolithic phases (Phases 5 and 6.1), with 24 perforated specimens, must be considered significant.

A Collection on Beaches from Thanatocoenoses

We know of no birds or terrestrial animal that eat *Columbella rustica* and could have deposited the shells in the cave. The shells of adult *Columbella rustica* are light enough (0.3 to 0.4 g as a mean) to be displaced by saltation by the wind, but it is unlikely they could have moved ca. 3 km or more on plant-covered ground. Conversely, the high rate of perforation and use-wear attests that most *C. rustica* were collected and deposited by humans.

The question of the agent of deposition can, nevertheless, be raised for the small fragments recovered in the < 5 mm residues among the assemblage of micromolluscs (Shackleton J. 1988), and for three small specimens in the lower units of FAS (FAS 218, 217, 212, Fig. 5.2). The latter are not perforated, they are the smallest specimens in the whole Palaeolithic and Mesolithic assemblages and much smaller than the average perforated Palaeolithic *Columbella* (0.67 to 0.9 cm instead of 1.37 cm). These small specimens and the fragments from the < 5 mm residues may be part of the assemblage of marine micromolluscs, which are especially abundant in the earliest Upper Palaeolithic strata (see discussion in Chap. 4).

Columbella rustica can be fairly easily collected live on rocks in shallow waters (Appendix 3.2), but the frequency of broken or rounded apices, together with characteristic pitting (Plate 5.1), shows that the Palaeolithic dove shells were mostly collected on beaches, from thanatocoenoses (Rigaud *et al.* 2014b; Stiner 1999). Collecting in thanatocoenoses is more time demanding than collecting live shells under water, especially for large and sufficiently intact specimens, but the beach shells have been cleaned of their concretions by the wave and sand action and display a far more colourful surface.

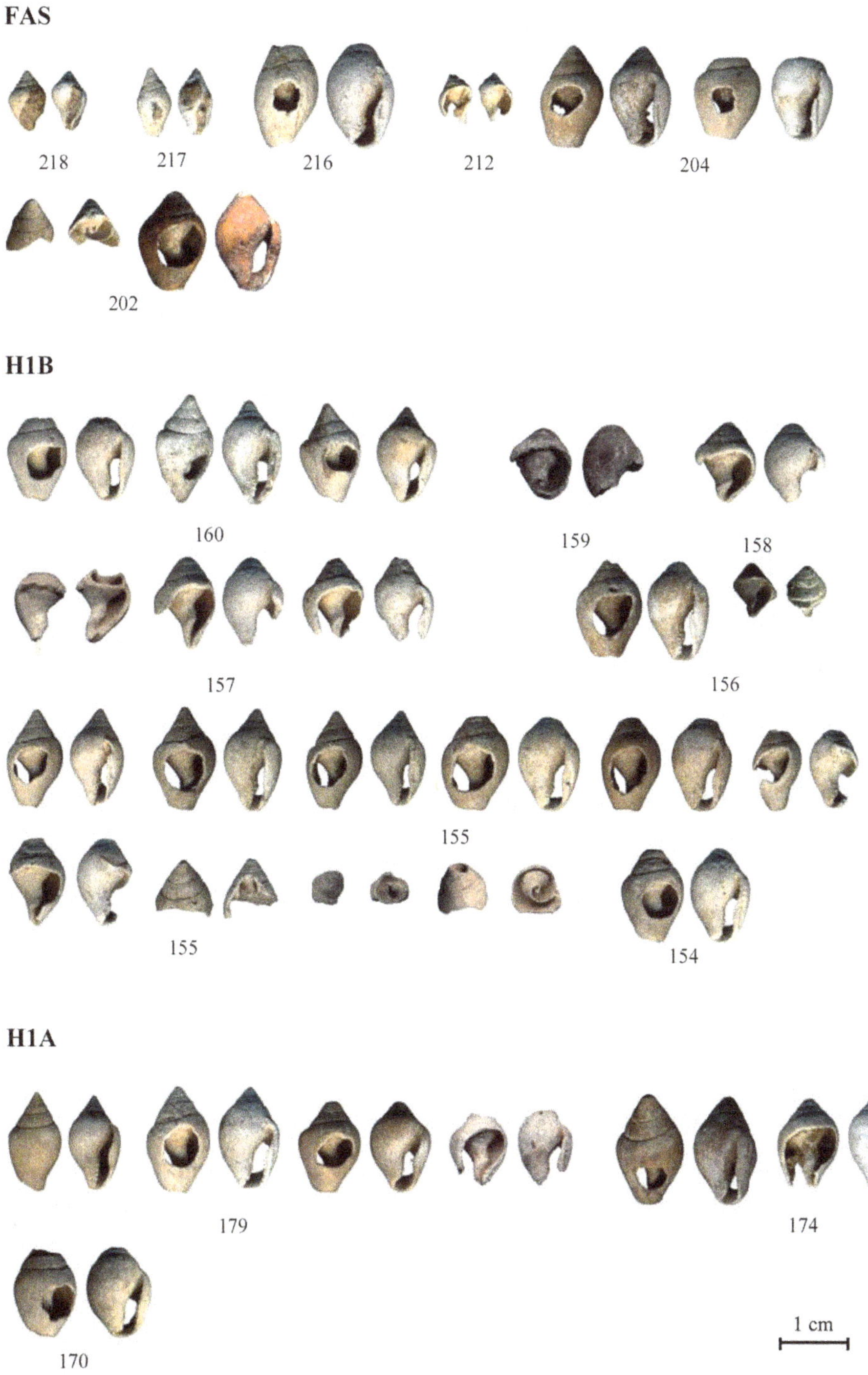

FAS

218 217 216 212 204

202

H1B

160 159 158

157 156

155

155 154

H1A

179 174

1 cm

170

Plate 5.1: Columbella rustica *from Palaeolithic levels. Fragments from the < 5 mm residues and one larger fragment from H1B 153 have not been scanned (DAO M. Vanhaeren).*

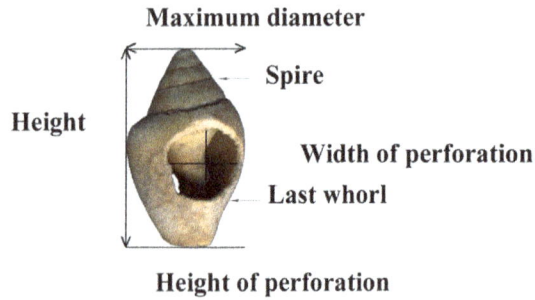

Fig. 5.2: Measurements and main parts of C. rustica.

A Selection of Large Specimens

After having collected hundreds of dove shells on beaches and admired the range of colours, one inevitably wonders whether the colours and/or the patterning could have been important selection criteria. Unfortunately, the shells have now all become a dull white or beige through bleaching and we shall never know whether some colours were preferred over others. On the other hand, the 10 specimens sufficiently well preserved to measure the height[1] reveal a clear selection in favor of large specimens (Fig. 5.3). The mean height (m = 1.42 cm, sd = 0.1) is substantially larger than the mean height in our collections from different Argolid beaches[2] (m = 1.14 to 1.17 cm, sd = 0.12 to 0.18. See Appendix 3.2).

Interestingly, this mean is nearer to the mean height of modern dove shells collected under water by sight, which are mostly inhabited by hermit-crabs (m = 1.37, sd = 0.13). Although we cannot rule out the possibility that prehistoric populations were larger than modern ones, this similarity rather suggests that the two populations had a similar size range and that, in both cases (but for different reasons!), the largest specimens were selected. A selection of the largest *C. rustica* for beads was also observed in several Croatian Mesolithic sites (Benghiat *et al.* 2009; Komšo & Vukosavljević 2011), where dove shells were of even larger dimensions. Large specimens are indeed far easier to perforate by percussion, the technique or range of techniques used in the Upper Palaeolithic at Franchthi and in the Croatian sites. On the other hand, searching for large shells increases the collecting time: in successive collections at Asini beach for instance, only 15% of intact *C. rustica* reached the mean height of the Upper Palaeolithic perforated dove shells[3].

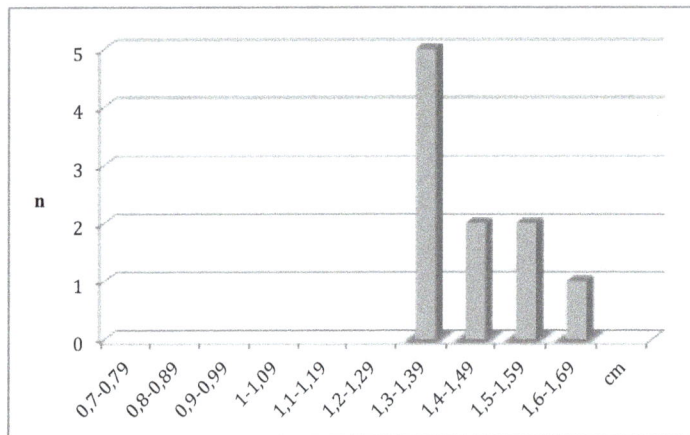

Fig. 5.3: Maximum height of intact perforated C. rustica.

The Production of the Dove Shell Beads

Contrary to Cyclopes, there is no indication that dove shells were heat-treated before (or after) perforation. Three specimens only, out of 44, are burnt: two fragments and a broken perforated bead. This low rate is within the range of accidental burning (Perlès & Vanhaeren 2010).

Almost all sufficiently well preserved Palaeolithic *C. rustica* have been turned into beads or pendants (Table 5.1). If one excludes the undiagnostic fragments and the three specimens well below average dimensions, only one large *C. rustica* (Plate 5.1, H1A 179) and one large fragment (H1B 153, not illustrated) were discarded without perforation. The high rate of perforation is comparable to the overall rate of perforation at nearby Klissoura Cave 1 (Stiner 2010) but higher than the rate of perforation on marine gastropods at Riparo Mochi in Italy (Stiner 1999) or on coniform shells—mostly *Columbella rustica*—at Üçağızlı Cave I in Turkey (Stiner 2014; Stiner *et al.* 2013). The rarity of unperforated specimens and frequency of wear traces lead us to wonder whether the ornaments were produced *in situ* or brought in as already-made beads, a question that will be addressed through use-wear analyses (*infra*).

Palaeolithic dove-shell beads from Franchthi display, as elsewhere in Palaeolithic and Mesolithic assemblages, characteristically large perforations (Fig. 5.4 and 5.5) with a high rate of correlation between height and width of the perforation (R= 0.81, p < 0.01).

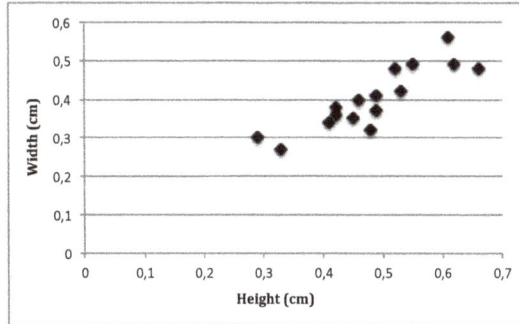

Fig. 5.4: Height and width of perforations on C. rustica.

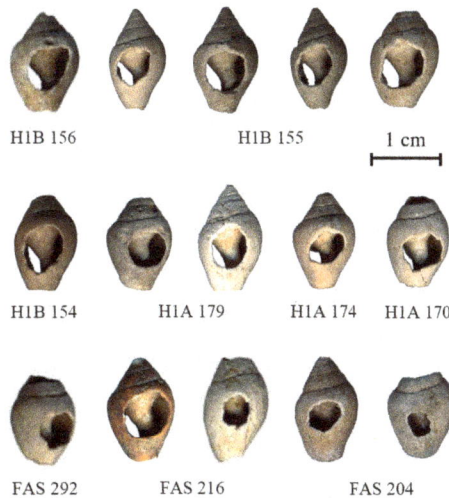

Fig. 5.5: Characteristic Upper Palaeolithic perforations on Columbella rustica.

Some perforations are oval or subcircular, others subrectangular, but in all cases they are located on the dorsal side of the last whorl and often invade its lower part, close to the columella. The delineation of the perforation is usually regular and the "ragged and amorphous" perforations of Mesolithic *Columbella* beads from Šebrn in Croatia (Benghiat *et al.* 2009) are rare here, probably because of intentional regularization and important use-wear (*infra*).

Both wave action and humans can produce these large perforations, easily distinguishable from predators' holes. Naturally perforated dove shells with invading perforations represent ca. 4 to 6 % of our modern collections (Appendix 3.2). The majority of naturally perforated *Columbella*, however, present either smaller and rounder perforations, equally suitable for use as ornaments, or more invasive breakage (Fig. 5.6). If the Palaeolithic perforated dove shells had been collected directly and exclusively in thanatocoenoses, we would thus expect perforations with a larger range of sizes, shapes and locations. Without excluding the use of naturally perforated specimens, the regular pattern of the Palaeolithic perforations indicates a systematic anthropic action. According to the rare published experiments (Benghiat *et al.* 2009; Cristiani 2009; Komšo & Vukosavljević 2011) and our own experiments (Appendix 3.2), the characteristics of the perforations shows that the majority was directly created by single blow percussion.

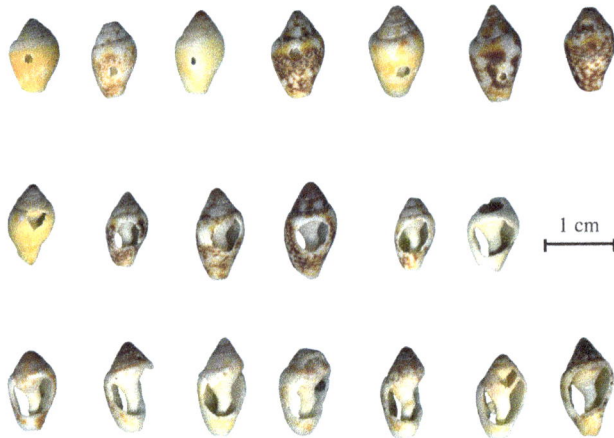

Fig. 5.6: Range of natural perforations on C. rustica *collected on Kastraki beach (2011), with predator holes on the top row, and wave perforations on the second and third rows.*

The use of this mode of percussion may be considered surprising. A reasonably large perforation can be easily initiated with a small hole made either by abrasion or direct or indirect percussion (Cristiani 2009), which is then enlarged by pressure with a flint tool placed in the perforation ("inward-outward snapping" *sensu* Benghiat *et al.* 2009). Some of our Palaeolithic perforations can have been produced by this technique, although we did not observe any traces of abrasion. The perforation can also be made by repeated light percussion on the dorsal face, a possibility we cannot exclude either. However, it is extremely difficult with these procedures to remove the lower part of the whorl, where the shell is thick and the action of the tool impeded by the columella. The removal of the lower part of the last whorl requires the use of direct or indirect percussion with a single blow. The rate of breakage in our experiments was high (about half of the attempts) possibly because we experimented mostly with small specimens (ca. 1.1 -1.2 cm) that, according to Benghiat and his colleagues (2009: 734) "almost invariably shatter, irrespective of the hard hammer used to pierce them". Conversely, on larger specimens, they consider direct percussion as "fast and effective" (*idem*). The choice of large specimens at Franchthi and in the Croatian Mesolithic sites would thus reflect functional rather than aesthetic considerations.

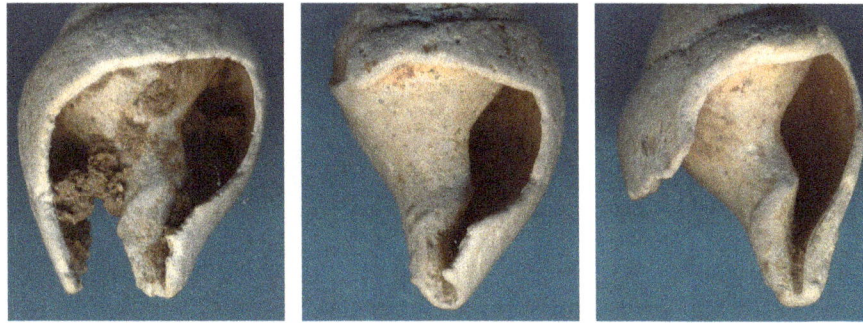

H1A 174   H1B 155   H1B 157

Fig. 5.7: Broken Columbella rustica *showing use-wear on the preserved part of the perforation.*

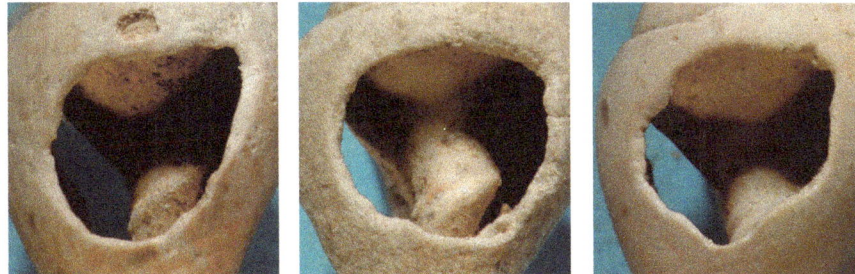

H1B 156   H1B 155   H1B 155

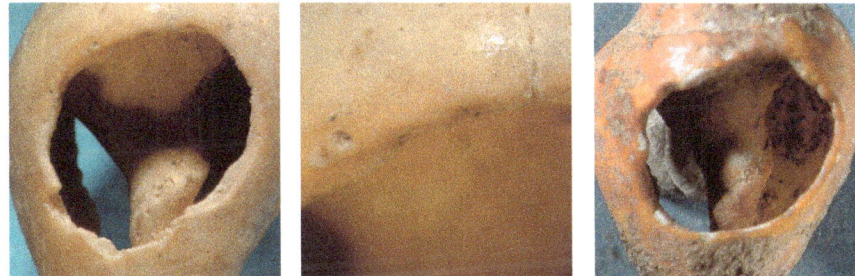

H1B 155   H1B 155 (détail)   FAS 202

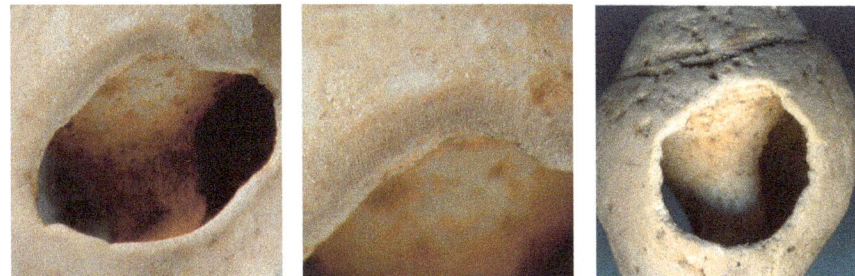

H1A 179   H1A 179 (detail)   H1A 179

Fig. 5.8: Use-wear on Columbella rustica *perforations. No scale. Photographs M. Vanhaeren.*

Even with large specimens, however, these authors also shattered an unspecified number of the shells. Thus, some of the broken specimens in archaeological assemblages could testify to unsuccessful attempts at perforating the shell. In the Franchthi Palaeolithic assemblages, however, all specimens with a broken perforation show use-wear on the remainder of the perforation, which indicates that they broke after having been worn (Fig. 5.7).

Most dove shells show well developed wear all around the perforation. This wear can be attributed to use rather than to soil erosion or chemical attacks since, in several cases, it also affects the lip on the ventral surface. Only one dove shell shows limited use-wear on the right upper corner (Fig. 5.8, lower right) and none can be considered freshly perforated. Thus, contrary to what was the case with Cyclopes, it is not possible to ascertain that these dove shells were perforated on the site, although newly perforated specimens may have been taken away. The distribution of the wear suggests a double binding to the left and the right upper part of the perforation. The dove shells were likely fixed on a garment, rather than suspended.

NOTES

1   Since we have shown a good correlation between the height and maximum diameter on modern collections (Appendix 3.2), only the height will be discussed here.

2   The difference is statistically highly significant. A Student's test on the Palaeolithic sample and the collections from Asini beach 2007 and 2008 (n = 76) gives a T value of 4.22, significant at $p < 0.01$.

3   However, Benghiat and his collaborators do not seem to have had problems finding large dove shell on the coast of Istria (Benghiat *et al.* 2009).

CHAPTER SIX

Rare Palaeolithic Ornament Types

Homalopoma sanguineum: An Early Upper Palaeolithic Ornament

Homalopoma sanguineum (L., 1758) is a small globular herbivorous gastropod with a hard and thick shell of distinctly bright red colour when alive. It lives on the rocky bottoms of medio- and infralittoral zones (Delamotte & Vardala-Theodorou 2001). According to some authors it is an exclusively Mediterranean species (Álvarez-Fernández 2001, 2005), but Delamotte & Vardala-Theodorou (2001) state it is also present on the Atlantic coast of France. It is rare nowadays in the Argolid: over several years of collecting we only found one specimen. Despite its small size (maximum diameter ca. 8 mm), *H. sanguineum* was a prized Upper Palaeolithic ornamental species (Taborin 1993; Vanhaeren & d'Errico 2006) that was traded up to 800 km from the coasts (Álvarez-Fernández 2001, 2005; Floss 2000).

Fourteen specimens only were identified at Franchthi (Fig. 6.1 and 6.2), all from the early Upper Palaeolithic phases (Phases 0 – 3). All were found in the > 5 mm residues. Since the conditions of preservation improve in the later Upper Palaeolithic phases, their absence in the more recent phases cannot be attributed to taphonomic factors and must be considered real.

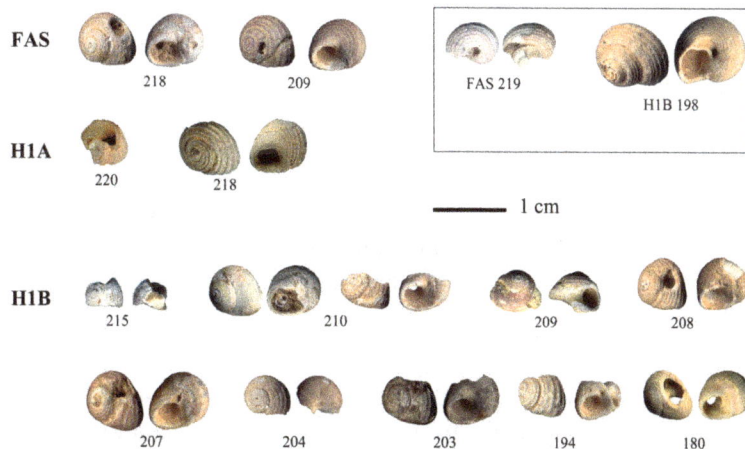

Fig. 6.1: Homalopoma sanguineum *from the Upper Palaeolithic levels. In the box, two similar-looking species:* Clanculus corallinus *(FAS 219) and* Gibbula *sp. (H1B 198). CAD M. Vanhaeren & C. P..*

Fig. 6.2: *Perforated* Homalopoma sanguineum *(from left to right: FAS 218, H1B 208, H1B 207, H1B 180).*

Of a total of 14 *H. sanguineum*, 4 are perforated, 6 are unperforated, and 4 are too fragmentary to tell. The perforation is large and located high on the last whorl. In the Palaeolithic series studied by Taborin, *H. sanguineum* was perforated by direct percussion on the external face, facilitated by one or two incisions (Taborin 1993: 199-202). A preparatory incision was also observed on one specimen from Upper Palaeolithic Klithi, in Epirus (Kotjabopoulou & Adams 2004: 44). We did not observe such traces on our *Homalopoma*: the perforation appears to have been done from the inside of the shell towards the outside by indirect percussion (Fig. 6.3). Three of the four perforated *H. sanguineum* bear a moderately developed use-wear, while the last one shows fresh breaks.

FAS 218   H1B 207   H1B 208   H1B 180

Fig. 6.3: *Details of the perforation and use-wear on* Homalopoma sanguineum. *No scale. Photographs M. Vanhaeren.*

The high rate of unperforated specimens does not necessarily imply that the shells were collected near the cave. *H. sanguineum* predominates in the very rich proto-Aurignacian ornament assemblage from Fumane (Verona, Italy). Yet, despite a distance to the sea of more than 300 km, only half of the shells were perforated (Broglio & Gurioli 2004). Since *H. sanguineum* is rare or absent from present-day Argolid beaches, it could also have been brought to Franchthi from elsewhere as raw material or valued shells.

Two other unperforated specimens belong to similar-looking taxa and may be part of the same ornament type. The first is a fragmentary *Clanculus corallinus* (Gmelin, 1791), a species visually very similar to *H. sanguineum* (Doneddu & Trainito 2005). The second is a *Gibbula* sp., again of similar shape but slightly larger than *H. sanguineum* (Fig. 6.2). Both taxa were used as ornaments at Klissoura Cave 1 in the Argolid, but there is no evidence that this was so at Franchthi. These two specimens may have been mistakenly collected as *H. sanguineum* and then rejected. Whatever the case, they demonstrate that both taxa were present around Franchthi and could have been included in the ornament assemblages.

Glycymeris sp.: Pendants or Ochre Recipients?

Glycymeris sp. (da Costa 1778), or dog-shells, are the only bivalves that were utilized during the Palaeolithic at Franchthi, and only during a brief period. Dog-shells are edible and live buried in the sand and pebbles. Their shell is solid, porcellaneous and variously coloured depending on the species (Delamotte & Vardala-Theodorou 2001). The coloration having disappeared on the archaeological specimens, it is difficult to distinguish between the different species nowadays present in Greek waters. The shape of our shells would suggest either *G. glycymeris* or *G. bimaculata*. The rounded margins of the Palaeolithic shells and abraded teeth indicate they were collected on beaches and had not been consumed before use. Fragmentary *Glycymeris* sp. can be found regularly on beaches in the Argolid, though never in high frequency.

Four *Glycymeris* sp. from Phase 5 (Fig. 6.4 and 6.5) and one from Phase 6 show definite traces of work and use. To these we have added a sixth specimen of similar size, workmanship and use, whose provenience is unknown[1]. Since perforated *Glycymeris* mainly occur in the Late Upper Palaeolithic[2], there is a high probability that it comes from the same levels. All six worked *Glycymeris* are small, or even very small for this genus (from 1.1 to 2.5 cm in length). Fragments of two much larger specimens were also recovered in deposits attributed to Phase 5. One is too fragmentary to tell whether it has been worked or used (H1B 155). The second one (H1A 177), nearly complete, is the only dog-shell that bears a natural perforation and no evidence of use. These two specimens indicate that large dog-shells were available, and that the choice of small shells for use as ornaments or containers was intentional. Taborin (1993: 284) similarly noted a selection in favour of small specimens in the Upper Palaeolithic of Western Europe.

H1B 160 FV 384   JFV 860   H1B 160

Fig. 6.4: Details of the perforation on H1B 160, FV 384, FV 860 and H1B 160, uncatalogued.

Although naturally perforated *Glycymeris* sp. are very frequent in thanatocoenoses (Sivan *et al.* 2006) and have been used as pendants (Bar-Yosef Mayer *et al.* 2009), natural perforations can be ruled out for the six small specimens. All were carefully perforated by abrasion, an operation that has removed a large part of the umbo. The very flat facet produced by the abrasion and the perforation itself bear use-wear. Even after the perforation broke (H1B 158), wear on the breaks shows that the piece continued to be manipulated. Several specimens (e.g. H1A 167, H1B 160 FV 385, H1B 158) also show heavily rounded and polished surfaces and margins, which suggest repeated manipulation overlying wave erosion. The same specimens, together with JFV 860, present clearly visible—and in one case (H1B 160 FB 385) thick—concretions, which can be tentatively identified as ochre or an ochre mix (Fig. 6.6). The ochre was deposited in the cavity, with a well-marked delineation. No ochre was noted on the outer surface of the shell. There can be no doubt that the pigment was intentionally and carefully deposited. Finally, two of the three *Glycymeris* sp. from H1B 160 and H1B 158 are burnt, but these units correspond to important hearths features and we cannot conclude that the heating was intentional.

H1B 160
FV 385

H1B 160
FV 384

H1B 160

H1A 167

H1B 158

JFV 860

1 cm

H1A 177

H1B 155

Fig. 6.5: Glycymeris *sp. from the Upper Palaeolithic levels (Phase 5). There is no evidence of work on the two specimens of the bottom row. CAD M.V. et C.P.*

Fig. 6.6: Details of the ochre deposits in H1B 160, FV 385 and H1B 158.

The presence of ochre in or on *Glycymeris* sp. has very ancient antecedents: a naturally perforated *Glycymeris* sp. stained with ochre on the outer surface was found in Mousterian level XXIV from Qafzeh (Israel), dated to ca. 92,000 ± 5,000 BP (Taborin 2003; Walter 2003). Two other naturally perforated shells with reddish or yellow stains were found in levels XXIV and XXII of the same site (Bar-Yosef Mayer *et al.* 2009). Similarly, hematite was identified in a perforated *G. insubricata* from a Mousterian level at Cueva de los Aviones (Spain), dated to ca. 45 – 50.000 BP (Zilhão *et al.* 2010).

Taborin (2003) interpreted the first shell from Qafzeh as an ochre recipient, an interpretation retained by Vanhaeren *et al.* (2006). On this basis, Zilhão (2007: 11) suggested that perforated *Glycymeris* sp. from the Ahmarian levels of Ksar' Akil and Üçağızlı Cave 1 were also used as containers rather than ornaments[3]. However, the hypothesis of ochre containers was later rejected for the Qafzeh shells, first because they were perforated, second because notches characteristic of suspension wear were present on some perforations, and, third because several other perforated valves did not show any colour staining (Bar-Yosef Mayer *et al.* 2009). Bar-Yosef Mayer and colleagues concluded in favour of suspended ornaments accidentally stained by the sediment or by rubbing against a skin painted with ochre.

Our specimens, although much more recent, demonstrate that the presence of a perforation—in this case intentional—does not contradict the thick, and equally intentional deposit of ochre, nor the important use-wear on the perforation. These dog-shells contained ochre *and* were suspended. They were also clearly repeatedly manipulated and, as stated above, still used after the perforation broke. Thus… are they suspended ochre containers or intentionally ochred pendants? The answer is probably far more subtle and rich in significance than offered by this simple dichotomy.

A Single Bone Bead …

Bone beads are extremely rare in the Palaeolithic and Mesolithic assemblages from Franchthi and only one, from H1A 216 in Phase 2, assuredly dates from the Upper Palaeolithic (Fig. 6.7). This tiny segment (0.73 x 0.32 cm) looks exactly like a smooth *Antalis* (cf. *Antalis vulgaris*) but M. Vanhaeren recognised, under high magnification, that the texture was osseous. According to M. Stiner (*in litt.* 6/2/15), the fact that the cross section is not perfectly round confirms this identification. Both she and N. Munro (*in litt.* 7/2/15) consider that the cortical wall on one extremity is too thick, in relation to the medullary cavity, to envision a bird bone. They suggest that the bead was manufactured on a small mammal metapodial, such as hare or fox, both present in the faunal assemblages (Munro & Stiner in prep.).

One extremity of the segment is broken and the other one has been sectioned perpendicular to the shaft of the bone. The sectioned extremity is smooth and polished. Manufacturing traces are no longer visible.

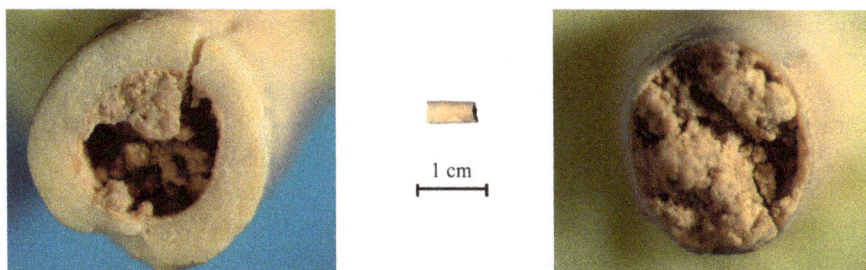

Fig. 6.7: Bone bead from H1A 216, actual size (centre) and details of extremities. Photograph M. Vanhaeren.

… And a Unique Perforated Ibex Tooth

The Franchthi Upper Palaeolithic ornament assemblage yielded only one perforated tooth, from H1A 198 (Phase 4). S. Payne and M. Stiner both identified it as a *Capra ibex* incisor. The state of preservation is not optimal and the tooth was broken after excavation. It measures 2.99 x 0.7 x 0.58 cm. There are no cut marks indicating extraction from the jaw with a flint tool (d'Errico & Vanhaeren 2002). The root bears a transversal hourglass perforation, so heavily worn that most manufacturing traces have been obliterated (Fig. 6.8). The remnant traces indicate a semi-rotary motion. The use-wear has also provoked an important reduction of the bridge on the buccal side (Fig. 6.8 and 6.9), showing that this pendant had been in use for a long period of time.

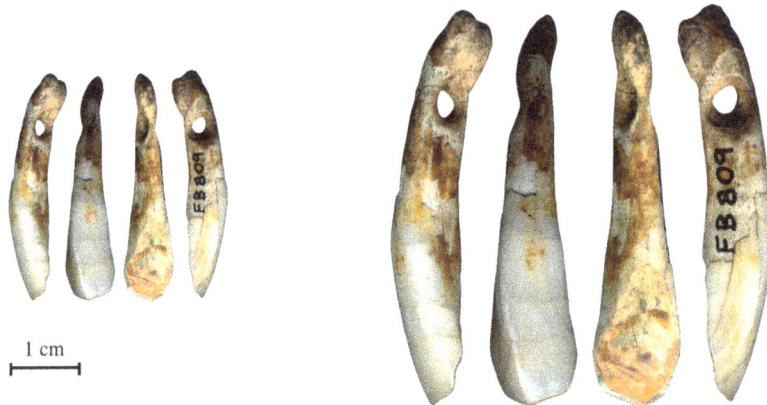

Fig. 6.8: Perforated Ibex incisor from H1A 198 (CAD M. Vanhaeren)

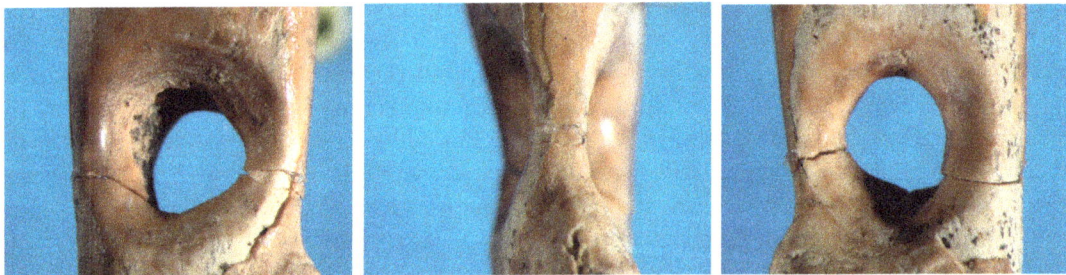

Fig. 6.9: Details of the perforation on the Ibex incisor. Photographs M. Vanhaeren.

Stone beads: Probable Intrusions

Two stone beads were found in the residues from the Palaeolithic deposits. The first (FS 697) was found in the residues from H1B 189 (Phase 2). The geologist Ch. Vitaliano identified it in the field as lapis lazuli, a semi-precious feldspathoid. The bead was intact when found, but has since deteriorated due to the removal of a sample for analysis (Fig. 6.10). The latter confirmed the original identification, as indicated in the Franchthi Stone (FS) catalogue entry[4]. The bead is very small (0.63 x 0.26 cm), very regular, circular, and shows an unusual plano-convex section. The perforation is slightly off-centre and perfectly cylindrical, with parallel striations. The shape of the perforation and orientation of the striations indicate the use of a mechanical device: at least a pump drill or a bow drill. The bead has been worn, as shown by the rounding of the ridges around the perforation.

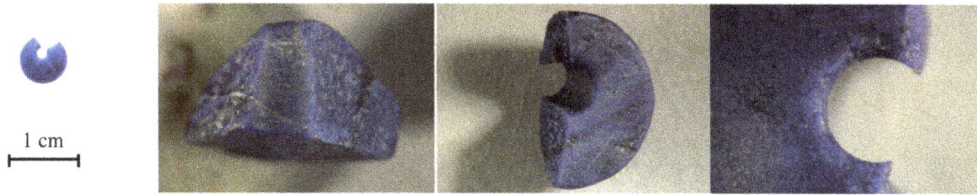

Fig. 6.10: The lapis lazuli bead from H1B 189.
Actual size and details.

Lapis lazuli is a very rare rock. The source of lapis nearest to Greece is Sar-i Sang in eastern Afghanistan, more than 4,000 km as the crow flies. Transfers on such distances are unknown in the Palaeolithic, and all the less plausible given that the sources were apparently not exploited at the time (Casanova 2013). The bead must be intrusive. It is highly unlikely, though, that it could have dropped in from Mesolithic or Neolithic levels: lapis lazuli beads are extremely rare in the Neolithic of the Near and Middle East, and the hemispheric shape is unrecorded (Casanova 2013). The most parsimonious explanation is to consider it as a modern contaminant.

The second bead (FS 797) comes from unit FAS 207, Phase 6. It is made of a green serpentinite, a local raw material frequent in Neolithic assemblages at Franchthi (Fig. 6.11). It is also very small (0.61 x 0.34 cm), discoid, with flat faces and straight sides. The hourglass perforation bears well-marked concentric striations, indicating a continuous rotary motion (by hand drill or bow drill). Wear facets from use are visible on each face, on the edges of the perforation, and within the perforation itself. This bead has no equivalent in Upper Palaeolithic or Mesolithic Greek assemblages, but is identical to numerous small Neolithic serpentinite beads from Franchthi. Given the thick Neolithic deposits in FAS, there is a high probability that it is a Neolithic contaminant. However, a tiny steatite bead (0.4 mm in diameter and 0.1 mm thick[5]) is reported from the late Upper Palaeolithic (between ca. 12,900 and 10,200 uncal BP) from Boïla rockshelter in Epirus (Kotjabopoulou & Adams 2004: 46). No Neolithic deposits are mentioned, but disturbances are noted in some parts of the shelter with a byzantine burial. The bead is not illustrated and cannot be compared with ours. Two other Palaeolithic stone ornaments were found at Kastritsa, in Epirus: they consist of two large and irregular pendants, entirely different from this geometric bead (*idem*: 43).

The manufacturing of very small geometric stone beads in the Greek Upper Palaeolithic cannot entirely be ruled out. However, it remains unlikely in view of their extreme rarity, their absence in other European Upper Palaeolithic contexts and the likelihood of simple contamination from the overlying Neolithic deposits.

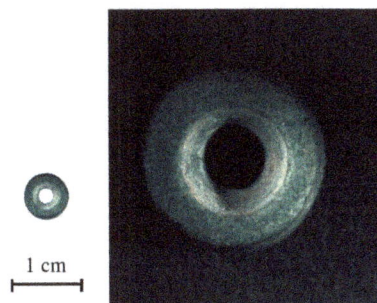

Fig. 6.11: Serpentinite bead from FAS 207.
Actual size and detail of the perforation.

A Note on Some Species that We Did *Not* Considered as Ornamental.

Several taxa, some of which were used elsewhere as ornaments, are present in various quantities in the Franchthi Palaeolithic deposits but have not been considered part of the ornament assemblage.

This applies first to the rich assemblages of 'micromolluscs', which comprise *Bittium reticulatum*, *Bittium latreilli*, Higromiidae gen. sp. ind., *Paracentrotus* sp., *Parvicardium* sp. *Pirenella conica*, *Rissoa ventricosa*, *Turritella* sp. etc. (Appendix 2). Neither A. Colonese nor M. Vanhaeren found any evidence of anthropic perforation or other kind of modification. There is no record of these species being used as ornaments in other prehistoric sites, and they are thus considered as non-intentional deposits (see discussion Chap. 4).

We similarly excluded *Patella* sp., *Cerithium vulgatum*, *Phorcus* (= *Monodonta* = *Osilinus*) *turbinatus*, *Gibbula divaricata*, *Gibbula rarilineata* and *Hexaplex* (= *Murex*) *trunculus*, abundant in the Palaeolithic marine molluscan assemblages (Colonese *et al.* 2011; Shackleton J. 1988). All these taxa have been used as ornaments in the European Upper Palaeolithic (Taborin 1993) and some of them are present in the ornament assemblages from Klissoura Cave 1 in the Argolid (Stiner 2010). However, the absence of anthropic perforation, the quasi-systematic breakage and the fresh state of the shells in the Palaeolithic levels from Franchthi indicate they were collected live and eaten. Limpets (*Patella*) and turbans (*Phorcus*) are familiar edible genera and were widely used as a source of food in prehistoric sites around the Mediterranean basin (Colonese *et al.* 2010). Conversely, doubts have been raised about *C. vulgatum* as an edible species and it was suggested it might have been used instead as bait (Colonese *et al.* 2010). However, there is no relationship between the frequency of *C. vulgatum* and the frequency of fish remains in the Palaeolithic levels at Franchthi (Perlès 2016a) and it is in fact eaten around the Mediterranean basin (Davidson 1972). Similarly, *H. trunculus*, better known as a source of dye, is professionally exploited in France to be served in restaurants (Besançon *et al.* 2013).

Finally, we also excluded a few other classical ornamental species, again because it could not be proven that any of the Palaeolithic specimens at Franchthi had been worked. These include examples of *Conus mediterraneus*, *Pisania striata*, *Pecten* sp., *Clanculus corallinus*, *Gibbula* sp. *Nassarius* sp. and a *Buccinidae*.

1 cm

Fig. 6.12: Naturally perforated Conus mediterraneus *(FAS 215, left), fragment of a large* Conus mediterraneus *(H1B 153, centre) and* Nassarius sp. *(H1B 155, right).*

NOTES

1   It had been extracted from its original bag and numbered by J. Shackleton (JVF 860), but we did not find a list giving the provenience of the " JVF " specimens.

2   Only one other was found, from a Lower Mesolithic level.

3   There is actually no *Glycymeris* mentioned at Üçağızlı (Stiner 2003; Stiner & Kuhn 2003; Stiner *et al.* 2013) and no mention of ochre in the *Glycymeris* from Ksar'Akil (Inizan & Gaillard 1978; Kuhn *et al.* 2001).

4   We do not know where the analysis was performed. The catalogue is kept at the Nafplion Archaeological Museum.

5   This seems to be a mistake. More likely 0.4 x 0.1 cm.

CHAPTER SEVEN

Diachronic Variations

Variations in the Intensity of Manufacturing, Use and Discard of Ornaments

As part of the diachronic perspective that sustains our work, variation in the intensity of the production, use and discard of ornaments is the first variable to investigate. The number of ornaments and ornamental shells in the Palaeolithic sequence at Franchthi fluctuates from phase to phase. It varies from three specimens in Phase 4 to 242 in Phase 2. Does this imply that the manufacturing, use or loss of ornaments varied drastically in intensity over the course of millennia? Or is it, alternatively, the simple consequence of variation in the duration and intensity of occupation of each occupational phase? If so, was the production of ornaments commensurate with the pace of subsistence and technical activities, or did it follow its own, independent rhythm?

Answering these questions poses several problems, some specific to Franchthi, others common to all stratified archaeological sites. The first problem is not specific to Franchthi but concerns all stratified sites: to assess variations in the intensity of ornament use and discard—or of any other archaeological category—one cannot compare directly the numbers of specimens from phase to phase since the duration of each phase and the intensity of occupation are themselves variable. A hundred ornaments in a phase that lasted three millennia are not comparable, in terms of intensity of production or discard, to a hundred ornaments from a phase that lasted 200 years. Consequently, the number of remains in each category must be weighted, or 'standardized' (*sensu* Stiner 2014), to compensate for these variations. Ideally, the number of specimens from each phase should be first weighted by its duration. Unfortunately, ^{14}C dates are of no help: besides the difficulties induced by plateaux in the calibration curve, especially important for the Mesolithic phases, the available 14C dates do not bracket the beginning and end of each phase, and some phases are still undated. However, even if the duration of each phase could be estimated, it would still have to be divided by the number of days, weeks or months the site was occupied each year. This is clearly impossible.

Despite variation introduced by changing climatic conditions, the volume of sediments within each phase, which in part depends on its duration for its geogenic component, and in part on the frequency of occupation for its anthropic component, can give us a first proxy for the duration and frequency of occupations. The ratio of the Number of Identified Specimens (NISP)/volume of sediment (in litres)[1] is the best method[2] to homogenize the data among phases and compensate for variations in the duration of each phase. If ornaments were produced and deposited at a regular pace through time, i.e. if there is no variation in intensity of deposition, their frequency should be directly correlated with the volume of sediment from each phase.

More likely, however, the production, use and loss of ornaments varied in intensity according to the nature of the cave's occupation, the activities that took place in and around the cave, the size of the human group, etc. If the production of ornaments was embedded in the other activities that took place at the site and varied at the same pace, the number of ornaments and ornamental shells represented should correlate with the number of remains related to subsistence activities and technical productions, such as faunal remains and chipped stones.

Alternatively, ornament production may constitute a specific sphere of activity, disconnected from subsistence and technical activities, and which varies according to independent factors such as the composition of the group, its preferences for ornaments or its symbolic conceptions. In this last case, no correlation would appear between the number of ornaments and the volume of sediment or the other categories of archaeological remains. Thus, after looking for simple correlations between the frequency of ornaments and the volume of sediment, we shall examine their variation in relation to mammal bones, shellfish and chipped stones, i.e. terrestrial resources, marine resources and technical activities.

These analyses will be based on the NISP of ornaments, ornamental shells, mammal bones, shellfish and chipped stones. Franchthi, however, poses specific difficulties for the apparently simple operation of counting the number of ornaments and ornamental shells in each phase and estimating their variations, both because it is a coastal site and because of the procedures used when sorting the residues. The proximity of the coast opens up the possibility of natural—or non-intentional—deposition of shells, a possibility that we did not entirely eliminate for a few very small *Columbella rustica* and for the smaller fraction of the *Antalis* sp. assemblage. Secondly, the morphological difference between the species represented induced different rates of recovery in the successive sieves. Due to their globular shape, a large majority of the *Cyclope, Homalopoma, Columbella* and *Glycymeris* could not pass through the mesh of the 5 mm sieve. They were thus mostly recovered in the residues from the 5 mm and 10 mm sieves, which were all completely sorted. By contrast, the elongated and narrow shape of tusk shells allowed them to pass through the 5 and 10 mm sieves, and the majority was recovered in the residues from the < 5 mm sieves. S. Payne sorted these residues, unit by unit, in fractions that comprised between 1/4th and 1/32th of their total volume. Consequently, the figures we have for tusk shells are well below the original figures and do not compare directly with other ornament types. Multiplying these figures by the fraction of the residues sorted, as compensation, would give spurious results given the small number of *Antalis* sp. segments in each unit. For instance, if two adjacent units, each containing five segments of *Antalis* sp., were sorted to 1/32th of their original volume, one segment might have been recovered by chance in the subsample from the first unit, but none in the other. An arithmetic multiplication would give 32 *Antalis* sp. segments in the first unit and zero in the second, a clearly unacceptable estimate.

A second option consists in eliminating the problematic *Antalis* sp. from relative frequency tables and graphs. This option, however, presents the disadvantage of obliterating chronological differences in the frequency of tusk shells and of artificially reducing the total number of ornaments when compared with other categories of remains. We shall thus present tables and graphs based on the total number of specimens of *Cyclope* sp., *Homalopoma sanguineum*, *Columbella rustica* and *Glycymeris* sp., excluding *Antalis* sp., but also present counts *of what was recovered*, without trying to compensate for the biases introduced by sorting procedures (Tables 7.1 and 7.2).

In both cases, tables and graphs will include perforated and unperforated specimens, to reflect all the activities related to the production, use and loss of ornaments and their variations over time. Here again, though, tusk shells pose some problems: we know that the smaller fragments cannot be threaded and that they represent neither beads nor raw material for beads, but instead manufacturing debris or unintentional deposits. We shall thus eliminate *Antalis* sp. posterior fragments with a minimal diameter < 1.5 mm, the lower limit that it has been possible to document for potential beads.

Phase	Units	Volume of sediment (litres)	*Cyclope sp.*	*Antalis sp.*	*Homalopoma sanguineum*	*Columbella rustica*	*Glycymeris sp.*	Others	Total
	H1A								
0									
1									
2	220-212 (211)	846	6	52	2			1	61
3	210-205	1104		4					4
4	(204) 203-190	1153		2				1	3
5	189-176 (175)	1563	18	8		3	1		30
6.1	174-169	782	50	2		2			54
6.2	168-167	259	50	2				1	53
	Total		124	70	2	5	2	2	205
	H1B								
0	215 - 214	74	1	3	1				5
1	213 - 208	440	11	9	4				24
2	207-181	3300	58	63	4	3		1	129
3	180-173 (172 -171)	>456	5	1	1				7
4	170-162	495							0
5	(161), 160-155, (154)	1289	170	4		21	5		200
6.1	153-151	710	19	2		1			22
	Total		264	82	10	25	5	1	387
	FAS								
0	227-223	2682	15	21		1			37
1	222-217	1729	41	23	2	2			68
2	216-209	2215	31	16	1	4			52
3	hiatus								0
4	hiatus								0
5	hiatus								0
6.1	(207), 206-203, (202)	1911	80	9		4		1	94
6.2	201-199	591	48	3		0			51
	Total		215	72	3	11	0	1	302
	H1A + H1B + FAS								
0		2756	16	24	1	1			42
1		2169	52	32	6	2			92
2		6361	95	131	7	7		2	242
3		1364	5	5	1				11
4		1648		2		0		1	3
5		2852	188	12		24	6		230
6.1		3403	149	13		7		1	170
6.2		850	98	5				1	104
	Total		603	224	15	41	7	4	894

Table 7.1: Synthetic list of Palaeolithic ornaments and ornamental shells by phase in H1A, H1B and FAS. Phase 6 has been subdivided because of shifts in proportions in the uppermost in FAS and H1A.

Phase	Units	Cyclope sp. perforated	Cyclope sp. unperforated	Cyclope sp. undetermined	Antalis sp. D. min. <1.5 mm	Antalis sp. D. min 1.5-3 mm	Antalis sp. D. min. >3 mm	Antalis sp. undetermined	C. rustica perforated	C. rustica unperforated	C. rustica undetermined	H. sanguineum perforated	H. sanguineum unperforated	H. sanguineum undetermined	Bone bead	G. glycymeris perforated	G. glycymeris undetermined	Stone bead	Incised tooth	Total
	H1A																			
0																				
1																				
2	220-212 (211)	4	1	1	18	23	11						1	1	1					61
3	210-205				1	3														4
4	203-190					1	1												1	3
5	189-176 (175)	13	2	3	5	2		1	2	1										29
6.1	174-169	20	11	19		2			2											54
6.2	168-167	31	14	5	0	2										1				53
	Total	68	28	28	24	33	12	1	4	1	0	0	1	1	1	1	0		1	204
	H1B																			
0	215 - 214			1			2	1			1									5
1	213 (212-208)	1	3	7	3	2		4			2	1	1							24
2	207-181	9	18	31	18	36	8	1			3	3		1				1		129
3	180-173 (172 -171)	1		4		1							1							7
4	170-162																			0
5	(161), 160-155, (154)	72	28	70	2	1	1		16		5					4	1			200
6.1	153-151	7	3	9		2			1											22
	Total	90	52	122	23	42	11	6	17	0	8	7	1	2	0	4	1	1	0	387
	FAS																			
0	227-223		2	13	3	14	3	1			1									37
1	222-217	2	8	31	3	18	2			1	1	1		1						68
2	216-209	1	4	26	7	8	1		1	1	2			1						52
3	hiatus																			0
4	hiatus																			0
5	hiatus																			0
6.1	(207), 206-203, (202)	12	21	47		8		1	3		1							1		94
6.2	201-199	27	14	7		2	1													51
	Total	42	49	124	13	50	7	2	4	2	5	1	0	2	0	0	0	1	0	302
	H1A + H1B + FAS																			
0	0		2	14	3	14	5	2			1			1						42
1	1	3	11	38	6	20	2	4		1	1	2	1	3						92
2	2	14	23	58	43	67	20	1	1	1	5	3	1	2	1		1	1		242
3	3	1		4	1	4								1						11
4	4					1	1												1	3
5	5	85	30	73	7	3	1	1	18	1	5					4	2			230
6.1	6.1	39	35	75		12		1	6		1								1	170
6.2	6.2	58	28	12		4	1									1				104
	Total	200	129	274	60	125	30	9	25	3	13	6	2	6	1	5	3	2	1	894

Table 7.2: Detailed counts of ornaments and Palaeolithic ornamental species in H1A, H1B and FAS.

Ornaments and Sediment: Independent Variations

In the Palaeolithic levels at Franchthi, the number of ornaments, whether or not *Antalis* sp. is included, is not correlated with the volume of sediments[3]. The ratio of ornaments/sediment tends to vary from trench to trench (Table 7.3), leading us to combine the trenches in order to limit the effects of spatial variations. Figure 7.1 shows that the scattergram of NISP ornaments/volume of sediments is only marginally modified by the inclusion of *Antalis* sp., and only for the early phases. We can therefore use the figures that include *Antalis* sp. segments in the following analyses. There are few comparative data for the density of ornaments, but the Franchthi Palaeolithic ratios are, overall, higher than the ratios obtained in the Klithi and Boïla rock shelters in Epirus—respectively 0.012 and 0.008—as might be expected from a near-coastal site compared to inland settlements (Kotjabopoulou & Adams 2004).

As shown by Table 7.3 and Fig. 7.1, the density of ornaments relative to sediment varies significantly through time. The rate of ornament deposition is not constant. Taken at face value and ordered chronologically, the ratios of ornaments/volume of sediment suggest a substantial increase in the density of ornaments from the early Upper Palaeolithic phases to the Late Upper Palaeolithic phases (Fig. 7.2).

However, the low ratios of ornaments to sediments in Phases 0 - 4 could be due to the presence of heavy rock falls in these deposits, which could have inflated the volume of sediments (Farrand 2000). At the other end of the spectrum, the ratio in Subphase 6.2 (H1A and FAS) appears suspiciously high: Cyclopes are far more abundant in the Mesolithic, so this could result from contamination from Mesolithic ornaments in these loose sediments, or from slight crosscutting of the strata during excavation. An examination of mammal bone data from H1B[4] (Stiner & Munro 2011) and of chipped stones (Perlès 1987) can help us evaluate the influence of rock falls on the figures obtained for the early phases: if the low values are due to the amount of fallen rocks, this should also affect mammal bones and chipped stones and lead to similarly low values of the ratio NISP mammal bones/volume of sediment.

Figure 7.3 shows that the rate of deposition of mammal bones and chipped stones follows different patterns, but neither supports the influence of rock falls on the ratios of ornaments to sediment for the early phases: in both cases the ratios are especially high in Phases 3 and 4, precisely when the ratio of ornaments/sediment is the lowest. This confirms that: (a) ornaments were not deposited at a regular rate over time; (b) the rarity of ornaments in Phases 3 and 4 is not due to especially sporadic or low-intensity occupations of the cave and, (c) the intensity of ornament-related activities and deposition was higher in Late Upper Palaeolithic phases than in Early Upper Palaeolithic phases. This, however, could simply reflect an intensification of the activities in the cave as a whole, rather than a feature specific to ornament assemblages. A comparison with the remains of cynegetic activities can shed a first light on this question.

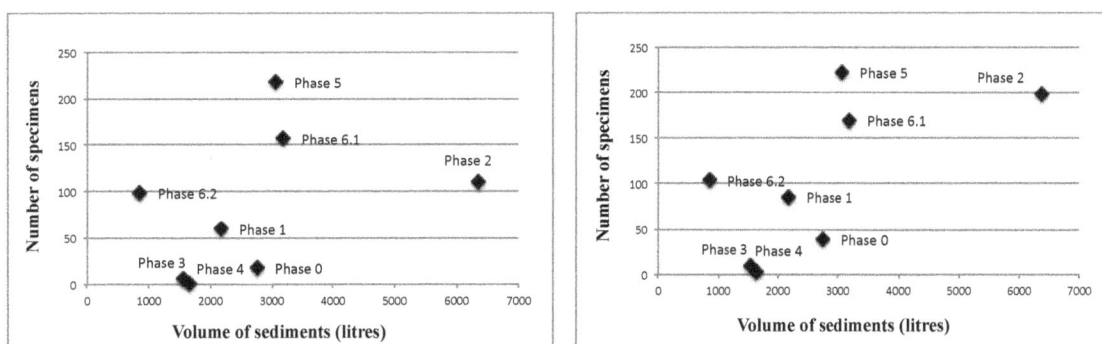

Fig. 7.1: Relation between the volume of sediments and number of ornaments in H1A, H1B and FAS combined. Left: without Antalis *sp. segments. Right: with* Antalis *sp. segments of a minimum diameter ≥ 1.5 mm.*

Phase	H1B			H1A			FAS		
	Vol. sed.	A	B	Vol. sed.	A	B	Vol. sed.	A	B
0	74	0.02	0.06				2682	0.006	0.012
1	440	0.03	0.047				1729	0.024	0.037
2	3300	0.014	0.033	846	0.01	0.05	2215	0.014	0.02
3	> 456	> 0.01	0.027	1104	0	0.002			
4	495	0	0	1153	0.0008	0.002			
5	1505	0.13	0.13	1563	0.014	0.019			
6.1	494	0.04	0.04	782	0.066	0.069	1911	0.042	0.05
6.2				259	0.196	0.2	591	0.08	0.08

Table 7.3: Abundance of ornaments and ornamental shells relative to the volume of sediment (NISP/nb. litres). A: without Antalis *sp. segments. B: with* Antalis *sp. segments of a minimum diameter ≥ 1.5 mm.*

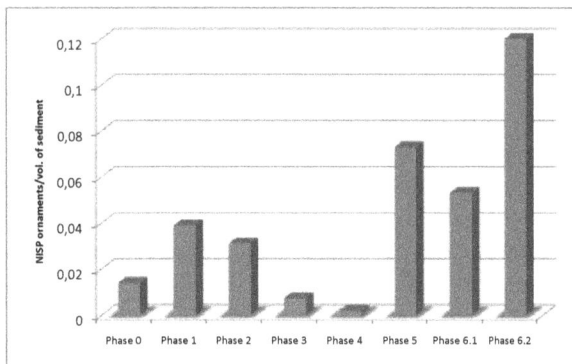

Fig. 7.2: Diachronic variation in the abundance of ornaments standardised by the volume of sediments (litres) in H1B, H1A and FAS combined, with fragments of Antalis *sp. D. min ≥ 1.5 mm.*

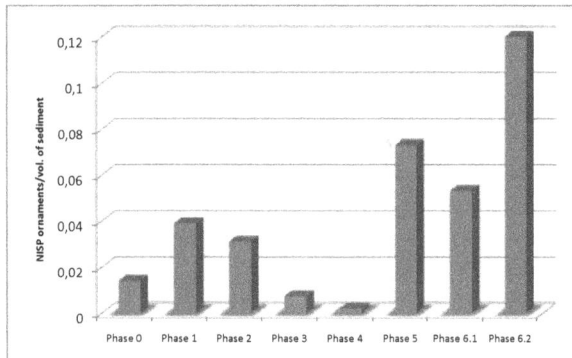

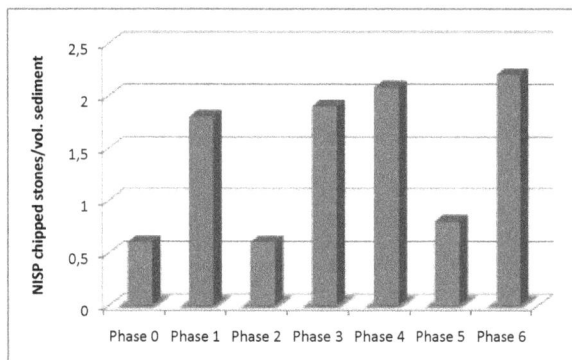

Fig. 7.3: Diachronic variation in the abundance of mammal bones (top) and chipped stones (bottom) from H1B, standardised by the volume of sediment (litres). Data after Stiner & Munro 2011, appendix 1 and Perlès 1987. There are no faunal data for Phase 0.

Mammal Bones and Ornaments: Again, Independent Variations

The abundance of ornaments in each phase is unrelated to the frequency of mammal bones in H1B[5], the only trench for which detailed counts of the mammalian remains are available (Stiner & Munro 2011).

Except for Phase 1, the ratios of ornaments/mammal bones fall within the range of the figures published for Üçağızlı Cave 1 in eastern Turkey (Stiner *et al.* 2013), but on the low side. The observed variation among phases indicates that the rate of deposition of ornaments was not proportional to the intensity of subsistence activities, or at least of cynegetic activities. The low ratios of ornaments in Phases 2 and 3 are confirmed, as well as a slight increase in the relative abundance of ornaments in the later Upper Palaeolithic phases. Phase 1 appears as a complete anomaly, with the highest ration of ornaments to mammal bone in the whole sequence. Unless bone was even more poorly preserved than shells (see Chap. 3), which appears unlikely, this would suggest that the collection of ornamental shells was one of the main motives for coming to the cave during the Aurignacian.

Phase	Mammal bones (NISP)	Total ornaments (NISP)	A	B
1	69	19	0.2	0.3
2	2106	91	0.03	0.05
3	515	7	0.01	0.013
4	618	0	0	0
5	3105	195	0.063	0.063
6	327	21	0.06	0.067

Table 7.4: Ratios of ornaments to mammal bones in H1B. A: without Antalis *sp. B: with* Antalis *sp. fragment, D. min ≥ 1.5 mm. Data on mammal bones from Stiner & Munro 2011.*

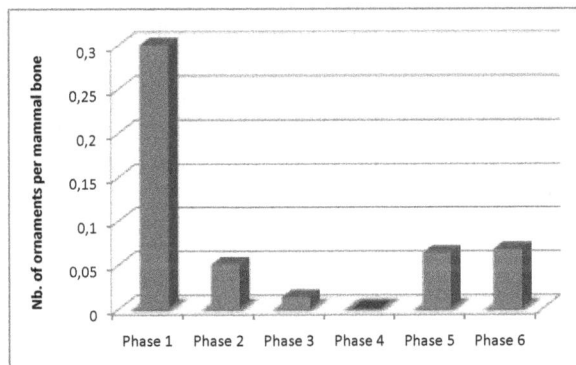

Fig. 7.4: Diachronic variation in the ratios of ornaments to mammal bones in H1B, with Antalis *sp. segments, D. min ≥1.5 mm.*

Collecting Ornamental Shells and Shellfish: Independent Activities

Collecting shellfish constitutes another subsistence activity, which we could logically consider more closely linked to the collection of ornamental shells than game hunting. This logical expectation, however, is again defeated. The presence of discarded juvenile *Cyclope* sp. (Chap. 3) demonstrates that Cyclopes were collected live near the cave for millennia before shellfish were collected, or, at least, brought back to the cave. *Cyclope* sp., *Homalopoma sanguineum* and *Antalis* sp. are already present in the pre-Aurignacian levels, below the ash layer identified as the Campanian Ignimbrite (Douka *et al.* 2011; Farrand 2000) and regularly present during Phases 1 – 3. The other coastal resources appear much later in the records, during the Late Upper Palaeolithic: fishing starts, on a modest scale, during Phase 4 (Rose, in prep.; Stiner & Munro 2011), while shellfish were not collected until Phase 5 (Shackleton J. 1988).

The collection of shellfish and ornamental species appear to have been largely independent activities[6]: the ratio of shellfish to sediment, for the three trenches combined, falls from 0.22 in Phases 5 and 6.1 to 0.02 in Subphase 6.2, precisely when the ratio of ornaments to sediment reaches its maximum for the whole Palaeolithic. The number of ornamental shells in Subphase 6.2 (n = 104) actually exceeds that of edible shells (n = 21) by a large margin.

The absence of correlation between the exploitation of ornamental species and edible shellfish may seem striking. It should be remembered, however, that the dominant ornamental species and shellfish species correspond to different coastal environments: in Phases 5 and 6, ornament assemblages are heavily dominated by *Cyclope neritea*, which thrives in lagoons and salt marshes. By contrast, the dominant shellfish are rock-dwelling species: *Patella* sp. and *Phorcus* [*Monodonta, Osilinus*] *turbinatus*. As shown by the reconstruction of the past shorelines (Chap. 2), collecting ornamental shells and edible shells implied exploring different sectors of the coast.

Ornaments and Chipped Stone Artifacts: Still Independent Variations

The rate at which ornaments were collected, used and discarded was independent not just of the rate of subsistence activities, but also of the intensity of technical activities[7] (Table 7.5). Phase 0 stands out with an anomalously high ratio of ornaments to chipped stones, even when *Antalis* sp. segments are excluded. This is difficult to interpret: we do not have faunal data as a control, nor any other remains of subsistence or technical activities. As for Phase 1, we may suggest that collecting ornamental shell species was a major incentive to visit the cave. With the exception of Phase 0, variations in the number of ornaments relative to chipped stone artifacts follow those between ornaments and sediment, although the relative increase in the later phases is less pronounced (cf. Figs. 7.2 and 7.5). In particular, subphase 6.1 now presents a lower ratio than Phases 1 and 2. The low relative density of ornaments in Phase 3 is confirmed, as well as their anomalous quasi-absence in Phase 4. Finally, the possible contamination by Mesolithic ornaments in subphase 6.2, which had been envisioned to explain the high ratio of NISP ornaments/sediment, is queried by the similar ratios of ornaments to chipped stones in Phases 5 and 6.2. This allows us to consider the high rate of deposition of ornaments in the very latest units of Phase 6 as real, with a marked increase during this phase. Compared with Klissoura Cave 1 (Stiner 2010), the ratio of ornaments to chipped stone artifacts is high at Franchthi, but this is probably due in large part to the inclusion of up to 50% of 'chips and chunks' in the lithic counts from Klissoura (Kaczanowska *et al.* 2010).

Phase	Total chipped stones	A	B
0	74	0.24	0.52
1	1385	0.04	0.06
2	2334	0.03	0.065
3	690	0.0086	0.014
4	3268	0.0003	0.0009
5	2699	0.08	0.08
6.1	4138	0.037	0.041
6.2	1250	0.08	0.08

Table 7.5: Ratios of ornaments to chipped stones artifacts in H1A, H1B and FAS combined. A: without Antalis *sp. B: with* Antalis *sp. fragment, D. min ≥ 1.5 mm. The numbers of chipped stones are minimum figures (after Perlès 1987).*

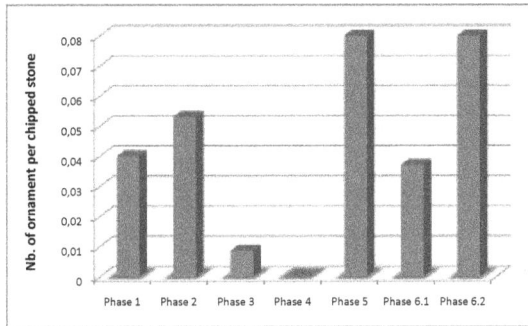

Fig. 7.5: Diachronic variation in the ratios of ornaments to chipped stone artifacts in H1A, H1B and FAS combined, with Antalis *sp. fragment, d. min ≥ 1.5 mm. Phase 0 has been omitted in order to better represent the variations in the other phases.*

Fluctuating Rates of Deposition of Ornaments and Unexpected Similarities

Overall, the variation in ornament abundance shows a similar pattern whether estimated in relation to the volume of sediments, to the remains of subsistence activities or to the remains of technical activities such as chipped stone artifacts. The pattern is also stable whether or not *Antalis* sp. segments are included, which suggests that the proportion of non-intentionally deposited tusk shells is low. The rate of deposition of ornamental shells was not constant through time, nor was it directly correlated with the intensity of subsistence and technical activities. Furthermore, the major differences in the relative abundance of ornaments do not correspond, either, to cultural discontinuities as inferred from the stone tools assemblages.

Phase 1 (Aurignacian) and Phase 2 (Gravettoid) present comparable ratios of ornaments relative to sediments and chipped stone artifacts, despite a chronological gap of several millennia. They only differ when the frequency of ornament is compared to the frequency of mammal bones, the latter being especially scarce (or badly preserved?) in Phase 1. Phase 3 (Gravettoid) presents, to the contrary, systematically lower ratios, despite the clear continuity with Phase 2 indicated by the chipped stone assemblages (Perlès 1987). There is no satisfactory explanation for this drop in the relative abundance of ornaments other than an actual decrease in the intensity of activities leading to the discard or loss of ornaments. The relative abundance of ornaments is even lower—quasi-null—in the following Phase 4. All other data demonstrates that this pattern is specific to ornament assemblages. It does not correspond to a quasi-abandonment of the cave. Phase 4 is separated from Phase 3 by a long chronological hiatus that covers the entire Late Glacial Maximum: therefore, the drop in ornament abundance in Phase 3, and their quasi-absence in Phase 4 do not reflect a long term trend, but two independent phenomena.

About one millennium later, during the Phase 5 occupation, ornament production knows a first peak, observable through all the comparative variables used. It would have been tempting to correlate this with the start of shellfish exploitation, if the later subphases did not show independent variations: the relative abundance of ornaments reaches a second peak in Subphase 6.2, when shellfish collection, to the contrary, is at its lowest. The same peak is observed when ornaments are considered in relation to the number of chipped stone artifacts, which, together with the absence of evidence for Mesolithic contaminations, lead us to consider that the relative abundance of ornaments at the end of Phase 6 (Subphase 6.2) reflects a past reality.

Fluctuations in the ratios of ornaments to the volume of sediment, mammal bones, shellfish and chipped stone artifacts show that ornaments did not accumulate regularly through time, nor in proportion to the intensity of subsistence and technical activities. The rate of deposition of ornamental shell species and ornaments at Franchthi thus differs drastically from what Stiner observed at several other sites, including Klissoura Cave 1 (Argolid), Üçağızlı Cave 1 (Turkey) and Riparo Mochi (Italy) where "ornament abundance closely paralleled the economic pulse of daily life" (Stiner 2014: 55). At Franchthi, ornament production, use and discard was an autonomous activity that fluctuated in intensity according to its own, independent rhythm.

Diachronic Variation in the Composition of Ornament Assemblages and Characterisation of Ornament Phases

Diachronic variation concerns not only the overall intensity of ornament procurement, use and discard, but also the relative proportions of the different shell taxa. To document these fluctuations, the discrepancies between the figures for tusk shell segments and for the other species represented again pose problems. We shall thus limit ourselves to the analysis of the relative proportions of *what was recovered* without trying to compensate for the recovery bias, while excluding *Antalis* sp. segments of a minimum diameter < 1.5 mm, too small to be considered as potential ornaments or as raw material (Chap. 4).

The relative proportions of ornamental taxa (Table 7.6, Fig. 7.6) reveal two homogeneous groups of phases, separated by the quasi-absence of ornaments in Phase 4. Phases 0-3 show a homogeneous composition, with a balanced representation of *Cyclope* sp. and *Antalis* sp., followed by *Homalopoma sanguineum* and *Columbella rustica* in much lower quantities. If all the < 5 mm residues had been sorted, *Antalis* sp. would have dominated in absolute numbers. The second group (Phases 5 and 6) is again homogeneous and characterised by the massive predominance of *Cyclope* sp., now probably mostly *Cyclope neritea*. *Antalis* sp. becomes much rarer and would have remained second to *Cyclope* sp. even if all the < 5 mm residues had been sorted. The proportion of *C. rustica* rises in Phase 5 and 6.1, while *H. sanguineum* completely disappears.

These fluctuations, together with the variations in overall abundance of ornaments, allow for the definition of three Upper Palaeolithic ornament phases (Franchthi Ornament Phase, or FOP): FOP 1 comprises the Franchthi General Phasing (FGP) Phases 0 to 3, FOP 2 only comprises FGP Phase 4, while FOP 3 groups FGP Phases 5 and 6.

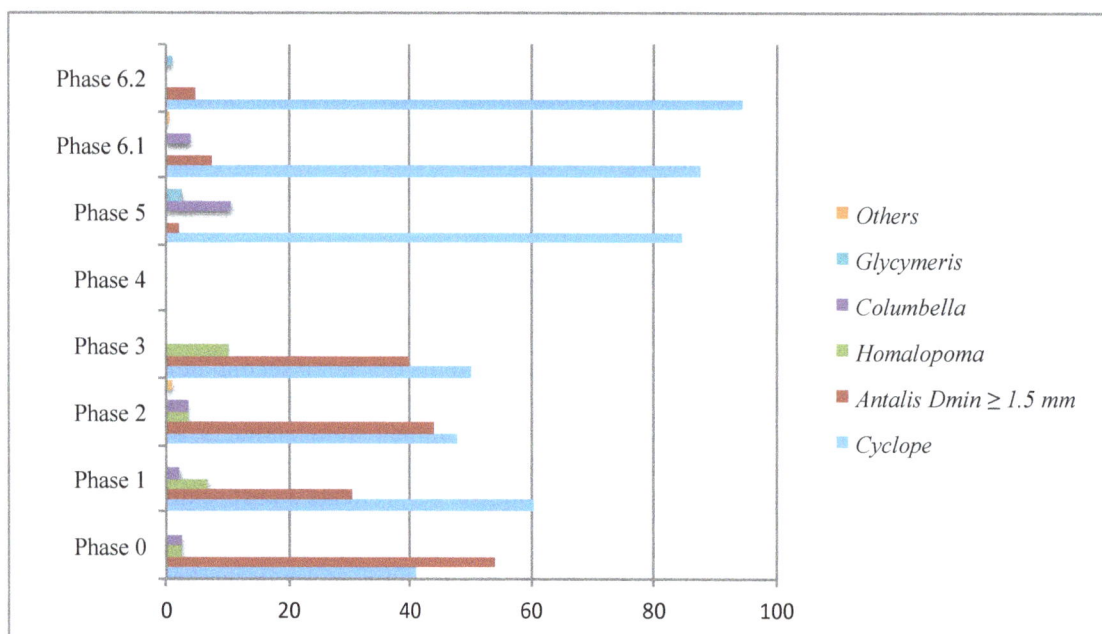

Fig. 7.6: Relative abundance (% of NISP) of the Upper Palaeolithic ornamental taxa.

Phase	Cyclope sp.	Antalis sp.	Homalopoma sanguineum	Columbella rustica	Glycymeris sp.	Others	N
		D min ≥ 1.5 mm					
0	41.03	53.8	2.56	2.56	0,00	0,00	42
1	60.5	30.2	6.9	2.3	0	0	92
2	47.7	44.22	3.5	3.5	0	1	242
3	50	40	10	0	0	0	11
4							3
5	81.7	5.2	0	10.4	2.6	0	230
6.1	87.6	7.6	0	4.1	0	0.6	170
6.2	94.2	4.8	0	0	0.96	0	104

Table 7.6: Relative abundance (% of NISP) of the Upper Palaeolithic ornamental taxa in H1A, H1B and FAS combined. Percentages have not been calculated for Phase 4, because of the low number of specimens (n= 3) and are unreliable for Phase 3 (n = 11).

Franchthi Ornament Phase 1: FAS 227-209, H1B 215-173(172-171), H1A 220-205[8]

Despite their poor preservation, the FOP 1 ornament assemblages from Franchthi are important: the small assemblage from (FGP) Phase 0 belongs to the very limited set of pre-Aurignacian ornament assemblages in Europe (Chap. 8), and the FOP 1 ornaments as a whole belong to the equally limited set of hunting halts—hunting field-camps, *sensu* Binford 1980—where collection and manufacturing of ornaments can be documented. FOP 1 (Fig. 7.7) is primarily characterised by the presence of *Homalopoma sanguineum*, unique to this ornament phase. The other shell taxa, *Cyclope* sp., *Antalis* sp. *Columbella rustica*, are, to the contrary, present in the entire Franchthi sequence. The relative importance of *Antalis* to *Cyclope*, however, is also characteristic of this phase. The tiny tubular bone bead, although unique (Chap. 6), is noteworthy since no further bone bead is documented until the beginning of the Lower Mesolithic[9]. The composition of the assemblages and proportions of the different species is relatively constant throughout FOP 1. No ornament subphases can be distinguished on this basis.

FOP 1 covers many millennia and spans over three Franchthi General Phases. Ornamental shells are already present in the deepest excavated levels (FGP Phase 0, Stratum P), below the tephra deposit (Stratum Q) identified as the Campanian Ignimbrite and dated to ca. 39,300 BP (De Vivo *et al.* 2001; Farrand 2000). The chipped stone assemblage from Phase 0 is undiagnostic but shows no Middle Palaeolithic features[10]. These pre-Aurignacian levels should be comparable in age to the Uluzzian levels from Klissoura Cave 1 (Argolid), the Upper Palaeolithic settlement nearest to Franchthi. No faunal data from Franchthi are available for this phase. Judging from the chipped stone tool assemblage, occupations seem to have been very sparse. The ornamental shells from Phase 0 are not contaminants: thanks to the use of improved procedures for the ^{14}C dating of shells (Douka *et al.* 2010), an *Antalis* sp. segment from H1B 215 has been dated to ca. 39,000–40,000 cal BP (Douka *et al.* 2011).

FGP Phase 1, in Stratum Q and R, just overlies the tephra and has been dated from ca. 36,500 cal BC to ca. 34,000 (Douka *et al.* 2011). The chipped stone tool assemblage is relatively small but contains diagnostic Aurignacian carenated cores and twisted bladelets. FGP Phase 2 yielded a very different lithic assemblage, heavily dominated by single-backed bladelets and narrow double-backed points (Perlès 1987). Although no sterile layers separate Phase 1 from Phase 2, the dates from Phase 2, around 26,500 – 26,000 cal BC indicate a long chronological hiatus. FGP Phase 3 has not been radiocarbon dated but is close, lithic-wise, to Phase 2 with a predominance of single-backed bladelets and the replacement of double-backed points by single, curved-backed points.

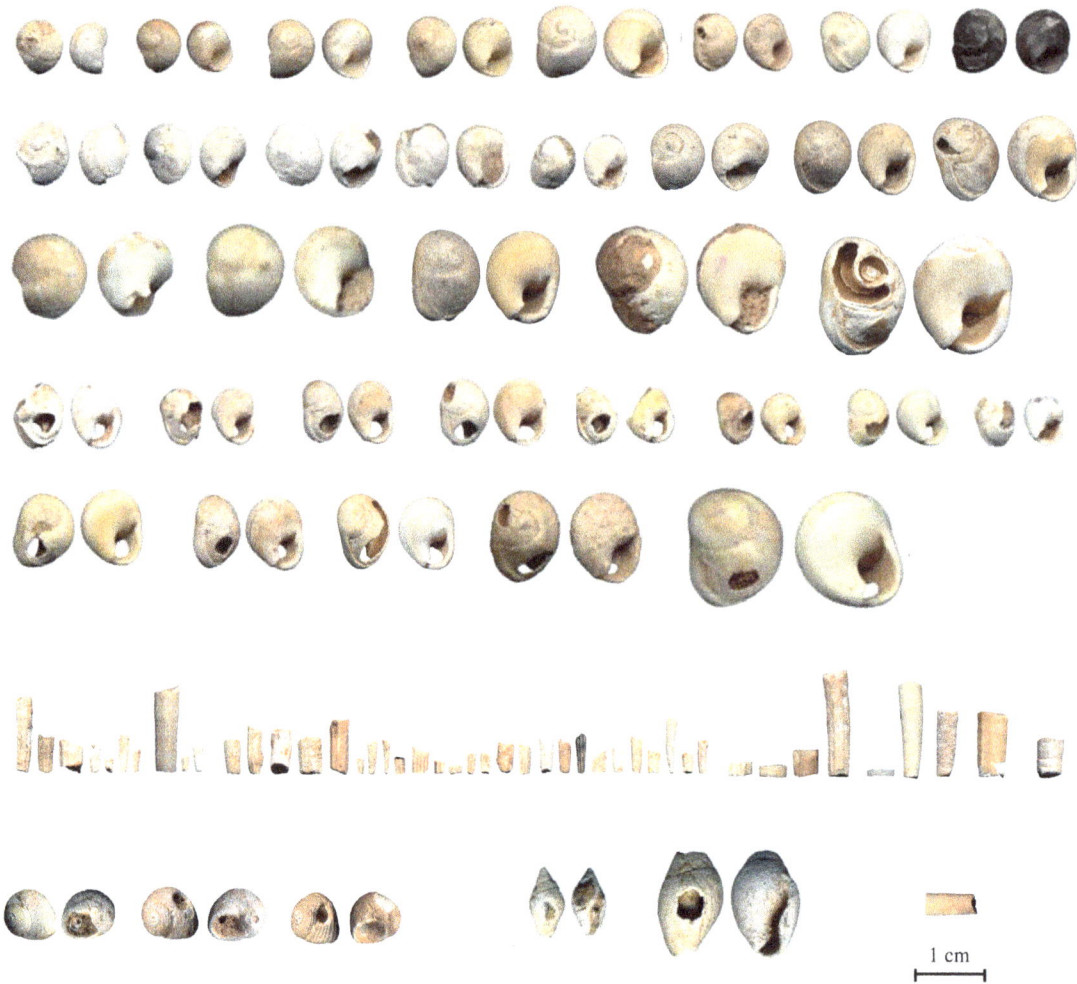

Fig. 7.7: Representative sample of Franchthi Ornament Phase 1 (FOP 1) assemblages.

FGP Phase	*Cyclope* sp.			*C. rustica*			*H. sanguineum*		
	perforated	unperforated	undetermined	perforated	unperforated	undetermined	perforated	unperforated	undetermined
0	0	2(1)	14	0	0	1	0	0	1
1	3	11(7)	38	0	1	1	2	1	3
2	14	23(13)	58	1	1	5	3	1	2
3	1	0	4	0	0	0	1	0	0

Table 7.7: Number of perforated and unperforated ornamental gastropods from FOP 1, in H1A, H1B and FAS combined. The figures in parenthesis indicate the number of juveniles among the unperforated Cyclope *sp.*

Phases 0 to 3 took place under a dry and cool climate[11], with a steppic environment in which red deer (*Cervus elaphus*), aurochs (*Bos primigenius*), European wild ass (*Equus hydruntinus*), boar (*Sus scrofa*), hares (*Lepus europaeus*) and partridges (*Alectoris* sp.) were hunted. Whereas hunting was relatively intensive, no gathering activity took place around the site: the numerous seeds recovered are minute uncarbonised nutlets of alkanet, gromwell and bugloss—*Alkanna* cf. *orientalis, Lithodora* (*Lithospermum) arvense* and *Anchusa* sp.—brought by the wind or washed down with the sediment. Fish and shellfish were not exploited, even though the distance from the site to the coast, of about 3.5 km, was no greater than in Phase 5 (Chap. 2). The quantity of land snails is too small to envision human collection, and slow moving animals such as tortoises are absent from the faunal record. All the evidence thus points to a use of the site as a hunting halt, which makes the presence of relatively abundant ornaments all the more interesting. Contrary to longer term hunting camps or base camps, the collection and manufacturing of ornaments is rarely documented at such sites (Bon *et al.* 2011; but see Orton 2008). At Franchthi, on the contrary, people seized the opportunity offered by the nearby shore to pick up ornamental species, while they did not bother to collect or bring back shellfish. This may indicates that their base camps were inland, and that the collection of ornamental shells was an important factor in their frequentation of the cave. Ornaments and ornamental raw material are indeed evenly distributed throughout FOP 1 deposits: they do not correspond to exceptional episodes of ornament manufacture, but to repeated and regular activities undertaken during visits to the cave.

In situ procuring of the ornaments is attested by the presence of juvenile *Cyclope* sp. In FOP 1, the proportion of juvenile *Cyclope* sp. is very high—29% of the specimens for which age class could be determined—and may indicate that a large proportion of finished beads, made on adult specimens, were taken away from the site. It may, however, also be simply related to the very high proportion of poorly preserved specimens, of which the determination is impossible. The presence of unperforated *Homalopoma sanguineum* may also indicate local procurement, but this does not constitute a decisive argument. Unperforated ornamental shells can be found at inland sites, sometimes in large quantities: at Fumane (Province of Verona, Italy), for instance, only 38.5 % of the ornamental shells, largely dominated by *H. sanguineum*, were perforated (Broglio & Gurioli 2004). Similarly, the inland rock shelters of Epirus, some 150 km from the ice-age coast, contained a notable proportion of unperforated *Cyclope* sp. (Kotjabopoulou & Adams 2004).

The state of preservation of ornamental shells in FOP 1 is very poor, due to a mix of chemical attacks and wave-induced damage. A very small minority of the ornaments is burnt: 3% of the *Cyclope* sp., 1% of the *Antalis* sp., and this can be considered accidental. The poor state of preservation constitutes a major handicap to ascertain not only the proportion of perforated specimens, but also the proportion of shells that bear wear traces and the distribution of those traces. The better-preserved specimens show that a relatively high proportion had been worn before being discarded: beads were not only produced at the site, but also recycled.

Franchthi Ornament Phase 2: H1B 204-183, H1A 170-162

FOP 2 corresponds to Phase 4 in the General Franchthi Phasing and is thus separated from FOP 1 by a long erosional hiatus. Deposits from Phase 4 are only preserved in H1A and H1B, and date to the second half of the 13th millennium cal BC, during the mild climatic episode of the Bölling. FOP 2 is characterised by the presence of a unique perforated Ibex tooth (Chap. 6), despite a quasi-absence of ornaments (n = 3). To my knowledge, no other perforated Ibex tooth is known in the Upper Palaeolithic of Greece.

The quasi-absence of ornaments in Phase 4 is all the more surprising in that it corresponds precisely to the period when the status of the site changed from a hunting halt to a base camp. Varied gathering activities were then practised, including a large variety of plants, some tortoises, and possibly some land snails. Small-scale fishing is also attested for the first time (Hansen 1991;

Perlès 2010; Rose in prep.; Stiner & Munro 2011). Franchthi can then be considered as a residential base for whole families (*sensu* Binford 1980), an interpretation supported by the presence of a shed milk tooth (Cullen & Papathanasiou in prep.). One would thus have (perhaps somewhat naïvely?) expected an increase in ornament output.

We considered early on the possibility that the bags containing shell remains had been mislaid[12]. We searched carefully, in many boxes at the Napfplion *apotheke,* but to no avail. The similar situation in both H1A and H1B[13] suggests instead that this quasi-absence is real. We consequently envisioned the hypothesis of a random sampling effect, since the volume of sediment excavated for Phase 4 is rather small (Table 7.1). This possibility cannot be completely ruled out, but the probability appears to be low: 11 ornamental shells were found in Phase 3, for a smaller volume of sediment, and 104 in Subphase 6.2, where the volume of sediment is approximately half that of Phase 4. It would seem, rather, that the procurement and discard of ornaments was not on the agenda during the occupation of Phase 4, even though members of the group occasionally went to the shore to fish gilt-head bream and grey mullet.

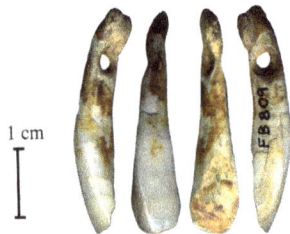

Fig. 7.8: The Ibex tooth from Franchthi Ornament Phase 2.

Franchthi Ornament Phase 3: FAS (207) 206-199, H1B (161) 160-155 (154), H1A 189-167

FOP 3 comprises Phases 5 and 6 of the Franchthi General Phasing, dated to the second half of the 12th millennium and the 11th millennium cal BC, i.e. overlapping the Alleröd and the cold episode of the Dryas III. We subdivided Phase 6 into two Subphases, 6.1 and 6.2, to reflect the increase in the abundance of ornaments in the latest Palaeolithic units of FAS and H1A.

FOP 3 is characterised by a marked predominance of *Cyclope* sp. (now probably mostly *C. neritea*), by a relative increase of *Columbella rustica* and by the absence of *Homalopoma sanguineum* (Table 7.6). In addition to *Antalis* sp., a few perforated *Glycymeris* sp. are also present. Their status as ornaments can be debated, but they are undoubtedly characteristic of FOP 3.

The hunting of the largest game, aurochs and wild ass, declined during Phase 5 (Stratum W) but taxonomic diversity was at its highest with the introduction of several fur animals such as lynx (*Lynx lynx*), wild cat (*Felis silvestris*), fox (*Vulpes vulpes*) and marten (*Martes* sp.) (Stiner & Munro 2011). Fishing or angling also reached a relative peak in intensity, in particular with abundant Sparids (Perlès 2016a; Rose in prep.; Stiner & Munro 2011). Shellfish were collected for the first time, with a focus on rock-dwelling species such as limpets (*Patella* sp.) and turbans (*Phorcus [Osilinus, Monodonta] turbinatus*) (Shackleton J. 1988). However, the most spectacular feature during Phase 5 is the massive accumulation of land snails, *Helix figulina,* forming thick middens (Whitney-Desautels, in prep.).

Despite the climatic change induced by the dry and cold episode of the Dryas III, the faunal and vegetal species exploited during Phase 6 remained essentially identical. The density of subsistence remains relative to the volume of sediments shows, however, a sharp decline (Perlès 2016a): land snails no longer constitute middens, large mammal bones are scarce, fishing is practiced on a much more modest scale.

Considering that the absence of *C. rustica* in Subphase 6.2 can easily be an effect of random distribution in a small sample[14], the composition of the ornament assemblages in the three FGP phases and subphases of FOP 3 can be considered fairly stable (Table 7.6). The state of preservation remains poor in Phase 5 and Subphase 6.1. It is much better in Subphase 6.2, possibly because the abundant "éboulis sec", constituted of small limestone fragments, induced a small but sufficient elevation in PH (Farrand 2000: Fig. 5.2). *Cyclope neritea* is by far the most abundant taxon. As in the earlier phases, it was collected locally. The proportion of juveniles, however, is much smaller than in FOP 1. This apparent drop may be due to environmental factors, since we observed similar variations during our present-day collections (Appendix 3.1). Alternately, it may indicate that fewer adult specimens left the site as finished beads, or that more worn beads were discarded.

Contrary to Cyclopes, very few dove shells (if any) appear to have been collected locally: there is only one unperforated specimen, and all the perforated ones show well-developed use-wear that indicates they had been worn a long time before being discarded at Franchthi. Approximately a quarter of the *Cyclope* sp. are burnt, a proportion that is higher than in any other category of remains, including animal bones and shellfish (Perlès & Vanhaeren 2010). Since Cyclopes were not eaten, this heat-treatment would have been implemented to change their colour from ivory to black (Chap. 3). The rate of perforation is much higher than in FOP 1: it varies between 62 and 76 % for *Cyclope* sp. and reaches nearly 100% for *C. rustica*. The proportion of undiagnostic specimens, which is comparable in FOP 1 and FOP 3, cannot account for the difference. The difference in ornament use that we suspected, with the introduction of embroidered beads in addition to strung beads (Chap. 3), may account for a higher rate of recycling and local discard of worn specimens.

These differences vis-à-vis FOP 1, however, can be considered as minor by comparison with the transformation in the status of Franchthi, in the activities that took place in and around the site in the subsistence base and in the conception of the tools and weapons, i.e. with all the variables that, together, constitute the basis for defining the Franchthi general phasing. The fact that ornament phases (FOP) do not present a one-to-one correlation with FGP phases reinforces the previous conclusions about the independence of ornament production, use and discard vis-à-vis subsistence and technical activities. It also shows that ornamental traditions lasted much longer than those of lithic production and the design of composite weapons with lithic inserts.

Phase	*Cyclope* sp.			*C. rustica*			*Glycymeris* sp.		Total
	perforated	unperforated	undetermined	perforated	unperforated	undetermined	perforated	undetermined	
5	85	30 (4)	73	18	1	5	4	2	230
6.1	39	35 (11)	75	6	0	1	0	0	170
6.2	58	28 (10)	12	0	0	0	1	0	104
Total	182	93 (25)	160	24	1	6	5	2	504

Table 7.8: Perforated and unperforated specimens from FOP 3, in H1A, H1B and FAS combined. The figures in parenthesis indicate the number of juveniles among the unperforated Cyclope sp.

The continuity in ornaments between FGP Phases 0, 1 and 2 in FOP 1 raises important issues and opens up new perspectives: Phase 0 is pre-Aurignacian, Phase 1 is typical Aurignacian in terms of lithic assemblage (Douka *et al.* 2011), whereas Phase 2, several millennia younger than Phase 1, is characterised by backed bladelets and backed points of Gravettian affinities (Perlès 1987). No continuity in the ornament assemblages would be expected if, as is often assumed, the pre-Aurignacian, the Aurignacian and the Gravettian corresponded to different human populations or, minimally, to different cultural complexes (Kozłowski 2004; Newell *et al.* 1990; Vanhaeren & d'Errico 2006). This is the first instance of arrhythmia in the pace of change between lithic assemblages, subsistence activities and ornament assemblages, an arrhythmia that actually characterises the entire Franchthi sequence. Before we discuss the potential meaning and implications of this pattern (Chapter 14), we need to ascertain whether this is unique to Franchthi, or, alternately, a generalised feature of ornament assemblages from Greece and south-eastern Europe.

NOTES

1   The volume of sediments derives from Hansen (1991) except for part of H1B where it was recalculated from the sections.
2   Or, perhaps, the least unsatisfactory...
3   For the three trenches combined, Pearson's R = 0.38 without *Antalis* sp., 0. 64 with *Antalis* sp. Neither is significant at p < 0.05.
4   H1B is the only trench where data on mammal bones are sufficiently complete to permit these calculations.
5   For H1B, R = -0.48 without *Antalis* sp., 0.65 with *Antalis* sp. ≥ 1.5 mm. Neither is significant at p < 0.05.
6   The number of phases when both categories are present in the Palaeolithic is too small to test statistical correlations.
7   For the three trenches combined, Pearson's R = 0.48 without *Antalis* sp. segments, 0.66 with *Antalis* sp. segments; neither is significant at p < 0.05.
8   Units in parentheses may be cross-cutting two phases or subphases.
9   As discussed in Chap.13, the determination of these Lower Mesolithic beads is not assured.
10 Although there is clear evidence that Middle Palaeolithic deposits are present in the cave (see Perlès 1987).
11 The abundance of uncarbonised Boraginaceae seeds, indicative of a dry and cool climate, is somehow surprising in Phase 0 when one would have expected a milder and moister climate.
12 Since shellfish was not yet exploited, the bags containing a few fragmentary shells and the shell ornaments were small and could easily have been misplaced.
13 The residues and artifacts from different trenches were kept in different boxes.
14 A χ^2 test comparing the number of *C. rustica* in each subphase to the total of ornamental shells shows no significant difference ($\chi^2 = 0.035$, df = 1).

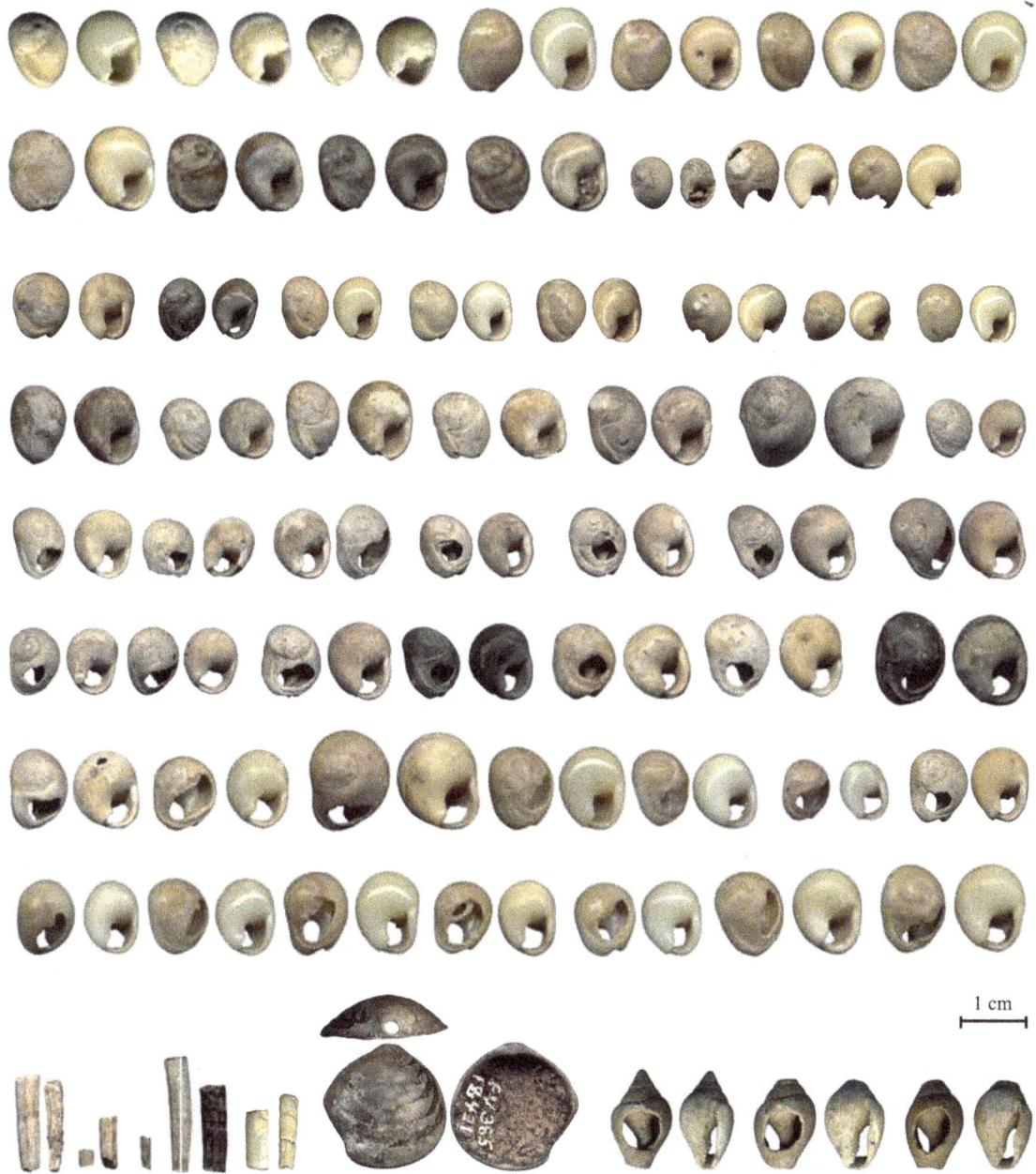

Fig. 7.9: Representative sample of Franchthi Ornament Phase 3 assemblages.

CHAPTER EIGHT

Franchthi Palaeolithic Ornaments: A Uniquely Restricted and Stable Range?

The preceding analyses have brought to light several highly diagnostic features in the Franchthi Upper Palaeolithic ornament assemblages:

- A massive predominance of marine shells,
- Among the marine shells, the predominance of small, basket-shaped species,
- The predominance of carnivorous gastropods,
- A very restricted range of ornaments, suggesting high selectivity,
- A marked continuity in the choice of ornaments.

To what extent does this narrow range of taxa reflect local availability? Does it, instead, reflect specific local or regional aesthetic and symbolic traditions? How do these compare with other Upper Palaeolithic Greek assemblages, and how do they fit into the broader context of the Mediterranean Upper Palaeolithic?

Few Upper Palaeolithic sequences have been excavated in Greece, and fewer still have yielded published ornament assemblages. Comparisons within Greece are limited to three sites from inland Epirus, Kastritsa, Klithi and Boïla (Kotjabopoulou & Adams 2004), to limited data from Kefalari Cave in the Argolid (Reisch 1980), and to the recently published assemblages from Klissoura Cave 1, also in the Argolid (Stiner 2010). Fortunately, the standard of recovery at Klithi, Boïla and Klissoura was high, including both dry-sieving and water-sieving. These assemblages can thus be directly compared with Franchthi.

Klissoura Cave 1, in the Gorge of Klissoura, is the Palaeolithic settlement nearest to Franchthi. It has revealed a long occupational sequence spanning from the Middle Palaeolithic to the Mesolithic (Kozłowski & Stiner 2010). Despite a distance to the sea that reaches today ca. 12 km and the lack of evidence for the exploitation of marine food resources, Klissoura has yielded a very rich Lower Aurignacian assemblage of ornamental shell species. Ornaments are less abundant in the other chronological phases, but remain important to place the Franchthi assemblages in context. Further north, in Epirus, Kastritsa, Klithi and Boïla provide interesting insights into the composition of ornament assemblages at inland sites, from ca. 27,000 cal BC to the beginning of the Holocene (see Facorellis 2013). The Kastritsa sequence, excavated long ago (Bailey *et al.* 1983a, b; Higgs *et al.* 1967) benefitted from new AMS dates (Galanidou & Tzedakis 2001) that bracket the main occupational sequence between 27-26,000 and 21,000 cal BC (Facorellis 2013). It thus overlaps with Franchthi FGP Phases 2 and 3. The Klithi rockshelter was excavated more recently, under the direction of G. Bailey (Bailey 1997a, 1997b). Its main occupational sequence concentrates between ca. 18,000 and 15,000 cal BC with sporadic occupations occurring between 12,000 and

10,000 cal BC (Facorellis 2013; Gowlett *et al.* 1997). Aside from these apparently brief late visits, the sequence from Klithi does not overlap with excavated deposits at Franchthi. To the contrary, the Boïla rockshelter, dated to 15,000 – 10,000 cal BC (Facorellis 2013; Kotjabopoulou *et al.* 1997), allows direct chronological comparisons to Franchthi Phases 4, 5 and 6.

The Predominance of Marine Shells

The predominance of marine shells at Franchthi (ca. 99% of the ornaments) is far from unique. It holds true for all the Greek reference sites. At Klissoura Cave 1, more than 1500 ornaments and ornamental shells were recovered. *Theodoxus* sp., a freshwater gastropod, and some fossil taxa are the only exceptions in assemblages that are, otherwise, exclusively composed of marine shells. No stone, bone or tooth ornaments was recovered (Stiner 2010). Marine molluscs also predominate in the inland Epirote sites, despite a distance to the sea that can be estimated between 115 and 150 km during the LGM. They constitute between 70 to 90 % of the ornament assemblages, accompanied by perforated deer canines, some *Theodoxus* sp. and rare stone or bone pendants (Kotjapopoulou & Adams 2004). At Kefalari, marine shells appear to dominate, though perforated deer canines are also present (Reisch 1980).

On a larger geographical scale, marine molluscs already predominate in early Uluzzian assemblages (Zilhão 2007) as well as in the large Proto-Aurignacian assemblage from Fumane, far from the coasts (Broglio & Gurioli 2004). They dominate also in the Aurignacian 'macro-set C', along the Mediterranean coast (Vanhaeren & d'Errico 2006), throughout the Upper Palaeolithic sequence of Riparo Mochi in Italy (Stiner 1999), in the Epigravettian from Riparo Tagliente (Cilli & Gurioli 2007) and at many Upper Palaeolithic settlements from southern France (Taborin 1993). Looking at the eastern end of the Mediterranean, marine molluscs also predominate in the early Upper Palaeolithic and Epipalaeolithic sequence from Üçağızlı Cave 1 (eastern Turkey) and at Ksar' Akil in Lebanon (Inizan & Gaillard 1978; Kuhn *et al.* 2001; Stiner *et al.* 2013). The importance of marine shells is clearly not a distinctive trait of the Franchthi Upper Palaeolithic ornament assemblages (Stiner 2014).

The Predominance of Small, Basket-Shaped Beads and Carnivorous Gastropods

The important volume "*Shells from the Greek Seas*" (Delamotte & Vardala-Theodorou 2000) lists dozens and dozens of different taxa, most of them with wide distributions in the Greek seas. Yet, five taxa only were selected at Franchthi: *Cyclope, Columbella, Homalopoma, Antalis* and *Glycymeris*, of which only the first four can be considered with certainty as 'ornamental'. This restricted choice is not random, nor is it specific to Franchthi. The preference for small shells of globular shapes has repeatedly been noted (Álvarez-Fernández & Jöris 2008; Stiner 2014; Taborin 2004), as has their resemblance to red deer canines and basket-shaped stone and ivory beads (White 1993, 2004; Zilhão 2007). The association of these globular or semi-globular shapes with the tubular *Antalis* is another feature common to many assemblages, and has no definite cultural significance.

In Franchthi Upper Palaeolithic assemblages, the most typical 'basket-shaped' taxon is the carnivorous *Cyclope* (C. *neritea* and C. *pellucida*); it predominates at Franchthi, but also at Klissoura Cave, Kastritsa, Klithi, and Boïla. Stiner has long pondered on the predominance of scavengers and carnivorous taxa in Upper Palaeolithic ornament assemblages, which, given their trophic position, should be much less abundant (ca. 10-15 %) in living biocenoses than herbivorous taxa (e.g. *Columbella rustica* or *Homalopoma sanguineum*) (Stiner 1999, 2010, 2014). However, this trophic scale may not apply to *Cyclope*, since *C. neritea* and *C. pellucida* are essentially scavengers that feed on bacteria, dead fish and dead crustaceans (Simon-Bouhet 2006; Southward *et al.* 1997). They form large colonies: densities up to 1600 snails per square meter have been reported (Southward *et al.* 1997; Tardy *et al.* 1985). We had no difficulty collecting 200 or 300 live specimens an hour, especially at sunset when they emerge from the mud to feed (Appendix 3.1). We may even suspect that the ease of collection may be one reason why *Cyclope* sp. were sometimes used so lavishly to decorate garments and head dresses, as exemplified by several burials from the Grimaldi caves in Liguria (Taborin 2004).

Highly Selective Assemblages

The preference for certain shapes and sizes automatically entails a selection amongst the available marine molluscs. This selectivity has been frequently underlined (Álvarez-Fernández 2010; Álvarez-Fernández & Jöris 2008; Stiner 2010, 2014; Stiner *et al.* 2013; Taborin 2004; Vanhaeren & d'Errico 2006), but it appears to be especially prevalent in Greek Upper Palaeolithic sites, with the notable exception of the Early Aurignacian from Klissoura Cave 1.

Referring to the three Epirote sites they studied, Kotjabopoulou & Adams (2004: 48) note that: "The use of a rather restricted assortment of shell species is evident, however, compared to the natural availability of the Mediterranean waters even in the face of changing sea levels and the waxing and waning of local littoral habitats". They then add with caution: "No doubt (...) we are dealing with skewed evidence, that is with assemblages recovered exclusively from *inland rockshelter habitation contexts*" (*idem*: 49. Emphasis by authors). The restricted range of species at Franchthi, a near-coastal site, demonstrates that the caution was unwarranted and that distance from the sea did not skew the evidence.

The early FGP phases from Franchthi (Phases 0-3), which together constitute FOP 1, correspond chronologically to Klissoura Cave 1 layers V, IV and III, i.e. successively to Early Upper Palaeolithic/ Uluzzian, Aurignacian, non Aurignacian Upper Palaeolithic and 'Mediterranean backed-bladelet' lithic industries (Kozłowski & Stiner 2010).

In the small Uluzzian ornament assemblage from Klissoura 1 (NISP = 34, MNI = 32), at least 10 taxa are represented. *Cyclope* and *Dentalium* (*Antalis*) sp. respectively amount to 34 and 29% of the MNI. *Columbella rustica* and undetermined bivalves make up 9% of the assemblage, completed by *Gibbula* sp., *Homalopoma* sp., *Hinia reticulata*, the fresh water gastropod *Theodoxus* spp. and a fossil lake species. The species richness[1] is one of the highest for the whole sequence: 9.30, or 6.6 if the different species of *Antalis* and *Cyclope* sp. are grouped, as we did for Franchthi[2] (Stiner 2010). At Franchthi, the levels just below the tephra (Phase 0) contained 16 *Cyclope* sp., 24 *Antalis* sp., 1 small *Columbella rustica* and 1 *Homalopoma sanguineum*, i.e. a species richness[3] of 2.46 if the counts are taken at face value. However, these figures are only indicative since the total number of *Antalis* sp. is underestimated by a large factor, while some of the smaller fragments may be unrelated to ornament manufacture and use (Chap. 4). In any case, adding more *Antalis* would only reduce the species richness and strengthen the contrast between the two sites. In this respect, the earliest assemblage from Franchthi compares better with the Uluzzian levels from Grotta del Cavallo (Palma di Cesnola 1993), also characterised by a very limited range of ornamental shell species, while the wide range of species at Klissoura Cave 1 evokes the diversified proto-Aurignacian ornament assemblage from Fumane (Broglio & Gurioli 2004) or layer G from Riparo Mochi.

The contrast between Franchthi and Klissoura Cave 1 (KC1) is exacerbated when one compares the Aurignacian assemblage from Franchthi (FGP Phase 1) with the Aurignacian assemblage from KC1, especially the Lower and Mid-Aurignacian (Layers IV and IIIe-g). The Lower Aurignacian from KC1 (NISP = 1300; MNI = 1218, species richness = 14.58[4]) is several times richer than the Aurignacian from Franchthi (NISP = 92). Contrary to figures for the pre-Aurignacian, where the assemblages were of similar size, such a difference can bias the comparisons in terms of species richness: rare taxa—such as *Haliotis lamellose, Calliostoma sp., Gibbula cf. umbilicus, Clanculus cruciatus (?), Littorina neritoides, Turitella communis, Cerithium vulgaris*, and several other species—are all represented by 1 to 3 specimens only at KC1, and have a low probability of being present in the much smaller Franchthi sample. Thus, the 45 taxa in the Lower Aurignacian at Klissoura cannot be directly compared with the 4 taxa present at Franchthi, *Cyclope* sp., *Antalis* sp., *Columbella rustica* and *Homalopoma sanguineum*, where the richness index barely reaches 2[5].

Phase	Actual counts			Counts without *Antalis* sp.		
	NISP	*N taxa*	*Taxa richness*	*NISP*	*N taxa*	*Taxa richness*
0	42	4	2.46	18	3	2.4
1	92	4	2.04	60	3	1.68
2	242	5*	2.1	111	4*	1.66
3	11	3	2.88	6	2	2.5
4	3	2	-	1	1	-
5	230	4**	1.69	218	3**	1.28
6.1	170	3*	1.34	157	2*	0.91
6.2	104	3**	1.49	99	2**	1

Table 8.1: Species diversity in the Palaeolithic assemblages based on actual counts with and without Antalis sp. * The stone bead is considered intrusive and has not been taken into account. **This figure includes the perforated Glycymeris sp., whose status as ornaments is uncertain.

However, the mid-Aurignacian assemblage from Klissoura Cave 1 (layers IIIe-g) is much closer in term of size to the Franchthi Aurignacian assemblage (NISP = 148, MNI = 138). Despite its relatively small size, it still contains 18 taxa, with a species richness index of 8.41[6]. Thus for the two phases so far examined, Franchthi systematically shows a much lower diversity than KC1, irrespective of the sample size. The phenomenon of 'high-grading' (Stiner *et al.* 2013: 381), according to which more 'junk' should accumulate on a coastal site and "ornament diversity should decline as people ventured inland" is not exemplified at Franchthi: the taxonomic diversity is actually higher in the inland site of Klissoura Cave 1 than at Franchthi.

Franchthi FGP Phase 2, AMS dated to 26,500 – 26,000 cal BC, possibly corresponds to part of the mixed layer 6a from Klissoura Cave 1[7]. Layers 6a and 7 only yielded 8 ornaments, but the latter still include, besides *Cyclope* sp., 2 *Theodoxus* sp., unrecorded at Franchthi. Franchthi Phase 2 also corresponds to the base of the Kastritsa sequence in Epirus, Strata 5+7 and 5, which yielded 36 perforated specimens and 48 unperforated or undiagnostic specimens. The comparison is relevant: whereas the relatively rich sample from Franchthi (n = 242) only contains the same four taxa as before (*Cyclope* sp., *Antalis* sp., *C. rustica, H. sanguineum*) and one tubular bone bead, the smaller sample from Kastritsa is composed of *Cyclope* sp., *Antalis* (*Dentalium*) sp., four perforated deer canines and a stone pendant. The range is similarly restricted at both sites, but the assemblage from Kastritsa demonstrates that perforated deer canines can be present even in small samples.

The presence of perforated red deer canines is confirmed at Klithi, whose main sequence takes place between our Phases 3 and 4. Altogether, the Klithi assemblages amount to 208 specimens, of which 188 are perforated (Adam & Kotjabopoulou 2004). Here again, *Cyclope* sp. predominates, followed by *Homalopoma sanguineum*. Besides *Theodoxus* sp., also well represented, a few rare species are present: *Nassarius* [*Arcularia*] *gibbosulus, Hinia* sp. and *Mitromorpha olivoidea*. Eight perforated red deer canine complete the assemblage.

Since the assemblages from FGP Phases 3 and 4 at Franchthi are too poor to evaluate the diversity, we shall now turn to the Final Upper Palaeolithic phases, dated to the 12th and 11th millennia cal BC. FGP Phases 5 and 6 (FOP 3) chronologically correspond to the main occupations of Boïla rockshelter, with close correspondences in the lithic assemblages from the two sites (Kotjabopoulou *et al.* 1997).

Despite reasonably large samples, the three FGP phases and subphases that belong to FOP 3 at Franchthi show remarkably low species diversity indices, between 1.34 and 1.69. All are indeed heavily dominated by *Cyclope* sp. (now probably mainly C. neritea), accompanied by a few *C. rustica*, *Antalis* sp. and the *Glycymeris* sp. of uncertain status (Chap. 6). Comparisons with the contemporaneous levels from Boïla are revealing: the ornament assemblage from Boïla comprises 46 perforated items and 59 unperforated or undiagnostic items, figures that are equivalent or lower than at Franchthi. Yet, 6 ornament categories are present at Boïla: *Cyclope* sp., *Homalopoma sanguineum*, *Theodoxus* sp., a perforated red deer canine, a worked red deer canine and a perforated stone (Kotjabopoulou & Adams 2004, table 1). Finally, mention must be made to the Zaïmis cave in Attica: the ornament assemblage has not been published, but Galanidou (2003: n.3 p. 105) signals a perforated *Turitella* sp. and a perforated *Nasa [Arcularia] reticulata* (now *Nassarius reticulatus* L.), both species unknown in Franchthi ornament assemblages.

Thus, even within Greece and even when compared with assemblages of similar sizes, the range of ornaments at Franchthi is systematically more restricted that at any other site. No environmental factor can be invoked: the rocky shores, the sandy shores and the marshes, the coastal plain with its small streams and the hills, all offered to the Franchthi inhabitants a diversified environment with many potential resources. N. Whitney-Desautels did not find *Theodoxus* sp. in her malacological survey around Franchthi, nor in the archaeological collection (Whitney-Desautels, in prep.). It is thus impossible to state whether it was available to the prehistoric inhabitants of Franchthi. On the other hand, deer canines and ibex incisors were available throughout the sequence (Munro & Stiner in prep.; Payne 1975; Stiner & Munro 2011), as was a whole range of marine shells that were, ironically, used as ornaments at more inland sites.

The fact that Franchthi was actually a nearly coastal site may, paradoxically, explain part of this pattern. Franchthi was close enough to the coast to allow for the exploitation of marine molluscs as food resources. The collection of shellfish started during the late Upper Palaeolithic (FGP Phase 5) and continued throughout the Final Palaeolithic and Mesolithic, albeit on a modest scale (Colonese *et al.* 2010; Perlès 2016a; Shackleton J. 1988; Stiner & Munro 2011). During the Upper Palaeolithic, the main species exploited were intertidal rock-dwelling species: *Patella* sp., *Cerithium vulgatum*, *Phorcus* (= *Monodonta* = *Osilinus*) *turbinatus*, *Gibbula sp.* and *Hexaplex* (= *Murex*) *trunculus*. *Gibbula*, *Phorcus* and to a lesser extent, *Hexaplex* were used as ornaments at Klissoura Cave 1, where shellfish were not consumed (Stiner 2010). The fact that several of these species were eaten at Franchthi would have precluded their use as ornaments, thus restricting the range of potential ornamental shell taxa. This, however, does not explain the absence of other species, well represented in the Aurignacian of Klissoura Cave 1, such as *Clanculus corallinus* or *Hinia reticulata* (also present at Klithi). Nor does it explain why certain species, known to have been present around Franchthi thanks to unworked specimens, such as *Pisania striata*, *Conus mediterraneus* or *Pecten* sp. were not transformed into ornaments.

The restricted range of ornaments at Franchthi cannot either be explained by the status of the site and the activities that took place in and around the cave: the status of the site changed repeatedly throughout the Upper Palaeolithic sequence. During the earlier phases, Franchthi can be interpreted as a hunting field-camp where, except for ornamental species, no gathering activity took place: carbonised seeds, land snail middens, shellfish, fish and tortoises are all absent (Perlès 2010, 2016a. For a different interpretation, see Stiner & Munro 2011). After the long depositional hiatus corresponding to the LGM, the status of the site changed markedly: during Phase 4 (FOP 2), the occupants of the cave collected plants, captured tortoises and started fishing from or near the shore. The site can then be considered as a base camp, and a shed milk tooth confirms the presence of whole families (Cullen & Papathanasiou in prep.). Shellfish exploitation is introduced during Phase 5 (FOP 3), together with the hunting of fur animals, more intensive fishing and a massive consumption of land snails (*Helix figulina*). During Phase 6 occupations seem to revert to much briefer stays, focussing each time on different resources: game, plants, fish and shellfish.

Overall, the status of the site appears to have shifted from a hunting halt to a residential base, albeit with different economic patterns even during these later occupations. It can thus be assumed that the numerical importance and the composition of the groups—in terms of gender and age— that occupied the site differed in the early and later phases. However, these social transformations did not impact upon the range of bead types[8]. Thus, the restricted range of ornament types cannot be attributed to the restricted social profiles of the cave occupants. It should, instead, most probably be taken at face value: a marked preference for a very limited number of ornament categories. This accords with the definition of 'conformism' put forward by Stiner and his colleagues (2013: 381). Their conclusion about the stability of the Üçağızlı Cave 1 assemblages appear to apply perfectly to Franchthi: "Thus, formal rules about what a bead ought to look like seem to have been responsible for the great consistency over time in bead size and shape" (*idem*: 396). What is most striking, indeed, is that in both sequences, the local preferences remained nearly unchanged throughout many millennia.

Stable Choices throughout Many Millennia

Besides variations in the relative importance of the different taxa, the only real change throughout the Upper Palaeolithic ornament sequence at Franchthi is the disappearance of *Homalopoma sanguineum* in the later phases and, if they are considered as ornaments, the presence of perforated *Glycymeris* sp. in phases 5 and 6. *Cyclope neritea* and *C. pellucida*, associated with smooth and ridged tusk shells, dominate the assemblages throughout. *Columbella rustica*, poorly represented in the early phases, becomes more important in the Late/Final Upper Palaeolithic. This relative stability is all the more impressive in that the sequence spans some 25 millennia, across fluctuating sea levels and with a hiatus of ca. 12 millennia in trenches H1A and H1B. This hiatus, however, is a *sedimentary, erosional* hiatus: there are no sterile layers indicating the prehistoric groups effectively abandoned the cave. In FAS the sedimentary hiatus is even longer and includes Phases 4 and 5. This shows that the erosion that removed the deposits could affect selectively different sectors of the cave. It is thus conceivable that the cave was occupied more or less continuously throughout the Late Glacial Maximum and that the deposits were eroded away when rainfall increased in the Late Pleistocene, or that they are preserved in an unexcavated sector of the cave. Consequently, we need not assume that the groups that occupied the cave in the Late Palaeolithic had no connection whatsoever with their predecessors.

Whichever is the case, the continuity observed at Franchthi is not unique. Indeed, diachronic continuity in the choice of ornaments might well be an under-explored characteristic of Upper Palaeolithic ornament assemblages. Kotjabopoulou & Adams (2004: 48), for instance, insist on the continuity in the Kastritsa, Klithi and Boïla sequences: "This lack of any significant diachronic variation points to a sustained symbolic/aesthetic preference interwoven with selectivity related to size (...), form/shape (...) colour/brilliance (...) and perhaps on occasion natural patterns (...)". Taxonomic diversity is much higher at Klissoura Cave 1, but one genus, *Cyclope*, dominates all through this long sequence (Stiner 2010).

Outside Greece, in the long Proto-Aurignacian to Epigravettian sequence of the Riparo Mochi in Liguria, Stiner (2014: 55) underlines the "remarkable consistency in the preferred molluskan taxa [*Cyclope* sp. and *Homalopoma sanguineum*] over thousands of years of occupation while many other aspects of material culture changed over this long time span". She notes a similar continuity of the dominant elements (*Nassarius gibbosulus, Columbella rustica* and *Theodoxus* sp.) at Üçağızlı Cave 1, "on the far eastern corner of the Mediterranean", from the Initial Upper Palaeolithic throughout the Late Ahmarian and Epipaleolithic. One can also observe a marked continuity from the Initial Upper Palaeolithic to the Ahmarian at Ksar' Akil in Lebanon, where *Nassarius gibbosulus*, and *Columbella rustica* are complemented by a high proportion of *Glycymeris glycymeris* (Kuhn *et al.* 2001).

Specific associations of ornament types are considered as identity markers that allow, from a synchronic perspective, the definition of cultural boundaries (Newell *et al.* 1990; Rigaud 2011; Rigaud *et al.* 2015; Vanhaeren 2010; Vanhaeren & d'Errico 2006; Wiessner 1982, 1984). The same should thus hold true from a diachronic perspective: the permanence of ornament assemblages should reflect enduring traditions and cultural continuity. If this is the case, ornament assemblages are in clear contrast with the lithic (and sometimes bone) assemblages from these long sequences, which display repeated discontinuities often interpreted as cultural breaks. Franchthi offers a good example with an absolute continuity in ornaments in Phases 0, 1 and 2, i.e., in lithic terms, between a Pre-Aurignacian, an Aurignacian and a Gravettoid phase (Perlès 1987). However, can we infer *cultural* continuity with such restricted assemblages, constituted of widely used shell bead types?

Where Local Preferences Come into Play: Choice of Species and Significant Absences

The Upper Palaeolithic shell bead types present at Franchthi are, as we have seen, absolutely commonplace and present at a great number of sites along the Mediterranean coasts. Arguing against cultural interpretations of Upper Palaeolithic ornament assemblages, Stiner (2014: 62) states that "The general uniformity in bead shape and size was far too extensive in its temporal and spatial scope to be explained by common linguistic or cultural heritage". Instead, she considers them as the basic units in a form of "information technology", i.e. as "media for communication" along spatially extensive interaction networks[9] (Kuhn 2014; Kuhn *et al.* 2001; Kuhn & Stiner 2007; Stiner 2014).

It cannot be disputed that neither the types of shell beads present at Franchthi, nor their associations can be considered as identity markers *per se*. However, one should also consider what species and materials were *not* used as ornament at Franchthi. As already mentioned, *Theodoxus* sp. is present in the Klissoura Cave 1 assemblages as well as in Epirus, but not at Franchthi. It is also widespread in Adriatic and Balkan Upper Palaeolithic sites (Cristiani *et al.* 2014b). We have no proof that it was locally available, but certainly no attempt was made to acquire it through exchange. The various species of *Gibbula*, abundant in the Aurignacian from Klissoura Cave 1, and the rarer *Clanculus* sp. were, to the contrary, locally available since unperforated specimens have been found in the equivalent levels at Franchthi (*supra*, p. 63-64). Conversely, *Antalis sp.* virtually disappears at Klissoura Cave 1 after the Uluzzian, while it remains present throughout the Franchthi sequence. *Homalopoma sanguineum* ceased to be used at Franchthi in the late Upper Palaeolithic phases, when it was second in importance to *Cyclope* sp. at both Klithi and Boïla. Red deer canines, present at Kefalari Cave and systematically present in Epirote sequences, are absent at both Franchthi and KC1 despite large assemblages and the continuous presence of deer in faunal assemblages. This absence distinguishes the two southern Greek sites from the northern ones, and, more generally, from the Adriatic and Balkan Upper Palaeolithic sites, where deer canines are consistently present (Cristiani *et al.* 2014b).

If these absences were sporadic and varied from one layer or phase to the next, one could simply invoke chance: no single bead of this precise type had been dropped or left behind during the occupation of the site at that time. When absences are systematic and independent of sample sizes, they demonstrate that these bead types were not part of the ornaments conception of the group and that this exclusion was maintained from generation to generation. Traditions are not only characterised by what is used, but also by what is *not* used (Cristiani *et al.* 2014b). In this sense, the restriction of ornament assemblages at Franchthi to a very small range of bead types can be considered as a cultural choice, within a very long lasting tradition that accepted only very limited changes. Stiner and his colleagues (2013: 381) alluded to the "formal rules about what a bead ought to look like". Since these rules vary from site to site or region to region, even within a broadly common conception, they must be considered as cultural. In turn, the cultural continuity exemplified in most long chronological sequences questions the discontinuities postulated on the basis of lithic assemblages, and, more precisely, on the basis of the stone weapon inserts (Perlès 2013).

NOTES

1   Calculated as N Species/log MNI. The use of log MNI corrects for sample size effects.

2   Given the overlap in dimensions between *C. neritea* and *C. pellucida* and the absence of morphological difference, we did not attempt to distinguish them in the counts (see Chap. 3). In addition, both can be found together and it would have been impossible for the prehistoric collectors or users to consider them as different species. Smooth and ridged *Antalis.* sp have not been counted separately since the distinction is difficult on small apical fragments.

3   Here calculated as N species/log NISP since we cannot exclude that two or more fragments of *Antalis* sp. came from the same shell.

4   Species richness at Klissoura is reduced to 13.6 if *Antalis* sp. and *Cyclope* sp. count for one entry only, as we did for Franchthi.

5   Species richness would reach 3.7 at Franchthi if it assumed that *Cyclope neritea* and *pellucida* are both present at the same time, as well as smooth and ridged *Antalis.*sp.

6   The index is reduced to 5.7 when *Antalis* sp. and *Cyclope* sp. are grouped.

7   Dates of the 28th and 27th millennia for layers III' and III", close to the dates for our Phase 2, are rejected as too young (Kuhn *et al.* 2010).

8   See the "neutral social factor" as a potential cause for variability on in the diversity of ornament assemblages in Stiner *et al.* 2013.

9   "The great redundancy in bead form and size and certain other characteristics therefore cannot be used to infer heritage or continuity among the cultural traditions. Shape and size constraints in the beads instead seems to relate to basic performance characteristics of beads, including geometry, weight, durability, and probably also their potential for recombination. In other words, beads were the irreducible elements of potentially complex artifacts, desirable for making larger compositions that may have been the main purveyors of meaning (e.g. Wiessner 1984). Beads may have had more in common with particles of language than did most other kinds of paleoart" (Stiner 2014: 59).

ORNAMENTS AND ORNAMENTAL
SHELLS OF THE MESOLITHIC

Mesolithic ornaments belong to three distinct chronological periods, each separated from the other by a chronological hiatus of several hundred years. The dates for the rich Lower Mesolithic (FGP Phase 7) concentrate between 8,600 and 8,300 cal BC. The Upper Mesolithic (FGP Phase 8) is dated to ca. 8,000 – 7,600 cal BC, while the Final Mesolithic occupations (FGP Phase 9) are dated between ca. 7,050 and 6,750 cal BC.

Perforated shells amount to no less than 99.9 % of the recorded Mesolithic ornament assemblages, which comprises almost 11,000 specimens. Shell ornaments are manufactured on the same three taxa that dominated Palaeolithic assemblages: *Cyclope* sp., *Antalis* sp. and *Columbella rustica*. The inhabitants of the cave also left behind a few perforated pebbles, several of which are unfinished, as well as extremely rare potential bird bone beads.

CHAPTER NINE

Continuity in a Changing Environment

The Same Shell Ornaments ...

In the introduction to the Palaeolithic ornament assemblages, we stated that "Palaeolithic ornament assemblages at Franchthi comprise almost exclusively perforated shells". It may therefore sound somewhat of a refrain to begin the analysis of Mesolithic ornaments with the assertion "Mesolithic ornaments comprise almost exclusively perforated shells"! Yet, the fact remains that perforated shells account for no less than 99.9 % of the recorded Mesolithic ornament assemblages. This high proportion is all the more significant given that the total ornaments and ornamental shells reaches nearly 11,000 specimens in only four trenches, H1A, H1B, FAS and FAN.

At Franchthi, the Mesolithic is separated from the Palaeolithic by a probable hiatus of a few hundred years, with no sterile deposits in between (Farrand 2000). The increase in the quantity of ornaments and ornamental species is perceptible in all trenches from the very beginning of the Mesolithic. The number can reach impressive figures: more than 150 specimens in a single excavation unit. The total number of ornaments quoted above is, nevertheless, below the actual number of pieces recovered during the excavations. First, except for the lowermost three Mesolithic units, trench H1A was not water-sieved and many fragmentary pieces are therefore missing. Second, after having recovered several thousand specimens from H1A, H1B and FAS, it was clear that the time-consuming process of sorting all the mixed snail and shell bags from the Lower Mesolithic in trench FAN would have resulted in little or no new information. Our counts from FAN are thus only partial. Third, Shackleton N. reports that: "In Mesolithic levels (both in G1 and areas excavated in 1969) there are enormous numbers of *Neritea* [*C. neritea*] shells. (Over 700 were recovered in one area excavated in 1969). Well over half of these appear to have been pierced, suggesting that they may have been used as beads." (N. Shackleton 1969: 379)[1]. In 1969, Mesolithic levels were excavated in H1A and we presume that the 700 shells recovered correspond to the specimens included in the present study. On the contrary, we were not able to locate the ornamental shells, or more generally the marine shells, from the 1968 and 1969 excavations in trenches G and G1. Finally, Mesolithic deposits were also excavated in trenches H, H pedestal and H2A but we shall not include the ornaments in the present study because they could not be assigned either to the Initial Neolithic or to a precise Mesolithic phase.

Even more striking perhaps that the sheer number of ornaments and ornamental species is their uniformity: shell ornaments are exclusively manufactured on the same three taxa that dominated Palaeolithic assemblages: *Cyclope* sp., *Antalis* sp. and *Columbella rustica*. Despite a far larger sample, the range of taxa is almost narrower than in the Palaeolithic: *Homalopoma sanguineum* is completely absent, *Glycymeris glycymeris* is represented by a single fragmentary specimen and *Conus mediterraneus* by one perforated specimen. However, to underline their affiliation to the European Mesolithic, the inhabitants of the cave also left behind a few perforated pebbles, several of which as unfinished preforms, and some extremely rare potential bird bone beads.

The ornaments belong to three distinct chronological periods, each separated from the other by a chronological hiatus of several hundred years. The dates for the rich Lower Mesolithic (Phase 7) concentrate between 8,600 and 8,300 cal BC[2]. The Upper Mesolithic (Phase 8)—a period when tuna fishing was intensively practised (Rose, in prep.; Perlès 2016a)—is dated to ca. 8,000 – 7,600 cal BC, while the Final Mesolithic occupations (Phase 9) are dated between ca. 7,050 and 6,800 cal BC. Despite a fairly large number of radiocarbon dates, the exact duration of these last two phases is impossible to define, as both correlate with plateaus in the calibrated ^{14}C curve (Fig. 9.1).

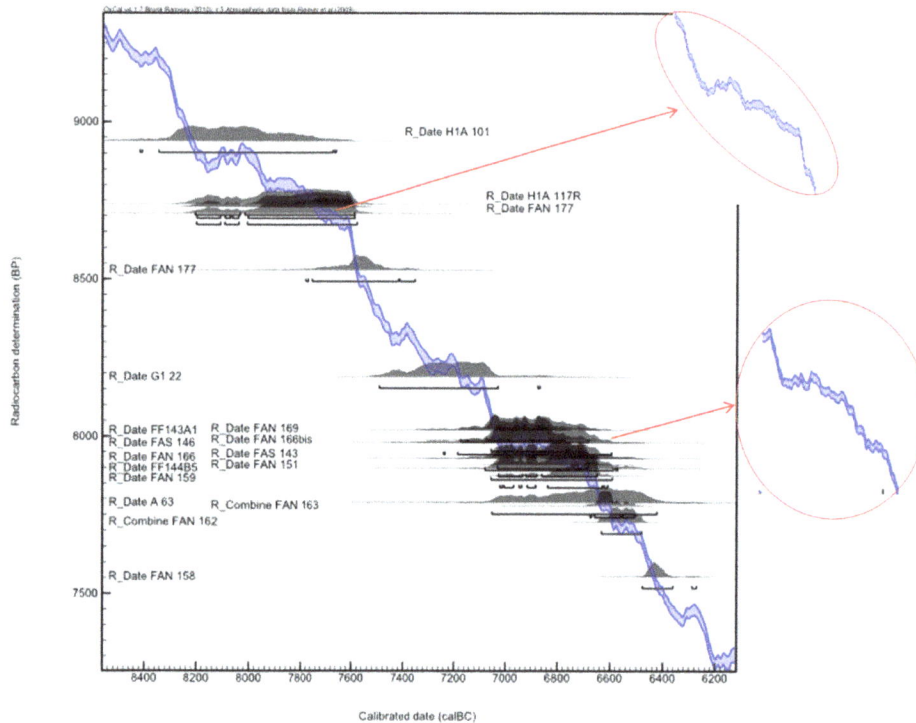

Fig. 9.1: Projection of the Upper Mesolithic, Final Mesolithic and Initial Neolithic dates from Franchthi on the IntCal09 calibration curve (Reimer et al. 2009). After Perlès et al. 2013.

… Despite a Transformed Coastal Environment

High-resolution cores from the northern Aegean show that the Early Holocene corresponds to a period of marked increase in precipitation and temperature (Peyron *et al.* 2011; Roberts *et al.* 2011; Schmiedl *et al.* 2010). Despite these climatic changes, neither the vegetation nor the fauna around Franchthi shows any difference compared with the Dryas III record. On the other hand, the end of the Pleistocene and the Early Holocene witnessed rapid sea-level rise (Lambeck 1996: fig. 5b; Siddall *et al.* 2003), which entailed important transformations to the immediate landscape around the site.

Van Andel and Lianos submarine profiling (van Andel & Lianos 1983) identified two submerged shorelines that should correspond to Mesolithic occupations, at – 38 and – 29 m below present-day sea level[3]. According to Lambeck's curve for the Argolid (1976: fig. 5b), the first would date approximately to 9,100 uncal BP, the end of the Lower Mesolithic (ca. 8,600 to 8,350 cal BC). The second would date around 8,000 uncal BP, corresponding to the Final Mesolithic (ca. 7,050–6,750 cal BC).

By the end of the Lower Mesolithic, the extension of the coastal plain had drastically reduced when compared with the Final Palaeolithic (Phase 6) palaeoshoreline at – 53 m. The sea, now about 1.5 – 2 km from the cave, deeply encroached the northern part of the plain (Fig. 9.2). According to Shackleton and van Andel (1986: 137), this would have substantially modified the shore habitats of the embayment, with a low rocky shore to the north, bars and large marshes in the centre of the bay, and low scarps fronted by gravel beaches and rocky shoals to the south. The open marshes, with their shallow muddy bottom, would have offered a perfect habitat for *Cyclope* sp., for thick-shelled *Cerastoderma glaucum* and also *Mactra corallina* (*idem*: 140). *Cerithium vulgatum* would be expected in the same environment. Other bivalves could have been present on the sandy beaches bordering the marshes, while limpets, trochids and dove shells could have been be found on the rocky shores. Gathering shellfish would have been less time-consuming, and gathering Cyclopes even easier.

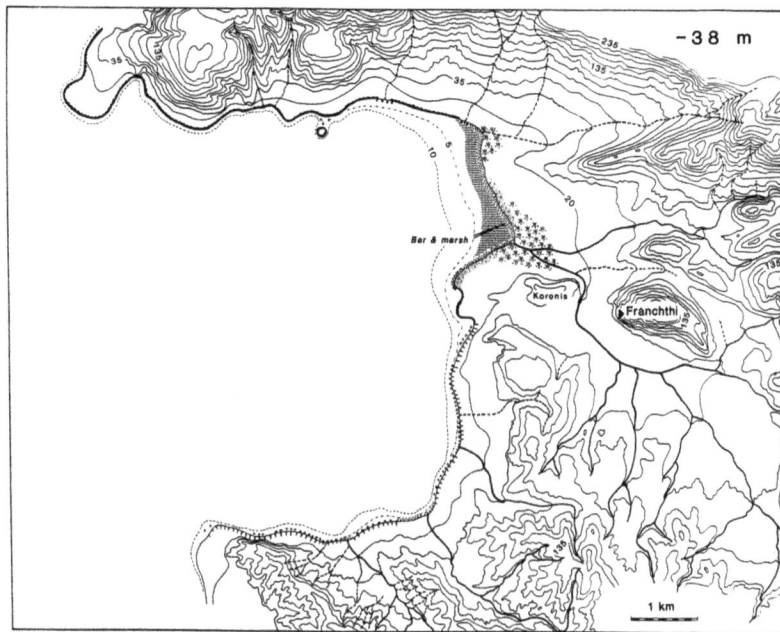

Fig. 9.2: Shores of the Franchthi embayment at ca. 8,300 cal BC (after van Andel 1987, dates corrected after Lambeck 1996). Elevation contours in metres a.s.l. at that time.

With the slowing rate of sea rise, the transformation of the coast between the beginning and the end of the Mesolithic, around 7,000 cal BC, appears to have been less pronounced (Fig. 9.3). The major change may have been a reduction of the marshes and the penetration of the sea deeper into the valley of the 'Franchthi river'. If this reconstruction is correct, the availability of *Cyclope* sp. and *Cerastoderma glaucum* would have been reduced, while the other potential resources, whether for food or ornaments, would have been unaffected by the environmental changes.

Once again, varied coastal environments can be reconstructed within one to two hours walk from the cave, with a wide range of edible and ornamental species available. Once again, in practice, the shellfish assemblages (Shackleton J. 1988) and the ornament assemblages reflect strong selection preferences. *Patella* sp., *Phorcus* (= *Monodonta* = *Osilinus*) *turbinatus*, *Gibbula divaricata* and *Gibbula rarilineata* all become conspicuously rare. Together with rare *Hexaplex (= Murex) trunculus* and *Cerastoderma glaucum*, *Cerithium vulgatum* now heavily dominates in the shellfish assemblages throughout the Mesolithic (Chap. 13).

As mentioned before, *Cyclope neritea* and *Cyclope pellucida* predominate in the ornament assemblages, associated with *Columbella rustica.* It would obviously be tempting to correlate the massive increase of Cyclopes in the Lower Mesolithic with the putative presence of extensive marshes (Fig. 9.2). However, their representation does not gradually decrease during the Mesolithic, as would be expected to result from the gradual rise of the sea level and associated reduction of marshy areas. In fact, the striking result of our analyses is that the marked transformations of the landscape from the end of the Palaeolithic to the end of the Mesolithic appear to have had little impact on the design and production of ornaments.

Fig. 9.3: Shores of the Franchthi embayment at ca. 7,000 cal BC (after van Andel 1987, dates corrected after Lambeck 1996). Elevation contours in metres a.s.l. at that time.

NOTES

1   The parentheses are part of the original quotation.
2   Calibration at one standard deviation. The uncalibrated BP dates tightly cluster between 9,300 and 9,100 BP, but have, unfortunately, large standard-deviations (see Jacobsen & Farrand 1987, plate 71).
3   See Chap. 2 for a discussion of the procedures and of Lambeck's corrections to global sea level rise curves.

CHAPTER TEN

A Massively Predominant Species: Cyclope neritea

The genus *Cyclope*[1], which was already predominant in Palaeolithic assemblages, no longer requires to be presented. Numbering more than 10.000 specimens in our main references trenches, it is even more predominant in Mesolithic ornament assemblages[2]. To this already impressive figure, we should add the hundreds of Cyclopes excavated in trenches G, G1, H and H2A, not included in the present study. The large quantity of Cyclopes is precisely what led J. Shackleton to define her "marine molluscan Zone II", roughly equivalent to the Mesolithic, as the "*Cyclope* (*neritea*) zone" (Shackleton J. 1988). Their abundance and the high proportion of perforated specimens leaves no doubt about the anthropic origin of the deposition. It will thus be interesting to see whether the change in the scale of exploitation, compared with the Palaeolithic, was paralleled by changes in the modalities of exploitation.

Given the number of Cyclopes (Table 10.1) we did not attempt to document in detail every specimen from our main trenches. Trench H1B was chosen as the reference trench[3], with all shells scanned, described, and measured. Most statistics will thus be based on H1B for the Lower and Upper Mesolithic (FGP Phases 7 and 8). As a control for spatial variations, a subsample of 1000 Lower Mesolithic and 600 Upper Mesolithic Cyclopes from other trenches were also recorded in detail, and will be analysed when dealing with smaller subsets, such as the perforated adults[4]. The Final Mesolithic (Phase 9), on the other hand, is only represented in undisturbed contexts in FAN and FAS: these trenches serve as references for this period. Unfortunately, the 'General Franchthi Phasing' was not definitive at the time of the study. Consequently, some units from FAS, now attributed to this phase, have not been studied in detail and the Final Mesolithic sample remains small.

Trench	H1A	H1B	FAS	FAN (partial counts)	Total
Phase 7 (LM)	1077	2125	3222	827	7251
Inter 7/8	33	168	71		272
Phase 8 (UM)	258	297	788	1002	2345
Phase 9 (FM)			175	91	266
Total	1368	2590	4256	1920	10134

Table 10.1: Recorded Mesolithic Cyclope neritea *and* C. pellucida *from the four main trenches.*

The preservation of Mesolithic shells is better than in the Palaeolithic, and there is no reason to suspect any bias due to taphonomic factors. Chemical attack ('altered' specimens) occurred less frequently and was also less invasive than in older deposits (Plates 10.1 – 10.22). This is particularly clear in the markedly anthropic deposits of the Lower and Upper Mesolithic, where sediments are rich in ash and land snails. The rate of altered specimens rises in the Final Mesolithic, but remains much lower than in the Palaeolithic. These variations, however, do not seem to follow closely the changes in pH of the sediments, as recorded by Farrand (2000: fig. 5.2). Conversely, many shells are broken into small fragments, thus reducing the number of diagnostic pieces for age classes and perforation.

Phase	Altered	Non altered	Undetermined	N
Phase 7 (H1B)	7.1	92.8	0.1	1932
Mixed 7/8 (H1B)	6	94	0	167
Phase 8 (H1B)	4.2	94.6	1.1	260
Phase 9 (FAN and FAS)	16.4	72	11.5	61

Table 10.2: State of preservation of Cyclope *sp. per phase, as percentages.*

Variations in Dimensions and Species Represented

We found no indication in the Palaeolithic phases at Franchthi that prehistoric hunter-gatherers tried to select especially large Cyclopes for their ornaments. Consequently, we attributed the progressive increase in dimensions throughout the Upper Palaeolithic to an environmental factor, coupled with a higher proportion of the larger *Cyclope neritea* and a decrease in the abundance of the smaller *Cyclope pellucida*.

Were the Mesolithic inhabitants of Franchthi equally non-selective when they collected Cyclopes? Do we observe a continuing increase in shell size in concert with the warming temperatures? Finally, did the large quantities of Cyclopes collected induce an over-exploitation of the molluscs and a consequent decrease in size, as is sometimes reported with food species (Álvarez-Fernández *et al.* 2011; Hunt *et al.* 2011)?

The unimodal, fairly Gaussian structure of the distributions by size (Figs. 10.1 – 10.4) corresponds to natural populations (Appendix 3.1) and indicates that no selection took place during shell collection. Taken as a whole, the Lower Mesolithic samples compare well, in terms of distribution and mean, to the younger Upper Palaeolithic assemblages (Phase 6). The mean maximum diameter of adult Mesolithic Cyclopes is 0.97 cm in H1B (s.d. = 0.09) and 0.95 (s.d.= 0.09) in the FAS and FAN subsamples. Their very slight difference, which is not statistically significant[5], may be due to the different procedures used to measure the shells (direct measurement for the FAS and FAN samples versus measurement on the 1 to 1 scans for H1B). Both figures are very close to the mean diameter in Phase 6 (0.97 cm, s.d. = 0.12), but about 2 mm smaller than our modern reference collections (Appendix 3.1). This could be due to the persistent presence of *C. pellucida* in the Mesolithic collections, but the Gaussian structure of the assemblages rather suggests a single population of *C. neritea*, smaller than modern ones. We shall henceforth consider them as *C. neritea* rather than the anonymous '*Cyclope* sp.', although the probable presence of a small number of *C. pellucida* is acknowledged.

There is no evidence that the snail population suffered from over-exploitation. In fact, more detailed analyses indicate a trend towards a progressive increase in dimensions from the base to the top of the Lower Mesolithic sequence. This trend, which is perceptible in both H1B and FA (Fig. 10.2), appears to be continuous and is probably related to progressively more favourable environmental conditions. Contrary to other marine gastropods (e.g. Álvarez-Fernández *et al.* 2011; Teske *et al.* 2007), our Cyclopes clearly seem to have preferred the warmer and moister conditions of the Alleröd and the Holocene than the cooler conditions of the early Upper Palaeolithic.

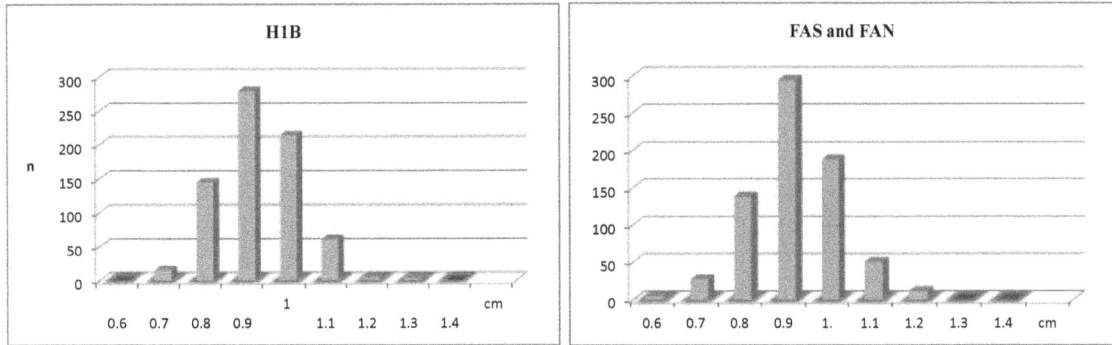

Fig. 10.1: Distribution of maximum diameter of Cyclope neritea *in Phase 7.*

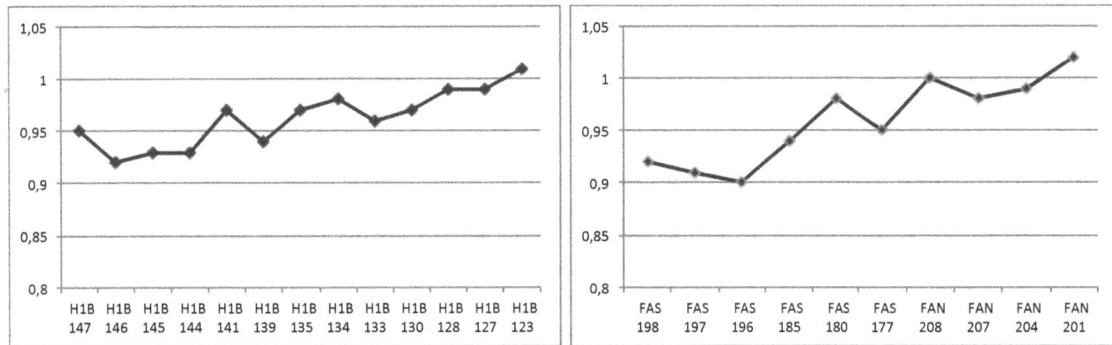

Fig. 10.2: Mean maximum diameter of Cyclope neritea *in selected Lower Mesolithic units of H1B, FAS and FAN in stratigraphic order. A minimum of 30 individuals in each unit was set for H1B and FAS. For the end of the period in FAN, the minimum number had to be set to 12.*

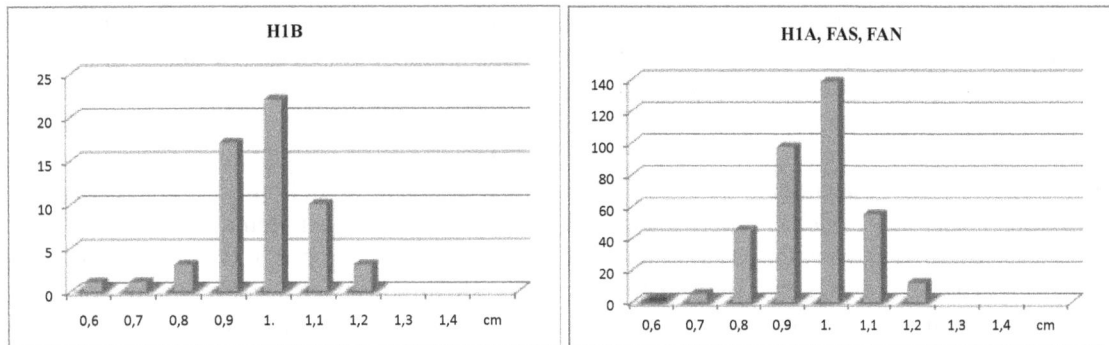

Fig. 10.3: Distribution of maximum diameters of Upper Mesolithic Cyclope neritea *in H1B and a subsample of H1A, FAS and FAN.*

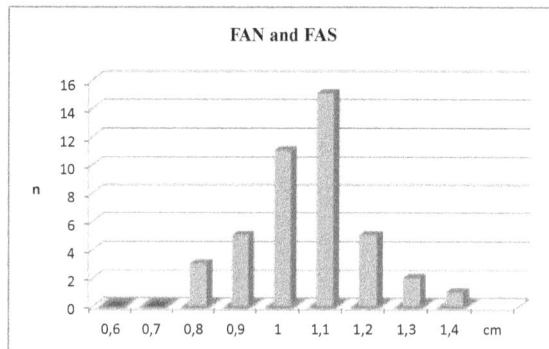

Fig. 10.4: Distribution of maximum diameters of Final Mesolithic C. neritea *in FAN and FAS (incomplete sample).*

The increase in size continues throughout the Mesolithic: from 0.97 cm in the Lower Mesolithic, the mean rises to 1.01 cm (s.d. = 0.1) in both H1B and the other trenches in the Upper Mesolithic (Phase 8), with a higher proportion of the 0.9 – 0.99 cm class in H1B (Fig. 10.3). The present-day value of 1.1 cm is reached in the smaller sample measured for the Final Mesolithic (Fig. 10.4). However, a deliberate selection of the larger specimens cannot be ruled out for this period: the relatively large Cyclopes are associated with perforated *Columbella rustica* that also present unusually large sizes, at a time (ca. 7,000 cal BC), when no particular climatic factor can be invoked (Chap. 11).

A Blind Collection of Adults and Juveniles

We argued for the Palaeolithic that collecting on beaches would have been extremely time consuming given the very low proportion of intact specimens in thanatocoenoses, at least under the present conditions of formation. The presence of discarded juveniles supported the hypothesis of a 'blind' collection of live specimens in muddy waters, where adults and juveniles cannot be distinguished. Both arguments hold true for the larger Mesolithic assemblages: it would have been very difficult to collect thousands of sufficiently well preserved specimens on beaches, juveniles are still present and, as stated above, the distribution of sizes corresponds to that of a natural live population (Appendix 3.1).

Despite a fairly high number of broken shells for which the age class could not be determined (Table 10.3), the ratio of juveniles to adults for aged specimens is remarkably stable throughout the Mesolithic (9-15%). It compares well to the ratios obtained in several of our own modern collections (Appendix 3.1) and suggests that *Cyclope neritea* were again gathered live, in bulk, and only sorted once back in the cave. Even for much more intensive collections than during the Palaeolithic, there was no need to use special devices to collect the snails: two or three people—including children—can collect two or three hundred individuals in an hour, especially at sunset (Appendix 3.1). Since *Cyclope neritea* and *Cerithium vulgatum*, the most abundant shellfish in the Mesolithic, can live in the same environments of quiet waters and lagoons, it is possible that both species were collected together. However, *C. neritea* predominates over *C. vulgatum* in the Lower Mesolithic, while they are found in equal quantities in the Upper Mesolithic: collecting shells for ornaments was not a by-product of the collection of shellfish. Indeed, until the Final Mesolithic, the reverse might well be true (Perlès 2016a).

Phase	Adults	Juveniles	Undetermined	Total
Phase 7 (H1B)	1089 85.7%	181 14.25%	662	1932 100%
Phase 7 (FAS. FAN)	748 85.0%	132 15.0%	118	998 100%
Mixed 7 x 8 (H1B)	111 91%	11 9.0%	45	167 100%
Phase 8 (H1B)	187 86.5%	29 13.5%	44	260 100%
Phase 8 (FAS. FAN. H1A)	454 87%	68 13,00%	153	675 100%
Phase 9 (FAS. FAN)	43 89.5%	5 10.4%	13	61

Table 10.3: Proportion of adult and juvenile Cyclope neritea *in the Mesolithic assemblages.*

From Snail to Ornament

How the flesh was removed from the shells remains unknown. The frequent heat-treatment may be part of the answer: besides changing the colour of the shell, it would have dried out the tiny flesh of the mollusc. A significant proportion of *C. neritea* show evidence of having been exposed to heat and turned grey or black (Lange *et al.* 2008; Stiner *et al.* 2013: 384). This proportion exceeds 43% of the shells in the Lower Mesolithic of H1B (Table 10.4, grey and black heated specimens) and approaches 30% in the other trenches. The proportion diminishes to ca. 32% in the Upper Mesolithic of H1B and becomes negligible in the Final Mesolithic. Heating conditions were the same as in the Palaeolithic, i.e. a long exposure to heat in a reducing atmosphere with good protection against direct contact with flames and glowing embers (Lange *et al.* 2008). Hearths are plentiful in the Mesolithic occupations at Franchthi and there is no doubt that a number of shells were accidently heated. The variable density of hearths may account for the observed difference among trenches, with a higher proportion of heated Cyclopes in H1B than in the other trenches[6]. However, comparisons with the other categories of remains—mammal bones, fish bones, shellfish and especially land snails—indicate that the fragile shells of the *C. neritea* always show higher rates of heating than other remains (Perlès & Vanhaeren 2010). This led us to suggest that, besides the 'background noise' created by accidentally burnt specimens, *C. neritea* were intentionally heated to create a contrast between ivory-white and black beads, a practice already envisioned for the latest Upper Palaeolithic phases. Heat-treatment, as in the Palaeolithic, was performed in bulk with little or no sorting beforehand, and before the shells were perforated. Some of the juveniles are burnt, but in the large Lower Mesolithic assemblage, the proportion is lower than for adults: ca. 18% in H1B, ca. 21% in the other trenches (Table 10.4). This suggests that some juveniles had already been discarded[7].

Many of the unperforated adult Cyclopes were also heated. In the Lower Mesolithic, where the rate of heated specimens reaches a peak, the proportion of perforated and non-perforated heated specimens is remarkably similar (Table 10.5). By contrast, during the Upper and Final Mesolithic, perforated shells are more often heated than non-perforated shells, suggesting that heat-treated Cyclopes were more often selected for perforation.

Phase	Age class	Not heated	Heated (Grey)	Heated (Black)	Undetermined	Total
Phase 7 (H1B)	Adults	593 *56.3%*	189 *18,00%*	267 *25.4%*	40	1089 *99.7%*
	Juveniles	147 *82.1%*	18 *10.05%*	14 *7.8%*	2	181 *99.9%*
Phase 7 (FAS. FAN)	Adults	529 *71.4%*		212 *28.6%*	7	748 *100%*
	Juveniles	104 *78.8%*		28 *21.2%*		132 *100%*
Mixed 7/8 (H1B)	Adults	60 *56.6%*	25 *23.6%*	21 *19.8%*	5	111 *100%*
	Juveniles	8	2	1		11
Phase 8 (H1B)	Adults	124 *67.9%*	31 *16.5%*	29 *15.5%*	3	187
	Juveniles	22	3	1	3	29
Phase 8 (FAS. FAN. H1A)	Adults	356 *83.9%*	24 *5.6%*	44 *10.37%*	30	454 *99.9%*
	Juveniles	59 *86.7%*	2 *2.9%*	7 *10.29%*	0 *0.00%*	68 *99.9%*
Phase 9 (FAS and FAN)	Adults	40	0	3	0	43
	Juveniles	5	0	0	0	5

Table 10. 4: Proportion of heat-treated C. neritea *among juvenile and adult specimens.*

Phase	Not heated				Heated			
	Unperforated	Perforated	Undetermined	**Total**	Unperforated	Perforated	Undetermined	**Total**
Phase 7 (H1B)	188 *32.1%*	398 *67.9%*	0 *0.00%*	586 *100%*	155 *33.5%*	296 *64,00%*	11 *2.4%*	462 *99.9%*
Phase 7 (FAS. FAN)	144 *27.2%*	385 *72.8%*	0 *0.00%*	529 *100%*	54 *24.6%*	165 *75.3%*	0 *0.00%*	219 *99.9%*
Phase 8 (H1B)	45 *75%*	15 *25%*	0 *0.00%*	60 *100%*	78 *61%*	46 *36.2%*	3 *2.36%*	127 *99.9%*
Phase 8 (FAS. FAN. H1A)	101 *85.6%*	10 *8.4%*	7 *5.9%*	118 *99,9%*	248 *81%*	56 *18.3%*	2 *0.6%*	306 *99.9%*

Table 10.5: Rates of unperforated and perforated specimens among adult non-heated and heated C. neritea. *Specimens with uncertain traces of heating have been excluded.*

To understand why so many heated specimens remain unperforated we need to consider unperforated adult Cyclopes as a whole. Table 10.6 summarises the data: in all periods and trenches, a quarter to a third of the Cyclopes were cached, discarded or lost with no perforation. This proportion may seem high, but it is comparable to the pattern observed in the Palaeolithic levels and at several other Palaeolithic sites (*supra*, Chap. 3). Tests on the shells mean dimensions show that they were not discarded because they were either too small or too large[8]. Selection by colour cannot be ruled out, but variation in the colour of *Cyclope neritea* is much less pronounced than for *Columbella rustica,* for instance. We can instead envision the creation of stocks of raw materials or of exchangeable goods, lost in the loose sediment that accumulated during Mesolithic occupations. Since Cyclopes were abundant and easily available, some loss would not have been of great concern. Alternatively, we can consider the possibility that unperforated shells were glued to garments or artifacts. However, it should be recalled that the pattern we observe only concerns the Cyclopes that were lost or discarded in the cave. Much larger quantities may have been originally perforated and taken away when the groups left the cave, as we shall discuss later. The real proportion of unperforated shells may thus have been substantially lower.

Phase	Unperforated	Perforated	Undetermined	Total
Phase 7 (H1B)	352 *32.2%*	717 *65.8%*	20 *1.8%*	1089 *99.1%*
Phase 7 (FAS. FAN)	198 *26.5%*	550 *73.5%*	0 *0%*	748 *100%*
Phase 8 (H1B)	60 *32.1%*	127 *67.9%*	0 *0%*	187 *100%*
Phase 8 (FAS. FAN. H1A)	114 *25%*	328 *72.2%*	12 *2.64%*	454 *99.8%*
Phase 9 (FAS and FAN)	16 *26.45%*	32 *52.5%*	13 *21.3%*	61 *100%*

Table 10.6: Perforated and unperforated adult C. neritea *per phase.*

Different types of perforation can be observed on the Mesolithic Cyclopes. Rare specimens were discarded or lost at the stage of the 'initial perforation', with a hole corresponding to the tip of a tool inserted through the natural aperture. 'Simple' perforations, slightly enlarged by exerting some pressure around the initial perforation, show unexplained difference in their proportion between H1B and the two FA trenches (Table 10.7), again exemplifying spatial variations. The most typical Mesolithic perforation, however, is the 'enlarged' perforation that invades the last whorl (Fig. 10.5). An enlarged perforation involves two steps: the initial perforation, made from the inside of the shell, is then enlarged by reinserting the tool from the outside. No special skill is required. Finally, 'half-shells', where the whole upper part of the shell has been removed (Fig. 10.7, FAS 197, H1B 146), only represent a small minority.

Phase	Initial	Simple	Enlarged	Half-shell	Total
Phase 7 **(H1B)**	13 *1.9%*	187 *27.1%*	472 *68.4%*	18 *2.6%*	690
Phase 7 **(FAS and FAN)**	24 *6.1%*	28 *7.1%*	329 *85.5%*	13 *3.3%*	394
Mixed 7 x 8 **(H1B)**	0	0	69 *93.24%*	5	74
Phase 8 **(H1B)**	1	39 *33.6%*	70 *60.3%*	6 *5.1%*	116
Phase 8 **(FAS. FAN. H1A)**	1 *0.3%*	99 *30.9%*	214 *66.8%*	6 *1.87%*	320
Phase 9 **(FAN. FAS)**	2	16	14	1	33

Table 10.7: Distribution of the types of perforation on C. neritea *by phase.*

Fig. 10.5: Typical enlarged perforations of the Mesolithic. CAD C.P.

Enlarged perforations appeared previously in the late Upper Palaeolithic levels, and became well represented in Phase 6. This denotes a technical, and probably also functional continuity from the Upper Palaeolithic to the Mesolithic. In both periods, the enlargement towards the back of the spire appears in part related to use: Cyclopes that bear no or limited use-wear traces (Fig. 10.6) tend, on the whole, to have smaller perforations than heavily used-ones (Figs. 10.6 - 10.9). This indicates that pressure was exerted through the perforation not only towards the lip, as for simple perforations, but also towards the back of the shell. This rules out simple threading and suspension in a necklace. Like *C. rustica* (*infra*, Chap. 11), which show similar use-wear patterns, *C. neritea* must have been embroidered onto garments by way of a double knot. This inference is supported by the very smooth and shiny worn surfaces, and by the absence of micro-chipping, as would be expected with loosely suspended beads.

A Mix of Shells with Very Different States of Use

The presence of use-wear on many specimens indicates that the perforated Cyclopes recovered during the excavation were not all recently manufactured beads, lost or rejected for one reason or another. Many were rejected only after they had been worn, sometimes for long periods. Significantly, unperforated, worn and unworn pieces are found in the same excavation units. This demonstrates that the collection of snails, the manufacturing of beads and the loss or rejection of worn Cyclopes do not constitute discrete, independent episodes of activity. On the contrary, the activities centred on these shells simultaneously involved unworked and freshly worked specimens, as well as beads already worn for a long time. Since we argued that most Cyclopes were embroidered rather than threaded, these activities would have involved the manufacturing of new embroidered garments, or the 'refreshing' of old ones with the replacement of old, worn-out beads, considered too fragile or already broken. At what stage of use was it deemed necessary to replace or reject a Cyclope bead is difficult to assess with certainty. My suspicion is that the main parameter was the thickness of the bridge between the lip and the perforation, which is reduced by use both on the dorsal and the ventral face (Fig. 10.9) and can then break very easily.

Many Cyclopes, indeed, have a broken lip and can no longer be threaded or sewn to a garment (Fig. 10.10). The exact proportion varies from phase to phase (Table 10.8), but is always high, as it also was during the Palaeolithic. Carelessness during manufacture may of course have occurred, but many broken Cyclopes show use-wear on what remains of the perforation. They may have fallen when the garments were manipulated, but they could also have been removed rather expediently from the garments on which they were sewn, to be replaced by freshly manufactured specimens.

However, here again the proportion of used and broken Cyclopes may appear higher than it was in reality: it can be assumed that many of the newly-manufactured beads left the site along with the bearers of the bracelets, necklaces, head dress, breastplates or coats that they adorned. The absence of grave goods associated with Lower Mesolithic burials at Franchthi, and with any other Mesolithic burial in Greece (Chapter 14), deprives us of any reliable reconstruction of the actual layout of the beads. But we can again gain some insight through the burials from the Ligurian caves (Taborin 2004) and from Vlasac in Serbia (Cristiani & Borić 2012). Some of these garments were probably not only embroidered with shells, but also coloured with ochre, as shown by the recovery of some ochred beads (Fig. 10.11). They also possibly displayed a mix of Cyclopes, dove shells and tusk shells, although Cyclopes would have been by far the most abundant component.

Phase	Perforated	Perforated. lip broken	Total
Phase 7 (H1B)	452 63%	265 37%	717
Mixed 7 x 8 (H1B)	55 78%	14 22%	69
Phase 8 (H1B)	96 75.6%	31 24.4%	127
Phase 9 (FAN. FAS)	22	10	32

Table 10.8: Proportion of intact perforated C. neritea *and specimens with broken lips.*

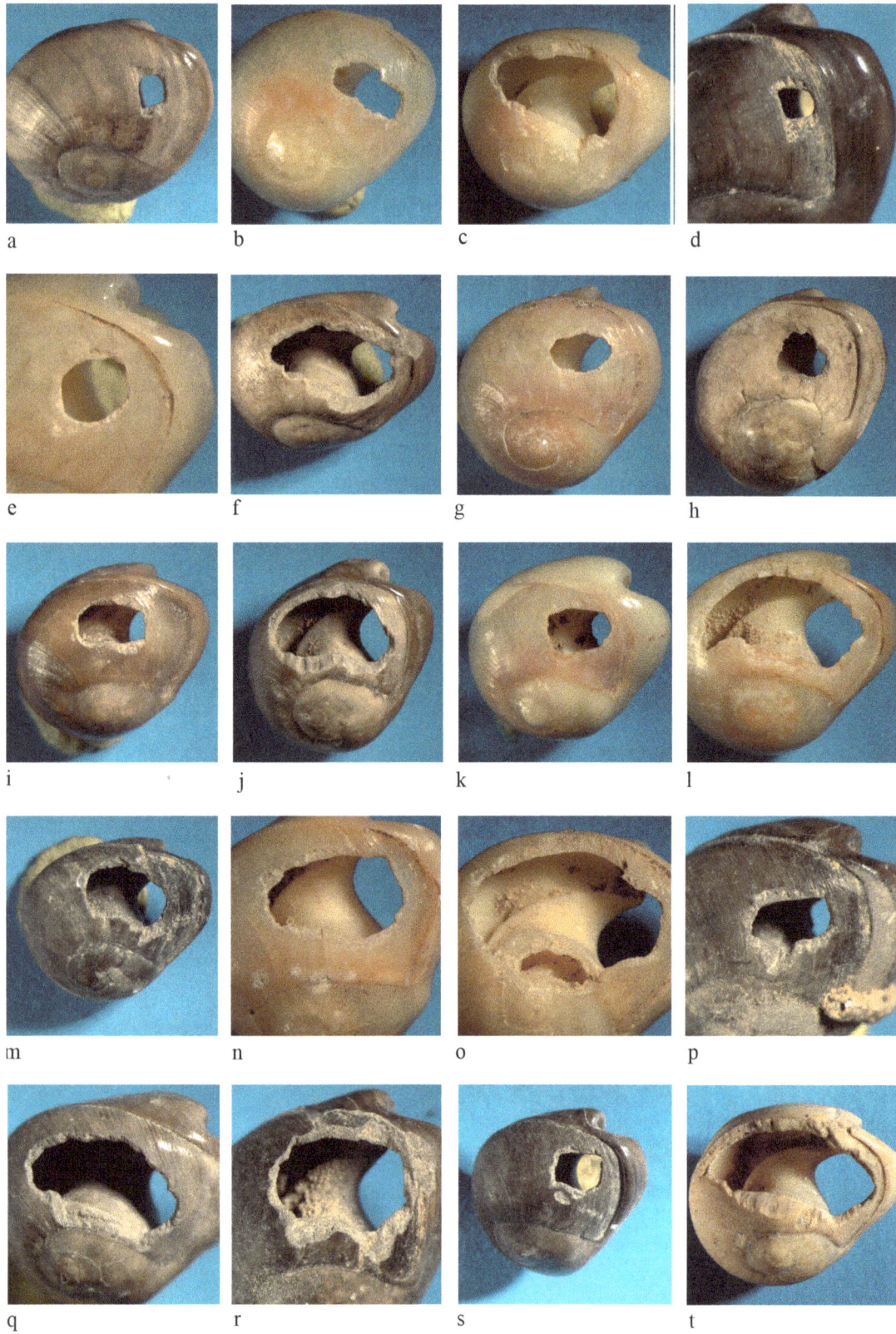

Fig 10.6: Perforated Cyclope neritea *with little or no use-wear. Photographs M. Vanhaeren. CAD C.P.*

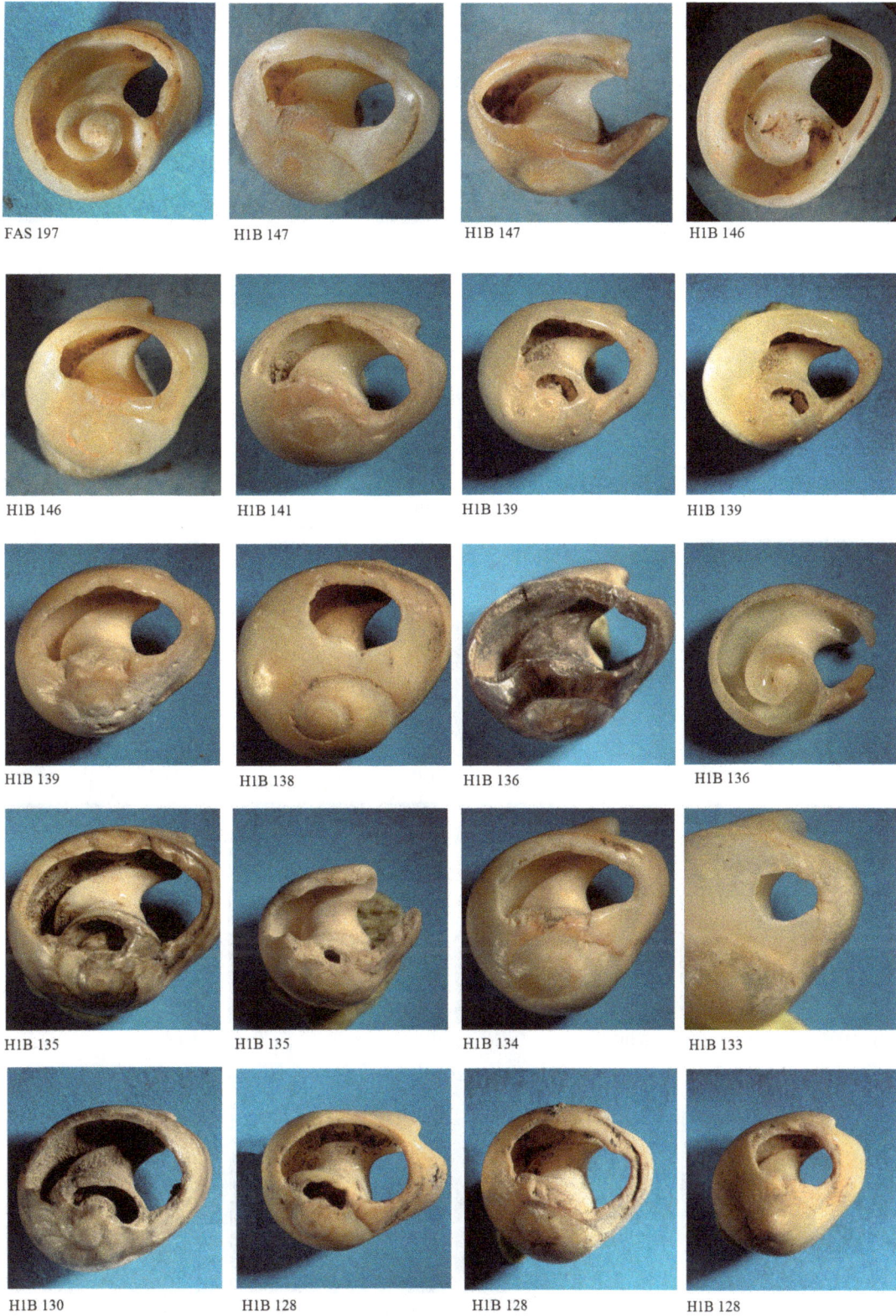

FAS 197	H1B 147	H1B 147	H1B 146
H1B 146	H1B 141	H1B 139	H1B 139
H1B 139	H1B 138	H1B 136	H1B 136
H1B 135	H1B 135	H1B 134	H1B 133
H1B 130	H1B 128	H1B 128	H1B 128

Fig. 10.7: Lower Mesolithic Cyclope neritea *with well-developed use wear. Photographs M. Vanhaeren. CAD C.P.*

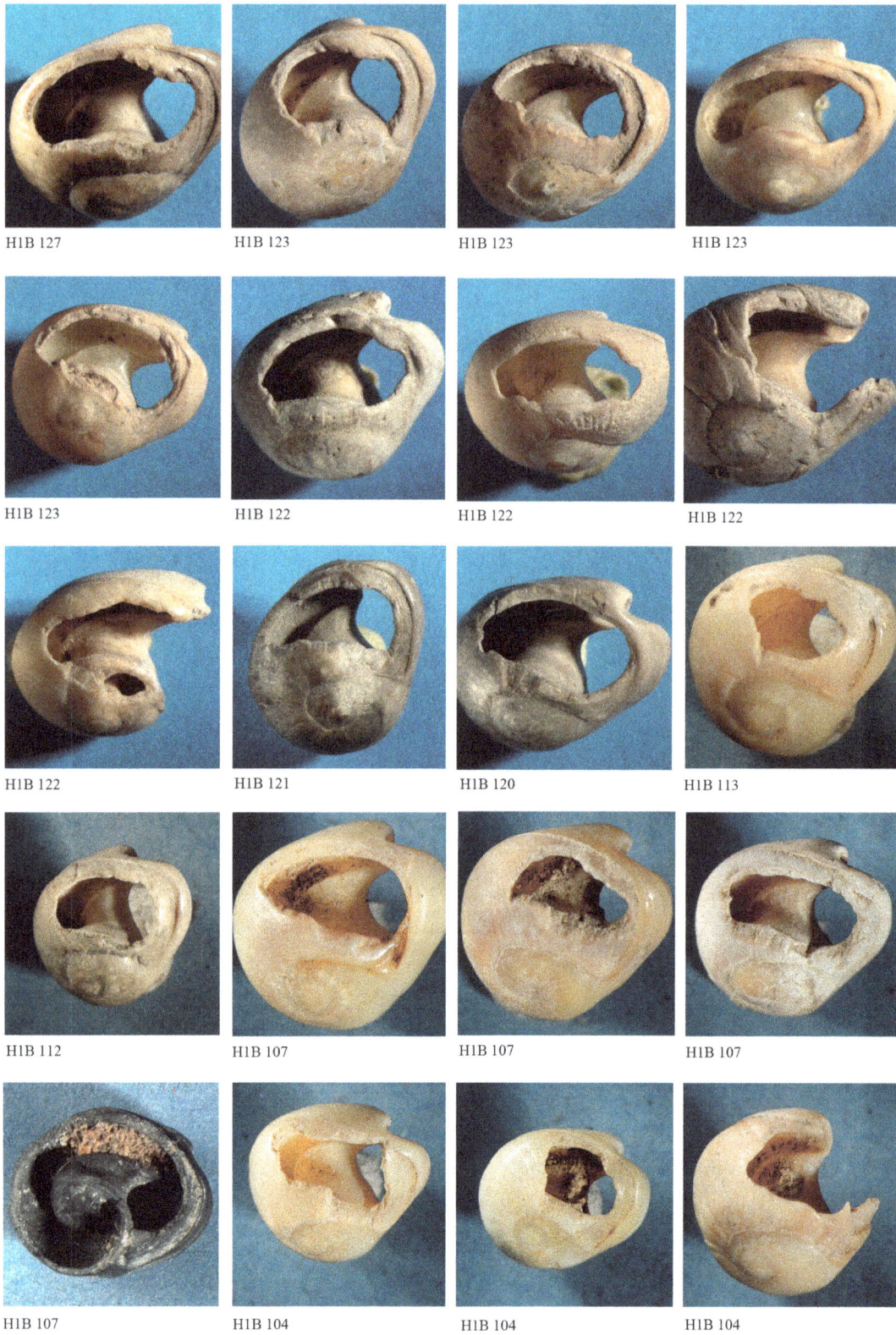

H1B 127   H1B 123   H1B 123   H1B 123

H1B 123   H1B 122   H1B 122   H1B 122

H1B 122   H1B 121   H1B 120   H1B 113

H1B 112   H1B 107   H1B 107   H1B 107

H1B 107   H1B 104   H1B 104   H1B 104

Fig. 10.8: Lower and Upper Mesolithic Cyclope neritea *with well-developed use-wear. Photographs M. Vanhaeren. CAD C.P.*

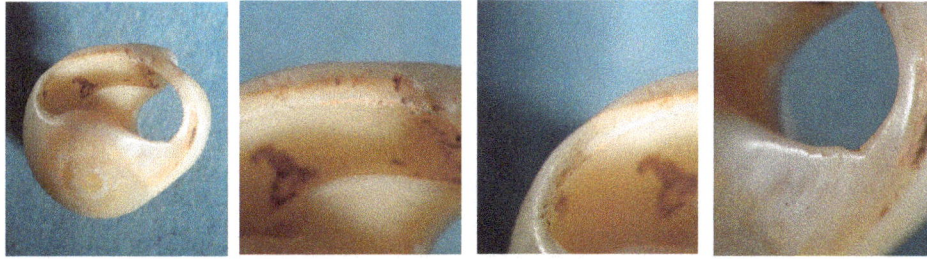

H1B 147

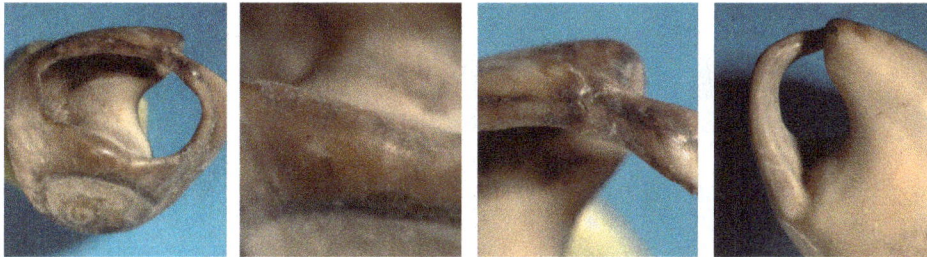

H1B 144

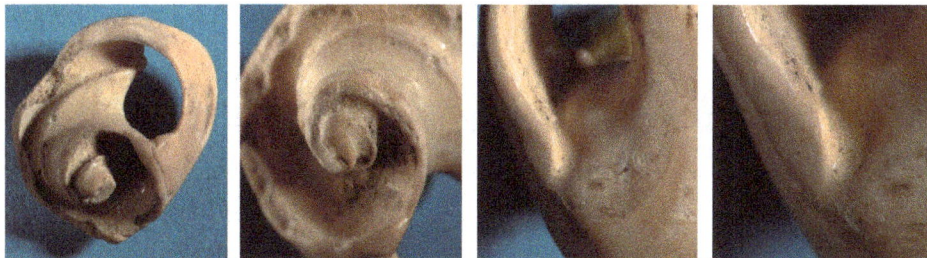

H1B 127

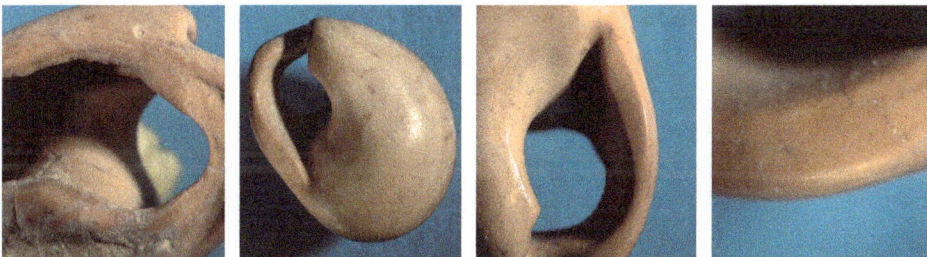

H1B 123

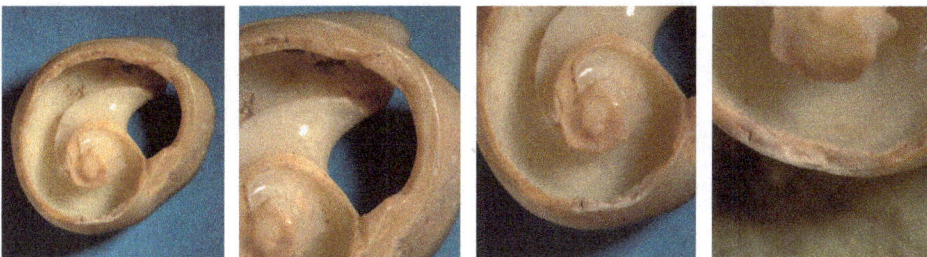

H1B 135

Fig. 10.9: Details of use-wear on C. neritea *showing deformations and furrows created by the thread. Photographs M. Vanhaeren. CAD CP.*

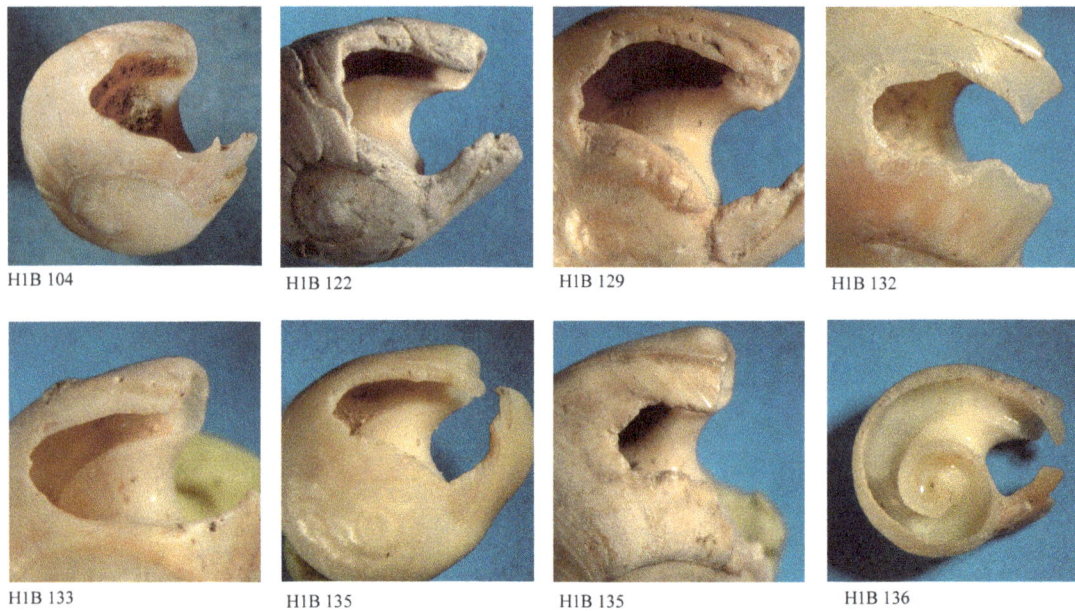

H1B 104

H1B 122

H1B 129

H1B 132

H1B 133

H1B 135

H1B 135

H1B 136

Fig. 10.10: Cyclope neritea *with a broken lip and well-developed use-wear.*

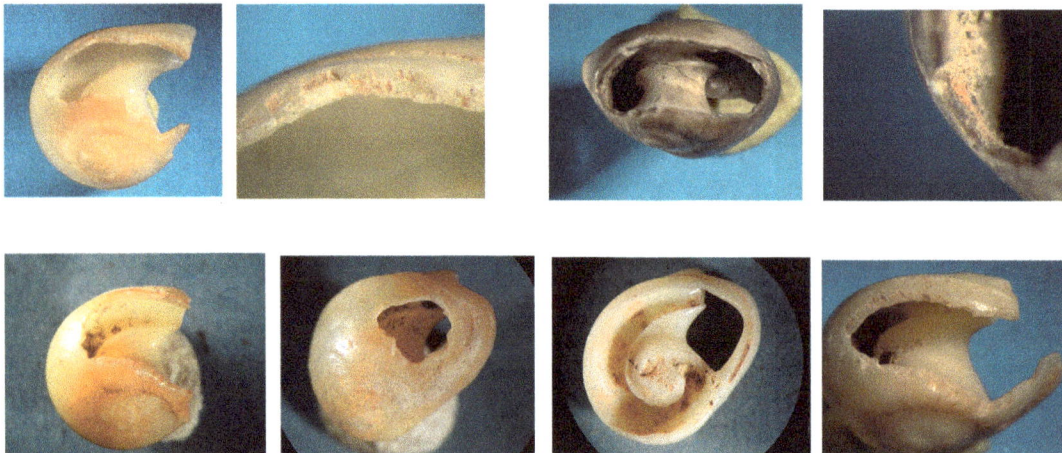

Fig. 10.11: Ochre-stained C. neritea *from Phase 7. Top row: H1B 144. Bottom row, from left to right: H1B 145, 146 (two specimens) and 134.*

NOTES

1 *Cyclope neritea, Cyclope pellucida* or *Cyclope* sp. will again be nicknamed 'Cyclopes', in the absence of a vernacular name.

2 This figure derives from the resorting of the shell and land snail bags (trench recovery and > 5 mm residues), as well as the identification of the < 5 mm residues fragments by A. Colonese. It thus slightly differs from Shackleton's counts (1988).

3 A few bags of shells from H1B were not located (H1B 124, 106 and 105). In this case, the figures for *C. neritea* were taken from J. Shackleton (1988) and are included in Table 10.1, but the assemblages are not included in the following analyses. H1B 116, a cleaning unit, is also excluded from the detailed analyses.

4 The Lower Mesolithic control subsample comprises units FAS 198-196, 185, 180, 177, FAN 208, 207 and 201. The Upper Mesolithic subsample comprises H1A 117 and 101, FAS 170, 168, 166, 158 and 157, FAN 189, 188, 179, 176, 175 and 166. For the Final Mesolithic, all units from FAN have been studied in detail except FAN 172. In FAS, only unit 149 was recorded in full detail.

5 Student's $t = 0.72, p = .47$. The difference is not significant at $p < .05$.

6 It is also possible that we were more conservative in defining shells as 'burnt' in the other trenches, which were recorded before H1B.

7 The difference is highly significant in H1B ($\chi^2 = 43.14$, df = 2, $p < 0.01$), but only slightly in the other trenches ($\chi^2 = 3.07$, df = 1, $p < 0.07$). It is also slightly significant for the Upper Mesolithic in H1B ($\chi^2 = 3.18$, df = 1, $p < 0.07$).

8 For instance, in the Lower Mesolithic of H1B, the mean diameter of perforated Cyclopes is 0.97 cm (n = 407, s.d. = 0.09) and the mean diameter of unperforated Cyclopes is 0.95 cm (n = 344, s.d. = 0.09). The difference is not statistically significant at $p < 0.05$ (Student's $t = -0.59, p = -0.27$).

PLATES

Plates 10.1 – 10.23: Mesolithic Cyclope neritea *and* C. pellucida *from trench H1B.*

H1B 150

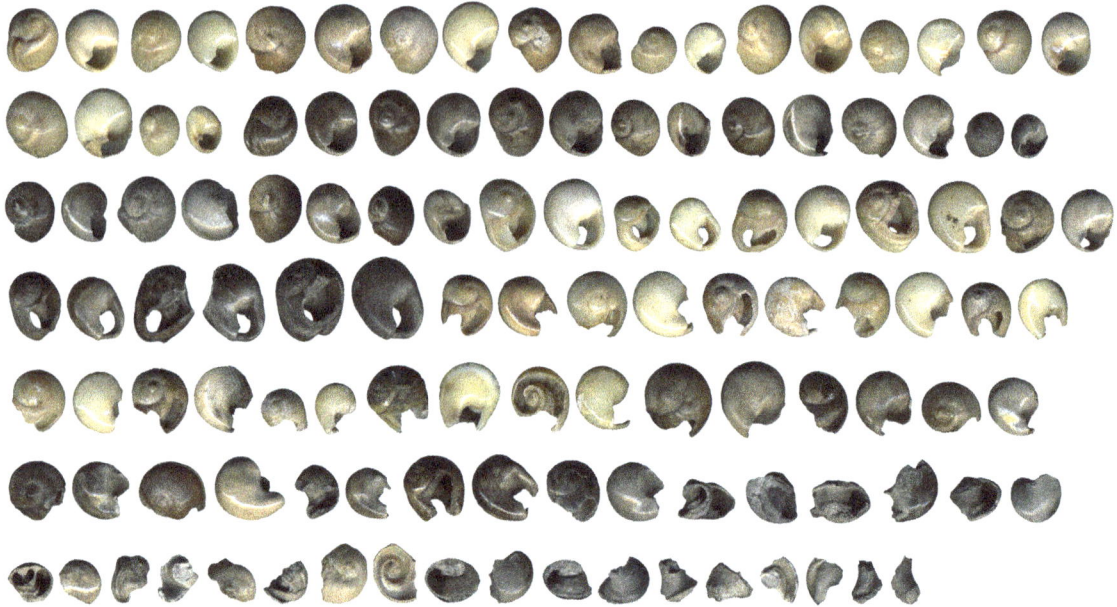

H1B 149

H1B 148

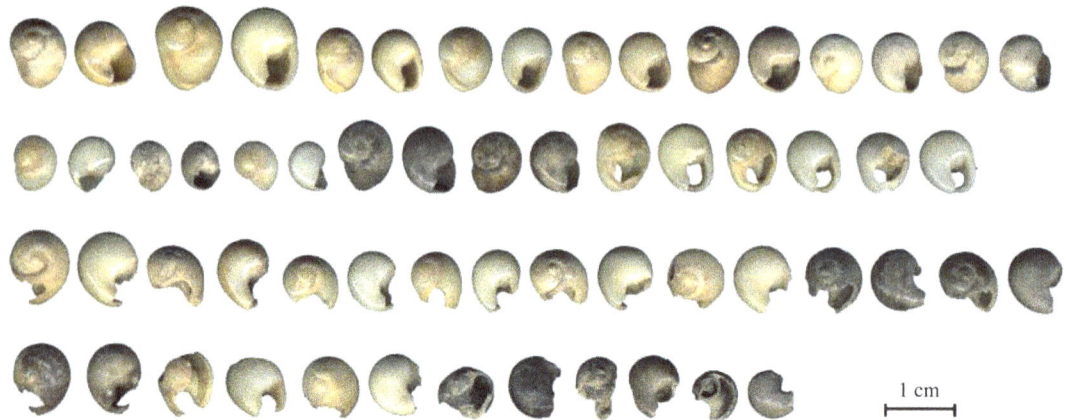

1 cm

H1B 147

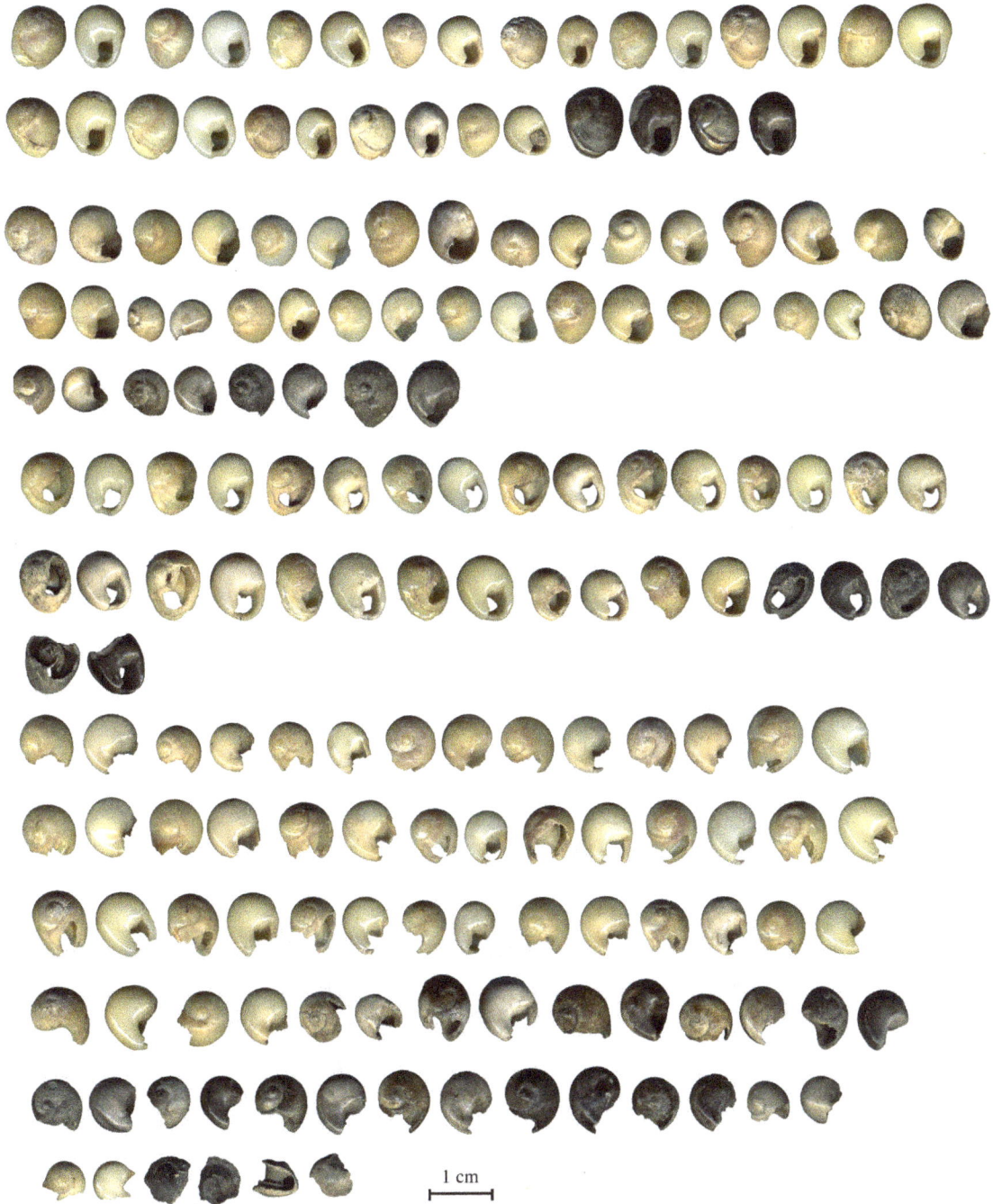

1 cm

H1B 146

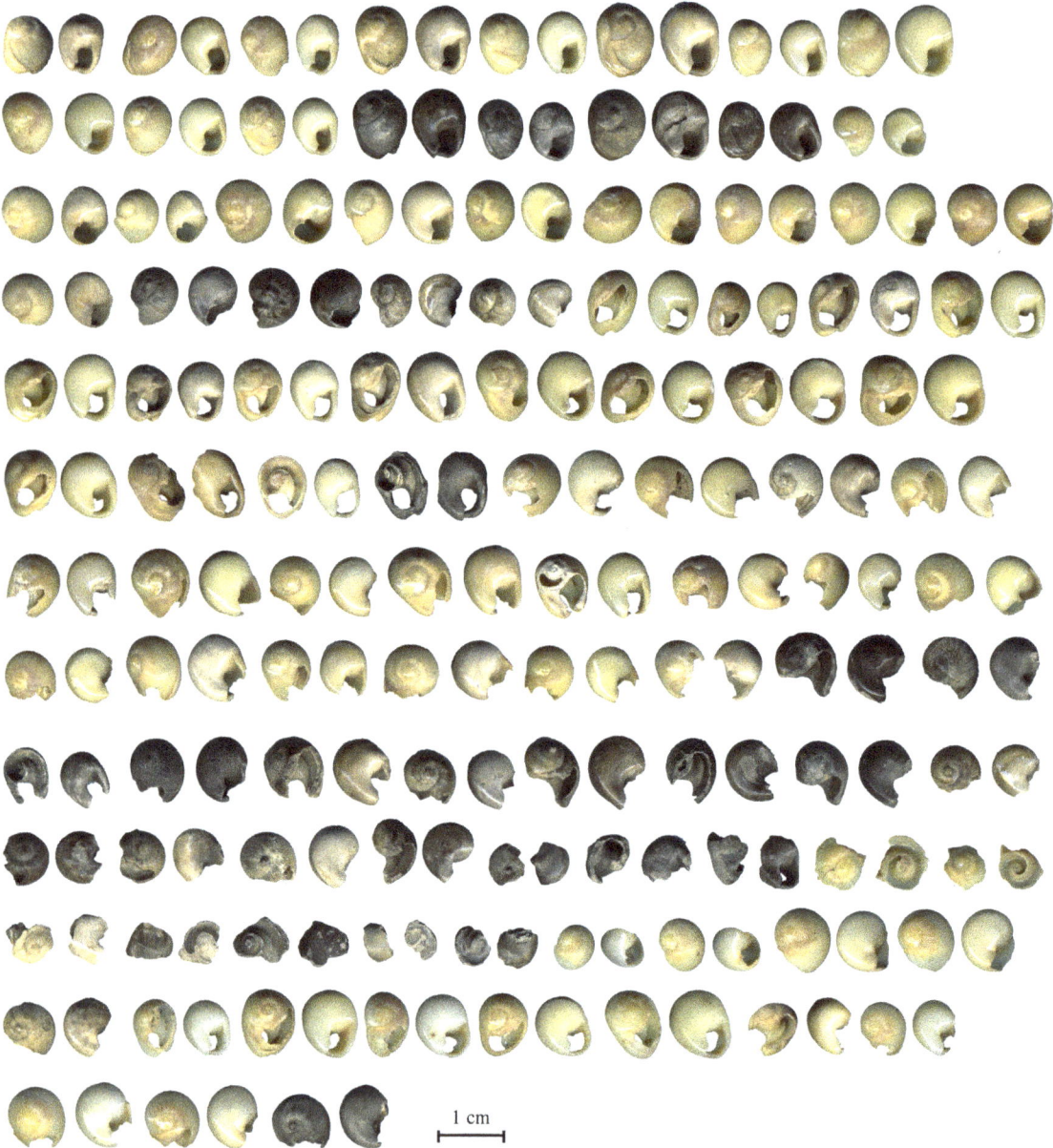

1 cm

H1B 145

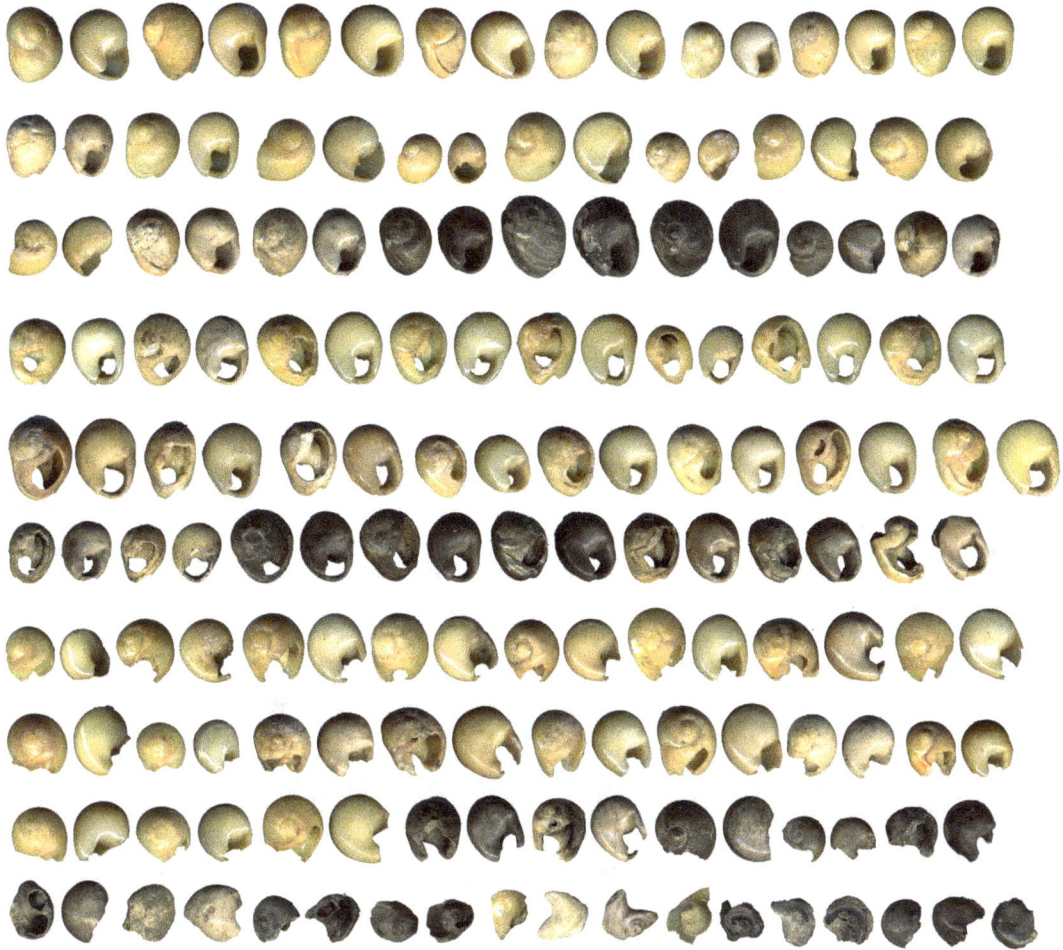

H1B 144

1 cm

H1B 144 (cont.)

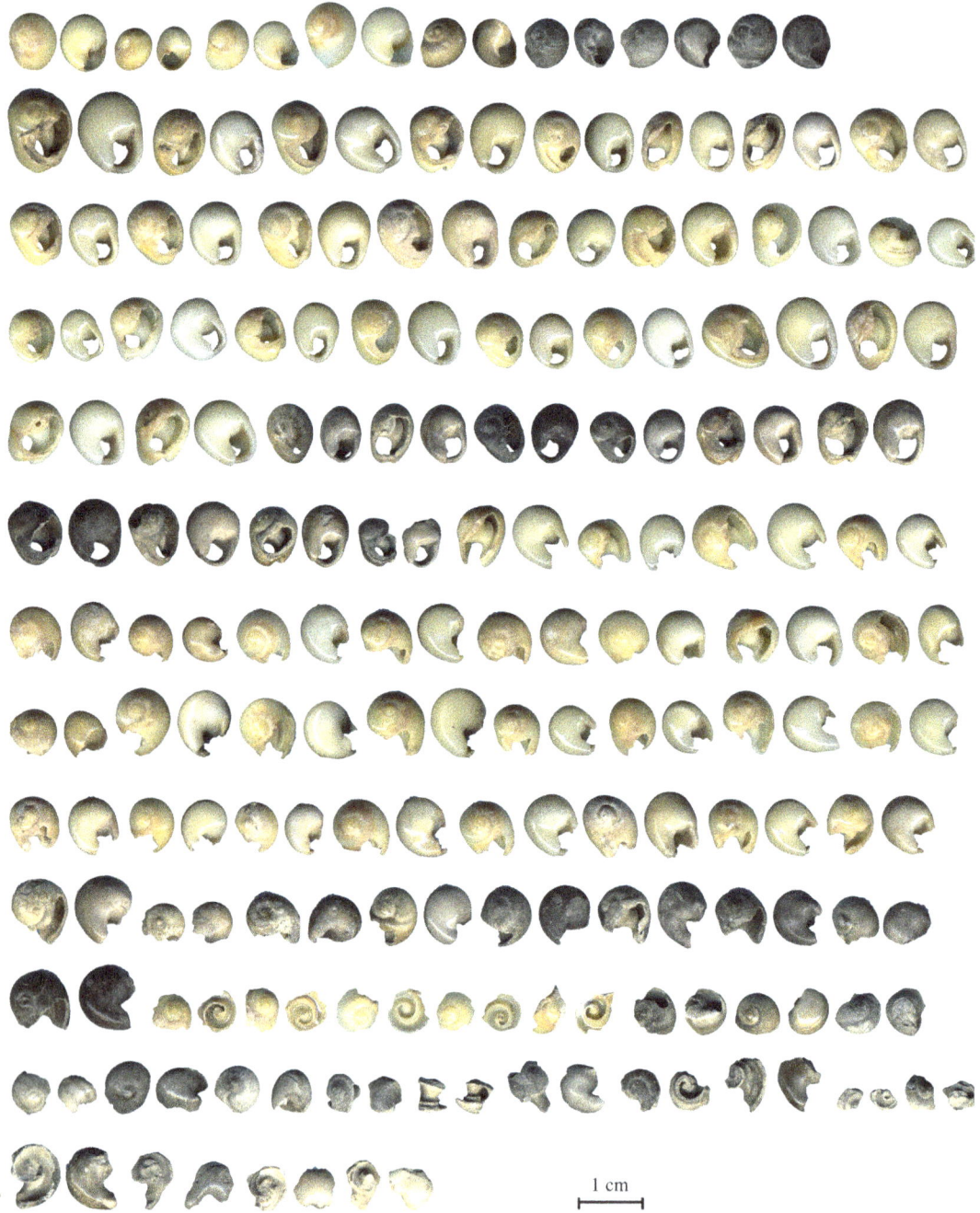

1 cm

H1B 143

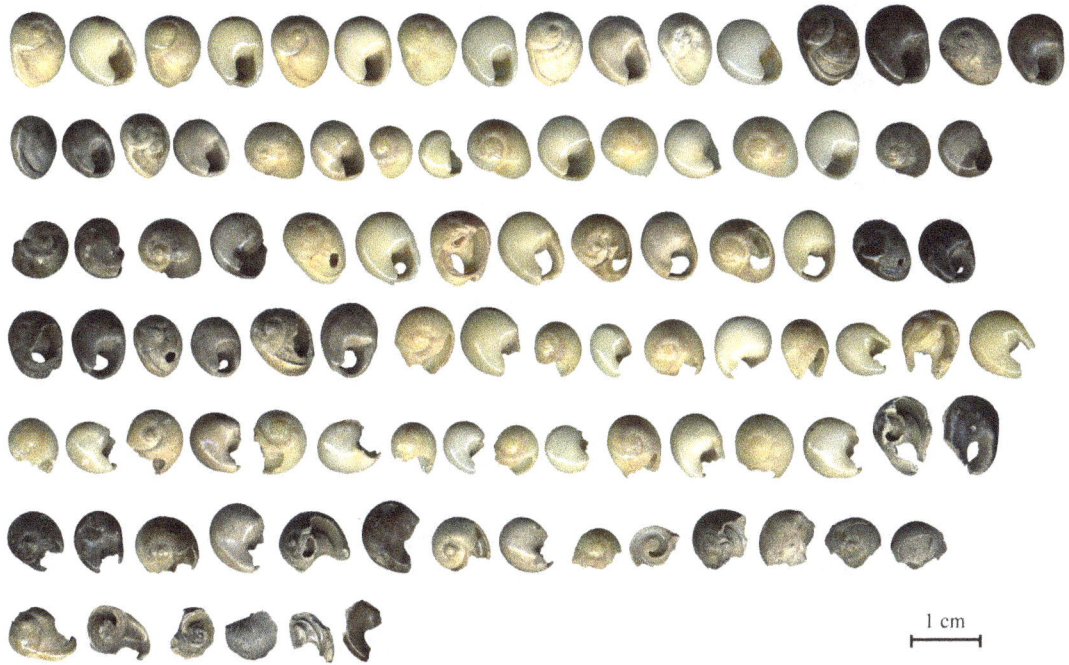

1 cm

H1B 142

H1B 141

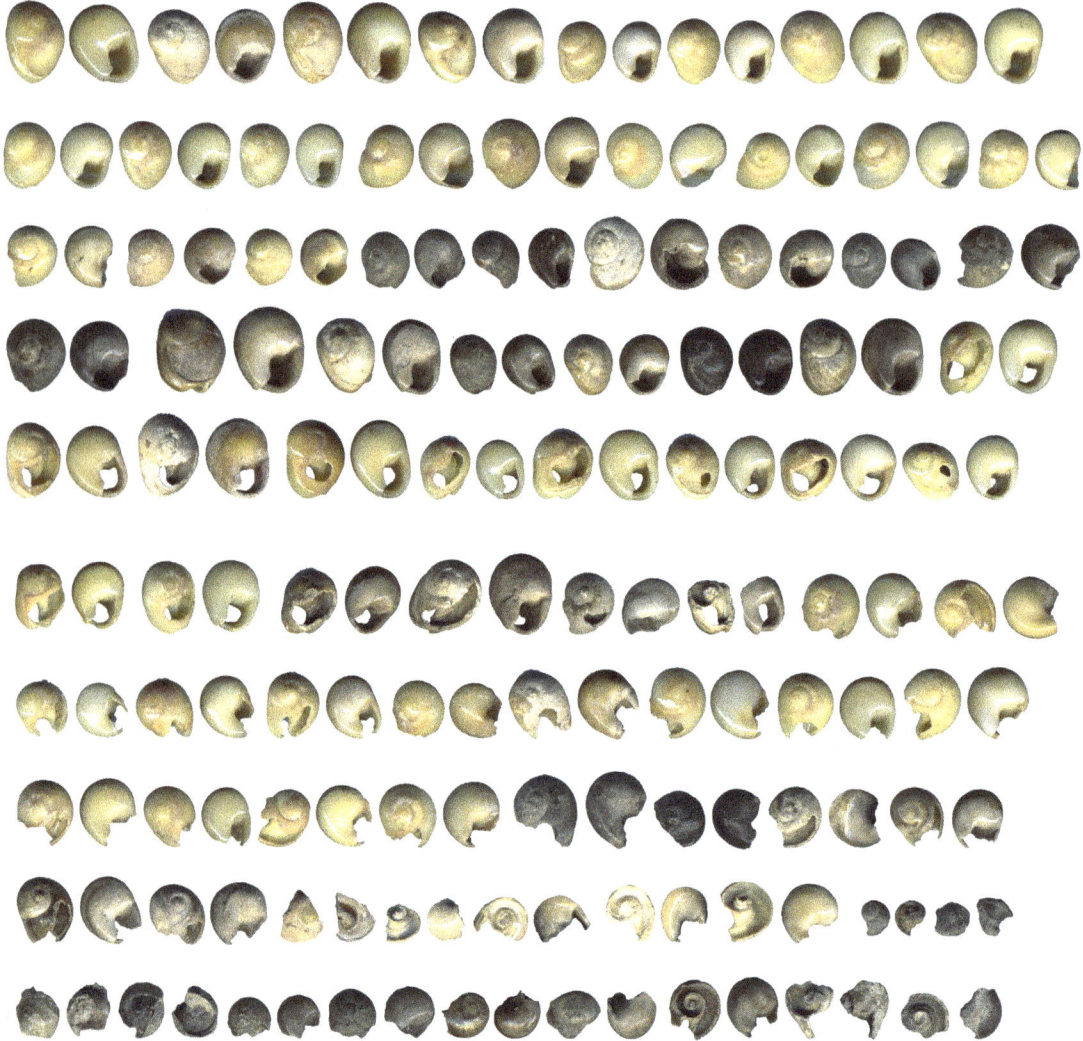

H1B 140

1 cm

H1B 139

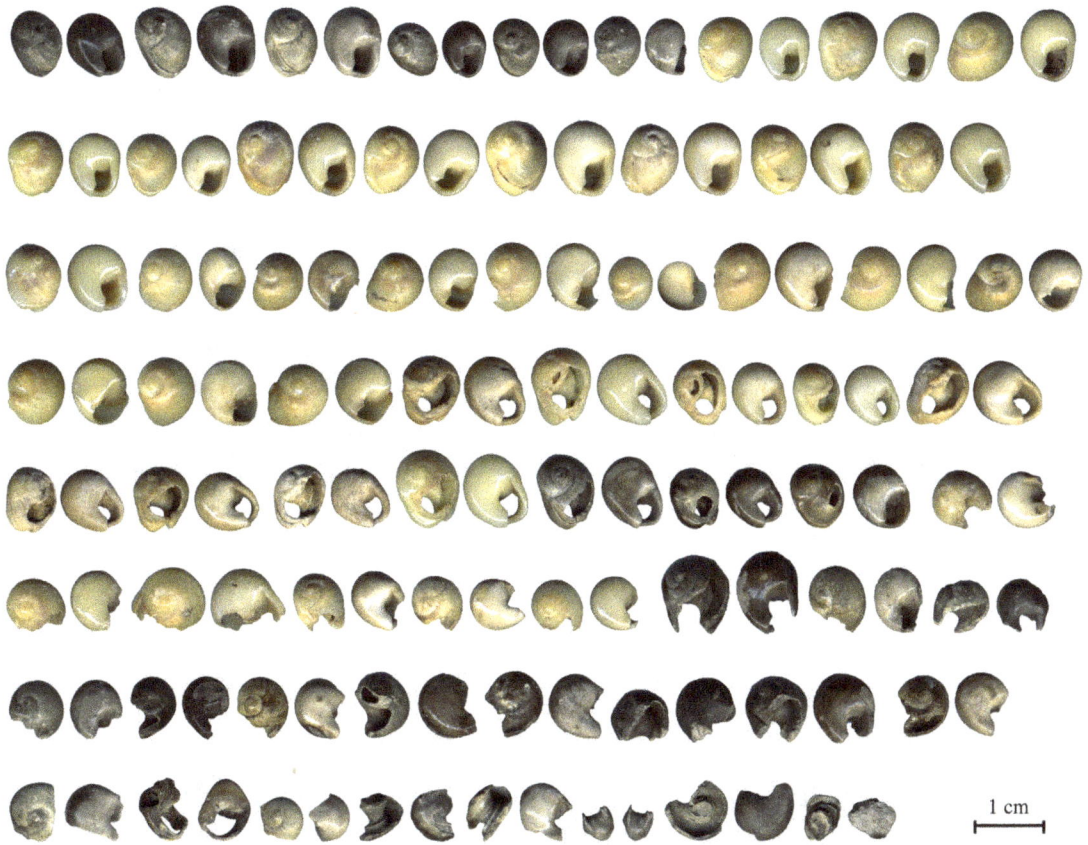

1 cm

H1B 138

H1B 137

H1B 136

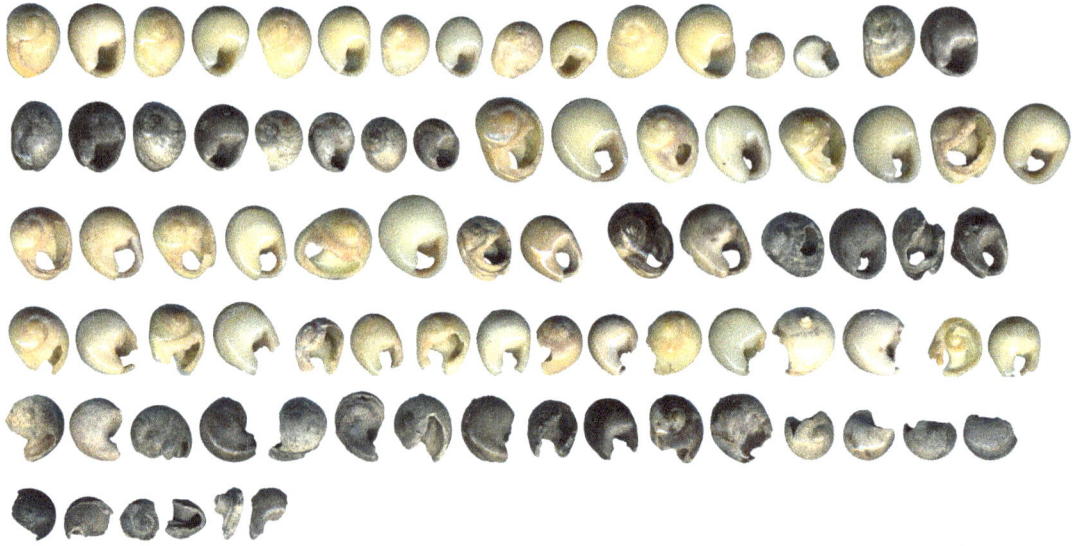

1 cm

H1B 135

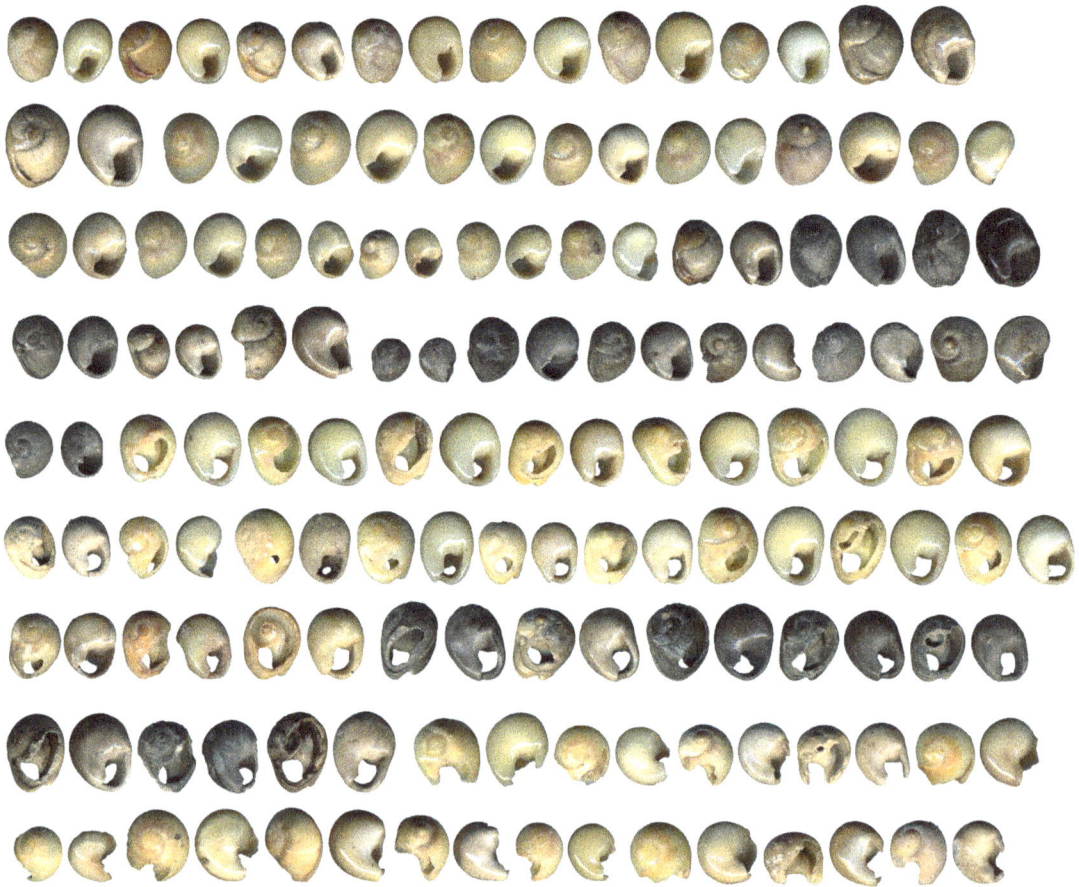

H1B 135 (cont.)

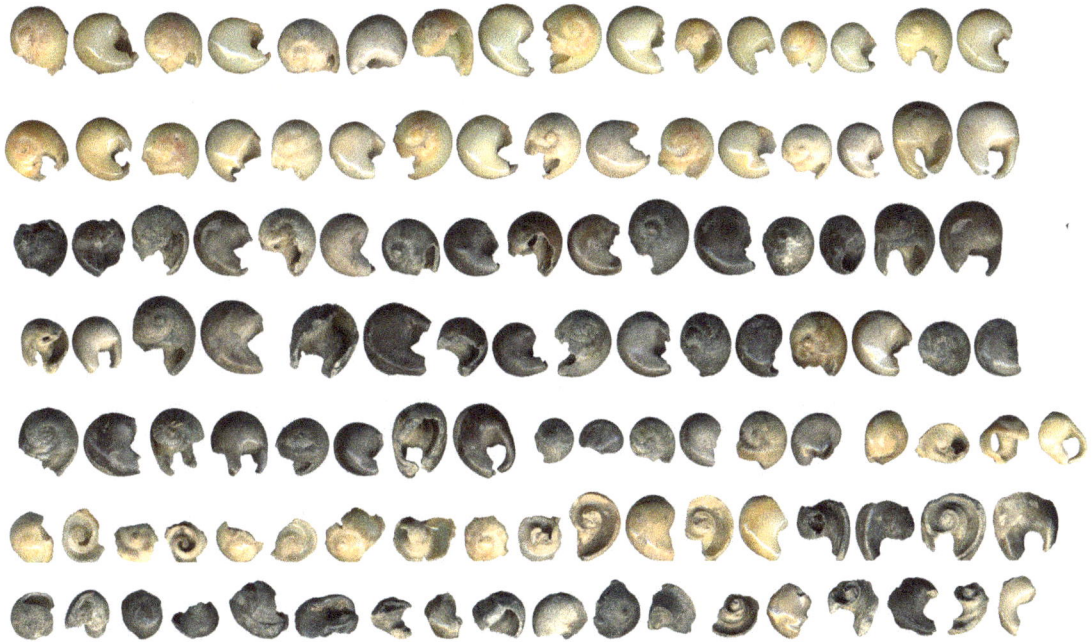

H1B 134

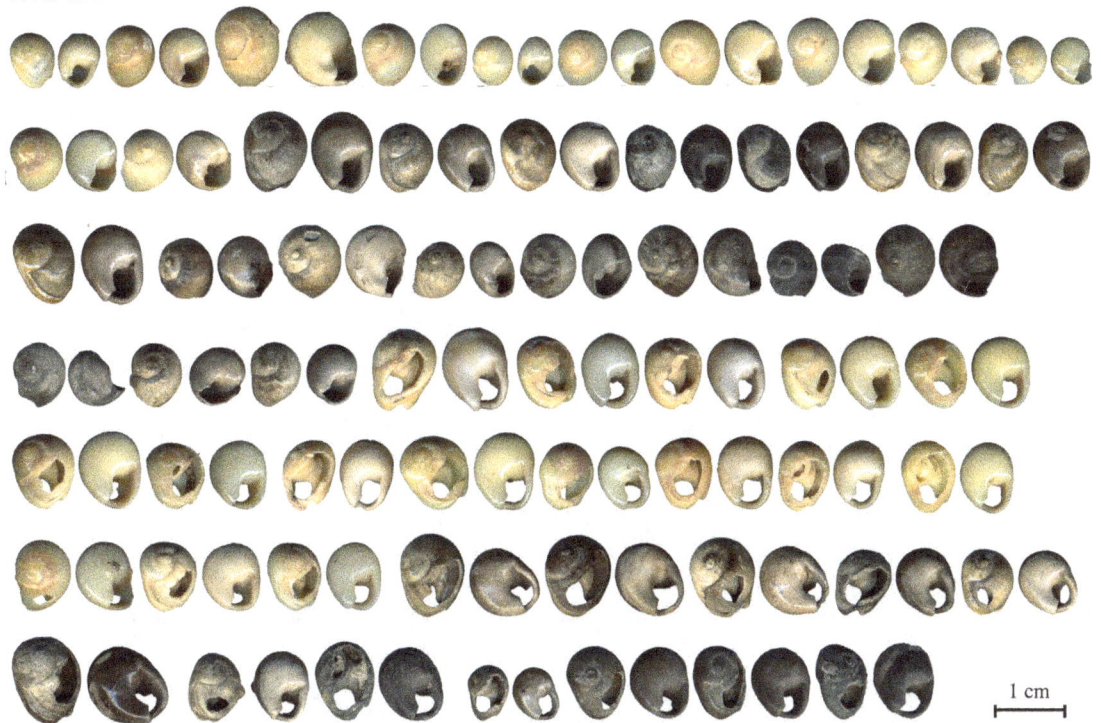

1 cm

H1B 133

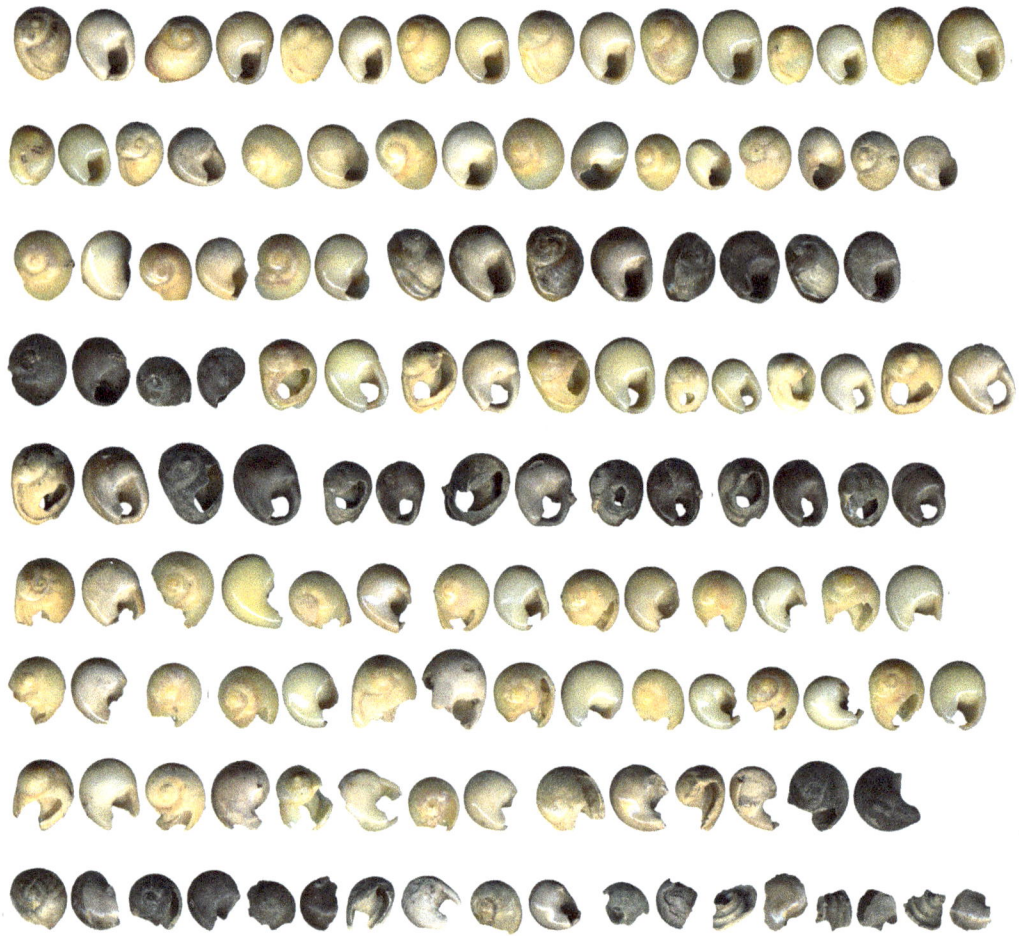

1 cm

H1B 132

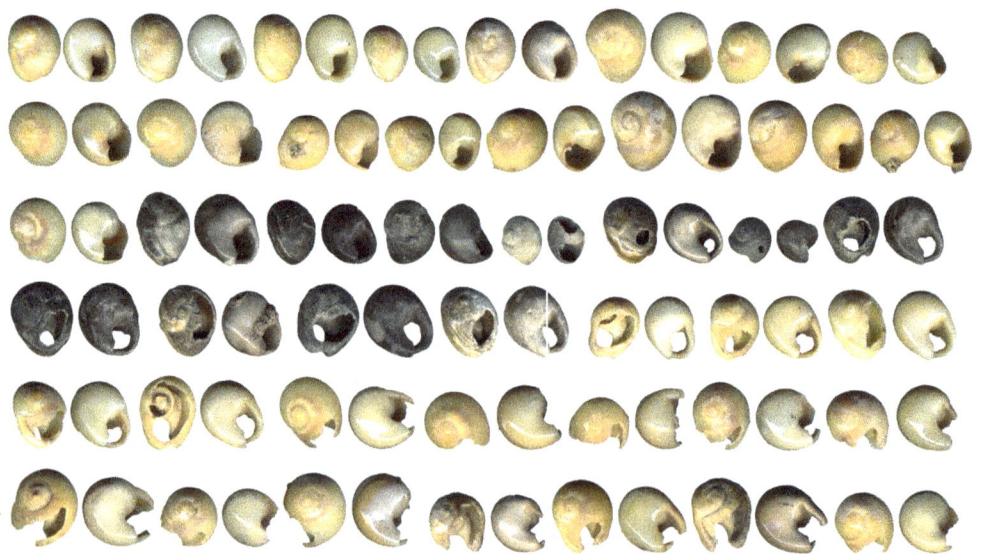

H1B 129 (uncomplete)

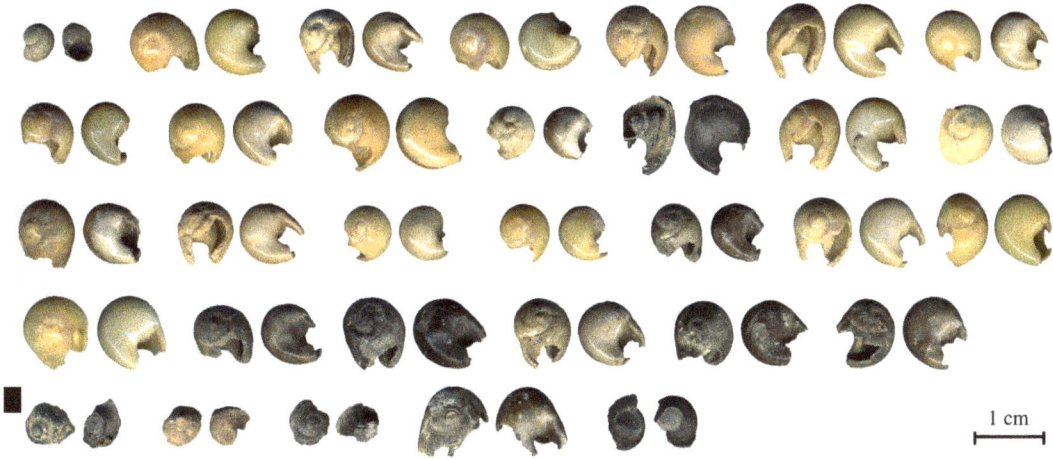

1 cm

H1B 128

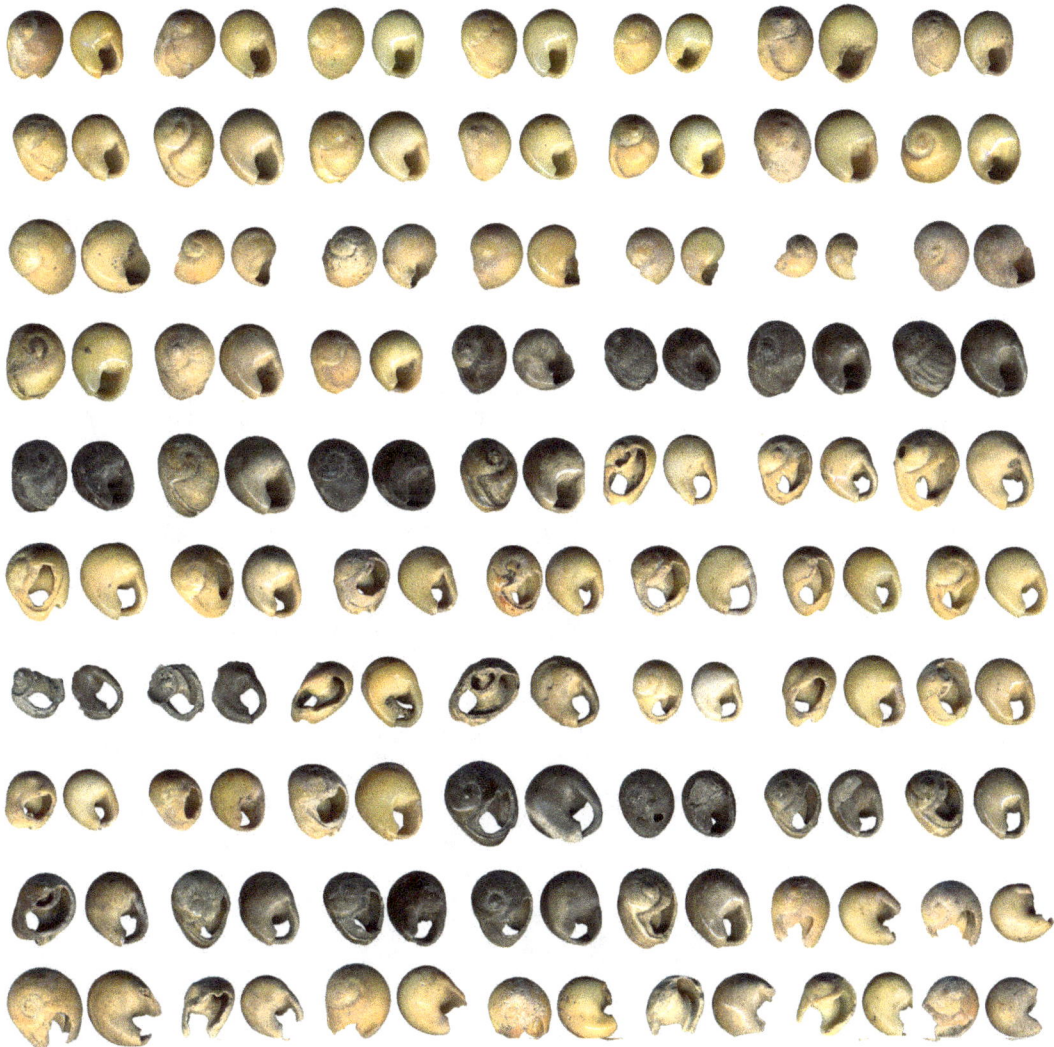

H1B 128 (cont.)

H1B 127

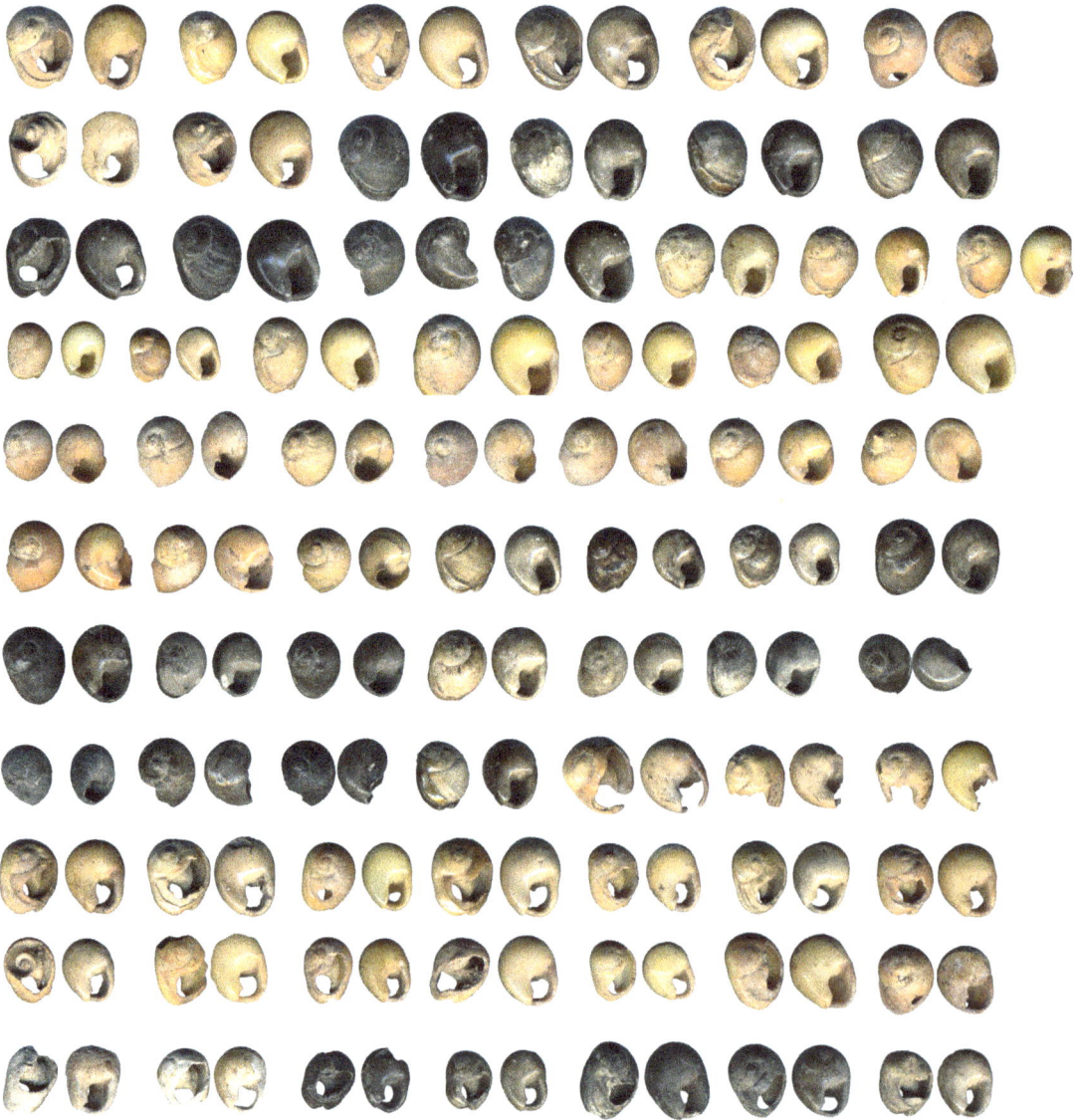

1 cm

H1B 127 (cont.)

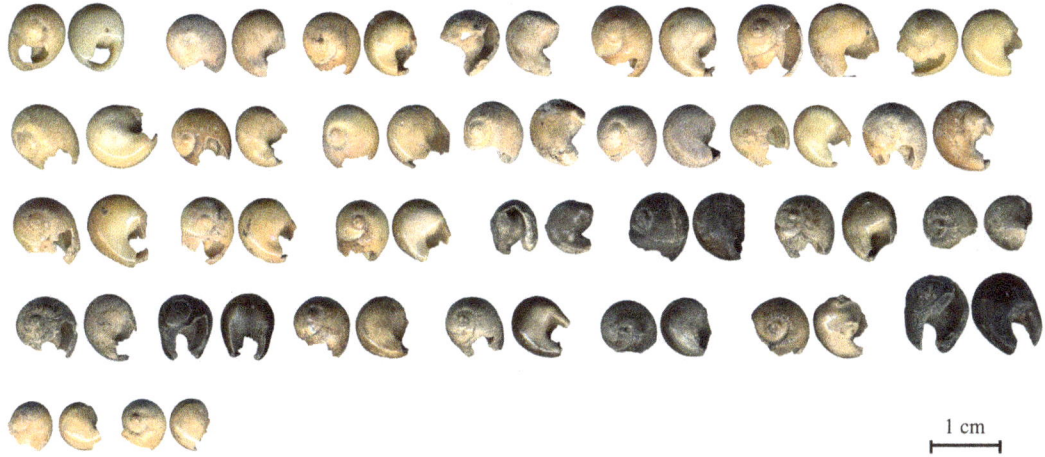

1 cm

H1B 126

H1B 125

H1B 124

1 cm

H1B 123

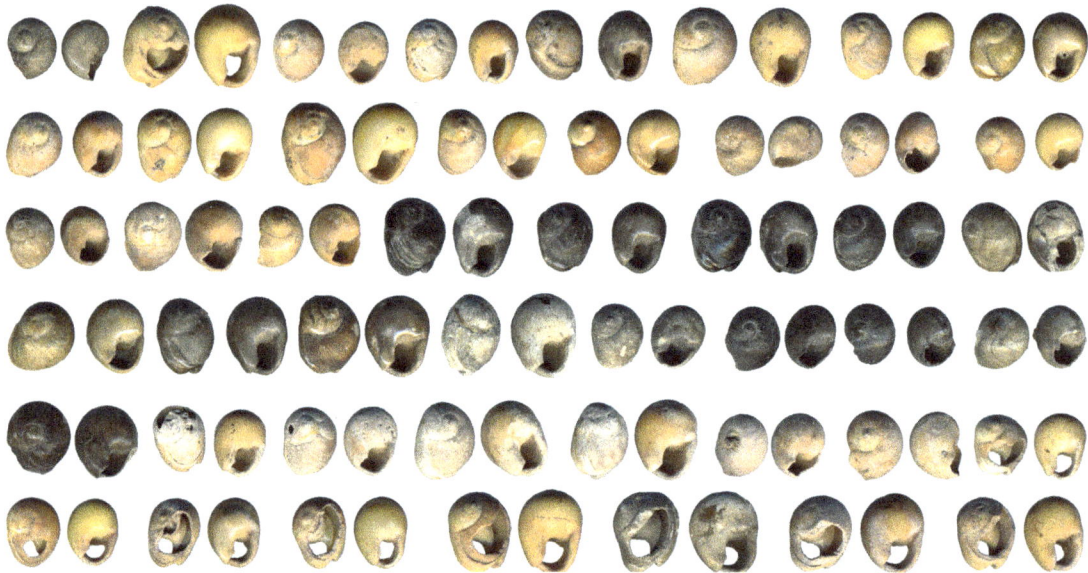

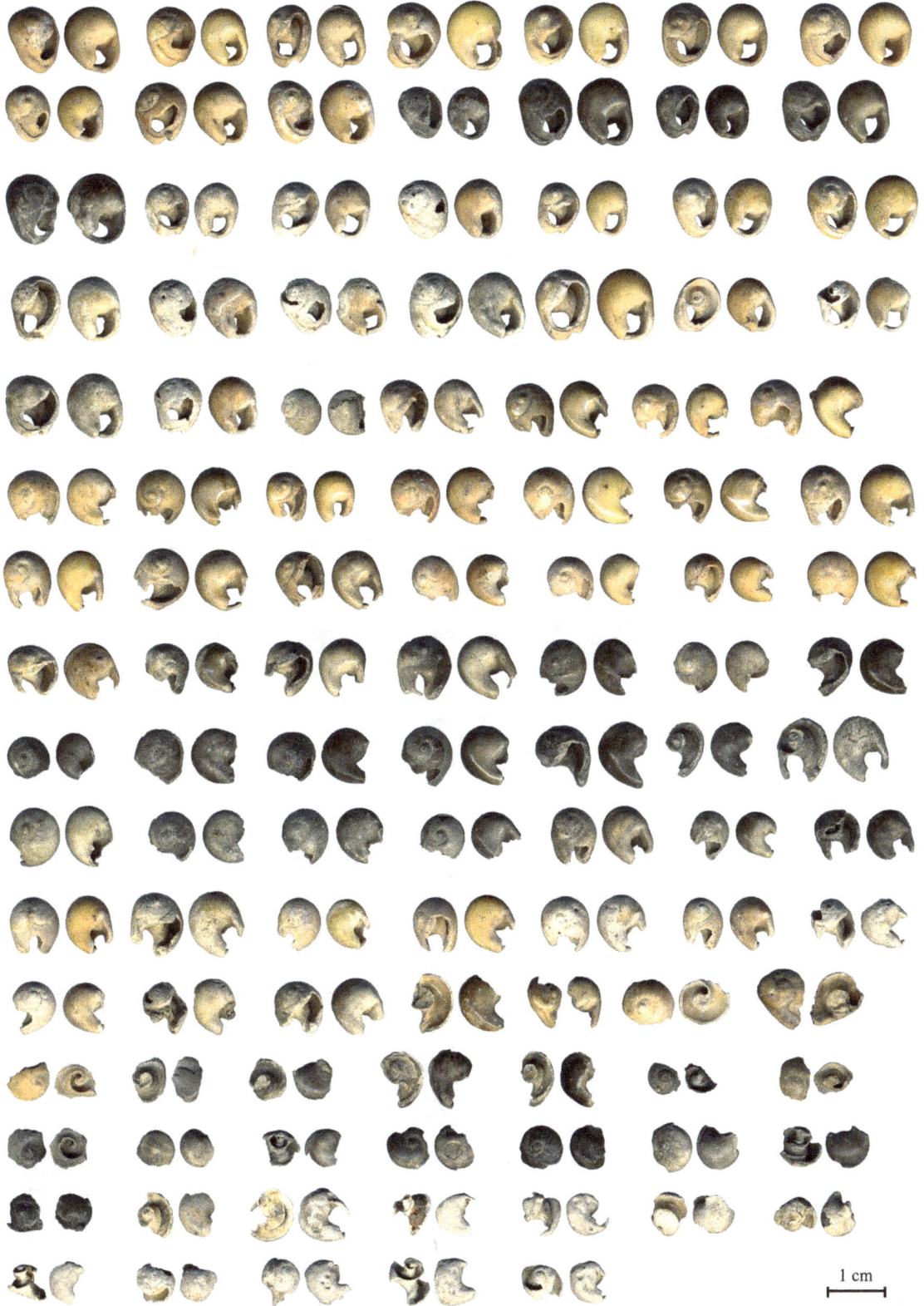

H1B 123 (cont.)

1 cm

H1B 122

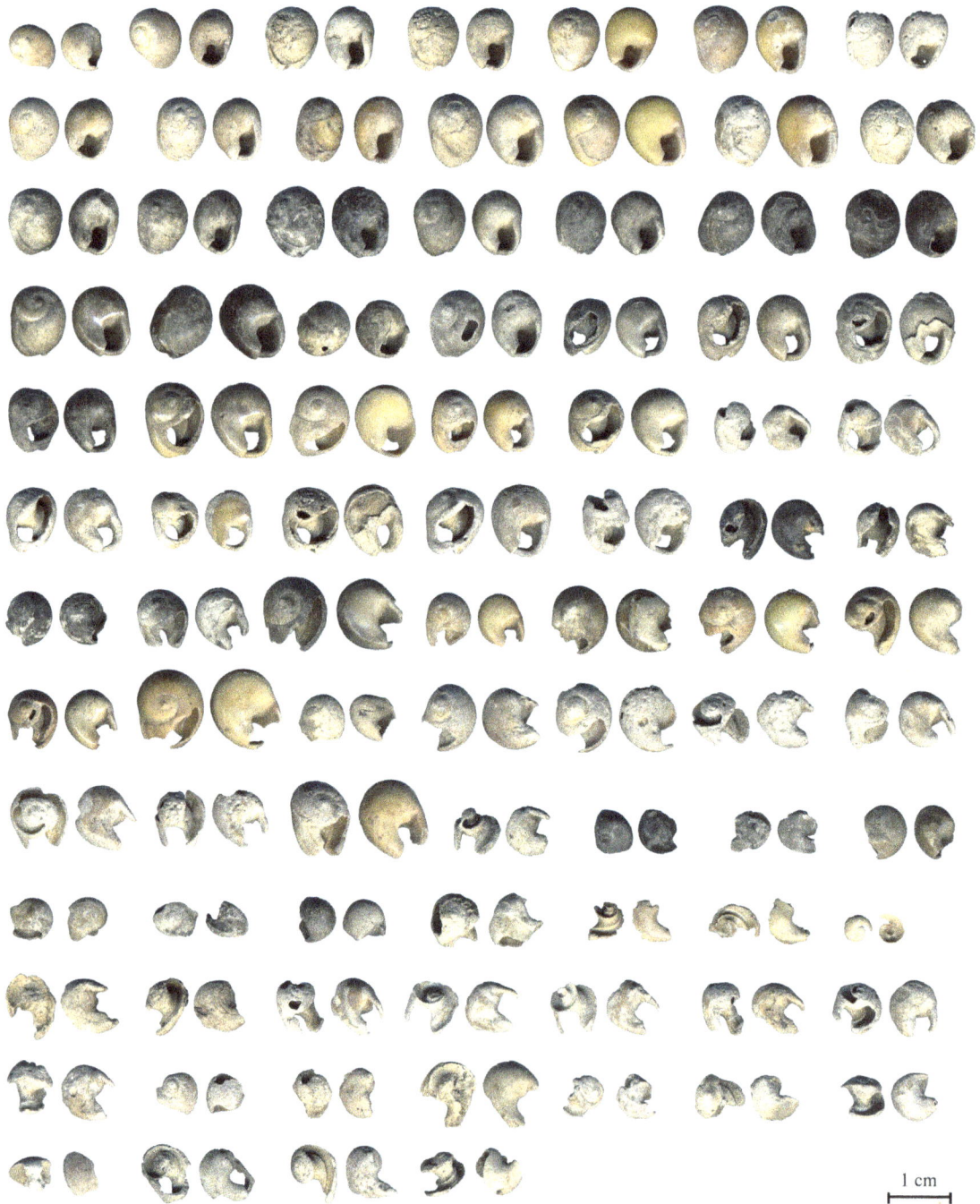

1 cm

H1B 121

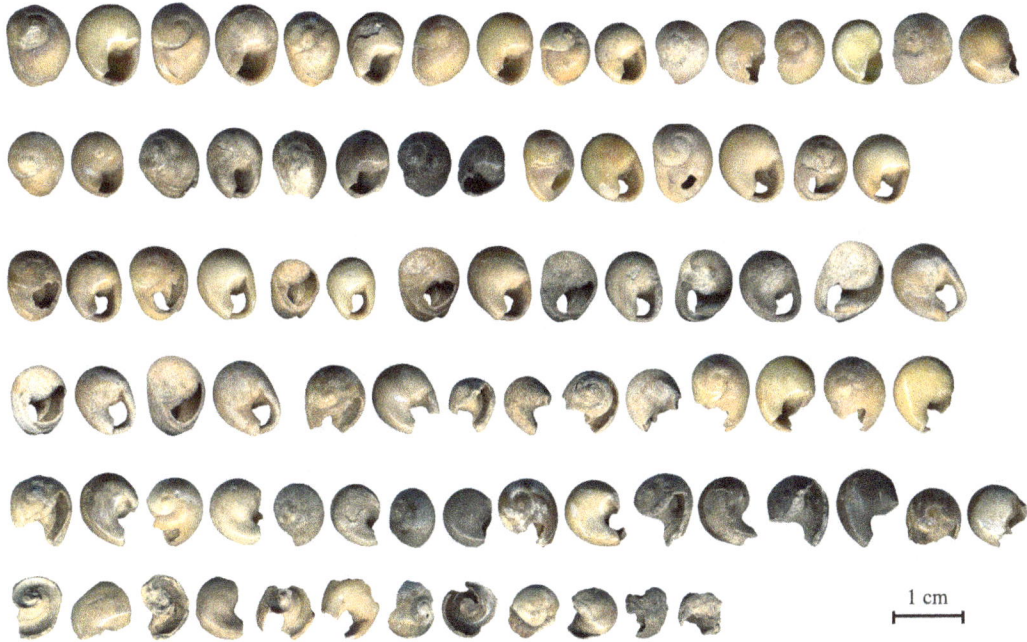

1 cm

H1B 120

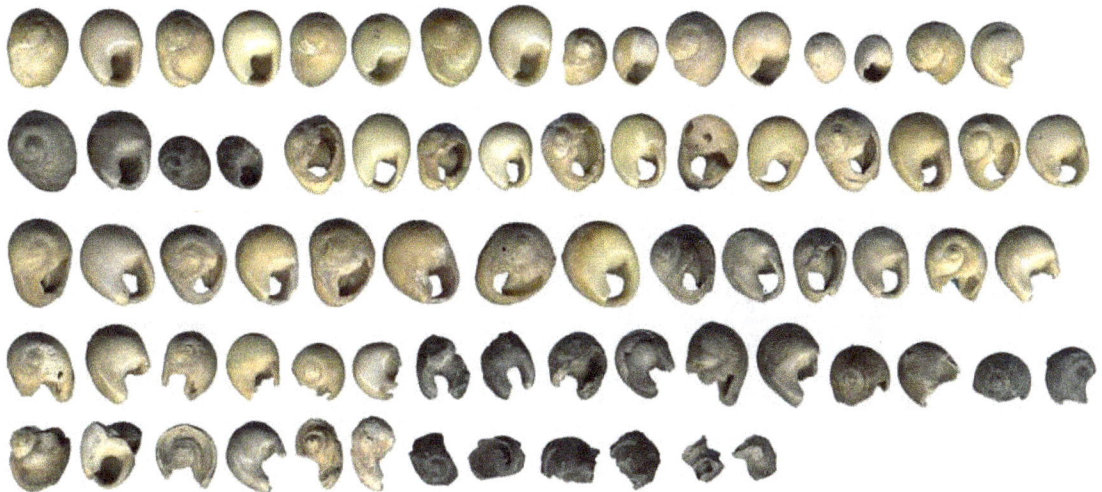

H1B 118

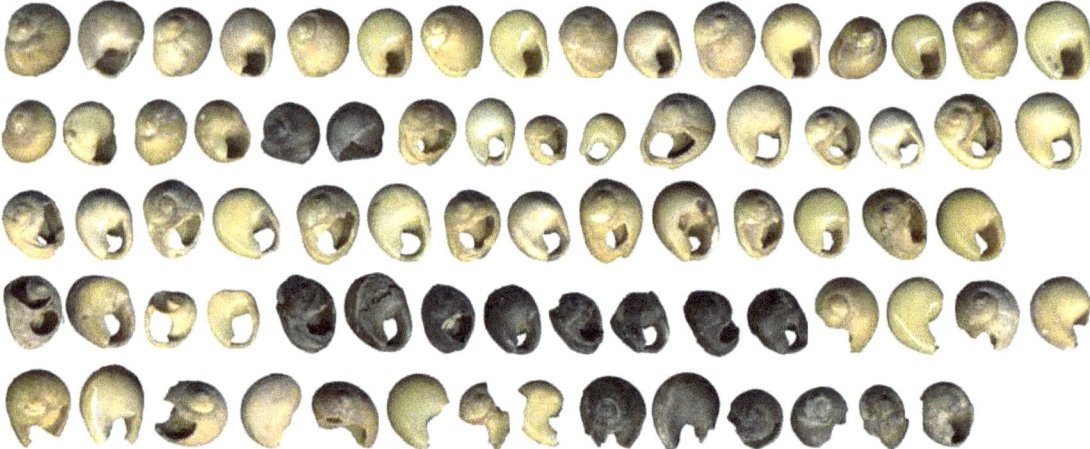

H1B 117

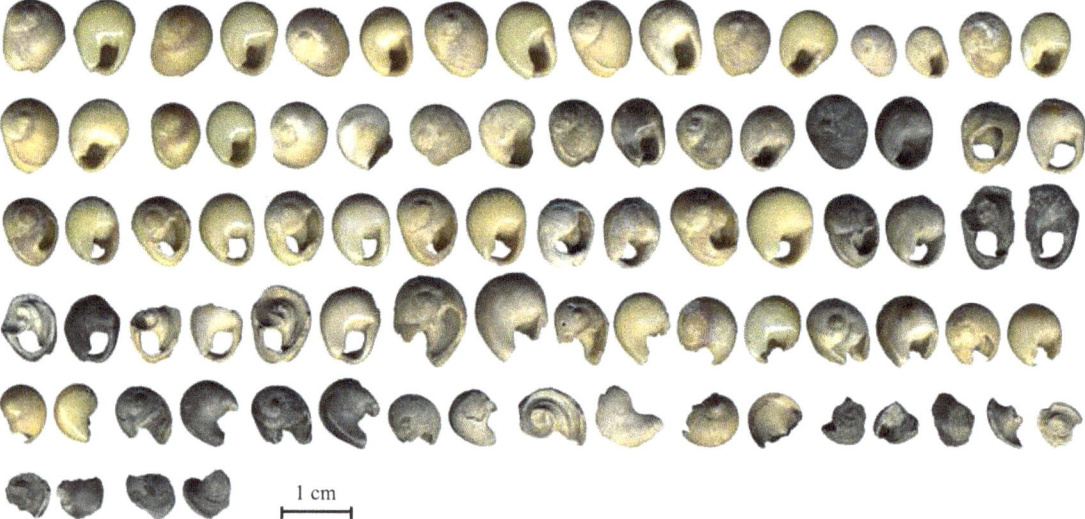

1 cm

H1B 115

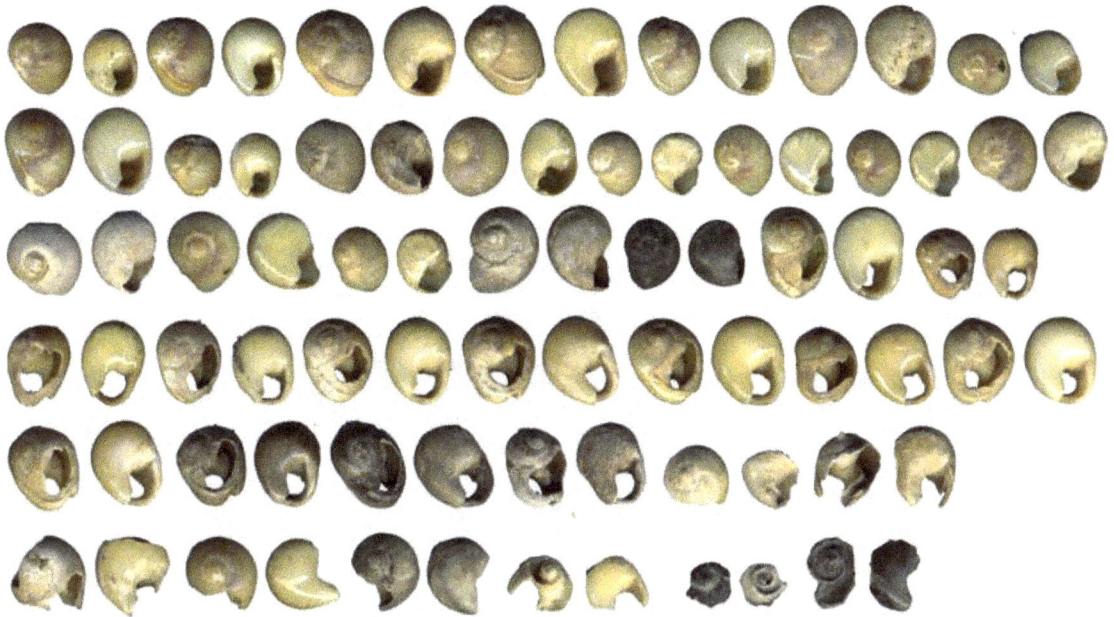

H1B 114

H1B 113

H1B 112

1 cm

H1B 110

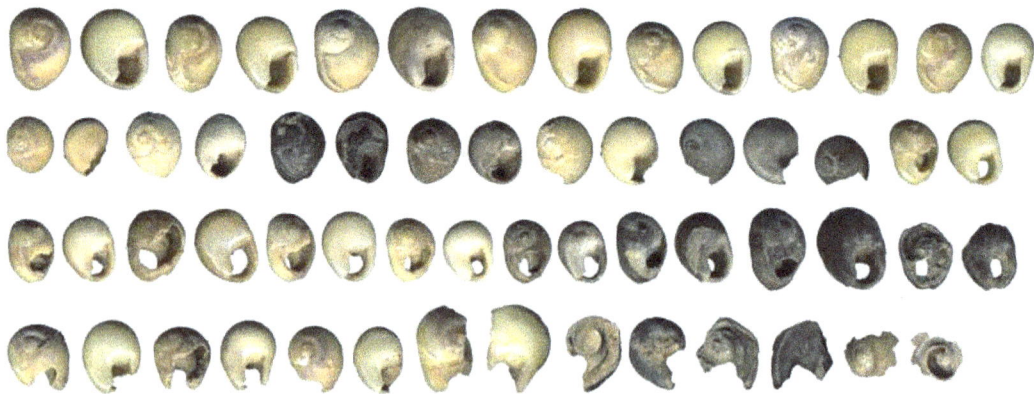

H1B 109

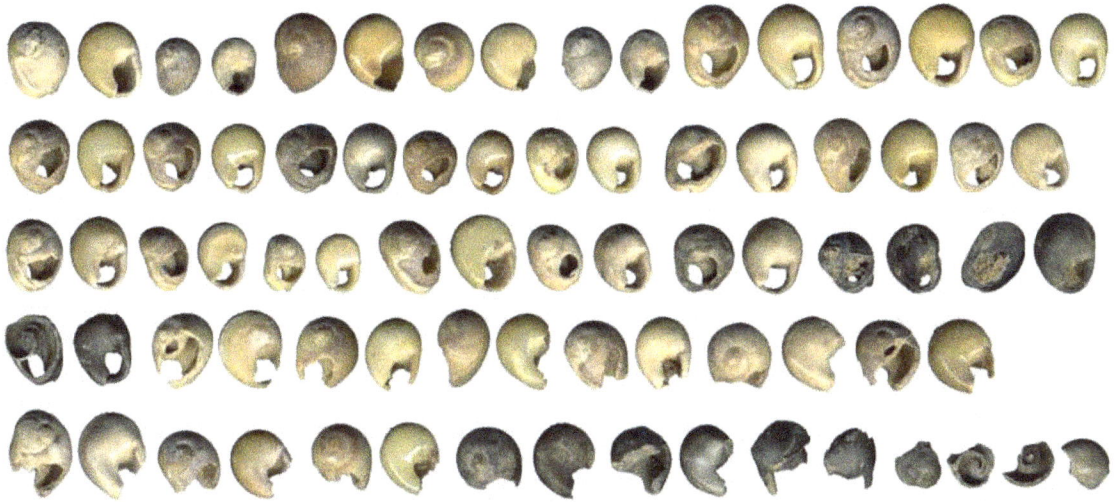

H1B 108

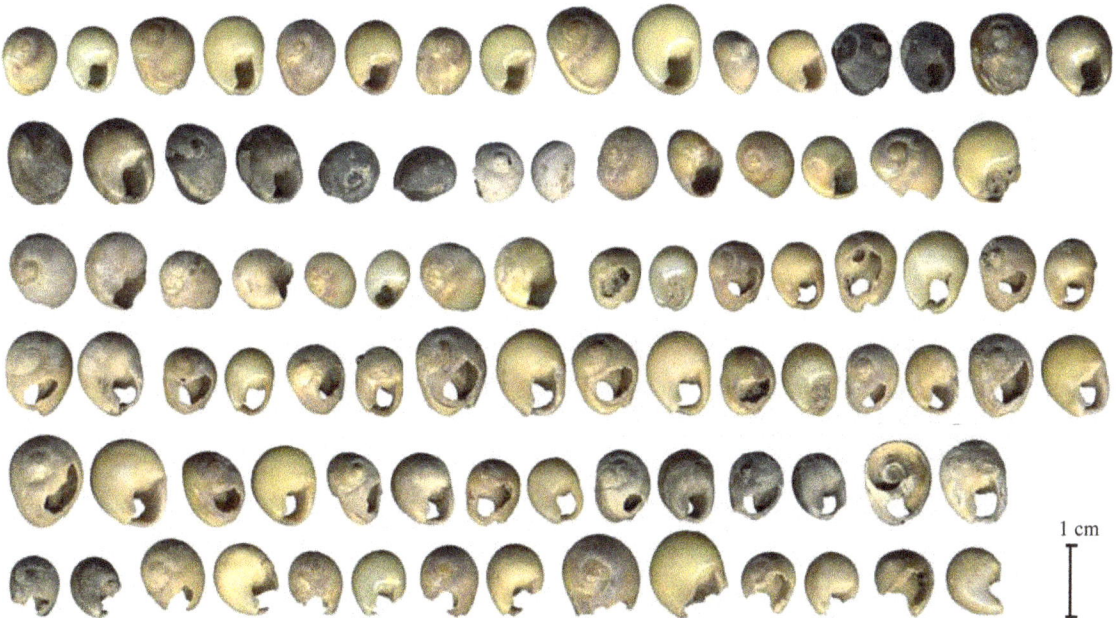

1 cm

H1B 108 (cont.)

H1B 107

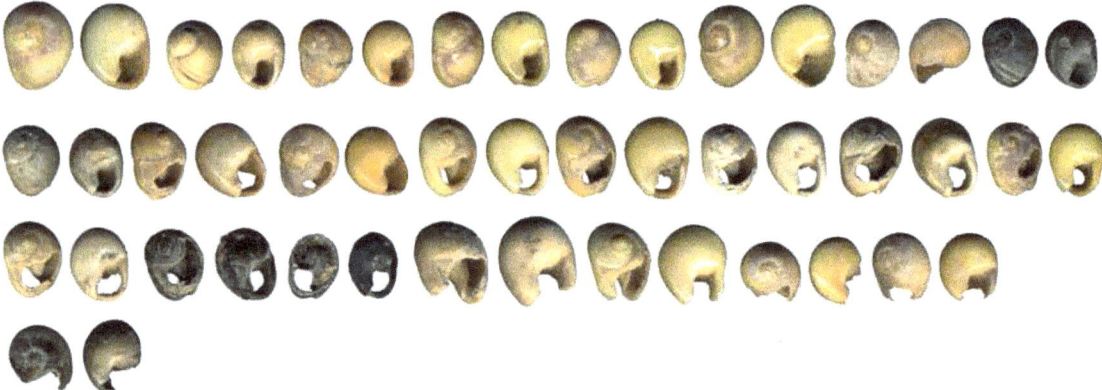

H1B 104

1 cm

CHAPTER ELEVEN

Abundant Mesolithic Columbella rustica

Like Cyclopes and tusk shells, dove shells at Franchthi are far more abundant in the Mesolithic levels than in Palaeolithic strata. This enlarged sample allows us to explore in more detail the modalities of collection of the shells, the production and use of the beads, and their diachronic variations. Despite only partial sorting of the FAN shell bags, nearly 480 specimens[1] were identified in our four reference trenches. All were recovered directly in the trench during excavation, or in the > 5 mm residues. No fragmentary specimen was identified in the subsample of < 5 mm residues. The fraction recorded in detail comprises nearly 400 specimens[2] and can be considered as representative, both qualitatively and quantitatively. Another fifty dove shells were also recovered from trenches G1 and H pedestal, but are not included in the present study for lack of precise chronostratigraphic attribution.

Two thirds of the dove shells are perforated and the majority are heavily worn. Their anthropic origin and use as ornaments can be in no doubt.

A Collection in Thanatocoenoses, and Variable States of Preservation

The state of preservation of C. *rustica* in the Mesolithic levels is highly variable, even within a single excavation unit. Some very rare specimens are in pristine condition, as though they had just been picked up yesterday under water. Conversely, many display a combination of beach alteration, use alteration and post-depositional alteration (Fig. 11.1). Only 49% can be considered as 'intact'[3], 27% are broken on the spire, 15% broken at the base, 2% on the main whorl, with the remaining 5% consisting of small fragments. The proportion of broken apices and the abrasion on the apical fractures, which compare well to our beach collections (Appendix 3.2), indicates that most shells were collected in thanatocoenoses. If, as suggested above, some were collected under water, this mode of collection remained marginal.

The proportion of broken bases, far higher than in our reference collections, as well as the presence of fragments restricted to the spire, indicate that breakage also occurred during use and after deposition at relatively high frequencies, though less so than in the Palaeolithic (*supra*, Chap. 5). Besides mechanical alteration, chemical alteration has also affected a number of specimens. The proportion of bleached and decalcified specimens actually increases throughout the three Mesolithic phases: 61.5 % of the dove shells from the Lower Mesolithic retained their original shine and colouration, while this proportion drops to just 18% in the Final Mesolithic (Table 11.1). The poor preservation conditions during the Final Mesolithic have already been observed for *Cyclope neritea*, but not the difference between Lower and Upper Mesolithic. As noted previously, the differences in the state of shell preservation do not appear to follow variation in the soil pH (Farrand 2000), and the middens of the Lower and Upper Mesolithic, rich in carbonates with the land snails, should offer good conditions of preservation. Why C. *rustica* have preserved more poorly in the Upper Mesolithic sediments is therefore difficult to understand, unless many specimens were brought into the cave already altered by use. Indeed, even in the Final Mesolithic, when preservation is generally poor, some exceptionally well preserved specimens are found side by side with heavily altered ones (Fig. 11.1). Thus, state of preservation is not only related to conditions of burial: the biography of each perforated dove shell, before it was abandoned at Franchthi, must also have influenced the state in which it was eventually recovered.

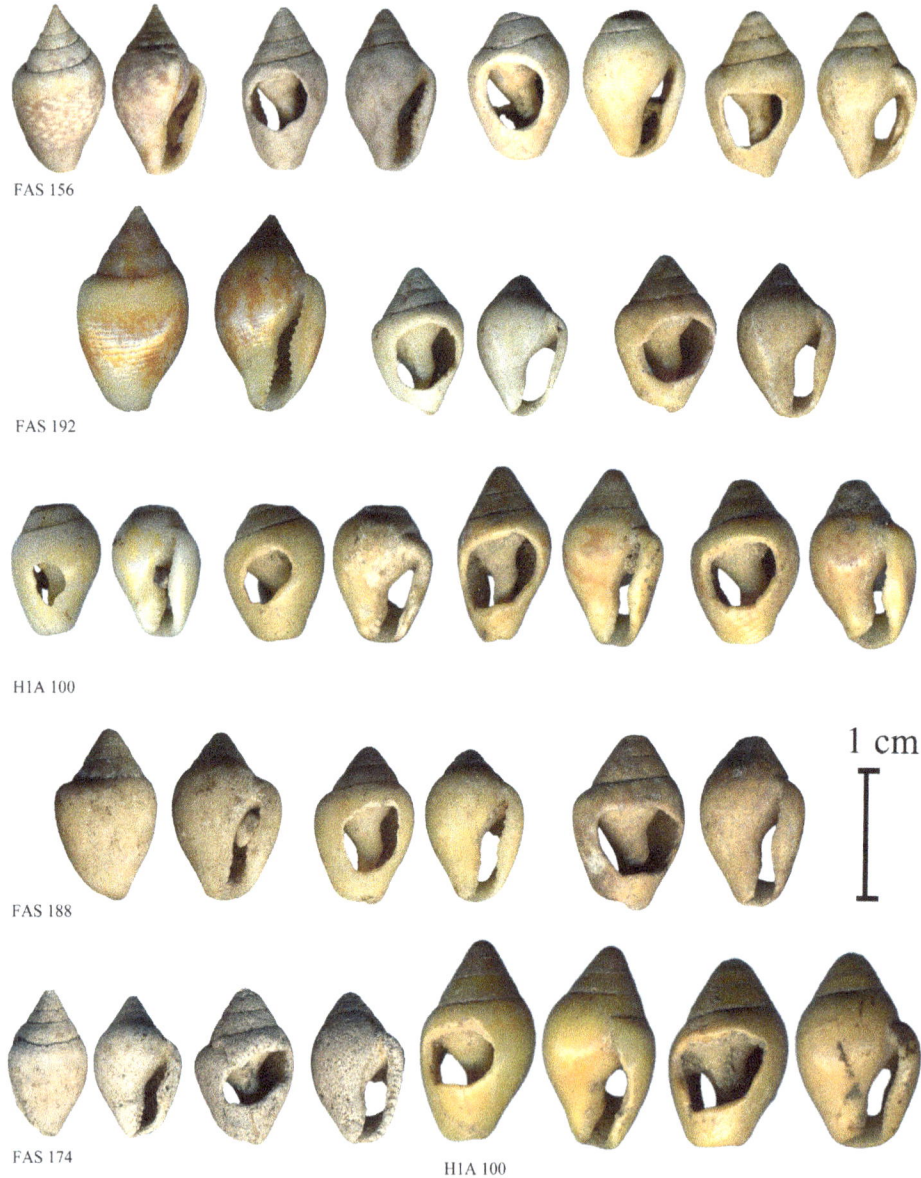

Fig. 11.1: Variable degrees of preservation and wear of Columbella rustica *in the same excavation units.*

Phase	Shiny	Mat	Mat, bleached	Decalcified	Total
Phase 7 (LM)	86 (61.5%)	30 (21.5%)	10 (7.1%)	14 (10%)	140
Inter 7/8	4	1	2	1	8
Phase 8 (UM)	41 (27.5%)	53 (35.5%)	15 (10%)	40 (26.8%)	149
Inter 8/9	1	4	1	10	16
Phase 9 (FM)	11 (18%)	23 (37.7%)	11 (18%)	16 (26.2%)	61

Table 11.1: State of preservation of Mesolithic C. rustica *by phase.*

A Double Process of Selection: on the Beach and in the Cave

The small sample of intact *C. rustica* from the Palaeolithic showed a mean height far above what we collected on Argolid beaches (m = 1.42 cm; s.d. = 0.1). We tentatively attributed this to cooler and more nutritious waters and to the selection of large specimens. The larger samples of the Mesolithic, when water temperatures were nearer to that of today, will help us explore further the influence of environmental conditions and human choice in the selection of the shells.

The mean height[4] of intact Mesolithic dove shells (Table 11.2) is slightly lower than in the preceding period, but still much larger than in our reference collections from thanatocoenoses (Appendix 3.2). The slight apparent increase in size in the Final Mesolithic is not statistically significant[5]. The size can thus be considered to be stable throughout the Mesolithic, and the sample can be treated as a whole.

Phase	Mean height	Standard-Deviation	N
Phase 7 (LM)	1.34	0.14	141
Phase 8 (UM)	1.34	0.11	77
Phase 9 (FM)	1.38	0.15	39

Table 11.2: Mean height of intact Mesolithic C. rustica *by phase.*

Does this greater size correspond with a naturally large natural population, or does it reflect deliberate selection when collecting the shells? As shown by Fig. 11.2, in which the Mesolithic sample is compared with our largest modern beach collection, both factors are operating simultaneously. The larger dimensional classes are clearly better represented in the Mesolithic sample, where the mode is 2 mm greater than in the modern sample. The conditions of growth must have been more favourable than today, but the reason for this is unclear given that water temperatures must have been comparable (Perlès 2016b). On the other hand, the non-Gaussian distribution of the Mesolithic sample, where the smallest classes are quasi-absent, demonstrates a strict selection: the shell collectors (why not children?) systematically rejected dove shells under 1.2 cm high. This limit is not aesthetic but rather practical: it corresponds to the minimum size required to perforate dove shells by percussion without hitting one's fingers or breaking too many of the smaller and more brittle shells (Benghiat *et al.* 2009: 734). It corresponds very precisely to the lower limit observed at Pupićina Cave and Zala Cave and is 1 mm lower than at Šebrn, three Croatian sites where deliberate selection of large specimens is also exemplified (Benghiat *et al.* 2009; Komšo & Vukosavljević 2011).

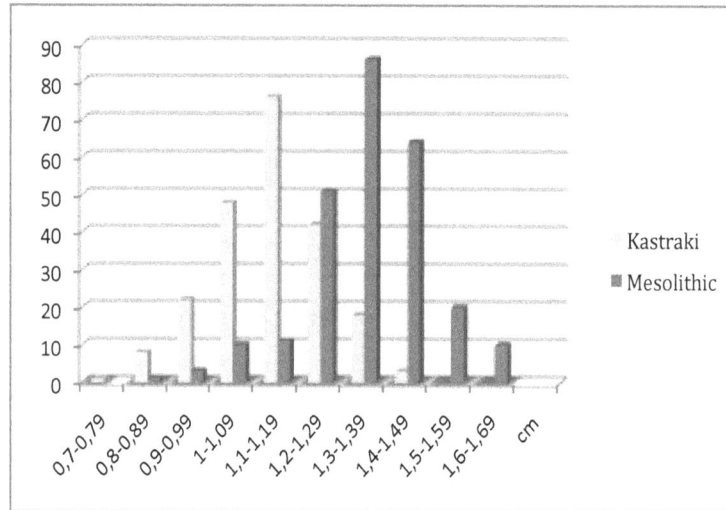

Fig. 11.2 : Comparison of the height distribution of intact C. rustica *from the modern collection of Kastraki (2010-2012) and the Mesolithic sample.*

The abundance of large shells in the Mesolithic sample may additionally suggest they were specially prized and were preferentially selected for perforation. The comparison of the distribution of unperforated and perforated dove shells (Fig. 11.3) shows that this is not the case : among the larger dimensional classes, the proportion of perforated and unperforated shells is comparable. However, it reveals that a second process of selection did take place when the shells were brought back to the cave : all dimensional classes show a roughly equal number of perforated and non perforated specimens, except for the class 1.3 – 1.39 cm, where the number of perforated shells is more than double those left unperforated[6]. Rather than looking for the largest dove shells, the craftsmen or craftswomen aimed at a standard dimension, centred around 1.35 cm. Graphs phase by phase[7] show no significant deviation from this pattern, and demonstrate a strong continuity in the conception of dove shell ornaments throughout the Mesolithic.

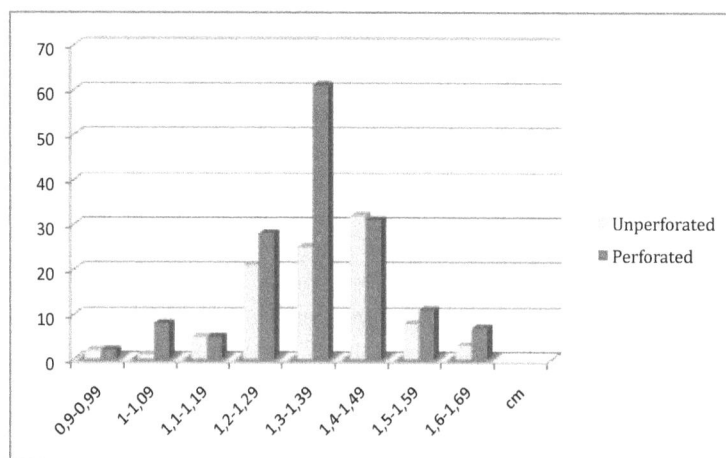

Fig. 11.3: Comparison of the height distribution of intact perforated and unperforated Mesolithic C. rustica.

Were *Columbella rustica* Heat-Treated?

We have seen that a large proportion of the *Cyclope neritea* had been heated, especially in the Lower and Upper Mesolithic, and more especially in trench H1B. While exposure to the heat must in part be considered accidental, the fact that the rate of burning among Cyclopes exceeded that of any other category of remains led us to conclude in favor of intentional heat-treatment. Some of the dove shells, both perforated and unperforated, have also been heated (grey) or burnt (black). The proportion, however, is lower than among Cyclopes, except in Phase 9 (Table 11.3). It is comparable to the proportion of burnt mammal bones and higher than the proportion of burnt fish bones (Munro & Stiner in prep.; Perlès & Vanhaeren 2010, table 1; Rose in prep.). However, both mammal bones and fish bones would have, at least in part, been burnt when cooked rather than by accidental contact with embers. Since this does not apply to *C. rustica*, the relatively high proportion of grey and black specimens suggests that heat-treatment was also practised, albeit on a smaller scale than with *C. neritea*.

Phase	Unburnt	Heated	Burnt	Ind.	Total
Phase 7 (LM)	108 (77%)	5 (3.5%)	27 (19.4%)	0	140
Inter 7/8	8	1	0	0	9
Phase 8 (UM)	126 (84%)	1 (0.6%)	19 (12.6%)	3 (2%)	149
Inter 8/9	15	0	1	0	16
Phase 9 (FM)	50 (82%)	0	11 (18%)	0	61
Total	307 (82%)	7 (1.8%)	58 (15.4%)	5 (0.8%)	375

Table 11.3: Proportion of heated and burnt C. rustica *by phase.*

Perforating the Dove Shells

A non-negligible number of dove shells, including many of the largest, were cached, lost or rejected without perforation (Table 11.4). This pattern, which contrasts with the Palaeolithic, increases throughout the Mesolithic to reach 40% of all *C. rustica* in the Final Mesolithic[8], a figure far higher than the 12.7 % unperforated dove shells from Mesolithic Vela Spila in Croatia, a coastal site considered a collection and processing centre (Cristiani *et al.* 2014b). Some may simply have been discarded because the small pebbles blocking the aperture could not be removed and impeded threading, but there is no reason why such pebbles should become more abundant over time! Several other interpretations, none of which can be tested, can be put forward: a more desultory use of the shells; the desire to cache some good specimens for future use; an increasing use of ornaments simply glued on artifacts, an increasing use of dove shells as exchangeable valuables, etc... However, it should be recalled that the actual proportion of dove shells left unperforated must have been originally lower: as for Cyclopes, we can assume that a large proportion of freshly perforated shells left the site.

The technique of perforation is similar to that employed in the Palaeolithic: the majority, if not all *C. rustica*, were perforated by direct or indirect percussion, two techniques which leave similar traces. They bear the characteristic large perforations that invade the lower part of the last whorl. The dimensions compare well with the scant comparative data, from Mesolithic Riparo Pradestel in northern Italy (Cristiani 2009), Pupićina Cave and Zala Cave in Croatia (Komšo & Vukosavljević 2011). No significant difference can be perceived among the three Mesolithic phases at Franchthi (Fig. 11.4). Here again, technical continuity prevails.

Phase	Perforated	Unperforated	Ind.	Total
Phase 7 (LM)	97 (80,1%)	22 (18,2%)	21	140
Inter 7/8	6	2	0	8
Phase 8 (UM)	88 (66,3%)	44 (33,3%)	17	149
Inter 8/9	8	5	3	16
Phase 9 (FM)	33 (60%)	22 (40%)	6	61

Table 11.4: Proportion of perforated and unperforated C. rustica *by phase. The percentages exclude indeterminate specimens.*

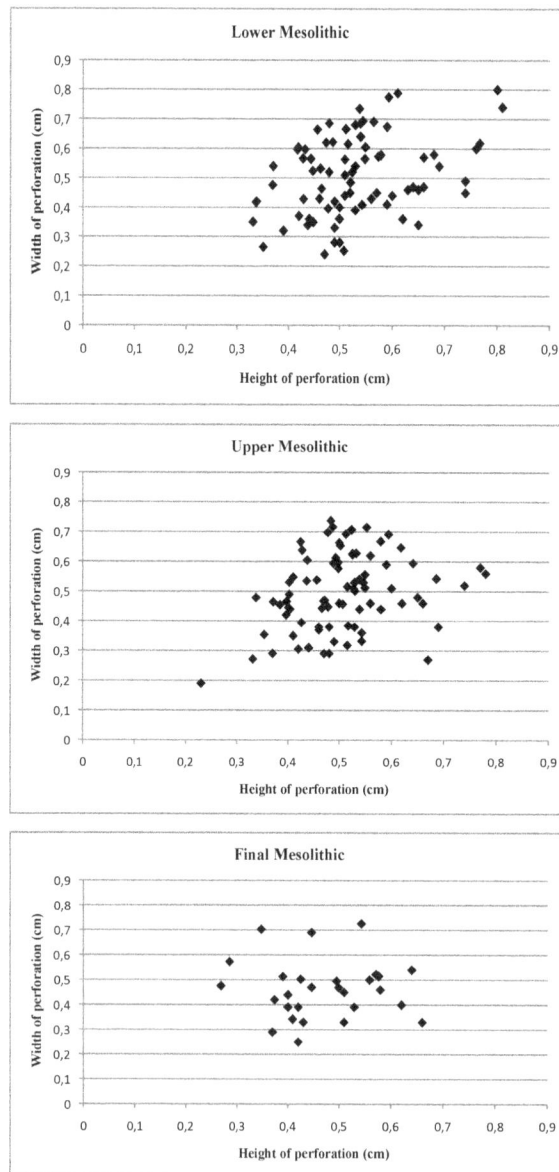

Fig. 11.4 : Height and width of perforations on C. rustica, *by phase.*

Dove Shell Beads: Heavily Used Ornaments

A large majority of perforated *C. rustica* show well-developed use-wear on both the dorsal and the ventral side. In early stages of use, the wear on the dorsal side tends to be more developed on the upper part, either in the left or right corner of the perforation. Later on, the use-wear eventually extends over its entire periphery. On average, heavily worn perforations are larger than fresh ones, which suggests that micro-breakage occurred along the perforation during use. On the ventral side, the teeth of the outer lip of the aperture are frequently completely worn down, when the lip itself is not broken and abraded by use (Fig. 11.5). More rarely, the teeth of the inner lip are also worn. All these features indicate that substantial pressure was exerted on both faces, probably due to tying the shell to a garment with a double knot.

Like their Palaeolithic counterparts, perforated *C. rustica* were worn for a long time before they were discarded at the site. Even broken specimens show wear-traces on the remaining edges of the perforation, demonstrating that breakage did not occur during perforation (Fig. 11.6).

Most dove shell beads or pendants were brought into the cave as already worn ornaments. Nevertheless, Franchthi's Mesolithic inhabitants collected fresh specimens and a minority of *C. rustica* bear perforations with little or no use-wear, suggesting ornaments were also produced at the site itself (Fig. 11.5). Within a single excavation unit, perforated and unperforated shells coexist, and the degree of wear on perforated specimens is highly variable[9] (Fig. 11.1). All through the Mesolithic sequence, unperforated, newly perforated and heavily worn dove shells were manipulated simultaneously. If these activities involved the replacement of heavily worn ornaments susceptible to breakage by newly manufactured ones, or the manufacture of new embroidered garments, then the relative rarity of freshly perforated specimens becomes logical: most of the latter would have left the site with the bearer of these garments, while worn ornaments would have been discarded *in situ*. Since *C. rustica* was widely traded to inland sites in the European Mesolithic (Álvarez-Fernández 2010; Cristiani *et al.* 2014b; Komšo & Vukosavljević 2011; Rigaud 2011), it is also probable that some of the newly manufactured beads left the site as exchange goods.

1 cm

Fig. 11. 6: Broken perforated C. rustica *showing pronounced use-wear traces.*

Abundant Mesolithic Columbella rustica

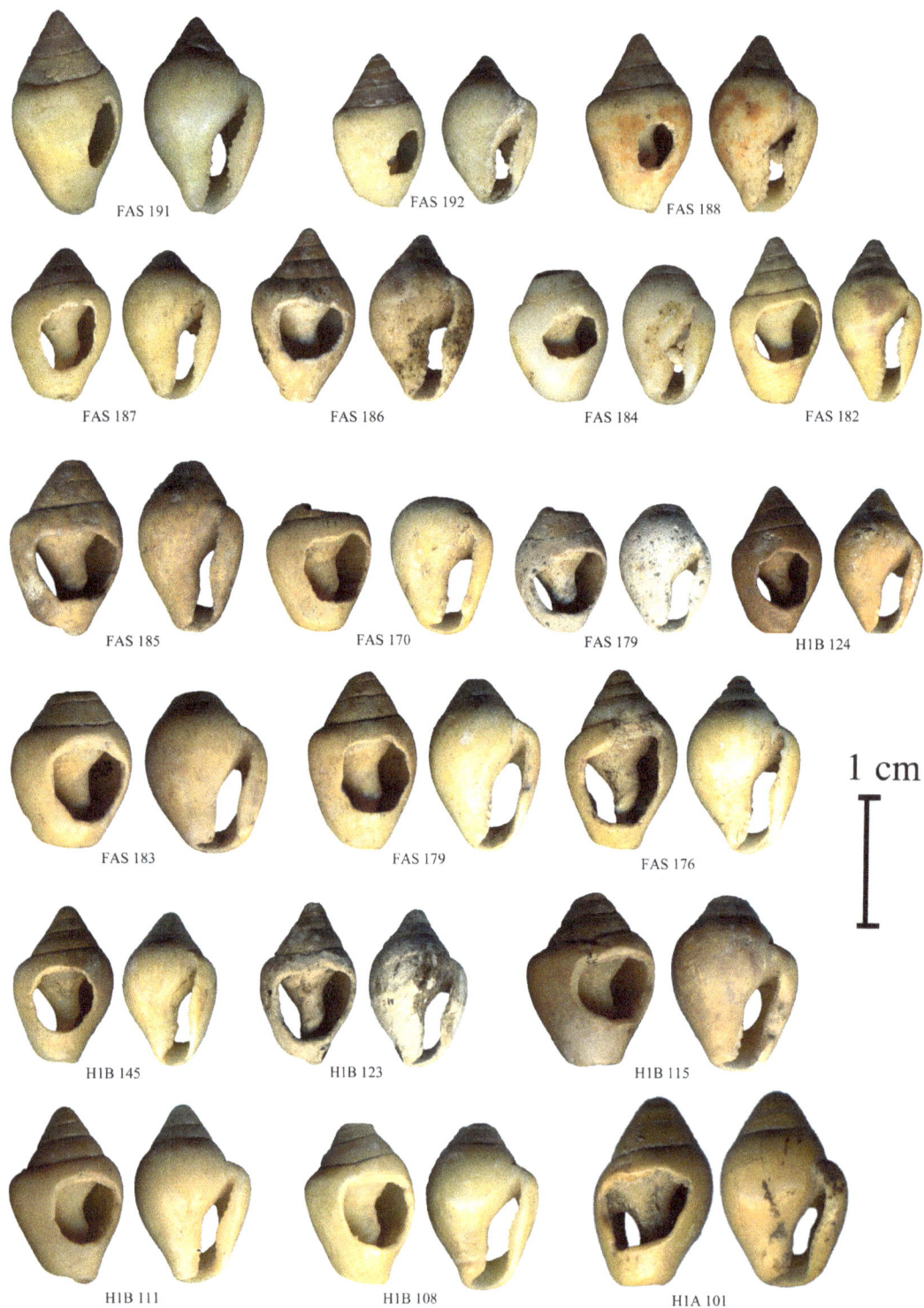

Fig. 11.5: *Variable degrees of use-wear on Mesolithic* Columbella rustica.

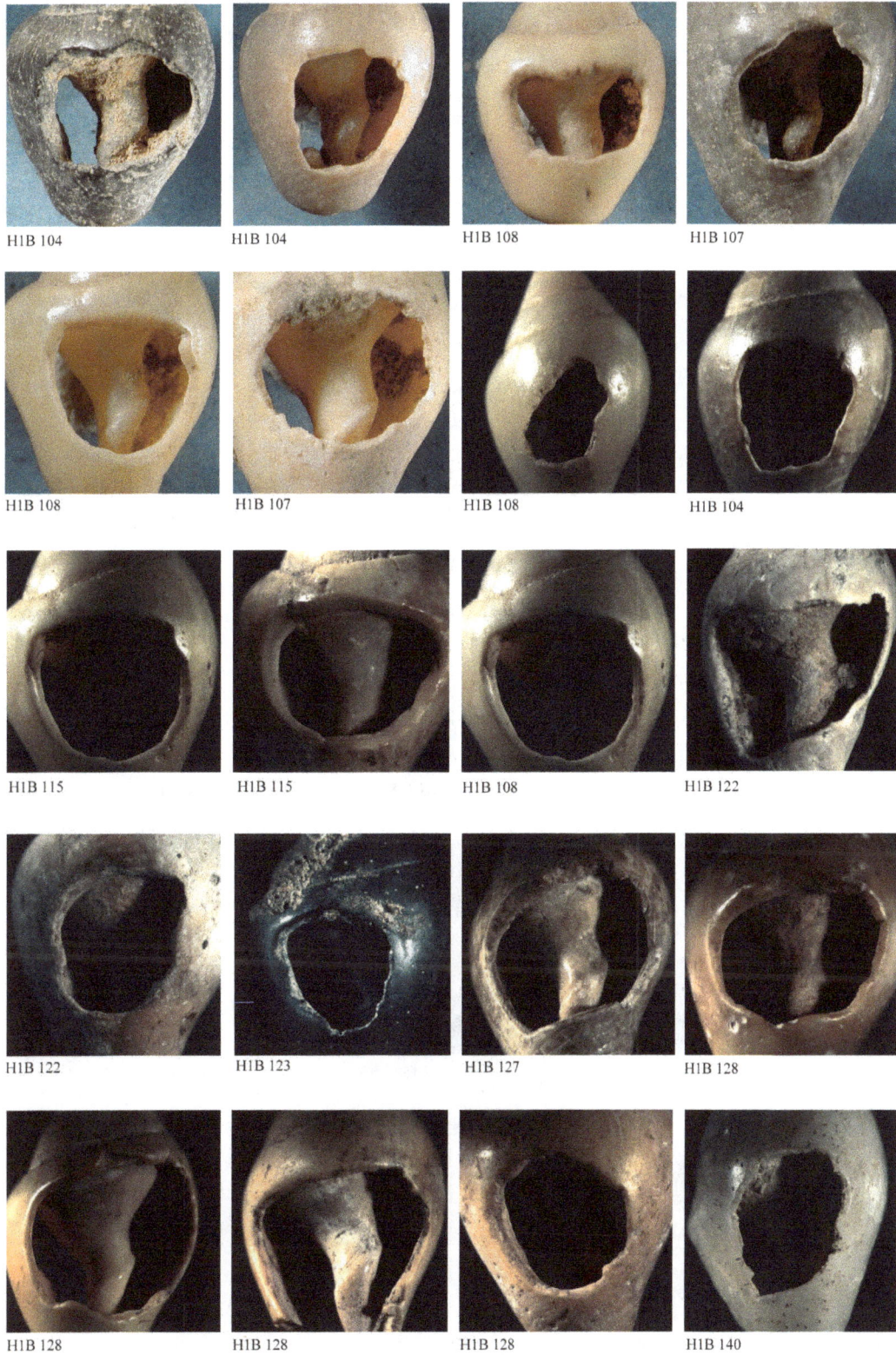

H1B 104

H1B 104

H1B 108

H1B 107

H1B 108

H1B 107

H1B 108

H1B 104

H1B 115

H1B 115

H1B 108

H1B 122

H1B 122

H1B 123

H1B 127

H1B 128

H1B 128

H1B 128

H1B 128

H1B 140

Fig. 11.7: Details of use-wear on the perforation of Columbella rustica *from H1B. Photographs J. Beck (x 8) and M. Vanhaeren (bottom right).*

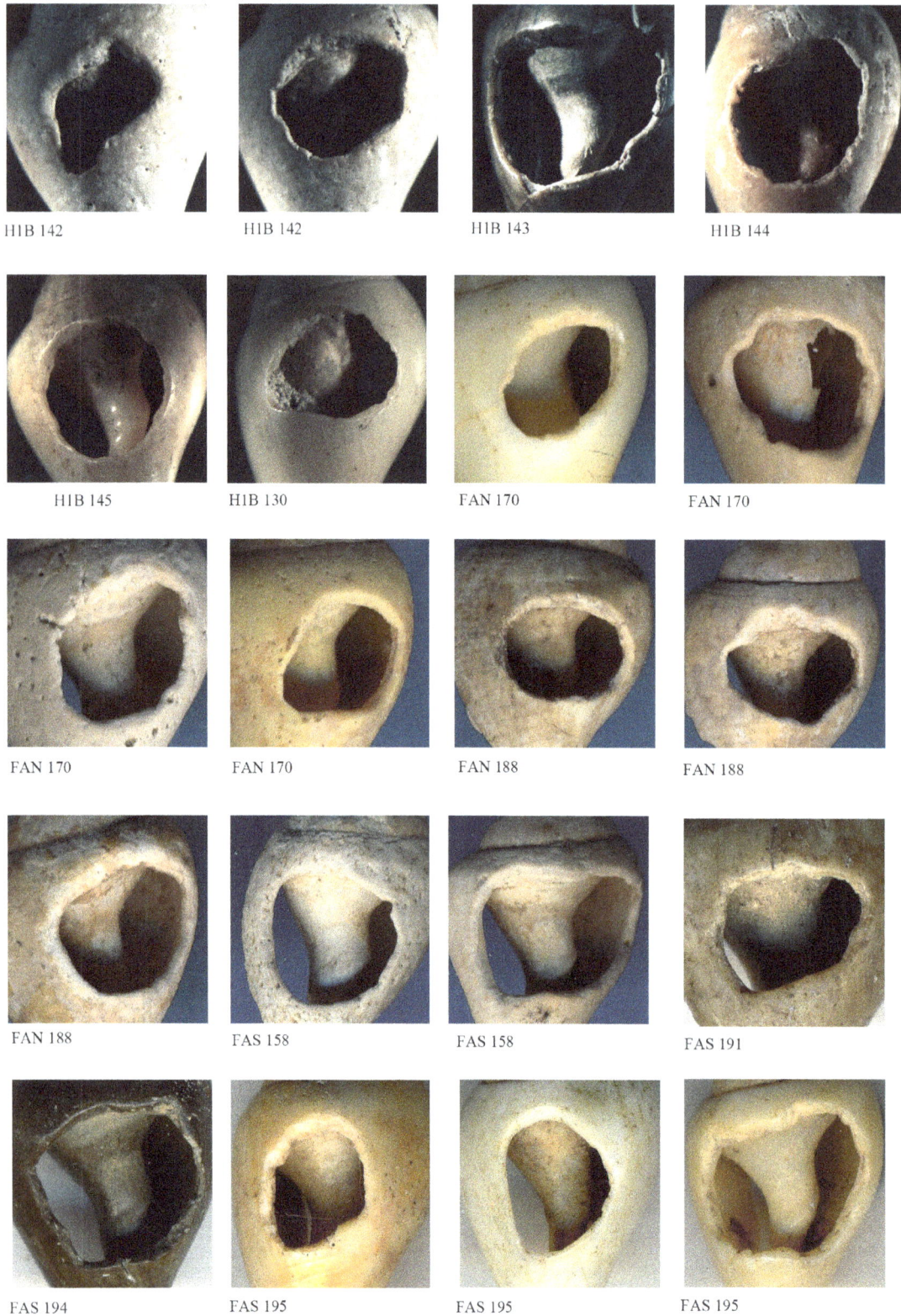

H1B 142   H1B 142   H1B 143   H1B 144

H1B 145   H1B 130   FAN 170   FAN 170

FAN 170   FAN 170   FAN 188   FAN 188

FAN 188   FAS 158   FAS 158   FAS 191

FAS 194   FAS 195   FAS 195   FAS 195

Fig. 11.8: Details of use-wear on the perforation of Mesolithic Columbella rustica *from H1B (photographs M. Vanhaeren), FAN and FAS (scans).*

NOTES

1   Including 18 from Mesolithic cleaning units, which will not be included in the statistics.
2   We only fully recorded the individual characteristics of *Columbella rustica* from FAN for the Final Mesolithic.
3   Since the last whorl is usually missing on specimens collected on beaches, we considered them « intact » when 4 whorls are preserved.
4   We have shown a strong positive correlation between height and diameter of *C. rustica* on modern collections (Appendix 3.2). The height is thus sufficient to describe the size distribution.
5   Student's $t = 0.69$, $p = 0.48$.
6   The difference of distribution of perforated and non-perforated shells between the three modal classes (1.2 – 1.5 cm) is highly significant ($\chi^2 = 9.74$, p < 0.01)
7   Not included here.
8   The difference between Phases 7, 8 and 9 is statistically highly significant, whether or not indeterminate specimens are included ($\chi^2 = 12.17$, d.f. = 4 with indeterminate specimens; $\chi^2 = 10.85$, d.f. = 2 without undetermined specimens. Both signicant at p < 0.02).
9   Which, incidentally, confirms that the alterations are not the result of taphonomic factors and soil erosion.

PLATES

Plate 11.1: Lower Mesolithic Columbella rustica *from trench FAS.*

Plate 11.2: Lower Mesolithic Columbella rustica *from trenches FAS and H1B.*

Plate 11.3: Lower Mesolithic Columbella rustica *from trench H1A.*

Plate 11.4: Upper Mesolithic Columbella rustica *from trench FAS.*

Plate 11.5: Upper Mesolithic Columbella rustica *from trenches FAS, H1B and H1A.*

Plate 11.6: Final Mesolithic Columbella rustica *from trenches FAN and FAS.*

FAS

198

197

197 (cont.)

196

195

195 (cont.)

194

192

192 (cont.)

191

190

188

187

186

185

184

183

182

180

180 (cont.)

179

177

1 cm

FAS (cont.)

176 174

174 (cont.)

173 172

H1B

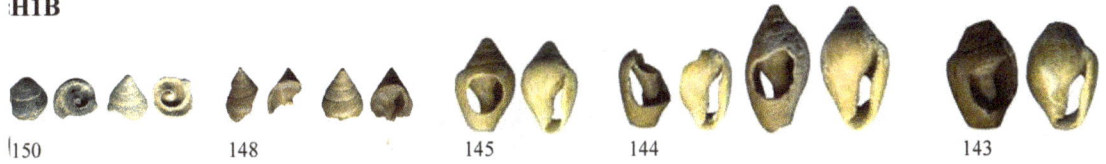

150 148 145 144 143

142 140 139 132

130 128 127

124 123

123 (cont.) 122

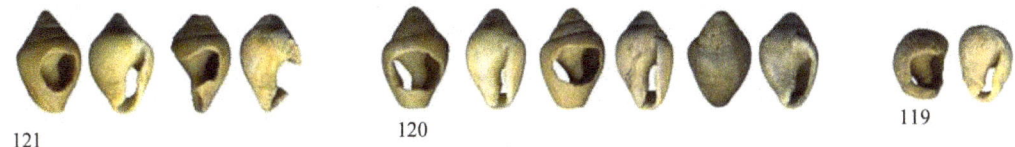

121 120 119

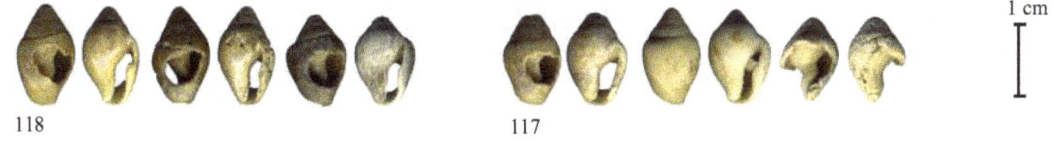

118 117

1 cm

H1A

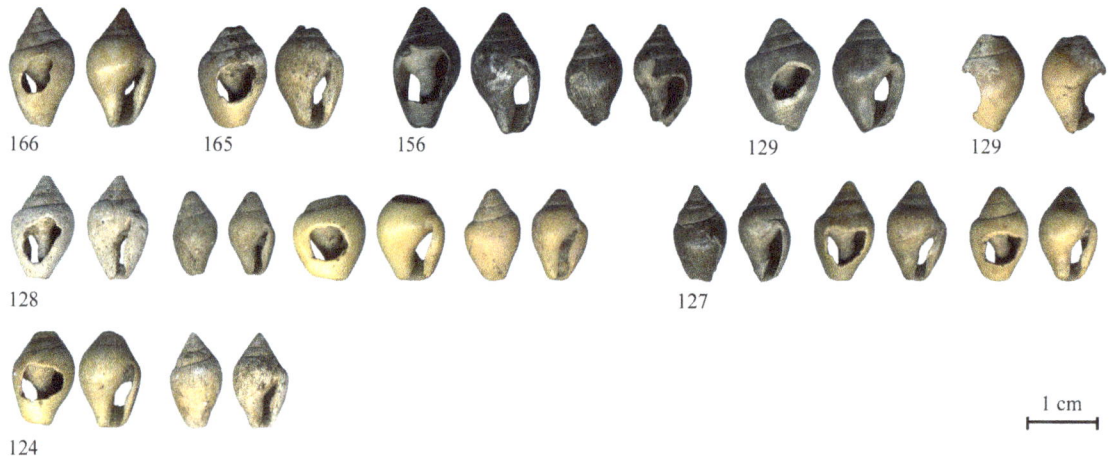

166

165

156

129

129

128

127

124

1 cm

FAS

170   168   167   164

162

161   160

159

159 (cont.)   158

158 (cont.)   157

157 (cont.)   156   1 cm

156 (cont.)

156 (cont.)

156 (cont.)

FAS (cont.)

156 (cont.)

156 (cont.)

H1B

115   114   113

112   111   110

109   108   107

104

H1A

117   116   114   112

108   107   103   101

100

1 cm

FAN

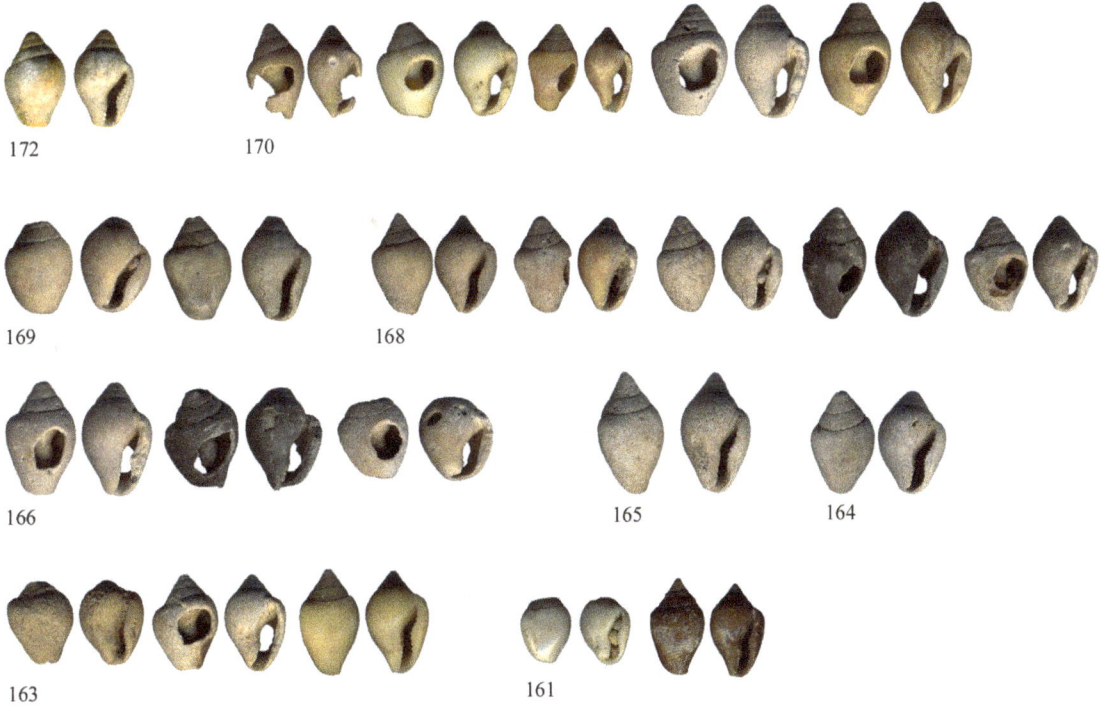

172   170

169   168

166   165   164

163   161

FAS

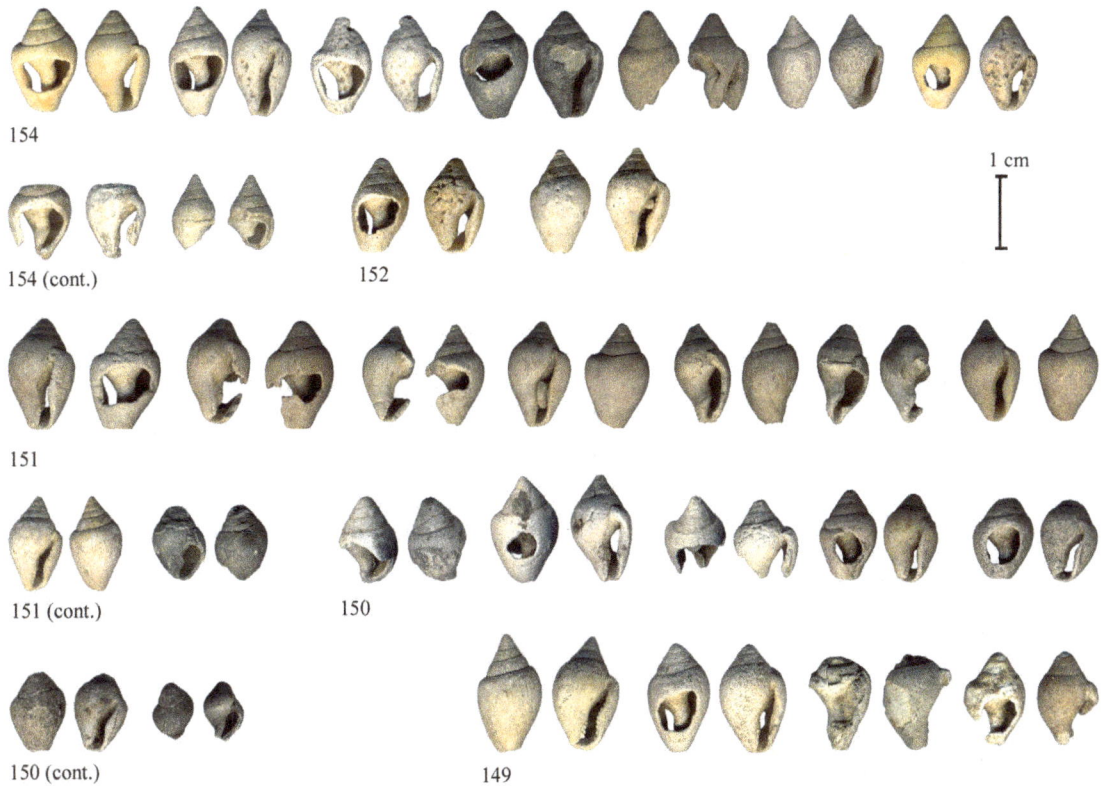

154

1 cm

154 (cont.)   152

151

151 (cont.)   150

150 (cont.)   149

CHAPTER TWELVE

Mesolithic Antalis *sp.: A Homogeneous Assemblage*

More than 400 tusk shells were recovered from the Mesolithic occupation levels (Table 12.1). They heavily concentrate in the Lower Mesolithic (96 %), so we shall consider here all Mesolithic tusk shells as a single assemblage. All *Antalis* sp. segments from trenches H1A, H1B and FAS were individually recorded, described, and the majority also scanned. A single look at Plates 12.1 and 12.2, compared with Plate 4.1, is enough to reveal profound differences between the Palaeolithic and Mesolithic tusk shell assemblages: in the latter, tiny posterior fragments are much rarer, the shells are larger, and the assemblage is far more homogeneous. Given the average size, the traces of intentional segmentation and the presence of ochre on a number of specimens, there can be no doubt that the vast majority of tusk shells was brought into the cave to be used as ornaments, if not as already used ornaments.

Trench	H1A	H1B	FAS	FAN (partial counts)	Total
Phase 7 (LM)	47	72	209	70	398
Inter 7/8	0	1	2		3
Phase 8 (UM)	3	5	6	3	17
Phase 9 (FM)			0	0	0
Total	50	78	217	73	418

Table 12.1: Distribution by trench and phase of Mesolithic Antalis *sp.*

Beads of Variable Length

The difference in average dimensions vis-à-vis the Palaeolithic becomes immediately apparent when the length and maximum diameter of the segments are plotted: in all three trenches the maximum diameter now concentrates between 3 and 4 mm, even if the length of the segments remains highly variable.

The clear differences with the Palaeolithic become even more striking when each variable is considered individually. No statistical test is needed to state that the size distributions differ significantly. For the three variables, length, maximum and minimum diameter, the Mesolithic assemblages approach Gaussian distributions that suggest a single, homogeneous population. The length of the segments, which can be variously reduced by natural or anthropic fracturing, logically shows a wider range of values than do their diameter.

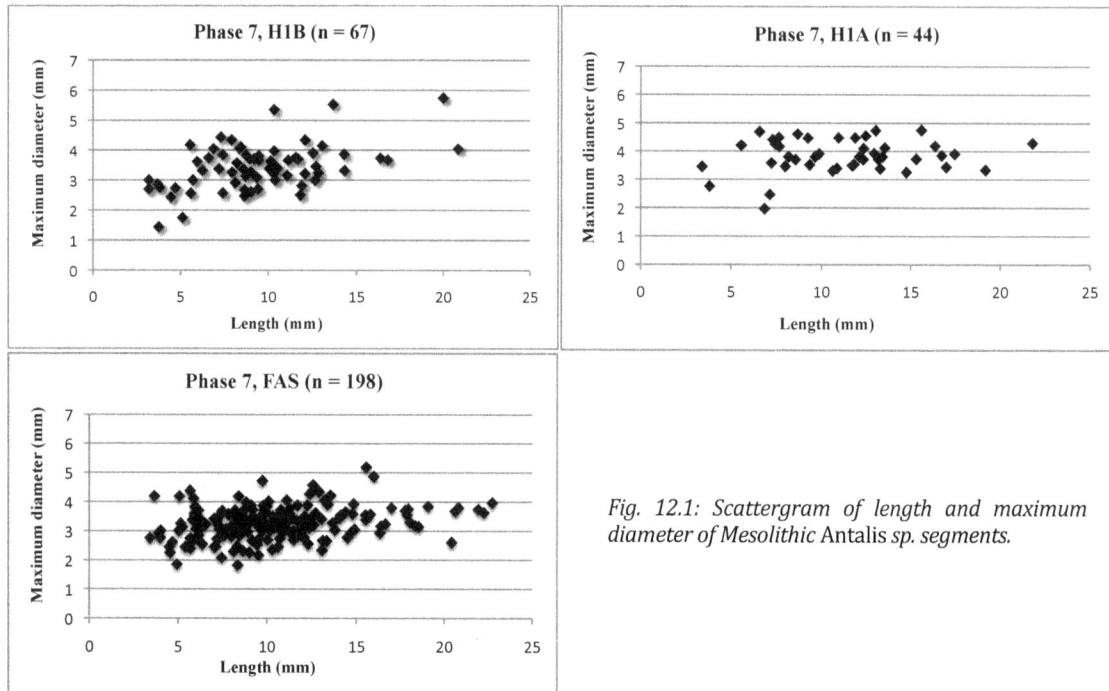

Fig. 12.1: Scattergram of length and maximum diameter of Mesolithic Antalis *sp. segments.*

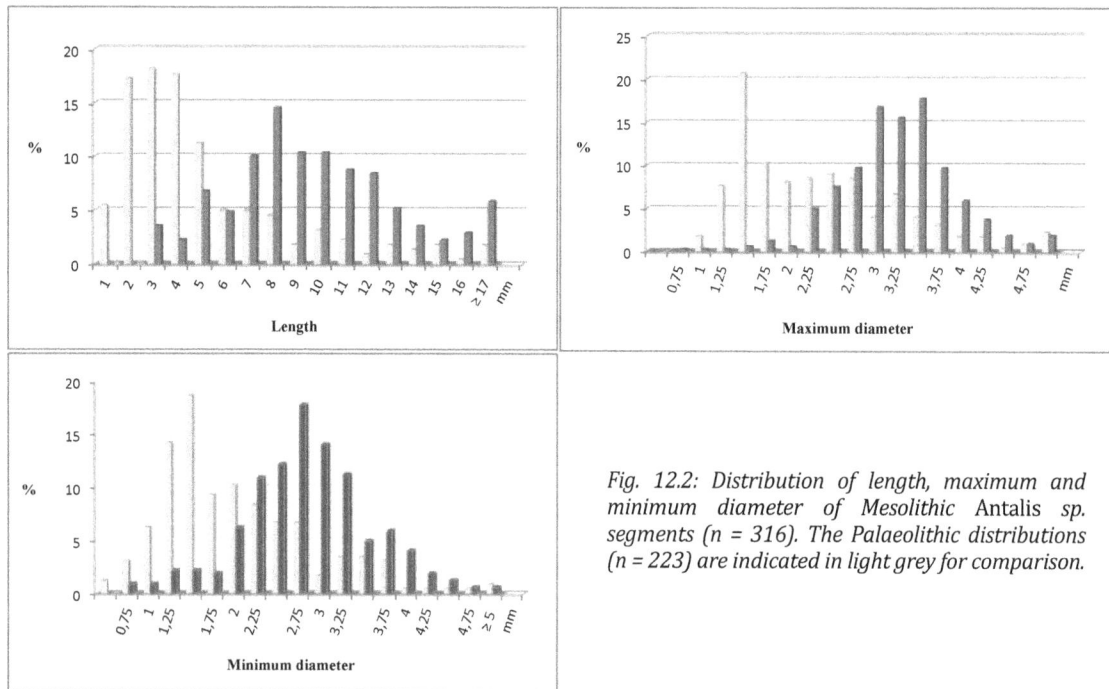

Fig. 12.2: Distribution of length, maximum and minimum diameter of Mesolithic Antalis *sp. segments (n = 316). The Palaeolithic distributions (n = 223) are indicated in light grey for comparison.*

H1B - Lower Mesolithic

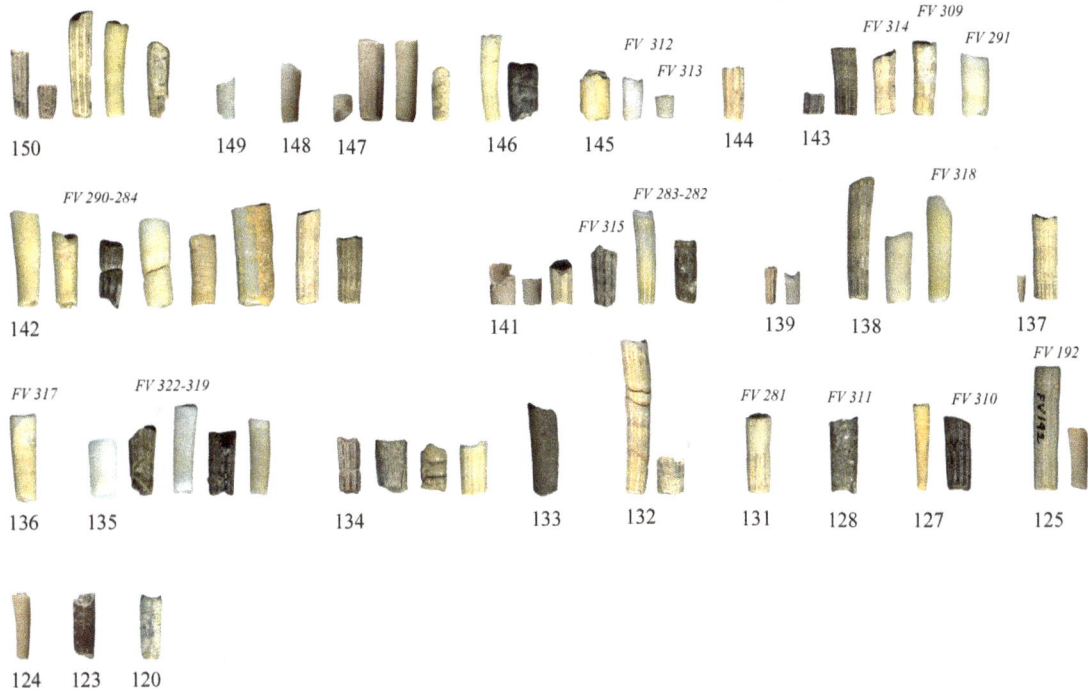

H1A - Lower Mesolithic

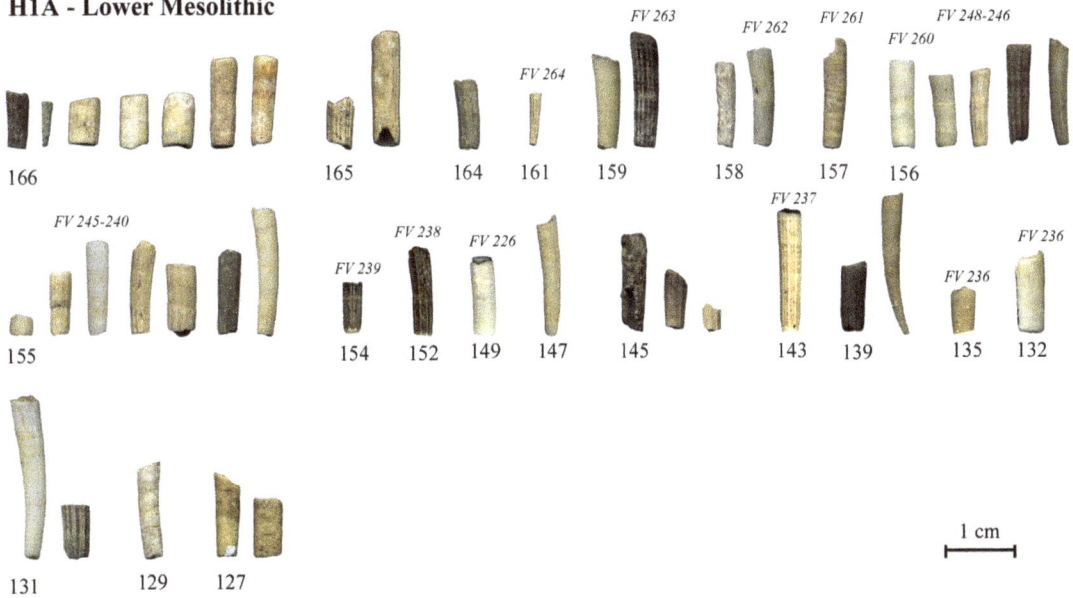

Plate 12.1: Lower Mesolithic Antalis *sp. from H1B and H1A.*

FAS - Lower Mesolithic

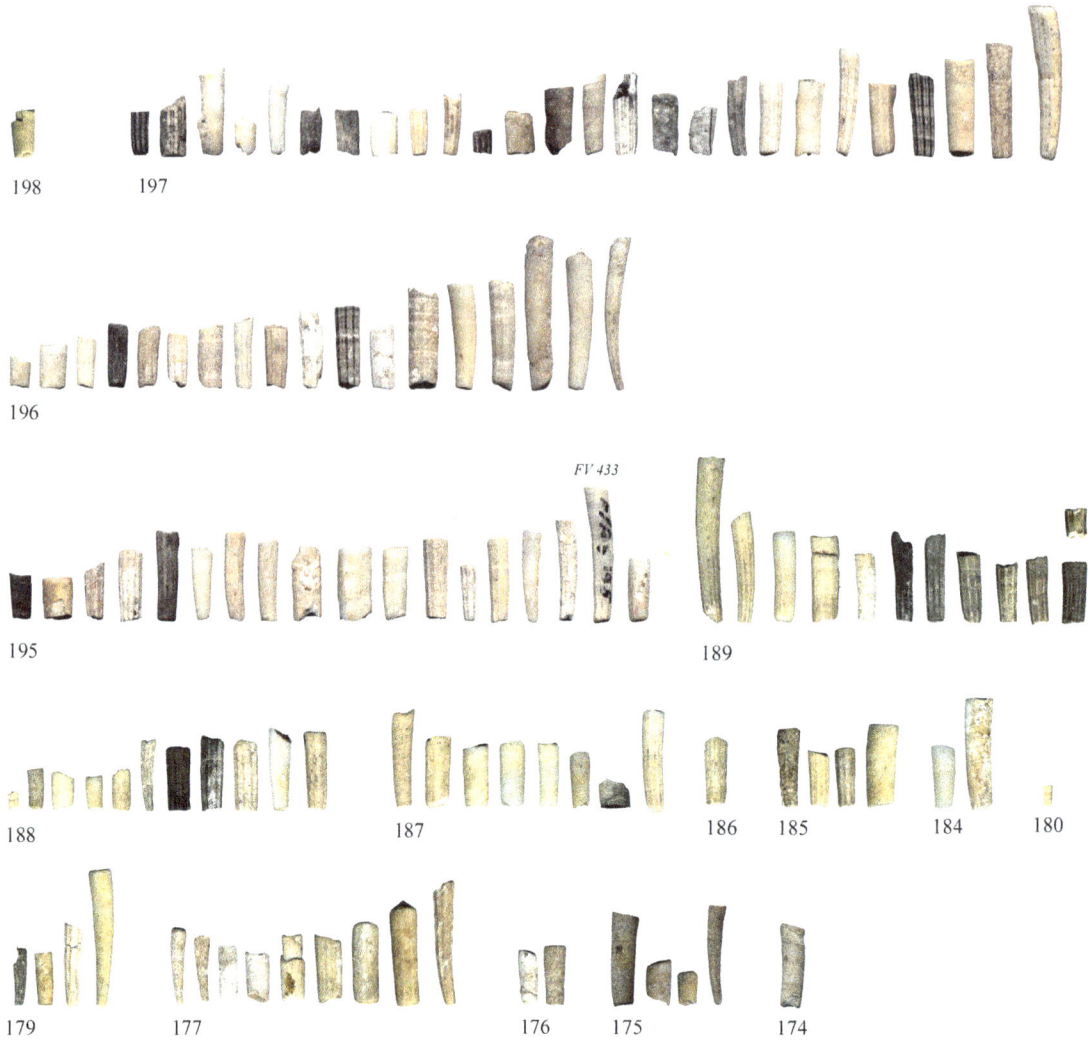

198 197

196

195 189
FV 433

188 187 186 185 184 180

179 177 176 175 174

INTERPHASE 7/8

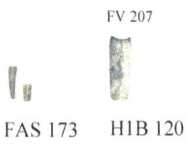

FV 207

FAS 173 H1B 120

UPPER MESOLIHIC

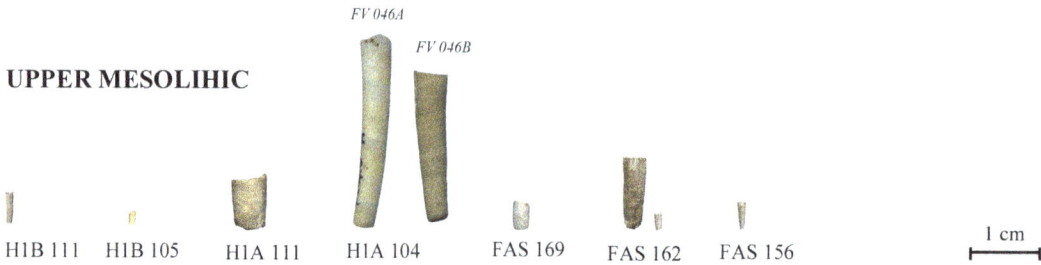

FV 046A
FV 046B

H1B 111 H1B 105 H1A 111 H1A 104 FAS 169 FAS 162 FAS 156

1 cm

Plate 12.2: Sample of Lower Mesolithic Antalis *sp. from FAS and Upper Mesolithic* Antalis *sp. from H1A, H1B and FAS.*

The Species Represented

The metric differences between the Palaeolithic and Mesolithic assemblages cannot be attributed to differences in the species represented, or, to be more precise, to the groups represented since no specific identifications were attempted (*supra*, Chap. 4). Thick-ribbed tusk shells still predominate (ca. 53 %), while thin-ribbed tusk shells and smooth tusk shells represent respectively ca. 30 % and ca. 10 % of the assemblages. There is again evidence that the latter may result from peeling off or from significant abrasion, as shown by specimens that retain a small part of the original ribbed surface (Fig. 12.3).

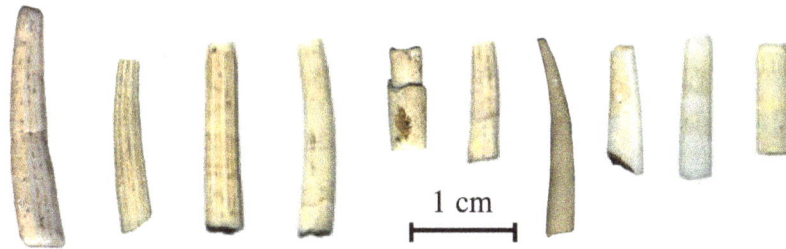

Fig. 12.3: Different type of Antalis *sp. from Mesolithic levels. CAD M. Vanhaeren.*

Representativeness of the Sample

The difference between the Palaeolithic and the Mesolithic assemblages is also unrelated to discrepancies in recovery procedures. S. Payne sorted subsamples of the < 5mm and < 2.8 mm residues from all FAS units, the richest trench for Mesolithic tusk shells, and for approximately every other unit in H1B. In these two trenches at least[1], Palaeolithic and Mesolithic samples are equally representative. However, in contrast with the early Upper Palaeolithic levels, very few tiny posterior fragments were recovered from the Mesolithic smaller fractions of residues. The average increase in size of the Mesolithic tusk shells and the scarcity of tiny segments is not an artifact of sieving or sorting. Rather, the activities that had previously brought numerous small posterior segments into the cave during the Palaeolithic were no longer practised. The few posterior fragments found in Mesolithic deposits may here correspond to manufacturing debris, i.e. segments that were snapped off to allow the threading of beads.

A Collection on Gravelly Beaches

In contrast to the small posterior segments, 'long' segments measuring 10 mm or more in length, are better represented in Mesolithic than in Palaeolithic assemblages. Mesolithic groups were deliberately searching for longer tusk shell segments than were their Palaeolithic predecessors. However, segments over 17 mm remain very rare. Compared with our reference collections (Appendix 3.3), the length distribution of the *Antalis* sp. segments corresponds closely to the sample collected on Fourni beach[2], very close to the site (Fig. 12.4). Fourni is a mixed gravelly-sandy beach, which yielded on average smaller segments than found on the sandy Karathona beach.

Despite the difference in species represented[3], it can be surmised that the Mesolithic occupants of the cave collected their tusk shells on a beach with a granulometry similar to that of modern-day Fourni beach.

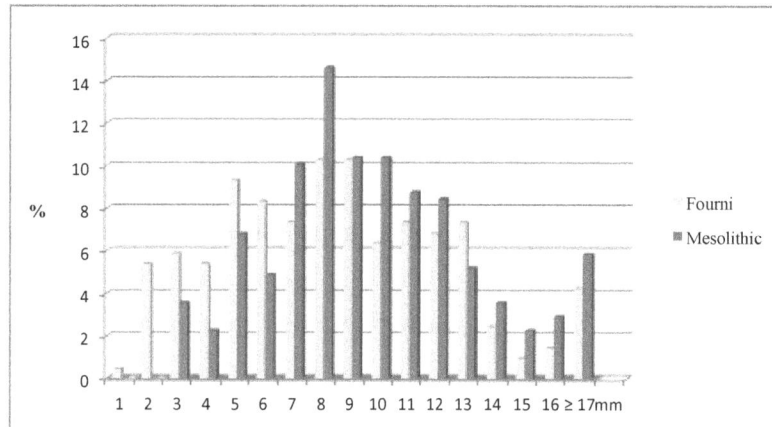

Fig. 12.4: Comparison of the length of the Mesolithic Antalis *sp. segment to our reference collection from Fourni beach, near Franchthi.*

Manufacturing the Beads

A majority of the tusk shells were directly used as they had been picked up on the beach: both extremities bear the heavy smoothing and polishing characteristic of wave and sand abrasion (Fig. 12.5 a-d). In FAS, the best-documented sample for this criterion, segments with marked abrasion and polish on both extremities represent 57% of the unbroken beads (Table 12.2).

| | *Anterior extremity* | | | | Total |
Posterior extremity	Smoothed	Light/partial sm.	No smoothing	Undetermined	
Smoothed	98	3	15	9	125
Light/partial sm.	6	5	3	1	15
No smoothing	20	12	10	1	43
Undetermined	9	2	3	9	23
Total	133	22	31	20	206

Table 12.2: Evidence of abrasion and smoothing on the anterior and posterior extremities of the tusk shells in FAS Lower Mesolithic. Undetermined extremities have suffered from post-depositional breakage or alteration.

Twenty per cent of the tusk shells, however, show a contrast between us smoothed extremity and a straight, non-eroded one. The latter can either be the large anterior extremity or the smaller posterior one, in roughly equal proportions (Fig. 12.5 e-f). More rarely (6%) both extremities show 'fresh' fractures. These fresher break(s) may be due to a natural fracture that occurred shortly before the shell was collected, but can also be part of the manufacturing process. Besides the removal of the narrow posterior aperture, standardisation in the dimensions of tusk shell beads by snapping or sawing has also been recorded in prehistoric contexts (Bar-Yosef Mayer 2010; Taborin 1993; Vanhaeren 2010). The wide range in the lengths of the segments in our assemblages, however, does not suggest that Mesolithic groups from Franchthi were particularly interested in standardised beads. The few examples of tusk shells inserted one into the other one confirm that shells of very different diameter could be threaded side-by-side (Fig. 12.5 g). Alternatively, if Mesolithic people collected tusk shells on gravelly beaches, as suggested by the lengths distribution, they would have frequently found their inner canal blocked by small pebbles that prevented threading. Snapping off the blocked extremity is the easiest solution to this problem.

A further 8% of the shells show a light or partial smoothing and polishing on one or two extremities (Fig. 12.5 h-j). Again, a short-duration natural abrasion should not be excluded, but this alteration can also be due to the friction of the beads one against one another. This may indicate that some tusk shell beads were brought into the cave as already used ornaments. While this is difficult to established with tusk shells, the presence of well-worn Cyclopes and dove shells suggests it was likely.

Changing the Colour: Potential Heat-Treatment and Deposits of Ochre

Artificial modification of the shells' colour has been documented for Franchthi ornaments during the late Upper Palaeolithic, and in the Lower Mesolithic for *Cyclope neritea*. Twenty per cent of the Lower Mesolithic *Antalis* sp. show traces of heating and a corresponding change in colour to grey or black (Pl. 1 and 2). However, the case for intentional heat-treatment is not as strong as with *C. neritea*, since this figure is below the corresponding figures for animal bones and shellfish (Perlès & Vanhaeren 2010, tables 1-2). Nevertheless, meat quarters and shellfish could have been heated for consumption, which cannot be the case with tusk shells. The relatively high proportion of burnt specimens may thus exceed what can be expected for accidentally heated remains.

Another colour modification relates to the presence of an ochre coating, which was observed on a number of specimens (Fig. 12.6). Here again, accidental deposition through contact with an ochreous soil or ochred garment cannot be excluded, but the thick deposit preserved in the furrows of the thick-ribbed tusk shell segments rather suggests intentional colouring.

Reconstructing the nature of the activities involving tusk shells in the—mainly Lower—Mesolithic levels is harder than with Cyclopes or dove shells, since the majority of tusk shells were directly used and threaded as they were found on the beach. In addition, the well-developed natural abrasion and polishing on their extremities masks most potential use-wear traces (Bonnardin 2009; Taborin 1993). It seems, however, that, like Cyclopes and dove shells, the assemblage comprises a mix of already worn and freshly picked beads, sometimes modified in the cave, indicating the production of ornaments or ornamented garments. Whether tusk shells were embroidered on garments or threaded as necklaces is difficult to determine. The developed, lustrous polishing on many of the tusk shells suggests a lengthy contact with fur or skin, but the latter can equally well be that of the bearer or of his or her garments!

NOTES

1   Trench H1A was not water-sieved until unit 161.
2   We learnt recently that the actual name of this beach is Lambayana beach.
3   We only found the thin-ribbed cf. *Antalis vulgaris*.

Fig. 12.5: Various combinations of wear on the extremity of Antalis *sp. segments: (a-d)* Antalis *sp. beads showing intense smoothing on both extremities, (e-f) a contrast between one smoothed and one non-abraded extremity, (g) a smaller tusk shell inserted in the anterior extremity, (h-i) a lightly-smoothed extremity opposed to an intensely smoothed one, or (j) to another lightly-smoothed extremity. a: H1A 156, FV 248. b: H1A 156, FV 245. c: H1A 155, FV 240. d: H1A 152, FV 238. H1A 155, FV 242. f: H1A 154, FV 239. g: H1A 149, FV 226. h: H1A 104, FV 046A. i: H1A 155, FV 241. j: H1A 135, FV 236. No scale. Photographs M. Vanhaeren, CAD C.P.*

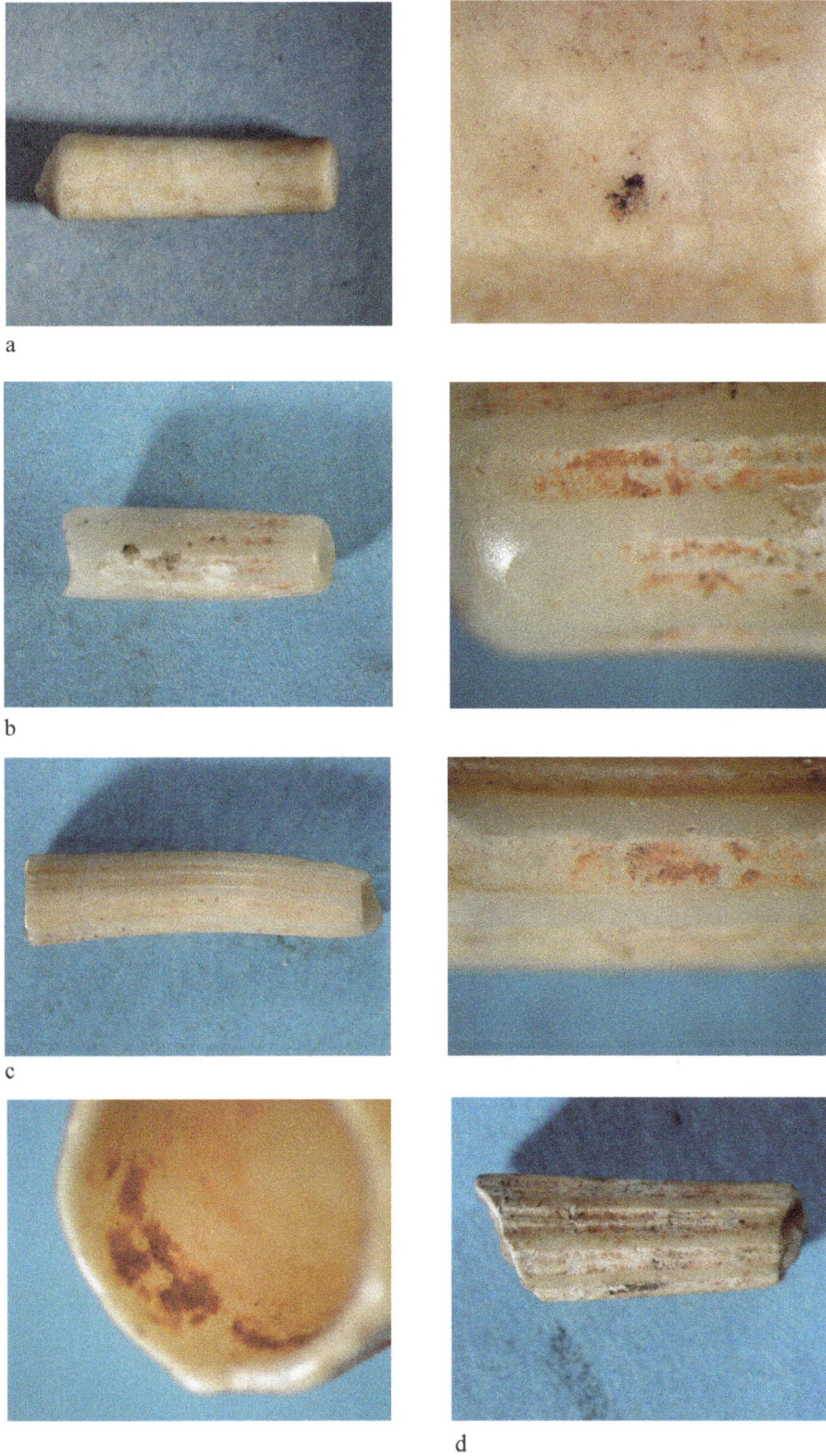

Fig. 12.6: Antalis sp. segments with remains of ochre. a: FAS 177. b: FAS 195 FV 433. c: FAS 195 (three shots). d: FAS 195. No scale. Photographs M. Vanhaeren.

CHAPTER THIRTEEN

Rare Mesolithic Ornament Types

Perforated Pebbles (M. Miller and C. Perlès)

Perforated pebbles, or "wide-drilled pebbles", constitute a new type of ornaments in the Franchthi repertoire and the first stone ornaments. Nine were recovered from Lower Mesolithic levels (Phase 7), and one at the interface of Phases 7 and 8 (Plate 13.1). None can be attributed with certainty to the Upper or Final Mesolithic (Table 13.1). However, one specimen (Fig. 13.1), near-identical to the Lower Mesolithic examples, was uncovered in H 50 (FS 162), a unit attributed by W. Farrand (2000: 50-51) to both the Upper Mesolithic (Stratum W3) and the Final Mesolithic (Stratum X1). According to the description of the sediment in the excavation notebook and to the section (Jacobsen & Farrand 1987, plate 22), it could also date to the Initial Neolithic. Large perforated pebbles indeed occur sporadically in Neolithic strata, and we shall present them in a forthcoming volume[1].

The pebbles were collected on a beach, and were carefully selected for their raw material since only limestone was used[2], as well as for their unusual dark colour, regular shape and flat section. The finer grained examples are also highly polished. Their size, on the other hand, does not seem to have mattered, since their lengths range from ca. 1.5 cm to nearly 4 cm, and even more for unfinished pendants. Their shape also varies, from round to elliptical. These dark flat limestone pebbles are uncommon on the beaches near Franchthi, where most pebbles are light coloured and thicker. Interestingly, the two complete unfinished specimens are larger and thicker than the perforated specimens (Pl. 1, H1A 132 and FAS 191), which suggests that the pendants makers did not find appropriate pebbles and abandoned their attempt.

Fig. 13.1: Perforated pebble (with an attempt at a second perforation) from uncertain context: H 50, FS 162.

H1A 132 FS 329

FAN 211 FS 800

FAS 176 FS 794

FAS 174 FS 705

H1B 121 FS 523

FAS 184 FS 704

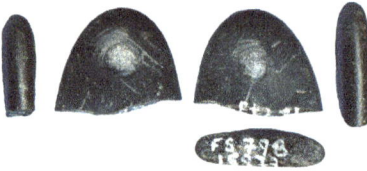

FAN 225 FS 798

H1A 132 FS 330

1 cm

FAS 191 FS 731

Plate 13.1: Perforated pebbles and unfinished specimens from the Lower Mesolithic.

Unit	Catalogue number	Phasing	Raw material	L (cm)	W (cm)	Th (cm)	Condition	Observations
H1A 132	FS 329	Phase 7	Limestone	1.36	1.17	0.3	Broken	Broken on perforation. Worn.
H1A 132	FS 330	Phase 7	Limestone	4.28	2.21	1.08	Intact	Unfinished: preparation for perforation on one face.
H1B 121	FS 523	Phase 7	Limestone	3	1.5	0.34	Broken	Broken on perforation. Worn.
FAS 191	FS 731	Phase 7	Limestone	4.46	2.6	1.11	Intact	Unfinished bifacial perforation.
FAS 184	FS 704	Phase 7	Limestone	5.58	1.47	0.71	Intact	Broken on 1st perforation, worn, then 2nd perforation and worn again.
FAS 176	FS 794	Phase 7	Limestone	na	na	> 0.5	Fragmentary	One half of perforation preserved. Worn.
FAS 174	FS 705	Inter-phase 7/8	Limestone	2.32	1.21	0.4	Intact	Hourglass perforation Worn.
FAN 225	FS 798	Phase 7	Limestone	1.49	1.85	0.48	Broken	Unfinished hourglass perforation
FAN 219	FS 799	Phase 7	Limestone	1.31	0.74	0.44	Fragmentary	Hourglass perforation
FAN 211	FS 800	Phase 7	Limestone	1.12	0.92	0.39	Broken	Broken on perforation. Worn.
H 50	FS 162	Phase 8, 9 or 10 ?	Limestone	3.28	2.54	0.42	Intact	Hourglass perforation. Worn. Second unfinished perforation.

Table 13.1: List of Mesolithic perforated pebbles.

These unfinished pendants and the manufacturing traces left around their perforations (Fig. 13.2) allow a precise reconstruction of the manufacturing sequence. A small circular area was first prepared by deep pecking and sometimes scratching on both faces, to ensure that the borer would not slip on the smooth natural surface. The pebble was then held in one hand and the borer, a sturdy chert borer (Fig. 13.3), held in the other hand, was placed in the small depression created by pecking. The tool was moved by oscillatory rotation of the wrist, at a more or less oblique angle; the process left characteristic semi-circular score-marks on the perforations. The same tool was then used on the other face of the pebble. Placing the tool exactly opposite to the first drilling area was not easy; the resulting perforations are highly biconical and often asymmetrical, of an average diameter of 7 mm on the surface of the pebble but only 3 mm at the centre of the perforation. We did not find appropriate pebbles and were not able to reproduce the manufacturing of these pendants, but our attempts show that the whole process must have been time consuming. This basically rules out potential functional uses of these pebbles: naturally perforated pebbles are plentiful on beaches nowadays, and the presence in a Mesolithic unit (G 25, FS 143, Fig. 13. 4) of an unworn pebble, perforated by a lithofagous mollusc, shows they could have been found in the past. The hand-made perforation was essential to the significance and value of these pieces. Two pendants retain ochre specks on the perforation but not on the surface (Fig. 13.5, FAN 211, FAS 174). They must thus have been strung on a thick ochred thread.

Surprisingly, these stone pendants appear to have easily broken, unless they were intentionally broken. Only two were recovered intact, and of these, one (FAS 184, FS 704) shows the remnants of a broken perforation. A second hourglass perforation was then made below the broken one, which shows that these ornaments were valuable to their bearer. All perforated pebbles bear use-wear traces (Fig. 13.5), but the latter are light enough that they did not obliterate the scoring within the perforations. As was the case for perforated shell ornaments, we are thus dealing with a combination of pendants in the process of manufacturing, of already worn specimens and of broken specimens. Despite the differences in raw material, manufacturing time and probably use (it is doubtful they were embroidered on garments), the pebble pendants are part of the same activities as the other ornaments: already worn pendants were brought into the cave, broken (?), and probably replaced by new ones that left the site.

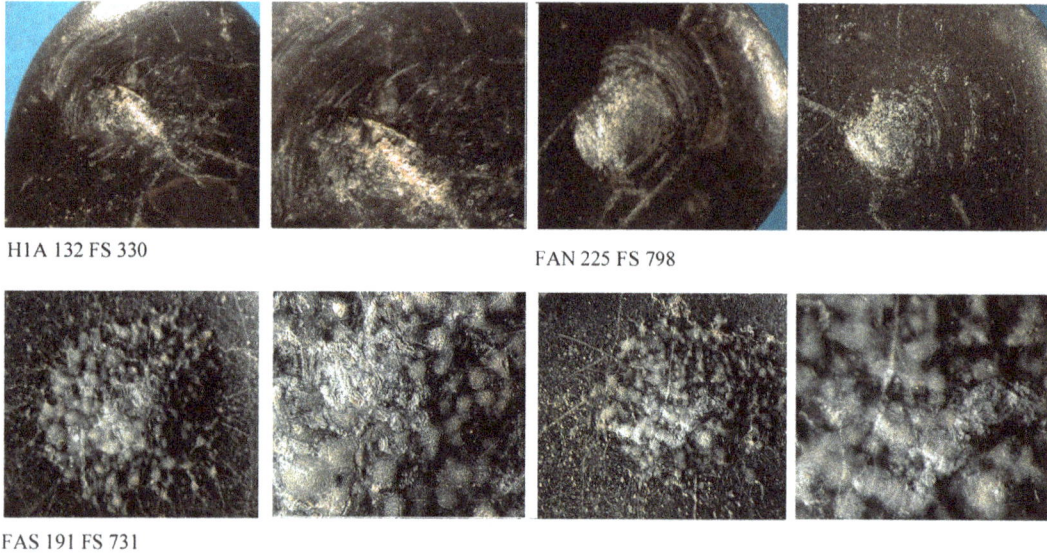

H1A 132 FS 330

FAN 225 FS 798

FAS 191 FS 731

Fig. 13.2: Details of manufacturing traces on unfinished Lower Mesolithic perforated pebbles.

1 cm

Fig. 13.3: Chert borer from H1B 142, which could have been used to perforate pebbles.

1 cm

Fig. 13.4: Naturally perforated and unworn pebble (G1 25, FS 143).

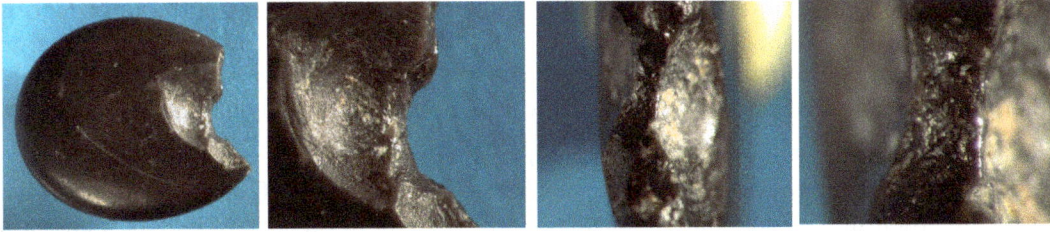

H1A 132 FS 329

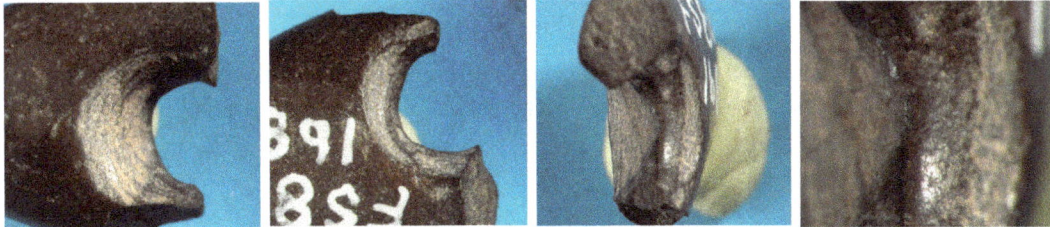

FAN 211 FS 800

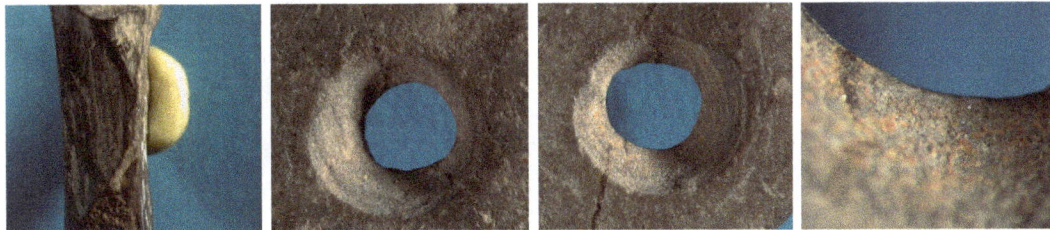

FAS 176   FAS 174 FS 705

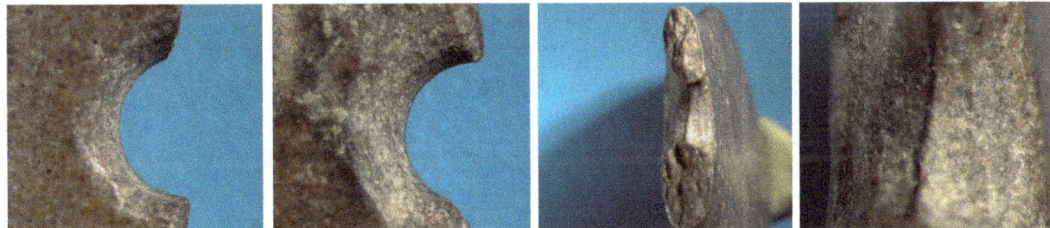

H1B 121 FS 523

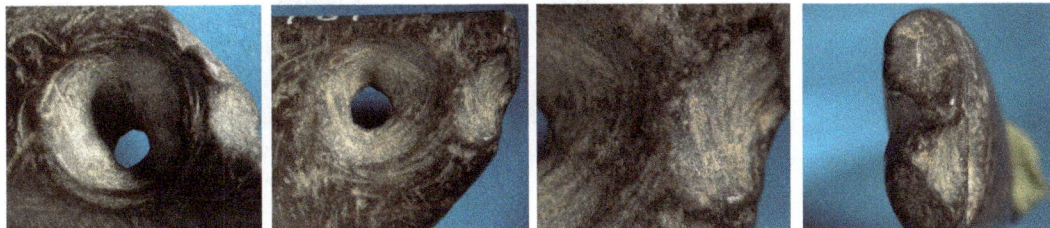

FAS 184 FS 704

Fig. 13.5: Details of use-wear and ochre on Lower Mesolithic perforated pebbles.

A Problematic Group: Bird Bone Beads or Tusk Shells?

Four tubular beads from H1B 150, including one badly burnt and fragmented specimen, and one bead from H1B 135, have been identified as possible bird bone beads. Without laboratory analyses, which proved difficult to implement, the possibility of unusually large non-ribbed *Antalis* sp. cannot either be ruled out, and both identifications were supported by different specialists.

We shall leave the question open for readers to decide, and present the documentation we have. Three remarks may be relevant. On the one hand, the dimensions of the beads plead in favour of bird bone: their maximum diameter equals or exceeds that of the largest indisputable *Antalis* sp. (Table 13.2). The irregular thickness of their walls, possibly due to significant use-wear, would also correspond better to bone than to shell. Conversely, the cracked appearance of their surfaces is similar to that of several burnt *Antalis* sp. (Fig. 13.6).

All five beads show well-developed use-wear, with rounded or flattened extremities, often with a sinuous edge (Figs. 13.7 – 13.8). The surface of the beads is smooth and polished, with no trace of any ribs.

Unit	Catalogue number	Original determination	L (cm)	Max. diameter (cm)	Min. diameter (cm)	Observations
H1B 150	na	Bird bone bead	1.61	0.54	0.49	
H1B 150	na	Bird bone bead	na	na	na	Fragmented
H1B 150	FV 357	*Antalis* sp.	1.03	0.53	0.48	
H1B 150	FV 356	*Antalis* sp.	2.0	0.57	0.51	
H1B 135	na	Bird bone bead	0.94	0.41	0.38	

Table 13.2: Dimensions of Lower Mesolithic potential bird bone beads.

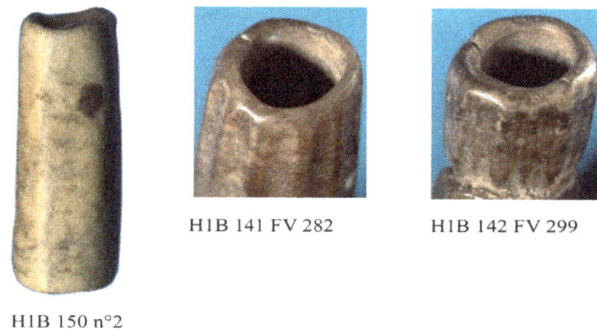

H1B 141 FV 282   H1B 142 FV 299

H1B 150 n°2

Fig. 13.6: Comparison of the cracked surface of potential bird bone bead from H1B 150 n°2 with two thick ribbed heated Antalis sp.

H1B 150 N°2

1 cm

a   b   c

d   e   f

H1B 150 FV 356

1 cm

a   b   c

d   e   f

Fig. 13.7: Top: tubular bead from H1B 150, n°2. a: scan of the bead. b and c: macrophotographs x 12. d, e: details one extremity, x 32. f: detail of the second extremity, x 32. Photographs: S. Ménard. Bottom: tubular bead from H1B 150, FV 356. A: scan of the bead. B: macrophotograph. c and d: details of the surface. e and f: details of the extremities. No scale. Photographs M. Vanhaeren.

H1B 150 FV 357

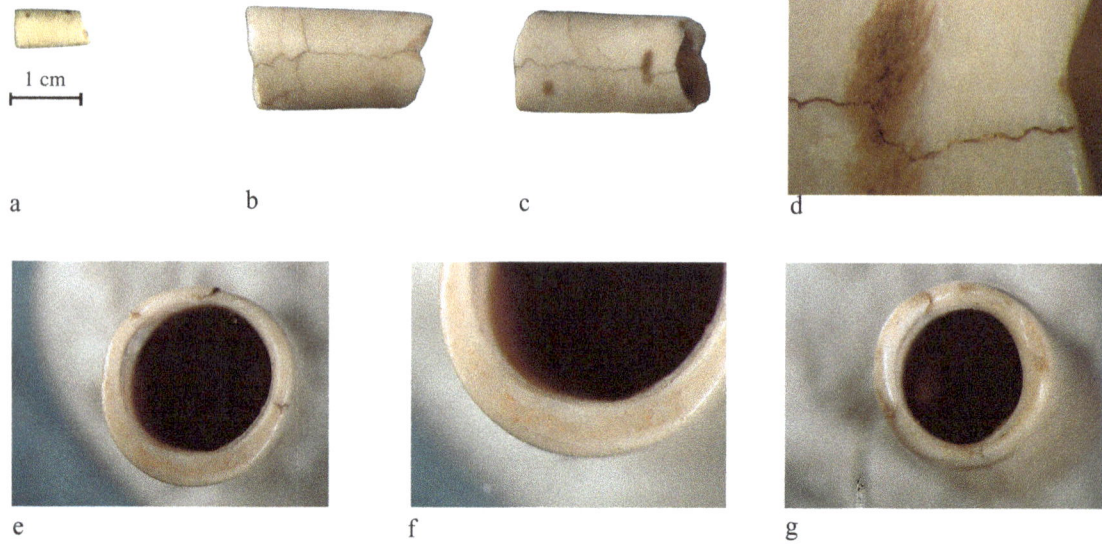

H1B 135

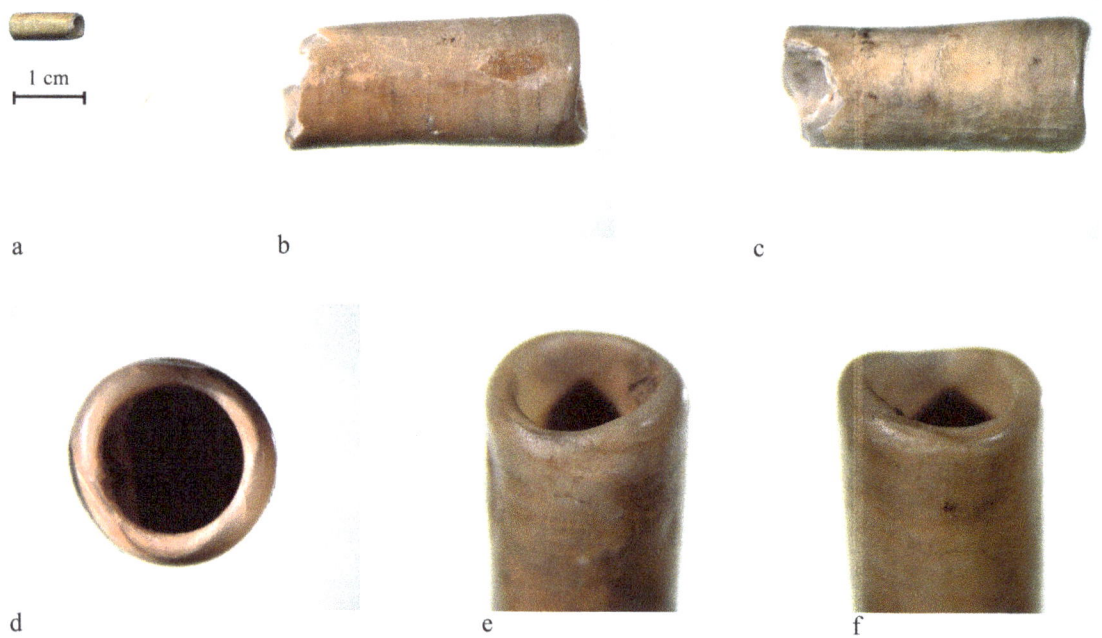

Fig. 13.8: Top: tubular bead from H1B 150, FV 357. a: scan of the bead. b and c: macrophotographs. d: detail of the surface. e and f: details of one extremity. g: detail of the second extremity. No scale. Photographs M. Vanhaeren. Bottom: tubular bead from H1B 135. A: scan of the bead. b and c: macrophotographs x 12. d-f: details of the preserved extremity x 32. Photographs S. Ménard.

A Single Perforated *Conus mediterraneus*: Mistake or Fancy?

A single perforated *Conus mediterraneus* was found in a Final Mesolithic unit from FAN (FAN 170). With its invasive perforation on the dorsal face, it mimics a dove shell with a broken spire and the subtle difference can only be observed on the ventral face, with the more rectilinear aperture. There can be little doubt that it actually belongs to the *Columbella rustica* ornament category, but its presence is interesting: it shows that *Conus mediterraneus* was available to the Franchthi Mesolithic inhabitants, but that they were careful not to collect them, and even more so, not to perforate them. Given the marked morphological similarity between *C. rustica* and *C. mediterraneus* and the ease with which they can be found on the same beaches, we had already wondered why they were not used during the Palaeolithic and the Mesolithic. Our experiments show that, in order to perforate cones, one has to use more gentle techniques than with dove shells: the shell is more brittle, and shatters easily under direct percussion. This single specimen, nevertheless, proves that they could have been used alongside dove shells, but were deliberately ignored.

Fig. 13.9: Perforated Conus mediterraneus *from FAN 170 (Final Mesolithic).*

We also recovered rare isolated *Conus mediterraneus* spires, naturally perforated. They could be mistaken for beads, but they occur frequently on beaches (Appendix 3.4) and we have no evidence they were used. Consequently, they have here been considered as accidental introductions.

A Lonely Fragment of *Glycymeris* sp.

A fragmentary specimen of *Glycymeris* sp. (FV 368) was recovered from H1B 133, a Lower Mesolithic unit. Like its Palaeolithic counterparts, it must have been a small specimen. The umbo is preserved and bears the characteristic perforation of Palaeolithic *Glycymeris*, by abrasion (Fig. 13.10). Again like several Palaeolithic specimens from Franchthi, it had been heated and the perforation is rounded by use. There are no traces of deposits within the shell and this very small fragment cannot help to solve the problem of the status of perforated dog-shells: were they ornaments or containers (Chap. 6)?

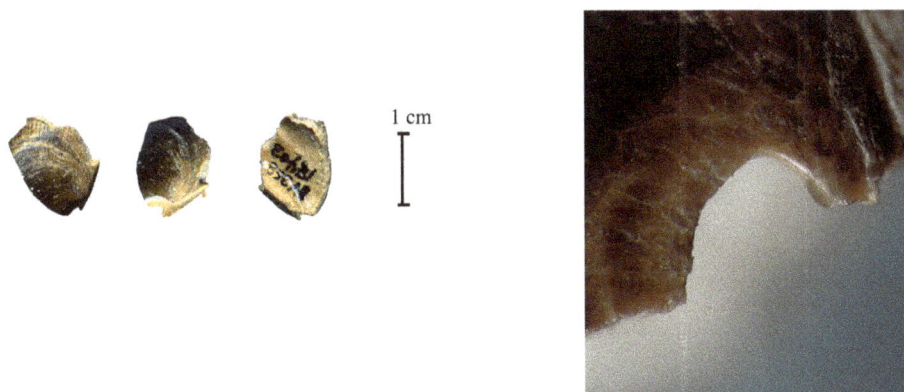

Fig. 13.10: Fragment of Lower Mesolithic perforated Glycymeris *sp. and details of perforation and use-wear (H1B 133, FV 368).*

A Note on Shells Species that We Did *Not* Considered to Be Ornamental

Several marine shell taxa, frequently used as ornaments in Palaeolithic or Mesolithic sites (Taborin 1993), have not here been considered as ornamental. The reasons are the same as for the Palaeolithic assemblages: none of these species yielded any specimen with an anthropic perforation. Several taxa or species are common to Palaeolithic assemblages: *Patella* sp., *Cerithium vulgatum*, *Phorcus* (= *Monodonta* = *Osilinus*) *turbinatus*, *Gibbula divaricata*, *Gibbula rarilineata* and *Hexaplex* (= *Murex*) *trunculus*. All are edible, even if some are not familiar as shellfish (Chap. 6). To these species we should add rare *Pinna nobilis* and *Pecten* sp. fragments, as well as a Cypraea. They may also have been eaten, or simply accidentally brought into the cave with seaweeds.

NOTES

1   M. Miller (1997) had discussed all "wide-drilled" pebbles, from Neolithic or from uncertain contexts, with the Mesolithic specimens given the morphometric and technical similarities.
2   All pebbles were tested with hydrochloric acid and all showed strong reactions.

CHAPTER FOURTEEN

Abundance and Restriction: An Overview of the Franchthi Mesolithic Ornament Assemblages

The three most prominent features of the Mesolithic ornament assemblages are, without doubt, their sheer abundance, their homogeneity, and, as in the Palaeolithic, their extremely restricted range. The high number of ornaments and ornamental species renders Franchthi exceptional in the context of the European Mesolithic, and we shall first discuss the factors that may account for this abundance. We shall then explore the diachronic variability, somehow hidden behind an overwhelming homogeneity, and assess its significance. Finally, to identify the potential cultural elements in the choice of species and their restricted range, the Franchthi assemblages will be set in their broader Mesolithic Mediterranean context.

Why So Many Ornaments?

Variations in the Density of Ornaments to the Volume of Sediment

We recovered about 11,000 ornaments and ornamental shells from the Mesolithic deposits from only four trenches (Tables 14.1 and 14.2). As discussed previously (Chap. 9), we know this figure to be below the original number of specimens. This represents more than a ten-fold increase when compared with the Palaeolithic. The Lower Mesolithic, the richest phase, alone yielded more than eight times the total number of Palaeolithic ornaments and ornamental shells. It is true, however, that the volume of Lower Mesolithic sediments excavated also greatly exceeds that of any other phase in the sequence (Tables 7.1 and 14.1*)*. Is the high number of ornaments, thus, simply a factor of the volume of sediments?

The ratio of ornaments to sediment, expressed by the NISP/litres of sediment, can be calculated for H1B and FAS, the two trenches that have been both water-sieved and completely sorted[1]. Figure 14.1 shows that there is indeed a weak correlation between the two variables: there are more ornaments and ornamental shells when the volume of sediment excavated is greater, i.e. in the Lower Mesolithic (Phase 7). Explaining the number of ornaments by a straightforward relationship to the volume of sediments is, however, unsatisfactory.

First, the sediments of Phases 7 and 8 are rich in material of anthropogenic origin, including massive land-snail middens and large quantities of ash (Farrand 2000; Whitney-Desautels in prep.). The sheer volume of sediment does not necessarily entail more intense or longer occupations of the cave and a consequent higher number of ornaments deposited than during previous periods. There is actually no correlation, over the entire Palaeolithic and Mesolithic sequence, between the volume of sediment excavated and the number of ornaments. The best comparison to the Lower and Upper Mesolithic shell middens is Palaeolithic Phase 5, which is also a land-snail midden (Fig. 14.2). In H1B, the volume of sediment from Mesolithic Phase 7 is two and a half times larger than in Phase 5 (3339 litres versus 1289 litres, respectively), while the number of ornaments and ornamental shells is ten times higher (2290 in Phase 7, versus 200 in Phase 5).

Phase	Units	Vol. sediment (liters)	*Cyclope* sp.	*Antalis* sp.	*Columbella rustica*	*Glycymeris glycymeris*	*Conus mediterraneus*	Bird bone beads ?	Perforated pebbles	Total
H1A	(No water-sieving)									
7	(166) 165-122	na	1087	47	16	0	0	0	2	1152
7 x 8	121, 120, 118	na	33	0	0	0	0	0	0	33
8	(119) 117-100	na	258	3	17	0	0	0	0	278
	Total		1378	50	33	0	0	0	2	1463
H1B										
7	150-122	3339	2114	72	39	1	0	5	0	2231
7 x 8	121-117	714	168	1	12	0	0	0	1	182
8	(116) 115-104	810	372	5	26	0	0	0	0	403
	Total		2654	78	77	1	0	5	1	2816
FAS										
7	(198-196) 195-174	6924	3222	209	81	0	0	0	4	3516
7 x 8	173-170	444	71	2	2	0	0	0	0	75
8	169-155	1090	788	6	89	0	0	0	0	883
9	(154) 153 (152) 151-149	982	175	0	45	0	0	0	0	220
	Total		4256	217	217	0	0	0	4	4694
FAN										
7	230-197 partial sorting		763	70	26	0	0	0	3	862
7 x 8	196-193 (192)		64	0	0	0	0	0	0	64
8	191-186 (185) 184-175 partial sorting		710	3	95	0	0	0	0	808
9	174-173 (172) 171-169 (168) 167-164	1449	90	0	36	0	1	0	0	127
	Total		1627	73	157	0	1	0	3	1861
H1A, H1B, FAS, FAN										
7			7186	398	162	1	0	5	9	7761
7 x 8			336	3	14	0	0	0	1	354
8			2128	17	227	0	0	0	0	2372
9 (FAS & FAN)			265	0	81	0	1	0	0	347
	Total		9915	418	484	1	1	5	9	10834
G1										
7			"Enormous quantities"							
8, 9 or 10			100		44					
H ped										
8, 9 or 10			15		5					

Table 14.1: General count of Mesolithic ornamental species and ornaments.

Phase	Units	Cyclope sp. perforated	Cyclope sp. unperforated	Cyclope sp. indeterminate	Antalis sp.	C. rustica perforated	C. rustica unperforated	C. rustica indeterminate	Bone bead?	G. glycymeris perforated	C. mediterraneus perforated	Perforated pebble
H1A												
7	(166) 165-122	na	na	na	47	10	5	0	0	0	0	2
7 x 8	121, 120, 118	na	na	na	0	0	0	0	0	0	0	0
8	(119) 117-100	na	na	na	3	11	4	2	0	0	0	0
	Total				50	21	9	2	0	0	0	0
H1B*												
7	150-122	1059	623	251	72	30	3	6	5	1	0	0
7 x 8	121-117	97	49	21	1	9	2	1	0	0	0	1
8	115-104	156	84	21	5	15	5	3	0	0	0	0
	Total	1312	756	293	78	54	10	10	5	1	0	1
FAS												
7	(198-196) 195-174	na	na	na	209	54	13	14	0	0	0	4
7 x 8	173-170	na	na	na	2	0	2	0	0	0	0	0
8	169-155	na	na	na	6	51	30	8	0	0	0	0
9	(154) 153, 151-149	na	na	na	0	24	15	6	0	0	0	0
	Total				217	129	60	28	0	0	0	4
FAN												
7	230, 219-197 partial sorting	na	na	na	na	na	na	na	0	0	0	2
7 x 8	196-193	na	na	na	na	na	na	na	0	0	0	0
8	195-175 partial sorting	na	na	na	na	na	na	na	0	0	0	0
9	174-173 (172)-164	26	12	12	0	19	14	3	0	0	1	0

*Table 14.2: Detailed counts of perforated and unperforated Mesolithic ornamental specimens
* Data for perforated or unperforated* Cyclope neritea *are missing for three units.*

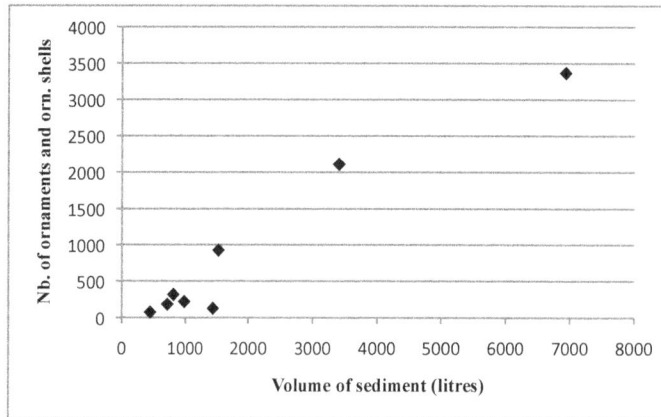

Fig. 14.1: Relation between the volume of sediment excavated and the number of ornaments and ornamental shells in the Mesolithic phases and interphases of trenches FAS and H1B.

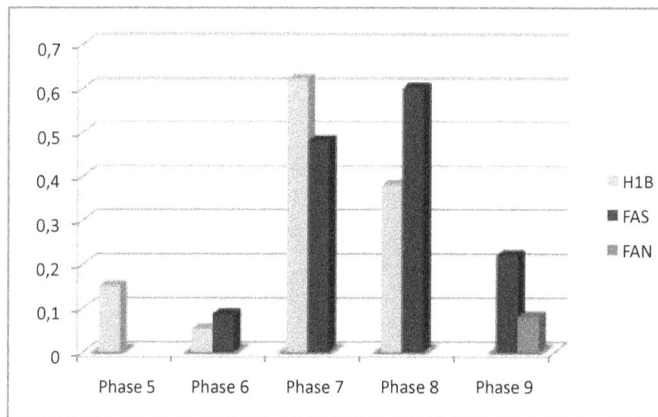

Fig. 14.2: Ratio of ornaments and ornamental shells (NISP) to sediment (litres) from Phase 5 to Phase 9.

Second, the correlation suggested by Fig. 14.1 is not one-to-one: the number of ornaments does not increase arithmetically according the litres of sediment excavated. The ratio of ornaments and ornamental shells to sediment varies from phase to phase and from trench to trench (Fig. 14.2). It is lowest for the Final Mesolithic (Phase 9) in both trenches, highest in H1B during the Lower Mesolithic (Phase 7), but highest in FAS during the Upper Mesolithic (Phase 8). This demonstrates important spatial and diachronic variations in the density of ornaments and leads us to reject the volume of sediment as the main factor behind the abundance of ornaments.

Detailed faunal counts are not available for the Mesolithic at the time of writing, so we cannot use this additional proxy to evaluate diachronic variation in the intensity of cave use. For the Palaeolithic, the ratios of ornaments to volume of sediment and to mammal bones showed very similar structures (Perlès 2016a). The abundance of stone tools is another potential indicator of the intensity of activity within the cave: there is no correlation between the total number of stone tools and ornamental shells for H1A and H1B (Phases 7 and 8), FAS (Phases 7–9) and FAN (Phase 9): Pearson's R = 0.29, p = 0.47[2].

If the variation in the density of ornaments and ornamental shells, as well as the high number of ornaments in Phase 7, cannot be explained by the intensity of activities in the cave, should it be instead related to the presence of human burials in the cave?

Ornaments and Human Burials

More than 20 years ago, Newell and his colleagues, in their analysis of European Mesolithic ornament variability, isolated a small group of sites conspicuously richer in ornaments than all the others, which they called the "Coastal Graves" (Newell *et al.* 1990: 136). Téviec and Hoëdic in Brittany (Péquart *et al.* 1937; Péquart & Saint-Just Péquart 1954), for instance, yielded, like Franchthi, thousands of ornaments, in sharp contrast with most open-air settlements, caves or even inland graves. More recent discoveries, however, lead one to nuance this opposition: Epipalaeolithic or Mesolithic burials rich in ornaments are also found some distance from the coast (e.g. Cristiani & Borić 2012; Duday *et al.* 1998; d'Errico & Vanhaeren 2000; Radovanović 1996; Rigaud 2011). Mesolithic burials, in addition, are not systematically associated with ornaments, and many contained neither ornaments nor grave goods (Radovanović 1996; Valentin *et al.* 2008; Verjux 2007).

Franchthi should clearly be included in the group of "Coastal Graves": it is a coastal site, and, besides the pit burial of a young adult male in G1 60, at the base of the Lower Mesolithic, T. Cullen was able to reconstruct the former presence of a burial ground, unrecognised during excavation, and located half a metre lower, in unit G1 65[3]. This burial ground comprised the partial remains of at least six inhumations: one infant, one adult male, three adult females, and an adolescent. It also yielded the remains of two cremations (Cullen 1995; Cullen & Papathanasiou, in prep.). Five human bones scatters in the vicinity (G1 62–65) derive from at least two other individuals. No burials were found in any other trench, but isolated bones or small groups of bones or teeth were also found in Lower Mesolithic units from H, H1A, H1B, FAS and FAN, totalling 14 occurrences[4]. In contrast, Upper Mesolithic deposits yielded the remains of only one possible infant burial (FAN 179) and three securely dated bone scatters, while in the Final Mesolithic only two bone scatters were found. It is consequently tempting to tie the high number of ornaments in the Lower Mesolithic to the human burials, especially considering N. Shackleton's observation concerning the "enormous numbers" of *Cyclope neritea* recovered from the Mesolithic deposits in G1 (Shackleton N. 1969).

In theory, the relationship between ornaments and burials could be either direct, if the ornaments were brought in or deposited with the dead, or indirect if the production of ornaments took place at Franchthi because it was a burial ground. In case of a direct relationship, the ornaments would have been brought into the cave as the personal jewellery of the deceased and as embroidery on their garments, or been specially manufactured for the deceased at the time of the burial. Both of these options can readily be ruled out for several reasons. First, the ornaments were neither all worn, nor all freshly manufactured, as is respectively implied by the two scenarios. Second, contrary to the human burials that concentrate in trench G1 and at the base of the Lower Mesolithic, ornaments are present everywhere in the cave and throughout the Mesolithic sequence. Even if we consider that some of the bone scatters could derive from disturbed burials—despite the lack of evidence for major disturbances and pits in these trenches—the stratigraphic distribution of ornaments remains far more continuous than that of human bones. Finally, we have no proof that the deceased were lavishly adorned, and in fact no definite evidence that they wore any ornaments at all. Despite what they describe as careful examinations (excavation notebook 510: 34-46), the excavators were unable to associate definite grave goods with the G1 60 burial. T. W. Jacobsen underlines the abundance of crushed shells—mostly land snails—around the skeleton, and the presence of one murex shell, but specifies: "no recognizable offerings were found" (Jacobsen 1969: 374). When N. Shackleton[5] underlined that ornaments were very abundant in G1 and in the trenches excavated in 1969, the figure he gave ("over 700" specimens recovered from "one area in 1969") must correspond to H1A, the only sector of the cave where Mesolithic deposits were excavated that year. Had they been strikingly more abundant around the Mesolithic burial from G1 60, he would probably have said so. Thus, the "enormous numbers" of Cyclope may reflect more the surprise of the excavators and specialists when first confronted with these ornaments in quantity than a particular overabundance in G1. It is also noteworthy that no ornaments or other grave goods have been reported from the other Mesolithic graves in Greece, at Theopetra in Thessaly and Maroulas on Kythnos (Honea 1975; Kyparissi-Apostolika 2003; Sampson *et al.* 2010). However, given the urgency of the excavations at the base of G1 and the taste for ornaments shown by the Mesolithic inhabitants of Franchthi, the burial of the deceased with their own ornaments should not be precluded. What is clear, nevertheless, is that the bulk of the collection does not come from the burials.

Alternatively, the abundance of ornaments could be indirectly linked to the human burials, with manufacturing activities taking place at Franchthi because the cave had acquired a special ceremonial or ritual status. Our analytical data have indeed shown that every trench and every unit yielded, for every category of ornaments, a mix of shells in varied conditions, ranging from unperforated shells in pristine condition to heavily used ornaments and broken ornaments. Since use-wear traces suggested the shells were embroidered onto garments, we concluded that garments were manufactured or re-embroidered, with worn elements removed and replaced by newly manufactured ones. These manufacturing activities, which probably bore some symbolic connotation, could conceivably be related to the ceremonial status of the cave. However, the fact that the highest density of ornaments in FAS dates to the Upper Mesolithic, with no human remains associated, and not to the Lower Mesolithic, does not support this hypothesis. Furthermore, if a case can be made for a special status of the cave in the Lower Mesolithic, with an overabundance of carbonised edible seeds and land snails (Perlès 2010), this does not hold true for the fishing settlement of the Upper Mesolithic or the limited occupations of the Final Mesolithic.

The continuous production of ornaments, jewellery and ornamented garments throughout the Mesolithic thus appears to have been primarily aimed at dressing the living, and only secondarily, if at all, the dead. Franchthi *is* a "Coastal Grave", but rather than 'grave', the main factor behind the abundance of ornaments at Franchthi appears to be, instead, the proximity of the coast. In this respect the social value given to embroidered garments and shell jewellery was such that the collection, production and use of ornaments constituted an autonomous sphere of activities, not a by-product of the exploitation of edible marine resources: the intensity of fish, shellfish and ornamental marine shells exploitation varied independently in the three Mesolithic phases, as exemplified in trench FAS (Fig. 14.3)[6].

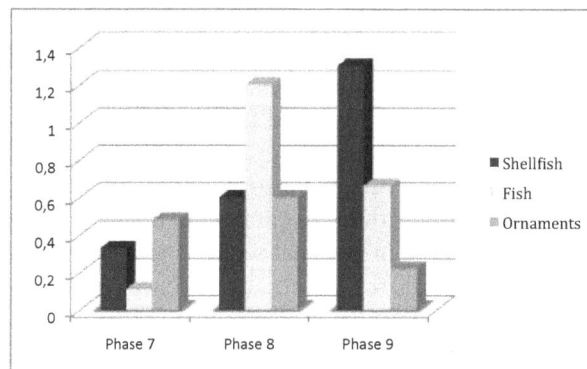

Fig.14.3: Variation in the density of the three main marine resources in NISP versus volume of sediment (litres) in trench FAS.

A Shift in Use between the Palaeolithic and the Mesolithic?

If the production of ornaments was meant to satisfy the needs of the living, as it already was during the Palaeolithic, how can we account for the striking contrasts in abundance between the two periods?

The density of ornaments is actually not the only difference between the two periods. Among the Cyclopes, by far the best-represented genus in both periods, we observe a shift from the predominance of simple perforations to enlarged perforations (Fig. 3.5). This shift occurs between Palaeolithic Phases 5 and 6 (from 30% enlarged perforation to 67%), and it is especially marked at the end of Phase 6 (Subphase 6.2), when enlarged perforations reach 85%, a figure similar to those observed for the Mesolithic (Table 10.7). Differences in the types of perforation go along with differences in use-wear traces. Palaeolithic simple perforations show an asymmetrical development of wear, mainly localised on the labial side of the perforation. This clearly corresponds to suspended pieces, strung as necklaces or bracelets. In contrast, the development of use-wear all around enlarged perforations evokes elements that were embroidered onto garments or head caps by a double knot (Cristiani *et al.* 2014a). The numerical increase from the Palaeolithic to the Mesolithic thus appears to be related to a progressively more important production of embroidered garments, requiring much larger quantities of shells.

Does this mean we should envision garments lavishly embroidered with Cyclopes, dove shells and tusk shells? Given the absence of data from the Franchthi burials, we can only tentatively look for external references. Well-excavated burials with a record of *in situ* ornaments are actually scarce in the Mesolithic of southern Europe[7]. They demonstrate an important inter-individual variability in the richness of ornaments within a single burial ground (e.g. Cristiani & Borić 2012; Rigaud 2011; Taborin 1974), but show that large quantities of shells can be found associated with a single or a few individuals. At Téviec (Brittany, France) several males wore one to three bracelets, each made of up to 150 *Trivia europea* or *Littorina obtusata,* small basket-shaped shells comparable to our *Cyclope neritea* (Taborin 1974: 165-166). One young woman wore a headdress comprising 527 *Littorina obtusata,* while, at the nearby site of Hoëdic, a young male was buried with several bracelets and necklaces, and a head cap comprising 442 *T. europea* and 99 *L. obtusata* (*idem*). At Vlasac (Iron Gates, Serbia), D. Borić and E. Cristiani carefully excavated two richly adorned burials (Cristiani & Borić 2012). Burial H2 contained the remains of an adult female, and yielded 674 ornaments comprising mainly carp teeth associated with some *Cyclope neritea.* The second burial, of a one-year-old child, was even richer with 723 ornaments, again constituted of carp teeth and *Cyclope neritea.* The ornaments were distributed on the back and the front of the two bodies, with a similar pattern for the woman and the baby, suggesting they wore either embroidered jackets and trousers, or long cloaks. As a last example, pit burial 7 from La Vergne (Charente-Maritime, France), which contained the remains of two adults, a newborn and one cremation, yielded more than 1900 *Hinia reticulata* and *Antalis* sp. (Duday & Courtaud 1998).

Given the quantities of shell ornaments that some Mesolithic men, women and children wore when they were buried, the number of ornamental remains at Franchthi no longer appears so remarkable, especially if, as we argued, Franchthi was a production site. But the comparisons are probably spurious: the majority, if not all ornaments and ornamental shells analysed from Franchthi correspond to pieces that were *lost* or *discarded*, rather than *deposited* as in a burial or in deliberate caches. Because it was a production site, the majority of freshly made or recycled ornaments must have left the site, leaving us with a pale reflection only of the quantity of ornaments that had been actually produced and used.

Variation behind Homogeneity

The overwhelming predominance of *Cyclope neritea* in the Mesolithic ornament assemblages may give a feeling of uniformity and profound continuity throughout the whole period. However, we already noted variation in the quantities of *Antalis* sp., *Columbella rustica* and perforated pebbles among the three phases, the maximal diversity occurring in the Lower Mesolithic (Phase 7). Are these variations meaningful, or are they simply related to the higher number of ornaments in this phase?

As shown by Table 14.3, the number of types represented, though always small, is not directly related to the total number of ornaments and ornamental shells: it is equal in Phases 8 and 9, despite a much smaller assemblage in Phase 9. However, this is due to the presence in FAN of a single perforated *Conus mediterraneus*, which is probably someone's idiosyncratic fancy or a plain mistake rather than a relevant type for the period. If the two types represented by unique specimens—this *Conus* and the *Glycymeris* sp. from Phase 7—are removed, a graphic correlation clearly appears between the number of types and the size of the assemblage (Fig. 14.4). The apparent decrease in the diversity of the ornament assemblages from the Lower to the Final Mesolithic[8] may thus simply result from a sampling effect and cannot be considered significant. In particular, the absence of perforated pebbles and potential bird bone beads in Phases 8 and 9 may be due to smaller assemblages and to the very low frequency of these types, when present: 0.16 % altogether.

Phase	*Cyclope* sp.	*Antalis* sp.	*Columbella rustica*	*Glycymeris glycymeris*	Perforated pebble	BBB?	*Conus mediterraneus*	Total
7	6423 *93.1*	328 *4.75*	136 *2*	1 *0.01*	6 *0.09*	5 *0.07*	0 *0*	6899 *100%*
8	1418 *90.7*	14 *0.9*	132 *8.4*	0 *0*	0 *0*	0 *0*	0 *0*	1564 *100%*
9	265 *76.3*	0 *0*	81 *23.3*	0 *0*	0 *0*	0 *0*	1 *0.3*	347 *100%*

Table 14.3: Absolute frequencies and relative abundance of Mesolithic ornament types per phase in trenches H1A, H1B and FAS combined. Interphases have been omitted. BBB? = potential bird bone beads.

Consequently, the relative richness of types in each phase cannot be used to discriminate the three Mesolithic phases. However, a χ^2 test demonstrates that the differences in the *proportions* of types among the three phases in H1A, H1B and FAS are highly significant[9], in particular for *Antalis* sp. and *Columbella rustica*.

The most conspicuous diachronic change is the progressive rise in importance of the dove shell, and the quasi disappearance of tusk shells after the Lower Mesolithic. Even if the overabundance of *Cyclope neritea* may lead one to minimise the importance of the variations in the other taxa, χ^2 tests clearly confirm that each phase significantly differs from the other two.

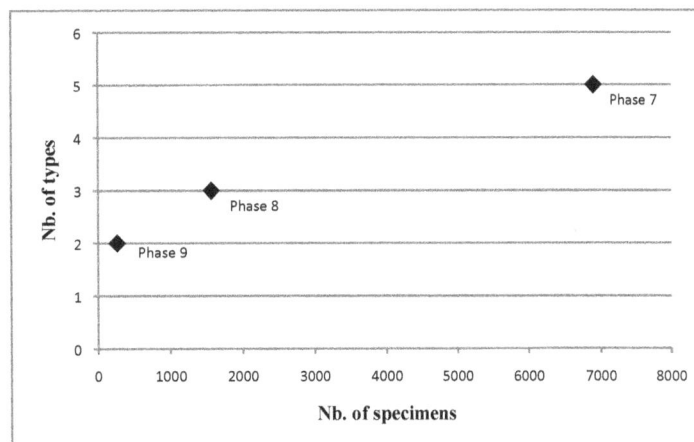

Fig. 14.4: Relation between the number of types and the size of the assemblage in the three Mesolithic phases.

In conclusion, since we cannot ascertain that the absence of perforated pebbles and potential bird bone beads in the Upper and Final Mesolithic is not a sampling artifact, the three Mesolithic phases cannot be differentiated by the presence/absence of specific ornament types. They do differ significantly, however, by the proportions of the three main types, and can thus be considered as three ornament subphases. Contrary to what obtained in the Palaeolithic, these subphases coincide here with the synthetic Franchthi phasing (FGP).

FOP 4.1 corresponds to the Lower Mesolithic (FGP 7), dated between 8,600 and 8,300 cal BC. It is characterised by the presence of a few perforated pebbles, by a massive predominance of *Cyclope neritea*, a comparatively good representation of *Antalis* sp., and a small percentage of *Columbella rustica*. A few potential bead birds and a single *Glycymeris* sp. complement the ornament assemblage (Fig. 14.5)

The Lower Mesolithic took place under a mild and wet Holocene climate, with a definite Mediterranean character (Peyron *et al.* 2011; Roberts *et al.* 2011). If deciduous oak forest covered most of Macedonia and Thessaly, the seed assemblage at Franchthi suggests an open garrigue vegetation comprising abundant *Prunus amygdalus*, *Pistacia* cf. *lentiscus*, *Pyrus amygdaliformis*, *Lens* sp., *Lathyrus* sp., *Vicia ervilia*, *Avena* sp., *Hordeum vulgare* sp. *spontaneum* (Hansen 1991). The Lower Mesolithic witnessed an intense occupation of the cave, perhaps related to the human burials. Subsistence activities then clearly focused on the gathering of plants and land snails, but their exceptional abundance poses questions. Lower Mesolithic assemblages indeed display several odd features: the scarcity of grinding tools compared with the overabundance of carbonised seeds (more than 28,000 were recovered from the four water-sieved trenches only, in about 18/20 m^3), the abundance of land snails (nearly 13,000 in trench H1B alone, for about 3.4 m^3) the very large quantities of ornaments, and the relative scarcity of chipped stone tools and bone tools.

Compared with the Upper and Final Mesolithic, the ratio of land snails per volume of sediment is 2 to 10 times higher, the ratio of seeds is 10 to 30 times higher, and, as we have seen, this holds true for ornaments also. On the contrary, large and small game, mainly red deer, wild boar, hare and fox, is scarce and the exploitation of marine resources, whether fish or shellfish, is rather limited when the actual number of specimens is considered. We should thus consider the possibility that the activities that took place in the cave were directly related to the presence of the dead, and that the cave was mostly a ceremonial locus.

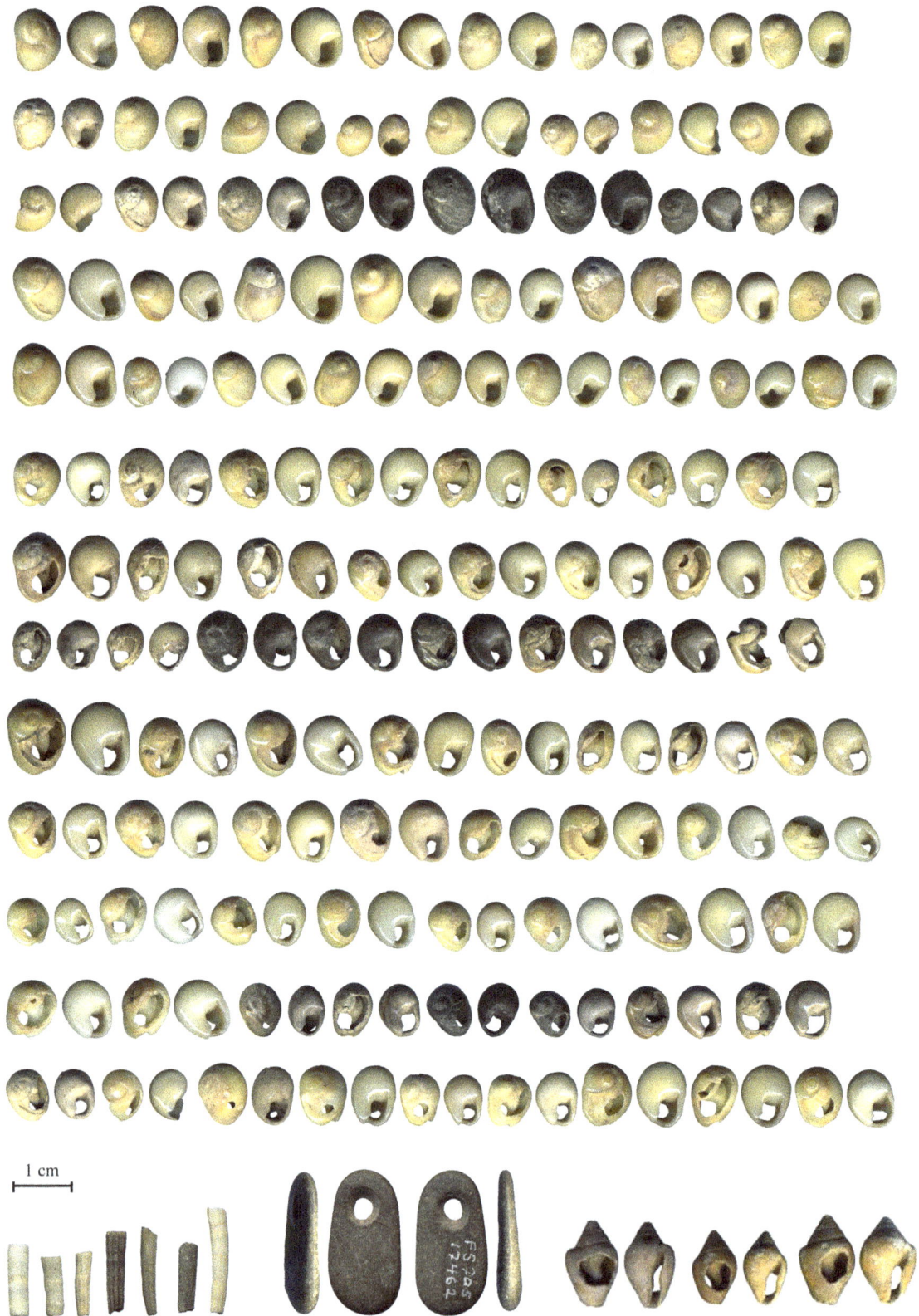

Fig. 14.5: Representative sample of Franchthi Ornament Subphase 4.1.. Cyclope neritea is under-represented in relation to the other types. CAD M. Vanhaeren and C.P.

FOP 4.2, the Upper Mesolithic (FGP 8), is dated to ca. 8,000 – 7,600 cal BC. It is characterised by a very low proportion of *Antalis* sp. and a better representation of *Columbella rustica. Cyclope neritea* is still massively predominant (Fig. 14.6). No other ornament type is present.

Franchthi was no longer used as a collective burial ground[10] and the most spectacular economic shifts at that time are the decrease in seed numbers and the importance of large tuna fishing (Rose 1995, in prep.). With more than 74,000 fish vertebrae in trench FAS alone (ca. 1,5 m³), the Upper Mesolithic is the only occupational phase when marine resources can indeed be considered as prevalent. There is no indication that this could be related to a further decline in terrestrial resources, even if temperatures had continued to rise (Marino *et al.* 2009). The temporary accessibility of large schools of fish is a more probable factor, since the rest of the fauna shows no conspicuous change (Stiner & Munro 2011). The seed assemblage is far more restricted in absolute and relative figures, but stable in terms of taxa represented. The stone tool assemblage now comprises a high proportion of geometric and non-geometric microliths, probably related to the preparation of the equipment for catching the tuna and to the processing of the fish for preservation.

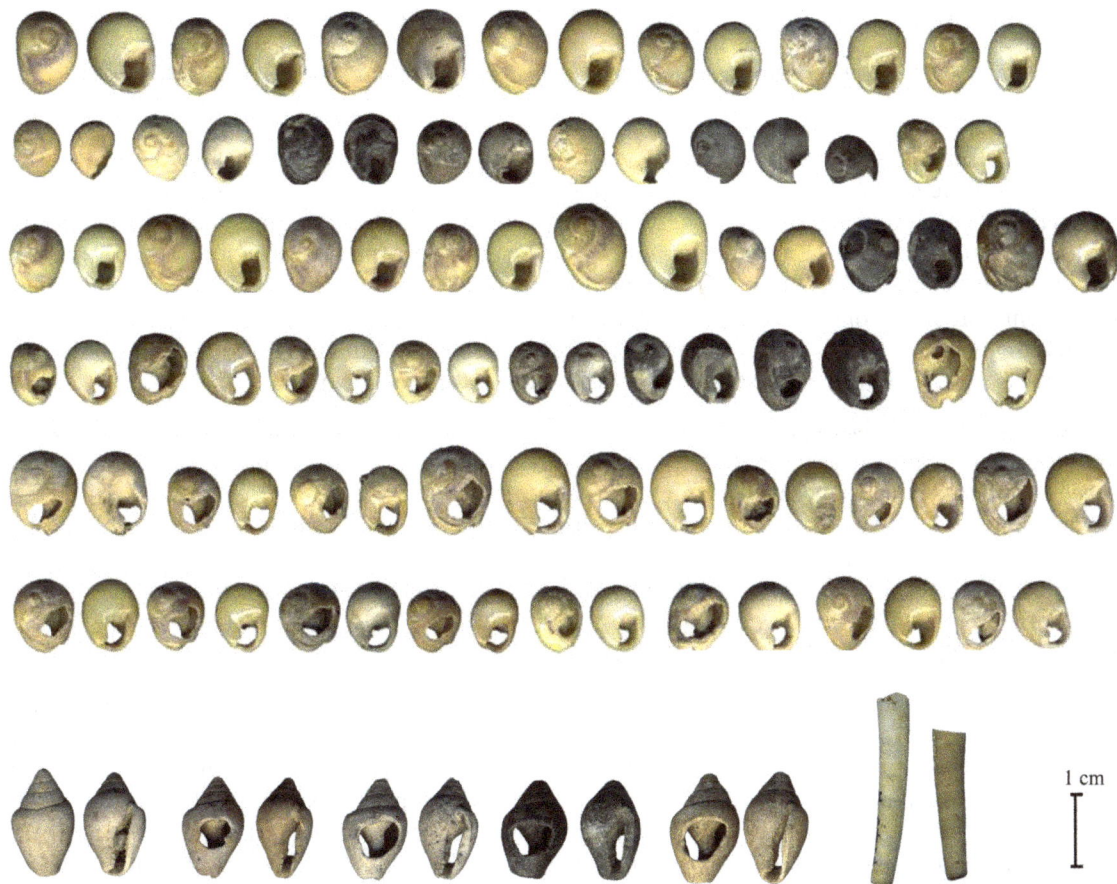

Fig. 14.6: Representative sample of Franchthi Ornament Subphase 4.2. CAD M. Vanhaeren and C.P.

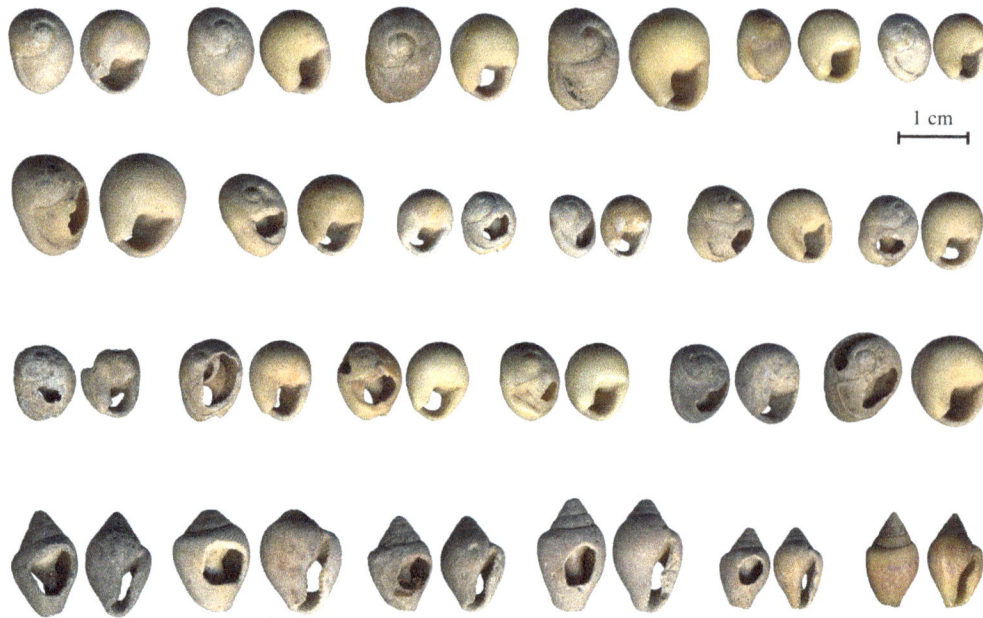

Fig. 14.7: Representative sample of Franchthi Ornament Subphase 4.3. CAD Fotis Ifantidis

FOP 4.3, the Final Mesolithic (FGP 9, ca. 7,050-6,750 cal BC), is the most distinctive of the three Mesolithic ornament phases: *Antalis* sp. is absent[11] and *C. rustica* now constitutes almost a fourth of the total assemblage. It is, conversely, the least distinctive in terms of subsistence and technical activities: the inhabitants of the cave reverted to a diversified diet mainly based on wild fruit, legumes, cereals, a few land snails and some game hunting. Fishing was no longer important, but shellfish gathering became more intense. The diet breath was comparable to that of the Lower Mesolithic in terms of taxa exploited and variety, but the proportion of seeds and land snails relative to the volume of sediments is 20 to 30 times lower.

Ornament assemblages poorly reflect these important changes in the status of the site, subsistence activities and technical production and, again, hint at a long persistence of cultural choices. All three subphases share several common points among which, most evidently, is a very restricted range of ornament types. Faced with a similar situation in the Palaeolithic, we had argued that this restricted range was specific to Franchthi. The insertion of the Franchthi Mesolithic assemblages in their broader European context will lead to an altogether different perspective.

Franchthi, a Typical Mediterranean Site for Ornaments

A decrease in the diversity of ornament types, compared with the Palaeolithic, is a common feature of Mesolithic ornament assemblages. At Vela Spila (Croatia) for instance, the number of ornament types drops from five in the Late Upper Palaeolithic to one in the Mesolithic, *Columbella rustica*, despite a massive increase in the quantity of ornaments (Cristiani *et al.* 2014b). At the Grotta della Serratura (Campania, Italy), the number of ornamental shell species drops from eight in the Final Epigravettian to three in the Mesolithic (Martini 1993: 210). At the other end of Europe, when discussing the marked predominance of two taxa only in the Mesolithic burials at Téviec and Hoëdic, Taborin (1974: 174) adds that in the other Mesolithic collections she studied: "la parure en coquillage est également composée de deux éléments principaux". On a wider geographic scale, half of the ca. 40 sites considered in Newell's survey of Mesolithic ornaments in Europe yielded one to three types of ornaments only (Newell *et al.* 1990, table 34). In Rigaud's updated data base, which contains 450 Mesolithic and Early Neolithic stratigraphic units[12], 48%

of the units contained only one of the 228 identified ornament types, and another 34% contained two or three types only (Rigaud 2011: fig. 115; Rigaud *et al.* 2015).

In other words, and contrary to what was the case for the Palaeolithic, the restricted range of ornaments is certainly not unique to Franchthi. It can be considered a characteristic of the European Mesolithic ornamental assemblages, largely independent of sample sizes, and in sharp contrast with contemporary eastern Anatolian or Levantine diversified assemblages (Alarashi 2014; Bar-Yosef Mayer 2013).

Are the types of ornaments present at Franchthi, alternatively, more characteristic of local or regional choices? The almost complete lack of data from Greece drastically limits direct regional comparisons. The Mesolithic levels (3-5a) from Klissoura Cave 1 in the Argolid yielded only one *Antalis* sp., one *Cyclope neritea,* one *Glycymeris* sp. and one *Acanthocardia tuberculata* (Stiner 2010: 302). Two fragments of *Pecten maximus* are also listed, but they are fragmentary: it cannot be ascertained whether they were perforated and used as ornaments (Stiner, *in litt.,* 19/3/16). Despite the poverty of the assemblage, it is richer in species than Franchthi! *Columbella rustica* and, to a lesser extent, *Cyclope neritea,* are also listed throughout the Mesolithic levels at the Cave of the Cyclops on Youra in the Sporades (Karali 2011: Table 5.2). Since ornamental species were not singled out from the global molluscan assemblage, we do not know whether more types were present. The same situation obtains for the very small assemblage of seashells associated with the 25 partial burials from Maroulas on Kythnos (Karali 2010). Of the 140 or so shells identified, four *Conus* sp., three *Antalis* [*Dentalium*] sp. segments, two *Glycymeris* sp., one *Columbella* sp. are potential ornaments. None is specifically associated with any of the burials, and no grave goods are mentioned. Again, despite the poverty of the assemblage, the range of ornament types appears larger than at Franchthi. Finally, no ornaments were found in securely dated Mesolithic deposits at Theopetra in Thessaly (Kyparissi-Apostolika, *in litt.,* 15/3/16)[13].

Franchthi thus stands out in the Greek Mesolithic context by its richness of ornaments, but not by the types represented. Except for perforated pebbles and potential bird bone beads, which would not be expected in the other, very small, assemblages, the ornament types at Franchthi are common to the other sites. A broader look at southern Europe confirms that the most important species are ubiquitous in the Mediterranean area. A distribution map based on the kernel density (Rigaud 2011, appendix 2; see also Álvarez-Fernández 2010, Fig.4) illustrates the dense and wide-ranging distribution of dove shells, often the dominant species in Mesolithic ornament assemblages. Tusk shells also are widespread in southern European sites, albeit in fewer sites. *Cyclope* sp. tend to concentrate in a restricted number of sites, with a discontinuous geographic distribution. Perforated pebbles can be found all over Europe, but again with a discontinuous distribution.

The types of ornaments, thus, do not single out Franchthi. To the contrary, they attest that the groups living in the cave shared common symbolic or aesthetic values with hunter-gatherers of the Mediterranean area, and that they participated in a vast interaction sphere through neighbouring groups. If a specific identity was expressed through the ornaments, it could only be, consequently, by the proportions of the different types they used and their combination.

Compared with the Franchthi assemblages, the striking feature of most Mediterranean ornament assemblages is the predominance of dove shells over Cyclopes or tusk shells (Álvarez-Fernández 2010; Cristiani *et al.* 2014b; Komšo & Vukosavljević 2011 and refs. therein). At the highest level of their classification, Newell and his colleagues thus defined a 'Columbella tribe', characterised by the association of *C. rustica* and *Cyclope neritea/Cyclonassa.* Its territory would have expanded from southern Spain to southern Italy and to the Main region in Germany (Newell *et al.* 1990: fig. 130). Rigaud similarly notes the presence of *C. rustica* in all the first eight groups defined by her Neighbor-Joining analysis, based on similar associations of types (Rigaud 2011). In particular, group 2 contains *C. rustica, Antalis* sp. and *Glycymeris glycymeris,* group 3 associates *Cyclope* sp. and *Columbella rustica,* and group 7 associates *C. rustica, Cyclope* sp., *Antalis* sp. and *Cerithium vulgatum.*

Each group presents a very wide geographic distribution, from the northern Mediterranean coasts to the Balkans and Germany (Rigaud 2011: figs 121, 122, 126). For instance, Franchthi appears in group 2 (on the basis of the single Lower Mesolithic *Glycymeris*), together with two German sites, one northern Italian one and several Spanish sites. Group 3 spreads from the Iron Gates to Italy and northern Spain, while group 7 spreads over France, Germany and northern Spain. The distribution of these groups is all but geographically continuous, and all overlap: nearby sites may belong to different groups, far-off sites may belong to the same group. This demonstrates that, on a largely common base of ornamental taxa, human groups could express their own identity and variously combine the taxa[14], even though other approaches suggest a more important degree of regional homogeneity (Cristiani *et al.* 2014b; Rigaud 2011: 303).

This overall variability in European Mesolithic ornament assemblages reinforces the significance of the continuous predominance at Franchthi of *Cyclope neritea*, as does the secondary role played by dove shells. If these species are all but 'cultural markers' by themselves, their relative proportions at Franchthi denote original and long-lasting choices.

NOTES

1   We shall also calculate this ratio in FAN for Phase 9, the Final Mesolithic, since this is our best assemblage for this phase. H1A is not included in these analyses since it was only water-sieved in units 163 to 220, which are almost all Palaeolithic units.
2   Not significant at $p < 0.05$.
3   This unit measured 1.5 m by 2.5 metres, with a depth of 10 to 36 cm.
4   Shed milk teeth are not taken into account in the figures for 'bone scatters'.
5   Here is the complete quotation again: "In Mesolithic levels (both in G1 and areas excavated in 1969) there are enormous numbers of *Neritea* [*C. neritea*] shells. (Over 700 were recovered in one area excavated in 1969). Well over half of these appear to have been pierced, suggesting that they may have been used as beads." (N. Shackleton N. 1969: 379. Parentheses from the original quotation).
6   A similar lack of correlation between the abundance of ornamental shells and shellfish was noted at Riparo Mochi in Liguria (Stiner 2014: 55).
7   Ornaments are so different, qualitatively and quantitatively, in the Mesolithic of northern Europe (see Newell *et al.* 1990; Rigaud 2011), that I prefer to limit comparisons to western and southern Europe.
8   The type richness, calculated as N types/logNISP of the total assemblage is 1.5 for Phase 7, 0.89 for Phase 8 and 1.2 for Phase 9. If the unique specimens are removed, they become respectively 1.28, 0.89 and 0.8. In all cases, the richness index is very low, even lower than in the Palaeolithic.
9   $\chi^2 = 569$, df = 10. The test was based on the figures from Table 14.1.
10 Human remains consist only of one potential baby burial and a few scattered bones.
11 13.5 specimens would have been expected if the proportion of *Antalis* sp. had been identical in the 3 phases.
12 A stratigraphic unit can be a site, a phase or a level.
13 A perforated tooth, most probably a red deer canine, has been found in Corfu at the Grava rockshelter (Sordinas 1969) in deposits dated to the early Holocene, thus potentially Mesolithic (Galanidou 2011). However, the presence of several equids and large bovids in the faunal remains leads me to suspect important Pleistocene contaminations and the real age of this bead remains uncertain.
14 The degree of diachronic variability behind this pattern is impossible to assess.

EPILOGUE

Lessons from a Monotonous Sequence

The Palaeolithic and Mesolithic ornament assemblages from Franchthi represent a unique collection. Its peculiar features and exceptional richness allows us to draw inferences about the production of ornaments, their social and symbolic value, which would have been impossible with more restricted assemblages.

Franchthi, a Rare Example of a Coastal Production Centre …

Marine shells were the predominant element used for ornaments around the Mediterranean basin during the entire Upper Palaeolithic and Mesolithic (e.g. Álvarez-Fernández 2010; Álvarez-Fernández & Jöris 2008; Newell *et al.* 1990; Rigaud 2011; Taborin 1993, 2004; Vanhaeren & d'Errico 2006). Because of eustatic sea level rise, however, few of the potential collection and production sites have been preserved. Thanks to its slightly elevated position[1], Franchthi is one of the few Upper Palaeolithic and Mesolithic sites that can be considered as 'coastal', even if the coast was located some 2 to 4 km away. It is also one of very few sites, if not the only one, where continuous *production* of shell ornaments has been documented. Both aspects are linked and have important bearings on the interpretation of the finds.

At a coastal site such as Franchthi, there are many ways shells could have made their way to the cave. The proximity to the coast was a clear incentive to collect and produce ornaments at the site, and we have even suggested that collecting marine ornamental shells was one of the main motives for the cave's occupation during the early Upper Palaeolithic (FGP Phases 0-3). Towards the end of the Upper Palaeolithic and during the Mesolithic, marine molluscs were also collected as a food resource and processed at the site. Secondly, we also considered it probable that shells were unintentionally introduced into the cave, together with driftwood, seaweeds, shellfish or fish packed in algae (Chap. 4). Finally, prehistoric children may also, like all children, have collected shells on the beach simply because they found them pretty or interesting.

While it is easy to demonstrate, on a large scale, that the collection of ornamental shells was a distinct activity from the collection of shellfish (Chap. 7 and 14), it is impossible to single out ornamental shell species unless some specimens at least bear anthropic perforations. We had to be very strict in the definition of 'ornamental species': with the exception of tusk shells, we only considered as 'ornamental' taxa that yielded unequivocally perforated specimens. This led us to eliminate from the ornament spectrum several species that, at inland sites, may have been considered as such: we had no proof they were used as beads and several other factors could account for their presence at a coastal site. We may, accordingly, have overlooked some ornamental species that, by chance, were only represented in our assemblages by unperforated specimens. Unperforated specimens of ornamental species can indeed constitute a non-negligible proportion, even at sites located far inland (see Chap. 8). I doubt, however, that we missed any ornamental species other than incidental: the samples for most phases are reasonably large, and sometimes extremely large. Had these species been used as (perforated) ornaments, we would have found some examples. There remains, of course, the theoretical possibility that some species or taxa were exclusively glued, without perforation, to adorn garments or objects. Tusk shells (*Antalis* sp.), which can be threaded without modification, also posed problems that would not have occurred at inland sites, since we suspected that some at least of the very small segments were not intentionally deposited (Chap. 4).

Even with this restricted definition, the total number of ornaments and ornamental shells studied, on the order of 12,000, is remarkable. It would be tempting to relate this high figure to the proximity of the coast and the ease of collecting ornamental species and producing ornaments. The relationship, in fact, is more subtle. First, some sites located further from the coast, such as Klissoura Cave 1, also yielded very rich assemblages: more than 1200 specimens were identified in the Lower Aurignacian level IV (Stiner 2010). Fumane, in Italy, located at the time hundreds of kilometres from the Adriatic and Mediterranean coasts, is well known for its unique Proto-Aurignacian assemblage, mostly composed of marine shells, and reaching 650 specimens (Broglio & Gurioli 2004). Thus, the sheer number of ornaments and ornamental shells does not, by itself, designate an *in situ* collection and production centre. Our argument to define Franchthi as a production centre has rested, instead, on the collection of live *Cyclope* sp. and on the presence in every unit of shells at different stages of manufacture and use: rejected unusable juvenile *Cyclope* sp., unperforated shells kept or lost as raw material, newly perforated beads, heavily worn and broken specimens. This demonstrates the production and recycling of ornaments, either to prepare new necklaces and bracelets, or to adorn garments.

Direct numerical comparisons with inland sites may, however, be misleading[2]. Because Franchthi was a production centre, we can logically assume that the majority of the ornamental shells and manufactured beads left the site. With the possible exception of the Lower Mesolithic burials from trench G1 (Chap. 14), Franchthi was not a site where ornaments were brought, deposited or intentionally cached. What we found are specimens that were *lost or discarded as no longer usable*. The high proportion of very worn beads seemed to me, at first, incompatible with the notion of a production site. It became comprehensible when I realised that most of the freshly manufactured beads were taken away, either adorning the Franchthi inhabitants themselves, or for exchange with inland sites. A fair number of unperforated specimens must also have been kept aside and taken away for exchange: an inland site such as Fumane presents a high rate of unperforated specimens (Chap. 7), demonstrating that unworked shells also circulated from the coast to the interior. As a consequence, the number of shells that were actually collected at Franchthi, and the number of beads and pendants that were produced, must have been considerably higher.

... But a Singularly Monotonous Sequence

Recovering several thousand ornamental shells in the excavation's storerooms was a long and fastidious task, even if we can be grateful to the Franchthi inhabitants for having taken away a good proportion of the ornaments! By far the majority of ornaments was still stored in the 'molluscs' bags and it took us weeks to sort the bags of mixed crushed marine shells and land snails. The effort was worth it, considering the quantities recovered. However, the exceptional abundance of ornaments and ornamental shells hardly compensated the disappointment of finding repeatedly the same three taxa, *Cyclope neritea*, *Columbella rustica* and *Antalis* sp. This meant, indeed, that our initial research model was clearly and irremediably contradicted.

This initial model was based on the premise of a succession of occupations by different cultural groups across the millennia, with corresponding changes in ornament assemblages. It postulated a correlation between environmental transformations, cultural changes as suggested by lithic assemblages, the fluctuating status of the cave, a shifting economic base and the design of the ornaments. We already knew that the cave had been successively a hunting halt, a base camp for families practising varied subsistence activities, then a residential or potentially ceremonial site associated with human burials, a fishing camp geared toward the capture of tuna fish, and, finally, a likely secondary settlement occupied by generalist hunter-gatherers (Perlès 1999, 2003, 2010). We therefore expected concomitant transformations in the ornaments, characterised by the choice of different ornament types, a different organisation of production and the use of different techniques. On the contrary, the most striking and unexpected result of our analyses was, beyond quantitative variations, the continuity of ornaments traditions throughout the Upper Palaeolithic and the Mesolithic.

This continuity can first be perceived by the marked predominance of shell ornaments and by the choice of the dominant taxa: from the beginning of the Upper Palaeolithic, in the Pre-Aurignacian, to the end of the Mesolithic, the bulk of the ornament assemblages is constituted by *Cyclope neritea/pellucida*, *Antalis* sp. and *Columbella rustica*. The only departures from this obstinate tripartite scheme are found in the Early Upper Palaeolithic (FOP 1), with the presence of *Homalopoma sanguineum*, and in the late Palaeolithic (FOP 3) with perforated *Glycymeris* sp., if the latter are indeed ornaments (see Chap. 6). Non-shell ornaments always represent a very, very small minority: one perforated Palaeolithic ibex tooth, a few potential bird bone beads and a few perforated pebbles in the Lower Mesolithic.

A similar continuity is observable in the strategies of collection: collecting live *Cyclope* in shallow waters, dead *Columbella* and *Antalis* on beaches. It is also identifiable in the techniques of perforation: by pressure for Cyclopes, by direct or indirect percussion for dove shells. The peculiar 'enlarged' perforations on many Cyclopes reinforce the continuity between the Late Upper Palaeolithic and the Mesolithic, as does heat-treatment to obtain black beads.

Of these different elements of continuity, the restricted range of shell species is undoubtedly the most striking, considering the size of the assemblages. However, the choice of shell ornament types was not constrained by available resources. The presence, in the shellfish assemblages, of a variety of species largely used elsewhere as ornaments, but here either eaten or simply discarded, shows that many other species could have been collected and used. Similarly, the abundance of deer, ibex, fox and birds in the faunal record (Stiner & Munro 2011, Munro & Stiner in prep.) offered ample opportunities to use perforated teeth and bird bones as ornaments, as they were in many other prehistoric settlements, including in Greece. Finally, we can exclude sampling biases since the Palaeolithic and Mesolithic ornament assemblages from Franchthi exceed 12,000 inventoried specimens, a figure higher than at any other site. No, the Palaeolithic and Mesolithic hunter-gatherers-fishermen from Franchthi simply did not want diversified beads and repeatedly used the same types. However, this stubborn restriction is also revealing. Once our initial disappointment was overcome, a series of unsuspected and important considerations opened up.

Basket-Shaped Beads, Yes, but Not Just Any Basket!

Cyclopes, dove shells and tusk shells are among the most commonplace taxa used as prehistoric ornaments. The preference for tubular, biconical, and globular—or "basket-shaped"—shell species, was noted long ago (Álvarez-Fernández & Jöris 2008; Taborin 1974: 128, 1993: 328, 2004). Beads and pendants of similar shape were also manufactured in other raw materials. R. White (1993, 2004), for instance, underlined the striking resemblance between "basket-shaped ivory beads" from the Aurignacian at Le Castanet (Dordogne, France) and *Cyclope neritea*. More recently, Stiner emphasised the formal similarity among dove shells, Cyclopes, *Nassarius* and deer canines, another prized Palaeolithic ornament (Stiner 2014).

There is more than shape or dimension in the selection of shell species, however. The exceptional size of the Franchthi ornament assemblages, which precludes any sampling bias, demonstrates that other basket-shaped or biconical species, also locally available, were systematically ignored. For instance, *Pisania striata* is hardly distinguishable from *Columbella rustica* on its dorsal face, and both species can be found together live (Appendix 3.2, Fig. A3.15*)*. Yet, the *Pisania striata* we occasionally found in the Franchthi archaeological assemblages—probably mistaken for *Columbella rustica* when collected—were never perforated. Similarly, when broken on the spire, *C. rustica* is very similar to *Conus mediterraneus*: they can only be distinguished by the shape of the aperture. Yet, only one perforated *Conus* was recovered, for more than 450 dove shells. *Clanculus corallinus* and *Gibbula* sp. are, in turn, very similar to *Homalopoma sanguineum*, but they too were rejected without perforation. All these similar-looking species are also colourful, so the absence of colour cannot be invoked for their exclusion.

There can be no doubt that, as advocated by Stiner (2014), Palaeolithic and Mesolithic hunter-gatherers chose shell species of a certain shape and size, which made them especially appropriate to be used as beads. However, within the spectrum of species that answered these criteria and were locally available, prehistoric beachcombers were attentive to collect particular species and, as keen malacologists, made few mistakes. It can thus be inferred that these species—or genus in the case of *Cyclope neritea*/*C. pellucida* and of the *Antalis* group—had a particular meaning, value or symbolic importance, which precluded their substitution by similar looking shells.

Cultural Continuity or Discontinuity: Which Proxy?

The preference for specific shells can be observed within each ornament phase at Franchthi, but, more importantly, it was maintained unchanged over many millennia. The few other long sequences we referred to similarly showed overall continuity in the choice of the shell ornament types (Chap. 8). The selection of taxa varied from site to site, and local availability and abundance no doubt played a role. Nevertheless, at every site, other potential ornaments were also available, yet the same dominant types persist throughout occupational sequences that can span over 25,000 years. Klissoura Cave 1 constitutes an interesting partial exception: whereas the Aurignacian and Gravettoid occupations show a continuous predominance of *Cyclope neritea/pellucida* and *Columbella rustica*, the basal Uluzzian deposits yielded mostly *Antalis* sp., which becomes conspicuously rare in the later levels (Stiner 2010). This confirms that local availability is not the guiding criterion behind the choice of ornamental species: it is improbable that all *Antalis* species would have disappeared after the Uluzzian and tusk shells actually constitute the second ornament type at Franchthi in all the early Upper Palaeolithic phases.

The overall stability observed in the choice of ornamental species for beads and pendants does not imply that the final compositions they were part of were rigorously copied from generation to generation. As aptly stated by Stiner and colleagues (2013: 397):

"Perhaps it is more productive to think of the beads not as the main objects of interest, but as the most conservative components of a flexible medium for visual signalling. Much of their conservatism may stem from shell beads' role as particulate or 'digital' units in more complex artifacts and the consequent technological constraints on them. A great number of distinct designs may be generated from one or a few small repeating units, such as strands of beads or panels of beads on garments. At the same time, design flexibility is enhanced by standardization of the component elements: it is much easier to recombine elements in a formulaic manner if they are similar and predictable in size and shape. The homogeneity of these individual digital elements probably disguises a great diversity in the larger objects, and messages, into which they were assembled".

In the absence of well-preserved adorned burials, potential changes in the final ornamental compositions elude us. Yet, even allowing for such transformations, the fact remains that at each of these sites the same basic 'units' were used over and over, in associations that are specific to the site. This suggests that ornamental traditions lasted for many millennia, disregarding the chronocultural boundaries defined on the basis of lithic assemblages. At Üçağızlı Cave I on the south-central coast of Turkey, the Initial Upper Palaeolithic, followed by an unnamed Upper Palaeolithic intervening layer and by the Ahmarian, are massively dominated by *Nassarius gibbosulus* and *Columbella rustica* (Stiner *et al.* 2013: 388). Their proportions vary through time, but it is noteworthy that the most important shifts do not correspond to the limits of the major technocomplexes, as delineated by chipped stone assemblages. The same two species also dominate at Ksar 'Akil on the coast of Lebanon, where, again, remarkably stable assemblages persist from early Upper Palaeolithic levels throughout a long Aurignacian sequence and a Kebarian occupation (*idem*). On the Italian Riviera, the Riparo Mochi inhabitants showed a marked preference for *Cyclope* sp. and *Homalopoma sanguineum*, followed by *Cerithium* sp. and *Nassarius* sp. Once more, the analysis reveals that there was "... little if any variation in these preferences across the five Epi- and Upper Palaeolithic phases at Riparo Mochi", i.e. across the Proto-Aurignacian, the Aurignacian, the Gravettian, the Early and Late Epigravettian (Stiner 1999: 748). At Franchthi, the ornament assemblages from the Aurignacian and Gravettoid occupations (Phases 1 and 2) are indistinguishable, and close to the Epigravettian and Mesolithic assemblages.

The arrhythmia of change between lithic and ornament assemblages raises the fundamental problem of the criteria we use to define archaeological "cultures" or technocomplexes. Even acknowledging that archaeological cultures bear little relation to anthropological cultures, but simply define stable associations of shared, learned behaviours (Valentin 2008), the problem remains: both the production of ornaments and of stone tools are learned and transmitted behaviours. If they do not vary together in time—or in space, for that matter—it implies, as we shall now discuss, that either ornament traditions have no cultural value, or that the traditional classifications based on lithics have no cultural value except at a most general and uninformative level.

The first option is that defended by Stiner (2014; see also Stiner *et al.* 2013). She considered that the prevalence of 'basket-shaped' beads in Palaeolithic assemblages was so marked that it was unlikely they referred to specific cultural entities. Instead, their prevalence would reflect transcultural standards in the choice of basic units of communication, linked to the shape and dimension of the ornaments. The absence of any specific cultural connotation is precisely what would have allowed the use of basket-shaped beads for interaction among different cultural groups, across very extensive social networks.

There is no doubt that Cyclopes, dove shells, tusk shells or deer canines cannot be considered, *per se*, as the mark of any particular cultural group. We have argued, nevertheless, that the specific association of species and their highly restricted range in each phase were a characteristic of the Franchthi assemblages, and should be considered as cultural choices. These two positions are not necessarily contradictory: the seven notes of the occidental heptatonic scale are also transcultural units of communication, but this does not preclude the existence of regional musical traditions. At Franchthi, the marked similarity in the choice of species from phase to phase implied that the traditions pertaining to personal adornment were maintained, locally or regionally, and with very little modification for about 30 millennia. This leads us, in turn, to envision an exceptional permanence of hunter-gatherer groups within their territory, in contradiction with what is, implicitly or explicitly, implied by the classical chronocultural divisions of the Upper Palaeolithic, based on lithic assemblages. Rigaud (2011: 300) similarly observed that Mesolithic ornament groups defined by the association of ornament types encompassed several chronological technocomplexes as defined by lithic assemblages.

Lithic assemblages have indeed traditionally constituted the main basis for the definition of 'cultural' entities in the Palaeolithic and the Mesolithic (Bon 2009; Guillomet-Malmassari 2012). Stone tools and weapons can certainly serve as excellent markers of learning lineages, of technical traditions and group affiliations, when subjected to detailed technological analyses that bring to light specific volumetric conceptions and '*manières de faire*' in their production (Bon 2002; Langlais 2010; Pelegrin 1995, 2005; Pesesse 2013; Pigeot 2004; Valentin 2008). However, the chronocultural label given to an assemblage is usually not based on this fine level of observation, which tends to reveal many idiosyncratic local or regional traditions. It is mostly based on the presence of characteristic weapon inserts, the infamous 'fossile directeur'. For instance, the Aurignacian is characterised by the presence of carenated end-scrapers, now understood as cores used to produce bladelets inserted on organic points, while the Châtelperronian is characterised by the Châtelperron point, the Gravettian by the Gravettian point, the Sauveterrian by the Sauveterrian point, etc. The broad chronocultural classification of the European Upper Palaeolithic and Mesolithic are thus based essentially on weapon inserts. However, new designs for weapons can spread rapidly over vast areas for simple reasons of effective or presumed gain in efficiency, disregarding 'cultural boundaries', as shown by many prehistoric, historic and contemporaneous examples (Bon 2009).

Ornaments, on the contrary, are not submitted to practical constraints. They function in a purely symbolic sphere, to assess a group's identity and the status of individuals within the group. Together with portable and parietal art, they should thus constitute better proxies of cultural identity and cultural continuity than do weapons, even if the duration of these traditions are so long that they are still difficult for us to apprehend. However, is not the Franco-Cantabrian parietal art an excellent example of symbolic traditions that developed for millennia in the same region, without spreading to other karstic areas?

Revisiting the Franchthi Occupational Sequence

This perspective invites us to re-examine the Franchthi sequence from a perspective different from that offered by the lithic assemblages: where the specialist in lithics observes, according to traditional interpretative frameworks, a succession of presumed cultural discontinuities, the specialist in ornaments sees instead far greater cultural continuity[3].

The identity of the taxa and similarity of proportions between the Aurignacian ornaments (FGP Phase 1) and the Gravettoid industries (or Mediterranean Gravettian) that followed after a long hiatus (Phases 2 and 3), contradict the hypothesis of two culturally different traditions and suggest that the makers of the backed-bladelet industries descended from the original Aurignacian occupants (Fig. E.1). The origins of the Gravettian are debated, but the notion of two different cultural complexes, if not of two different populations (Conard & Bolus 2003; Djindjian *et al.* 1999; Kozłowski 2004), cannot be sustained at Franchthi. To the contrary, the Franchthi record supports the hypothesis of an autonomous development of the Gravettian in the Mediterranean zone (Kozłowski 2015: 9), and, for the Argolid, a permanence of occupation by the same hunter-gatherers.

The long erosional hiatus[4] between Phases 3 and 4, together with the absence of ornaments in FGP 4, marks the sharpest shift in the ornament sequence at Franchthi. *Homalopoma sanguineum* disappears and *Columbella rustica* becomes more important. Nevertheless, the continuity in the restricted choice of species and the continued dominance of *Cyclope neritea/pellucida* suggests we are still within the same ornaments tradition. With passing time, however, the respective proportions of the three main bead types changes, perhaps in line with the suggested transition from strung beads, constitutive of necklaces and bracelets, to beads mostly used as garment embroidery (Chap. 14).

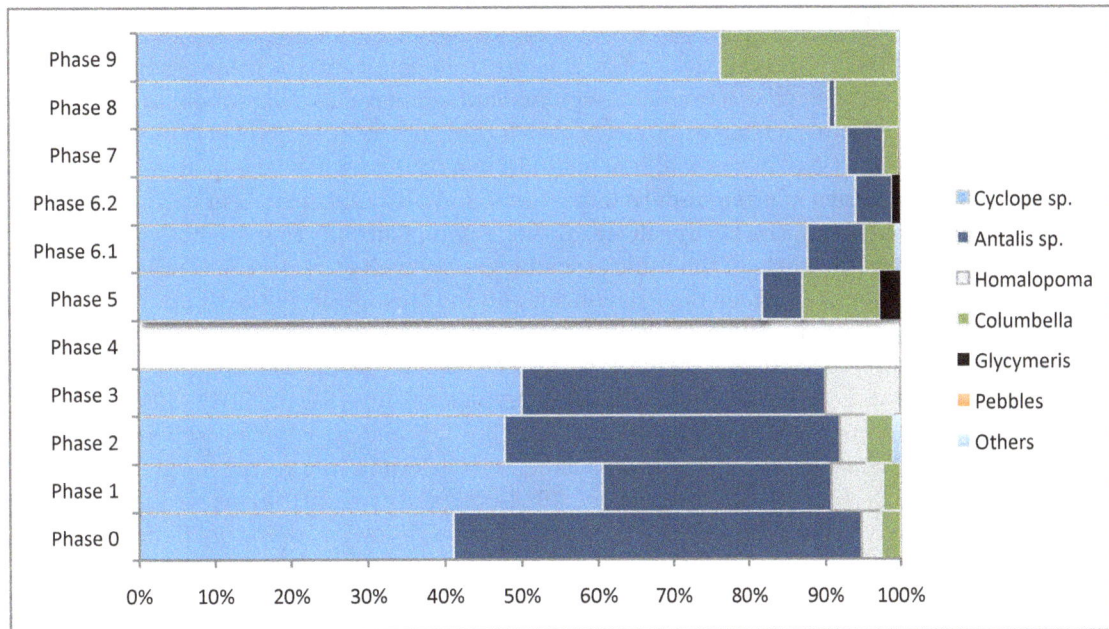

Fig. E.1: Relative proportions of the ornament types from the Pre-Aurignacian (Phase 0) to the Final Mesolithic (Phase 9). There are no ornaments in Phase 4 (Epigravettian). Percentages in Phase 3 (Gravettoid) are unreliable due to the small sample size.

The latest Upper Palaeolithic ornament assemblages (Phases 5 and 6) and the Lower Mesolithic one (Phase 7) are strikingly similar in their composition and proportions (Fig. E.1), despite important differences in absolute numbers and the presence of a few perforated pebbles. The similarity is reinforced by the common use of unusual techniques such as enlarged perforations and heat-treatment of Cyclopes. This can only reflect a continuity of traditions between the Palaeolithic and Mesolithic hunter-gatherers inhabiting Franchthi, even though the lithic assemblages, marked by the quasi-disappearance of microliths (Perlès 1990), are in turn strikingly different! The continuity in ornament traditions supports a functional interpretation of the transformations in lithic assemblages, which would be related to a marked decline of hunting with stone-inserted weapons, and leads us to reject the hypothesis of a cultural break related to the arrival of migrant seafarers from Anatolia (e.g. Runnels 1995, 2003).

The spectrum of species gets narrower between the Lower and Upper Mesolithic with the quasi-disappearance of *Antalis* sp. and an increase in the importance of *Columbella rustica*. While these two trends are statistically significant, the absence of perforated pebbles or other rare types in the Upper Mesolithic (Phase 8) may simply be due to a sampling effect and cannot be considered significant. At any rate, these quantitative variations concern the same species as before, and take place within the well-defined traditions of earlier phases. The cave no longer was an important burial ground and turned into a fishing camp, but the ornaments suggest that the tuna fishers of the Upper Mesolithic were actually related to the snail and seed eaters of the Lower Mesolithic. In parallel, the introduction of original microliths in the Upper Mesolithic would be linked to new fishing techniques, rather than to a new conception of stone tools or too different technical traditions. The trend towards a more and more restricted range of ornaments culminated in the Final Mesolithic, where, except for one *Conus mediterraneus* mimicking a dove shell, the assemblage only contains *Cyclope neritea* and *Columbella rustica*. The rise in dove shells is conspicuous, and statistically significant. For the first time, this species, which has been considered as emblematic of the Mediterranean Mesolithic, constitutes more than a small minority at Franchthi.

Lithics and Ornaments: Similar Discrepancies from a Synchronic Viewpoint

The radically different perspectives offered by the ornaments and the lithic assemblages can also be illustrated from a more synchronic viewpoint. Vanhaeren & d'Errico brought to light a clear regional patterning of Aurignacian ornaments, which they interpret as an expression of distinct ethno-linguistic groups (Vanhaeren & d'Errico 2006), in a context where the homogeneity of the stone and bone industries is often underlined. Newell and his colleagues also defined, through the analysis of ornaments in the European Mesolithic, regional groups that did not coincide with the groups defined on the basis of the lithic assemblages (Newell *et al.* 1990). On the whole, the situation seems to reverse between the Palaeolithic and the Mesolithic. In the Upper Palaeolithic, ornament traditions have a smaller geographic range than lithic traditions. On the contrary in the Mesolithic, where specialists have defined many regional groups on the basis of weapon inserts, ornament traditions tend to overlap several regional entities (Rigaud 2011: 300). A striking example is provided by the very characteristic "Fish Teeth Band", as labelled by Newell and his colleagues (1990), which uses carp teeth as ornaments, with the same recipe for gluing them to garments (Cristiani & Borić 2012; Cristiani *et al.* 2014a; Rigaud *et al.* 2014a). As we know it today, this group is split between the Upper and the Lower Danube Valley, hundreds of kilometres apart, with no correspondence in the toolkits.

Franchthi itself shows similar discrepancies between the regional affiliations suggested by stone tools on the one hand, and ornaments on the other. The succession of Palaeolithic lithic assemblages at Franchthi finds clear parallels in the rest of southern Europe, with Aurignacian and Gravettoid phases, now sometimes called the "Mediterranean Gravettian", followed by Epigravettian occupations. In contrast, the ornament assemblages, with their extremely restricted range of types, differ from contemporaneous assemblages, including from Greece. The reverse holds true in the Mesolithic: whereas there is no known equivalent to the lithic sequence, with two phases very poor in microliths (Phases 7 and 9) bracketing a phase rich in geometric and non-geometric microliths (Phase 8), the ornament assemblages fit perfectly within their European context. In particular, the restricted range of ornament types, which singled out the Franchthi Palaeolithic assemblages, is now shared with many other Mediterranean Mesolithic settlements, and the ornament types themselves are the most common at these sites (Chap. 14). The similarity in the choice of symbolic elements is echoed by the similarity in funerary rituals: the joint practice of inhumations and cremations is another current feature of the European Mesolithic.

Interestingly, no influence from the East can be perceived. Connections with the Near East were suggested by the presence of 'La Mouillah points' in the lithic assemblage of Phase 4, but this phase is precisely devoid of ornaments, and thus mute in this respect. Later on, connections with Anatolia have been suggested for the Mesolithic (Runnels 1995), again on the basis of the lithic assemblages. These connections would certainly have been possible given that Mesolithic inhabitants of Franchthi (or their neighbours) were skilled seafarers, who already exploited Milian obsidian. But our ornament assemblages differ drastically from the rich and highly diversified Pre-Pottery-Neolithic ornament assemblages (Alarashi 2014; Bar-Yosef Mayer 2013). The Initial Neolithic ornaments from Franchthi, which contain several typical Near Eastern types of geometric beads and pendants, will therefore mark a clear break in the sequence, and reinforce the notion of a sudden irruption of colonists (Munro & Stiner 2015; Perlès 2001).

The re-evaluation of the Franchthi sequence in light of the ornaments is an important outcome of this study, but it can be considered anecdotal compared with the broader implications of these analyses. Franchthi is not an isolated case. Several other sites with very long occupational sequences have revealed a comparable continuity in ornament assemblages. Based mainly on lithic assemblages, traditional scenarios for the Upper Palaeolithic imply population ruptures, movements, and dispersals. If recent studies tend to nuance this picture, our monotonous sequence leads, more radically, to question the relevance of stone weapons as the basis for chronocultural classifications: between the important changes in lithic assemblages and the persistence through time of symbolic choices expressed by ornaments or parietal art, should we not privilege the latter as a witness of socio-cultural traditions? If so, the very long duration of these ornaments traditions should lead us to rethink the Upper Palaeolithic cultural palaeogeography of Europe from a far more regional and stable perspective than has been traditionally the case. Many recent studies, which take into consideration the technological study of whole lithic assemblages, are leading this way (e.g. Klaric 2007; Langlais 2010; Moreau 2011; Pesesse 2013), yet they do not, unfortunately, integrate ornaments or art into their reassessment of cultural entities. Conversely, Mesolithic Europe has been divided by lithic specialists into myriads of small geographic groups, mostly characterised by subtle differences in the production of weapon inserts. Whereas complete weapons can carry significant visual information (Wiessner 1984), this is far more doubtful for the half hidden stone tip or lateral insert of a composite weapon (Valentin 2008: 63). Such non-visible subtleties are ideal for defining learning lineages, but not necessarily wider sociological units. Ornaments traditions, as they have been recognised so far in the Mesolithic, would point to larger geographical interaction networks, larger social groups and cultural entities (see Marchand 2014: 403 ff.). One may wish that for both periods, symbolically laden expressions such as portable art, parietal art and ornaments would participate in the definition of the human groups that, at different spatial and social scales, shared common traditions and cultural background.

NOTES

1   The mouth of the cave is presently located at about 15 m above sea level.
2   Without even going into the question of the volume of sediment excavated in each site.
3   It is by pure chance that the two specialists happen to be the same person, but this at least should limit the risk of individual variation in the perception of the importance of change.
4   It must be recalled that these are erosional hiatuses and that the cave may have been occupied more or less continuously during these periods.

APPENDIX 1

Lists of Ornaments and Ornamental Shells per Trench and Unit

Table A1.1: List of Palaeolithic ornaments and ornamental shells from trench H1A.

Trench	Unit	FGP	FOP	Cyclope sp.	Homalopoma sanguineum	Antalis sp.	Columbella rustica	Glycymeris sp.	Bone beads	Stone beads	Perforated teeth
H1A	220	2	1	2	1	7					
H1A	219	2	1	2		7					
H1A	218	2	1	1	1	1					
H1A	217	2	1			9					
H1A	216	2	1			6			1		
H1A	215	2	1			12					
H1A	214	2	1								
H1A	213	2	1			3					
H1A	212	2	1			1					
H1A	211	2 or 3	1	1		4					
H1A	210	3	1			1					
H1A	209	3	1			1					
H1A	208	3	1			2					
H1A	207	3	1								
H1A	206	3	1								
H1A	205	3	1								
H1A	204	3 or 4	2								
H1A	203	4	2								
H1A	202	4	2								
H1A	201	4	2								
H1A	200	4	2								
H1A	199	4	2								
H1A	198	4	2								1
H1A	197	4	2								
H1A	196	4	2								
H1A	195	4	2								
H1A	194	4	2								

Trench	Unit	FGP	FOP	Cyclope sp.	Homalopoma sanguineum	Antalis sp.	Columbella rustica	Glycymeris sp.	Bone beads	Stone beads	Perforated teeth
H1A	193	4	2								
H1A	192	4	2								
H1A	191	4	2			2					
H1A	190	4	2								
H1A	189	5	3								
H1A	188	5	3								
H1A	187	5	3								
H1A	186	5	3			1					
H1A	185	5	3			1					
H1A	184	5	3								
H1A	183	5	3			1					
H1A	182	5	3			1					
H1A	181	5	3								
H1A	180	5	3								
H1A	179	5	3	13		2	3				
H1A	178	5	3	2		2					
H1A	177	5	3					1			
H1A	176	5	3								
H1A	175	5 or 6.1	3	4		1					
H1A	174	6.1	3	15		1	1				
H1A	173	6.1	3	16		2					
H1A	172	6.1	3	5							
H1A	171	6.1	3	1							
H1A	170	6.1	3	1			1				
H1A	169	6.1	3	12		1					
H1A	168	6.2	3	31		2					
H1A	167	6.2	3	20		1		1			

Table A1.2: List of Palaeolithic ornaments and ornamental shells from trench H1B.

Trench	Unit	FGP	FOP	*Cyclope sp.*	*Homalopoma sanguineum*	*Antalis sp.*	*Columbella rustica*	*Glycymeris sp.*	Bone beads	Stone beads	Perforated teeth
H1B	215	0	1		1	2					
H1B	214	0	1			1					
H1B	213	1	1			1					
H1B	212	1	1								
H1B	211	1	1	2		1					
H1B	210	1	1	5	2	2					
H1B	209	1	1		1	3					
H1B	208	1	1	3	1	2					
H1B	207	2	1		1	6					
H1B	206	2	1	1		1					
H1B	205	2	1			5	1				
H1B	204	2	1	9	1	4	1				
H1B	203	2	1	8	1	7					
H1B	202	2	1	7		3					
H1B	201	2	1	1							
H1B	200	2	1	5		26					
H1B	199	2	1								
H1B	198	2	1	5							
H1B	197	2	1	2							
H1B	196	2	1	2							
H1B	195	2	1	3							
H1B	194	2	1	6	1						
H1B	193	2	1								
H1B	192	2	1								
H1B	191	2	1			FV 418					
H1B	190	2	1								
H1B	189	2	1	1						1	
H1B	188	2	1	3		FV 406-409					
H1B	187	2	1	2							

Trench	Unit	FGP	FOP	*Cyclope sp.*	*Homalopoma sanguineum*	*Antalis sp.*	*Columbella rustica*	*Glycymeris sp.*	Bone beads	Stone beads	Perforated teeth
H1B	186	2	1								
H1B	185	2	1	1		1+ FV 404-405					
H1B	184	2	1	1							
H1B	183	2	1				1				
H1B	182	2	1	1		FV 416 and 417					
H1B	181	2	1				1				
H1B	180	3	1		1						
H1B	179	3	1								
H1B	178	3	1								
H1B	177	3	1								
H1B	176	3	1								
H1B	175	3	1	1		1					
H1B	174	3	1	4							
H1B	173	3	1								
H1B	172	3 or 4	2								
H1B	171	3 or 4	2								
H1B	171	3 or 4	2								
H1B	170	4	2								
H1B	169	4	2								
H1B	168	4	2								
H1B	167	4	2								
H1B	166	4	2								
H1B	165	4	2								
H1B	164	4	2								
H1B	163	4	2								
H1B	162	4	2								
H1B	161	5	3	1							
H1B	160	5	3	11			3	1 + FV 384-385			

Trench	Unit	FGP	FOP	*Cyclope sp.*	*Homalopoma sanguineum*	*Antalis sp.*	*Columbella rustica*	*Glycymeris sp.*	Bone beads	Stone beads	Perforated teeth
H1B	159	5	3	12		1	1				
H1B	158	5	3	21		2	1	1			
H1B	157	5	3	17		FV 415	3				
H1B	156	5	3	48			2				
H1B	155	5	3	38		1	10	1			
H1B	154	5	3	22			1				
H1B	153	6.1	3	7		FV 366	1				
H1B	152	6.1	3	1							
H1B	151	6.1	3	11		1					

Table A1.3: List of Palaeolithic ornaments and ornamental shells from trench FAS.

Trench	Unit	FGP	FOP	*Cyclope sp.*	*Homalopoma sanguineum*	*Antalis sp.*	*Columbella rustica*	*Glycymeris sp.*	Bone beads	Stone beads	Perforated teeth
FAS	227	0	1	1		2					
FAS	226	0	1			3					
FAS	225	0	1	4		1	1				
FAS	224	0	1	2		9					
FAS	223	0	1	8		6					
FAS	222	1	1	14		9					
FAS	221	1	1	7		3					
FAS	220	1	1	3		2	1				
FAS	219	1	1	2	1	4					
FAS	218	1	1	3	1	1					
FAS	217	1	1	11		4					
FAS	216	2	1	1		3	1				
FAS	215	2	1	7		4					
FAS	214	2	1	5		5	1				
FAS	213	2	1	3		1					
FAS	212	2	1	6		1					
FAS	211	2	1	0							
FAS	210	2	1	0		1					
FAS	209	2	1	5	1	1	1				
FAS	208	mixed	mixed	2							
FAS	207	6.1	3	16						FV 797	
FAS	206	6.1	3	7		2					
FAS	205	6.1	3	10		2					
FAS	204	6.1	3	17		2	2				
FAS	203	6.1	3	20		1					
FAS	202	6.1 or 6.2	3	10		2	2				
FAS	201	6.2	3	2							
FAS	200	6.2	3	7							
FAS	199	6.2	3	39		3	1				

Table A1.4: List of Mesolithic ornaments and ornamental shells from trench H1A.

Trench	Unit	FGP	FOP	Cyclope sp.	Antalis sp.	Colombella rustica	Perforated pebbles
H1A	166	7 cont.	4.1	42	7	1	
H1A	165	7	4.1	1	2	1	
H1A	164	7	4.1	3	1		
H1A	163	7	4.1	9			
H1A	162	7	4.1				
H1A	161	7	4.1		FV 264		
H1A	160	7	4.1	61			
H1A	159	7	4.1	32	2 + FV 263		
H1A	158	7	4.1	55	1 + FV 262		
H1A	157	7	4.1		FV 261		
H1A	156	7	4.1	10	1 + FV 265-248, 260	2	
H1A	155	7	4.1	53	1 + FV 240-245		
H1A	154	7	4.1	13	FV 239		
H1A	153	7	4.1	3			
H1A	152	7	4.1	37	FV 238		
H1A	151	7	4.1	9			
H1A	150	7	4.1	12			
H1A	149	7	4.1	24	FV 226		
H1A	148	7	4.1	8			
H1A	147	7	4.1	17			
H1A	146	7	4.1	26			
H1A	145	7	4.1	22			
H1A	144	7	4.1	8		1	
H1A	143	7	4.1	8			
H1A	142	7	4.1	33			
H1A	141	7	4.1	1			
H1A	140	7	4.1	28			
H1A	139	7	4.1	9			
H1A	138	7	4.1	8			

Trench	Unit	FGP	FOP	Cyclope sp.	Antalis sp.	Colombella rustica	Perforated pebbles
H1A	137	7	4.1	7			
H1A	136	7	4.1	13			
H1A	135	7	4.1	68			
H1A	134	7	4.1	8			
H1A	133	7	4.1	9			
H1A	132	7	4.1	89			FS 329-330
H1A	131	7	4.1	110			
H1A	130	7	4.1				
H1A	129	7	4.1	69		2	
H1A	128	7	4.1	38		4	
H1A	127	7	4.1	51		3	
H1A	126	7	4.1	FV 53, 48			
H1A	125	7	4.1	18			
H1A	124	7	4.1	31		2	
H1A	123	7	4.1	4			
H1A	122	7	4.1	14			
H1A	121	7 x 8	4.1 x 4.2	6			
H1A	120	7 x 8	4.1 x 4.2				
H1A	119	8 cont.	4.2	16			
H1A	118	7 x 8	4.1 x 4.2	11			
H1A	116	8	4.2	5		1	
H1A	115	8	4.2	1			
H1A	114	8	4.2	12		1	
H1A	113	8	4.2				
H1A	112	8	4.2	6		2	
H1A	111	8	4.2	13			
H1A	110	8	4.2				
H1A	109	8	4.2	4			
H1A	108	8	4.2	4		1	

Trench	Unit	FGP	FOP	*Cyclope sp.*	*Antalis sp.*	*Colombella rustica*	Perforated pebbles
H1A	107	8	4.2	13		2	
H1A	106	8	4.2				
H1A	105	8	4.2				
H1A	104	8	4.2				
H1A	103	8	4.2	9		1	
H1A	102	8	4.2				
H1A	101	8	4.2	21		2	
H1A	100	8	4.2	8		4	

Table A1.5: List of Mesolithic ornaments and ornamental shells from trench H1B.

Trench	Unit	FGP	FOP	Cyclope. sp	Antalis sp.	Columbella rustica	Perforated pebbles	Bird bone ?	Glycymeris. sp
H1B	150	7	4.1	60	2 + FV 354-358	2		2 + FV 356, 357	
H1B	149	7	4.1	20					
H1B	148	7	4.1	30		1			
H1B	147	7	4.1	169	5 + FV 395-307	2			
H1B	146	7	4.1	103	FV 342-343				
H1B	145	7	4.1	82	FV 312, 313, 318	1			
H1B	144	7	4.1	156	FV 341	3			
H1B	143	7	4.1	49	1 + FV 291, 309, 314, 340	1			
H1B	142	7	4.1	12	FV 284-290, 339	4			
H1B	141	7	4.1	85	2 + FV 282, 283, 315, 325				
H1B	140	7	4.1	7		1			
H1B	139	7	4.1	68	2 + FV 281	1			
H1B	138	7	4.1	8	FV 206, 318, 324				
H1B	137	7	4.1	32	1 + FV 214				
H1B	136	7	4.1	42	FV 317				
H1B	135	7	4.1	138	FV 319-323	1		1	
H1B	134	7	4.1	97	FV 326-328				
H1B	133	7	4.1	70	FV 316				FV: 368
H1B	132	7	4.1	55		1			
H1B	131	7	4.1	1					
H1B	130	7	4.1	88		1			
H1B	129	7	4.1	67					

Trench	Unit	FGP	FOP	*Cyclope. sp*	*Antalis sp.*	*Columbella rustica*	Perforated pebbles	Bird bone ?	*Glycymeris. sp*
H1B	128	7	4.1	100	FV 311	4			
H1B	127	7	4.1	118	2 + FV 310	1			
H1B	126	7	4.1	12					
H1B	125	7	4.1	15	1 + FV 192				
H1B	124	7	4.1	2		5			
H1B	123	7	4.1	159		7			
H1B	122	7	4.1	88		3			
H1B	121	7 x 8	4.1x .4.2	43		2	1		
H1B	120	7 x 8	4.1x .4.2	37	FV 207	3			
H1B	119	7 x 8	4.1x .4.2	7		1			
H1B	118	7 x 8	4.1x .4.2	38		3			
H1B	117	Cleaning	Cleaning	43		3			
H1B	116	8	4.2	61		3			
H1B	115	8	4.2	41	FV 280	3			
H1B	114	8	4.2	10	FV 279	3			
H1B	113	8	4.2	12		1			
H1B	112	8	4.2	16		2			
H1B	111	8	4.2	29		2			
H1B	110	8	4.2	30		1			
H1B	109	8	4.2	40		1			
H1B	108	8	4.2	51		3			
H1B	107	8	4.2	24		3			
H1B	106	8	4.2						
H1B	105	8	4.2						
H1B	104	8	4.2	8		2			

Table A1.6: List of Mesolithic ornaments and ornamental shells from trench FAS.

Trench	Unit	FGP	FOP	Cyclope. sp	Antalis. sp	Colombella rustica	Perforated pebbles	Perforated Conus mediterraneus
FAS	198	7 cont.	4.1	75	2	10		
FAS	197	7 cont.	4.1	53	7	0		
FAS	196	7	4.1	135	6	14		
FAS	195	7	4.1	147	4	23+ FV 433		
FAS	194	7	4.1	55	1	13		
FAS	193	7	4.1	17		1		
FAS	192	7	4.1	235	6	27		
FAS	191	7	4.1	143	5	15		
FAS	190	7	4.1	79	3	17		
FAS	189	7	4.1	55		11		
FAS	188	7	4.1	106	3	10		
FAS	187	7	4.1	88	2	9		
FAS	186	7	4.1	118	2	1		
FAS	185	7	4.1	118	2	3		
FAS	184	7	4.1	263	5	2		
FAS	183	7	4.1	119	1			
FAS	182	7	4.1	235	5			
FAS	181	7	4.1	59	0	1		
FAS	180	7	4.1	236	3			
FAS	179	7	4.1	219	6	4		
FAS	178	7	4.1	58	0	2		
FAS	177	7	4.1	268	4	10		
FAS	176	7	4.1	143	6	2	FV 794	
FAS	175	7	4.1	0	0	3		
FAS	174	7	4.1	139	8	1		
FAS	173	7 or 8	4.1 or 4.2	18	0	2		
FAS	172	7 or 8	4.1 or 4.2	20	1			
FAS	171	7 or 8	4.1 or 4.2	8	0			
FAS	170	7 or 8	4.1 or 4.2	25	1			
FAS	169	8	4.2	0				

Trench	Unit	FGP	FOP	*Cyclope.* sp	*Antalis.* sp	*Colombella rustica*	Perforated pebbles	Perforated *Conus mediterraneus*
FAS	168	8	4.2	11	1			
FAS	167	8	4.2	7	1			
FAS	166	8	4.2	77	3	1		
FAS	165	8	4.2	59				
FAS	164	8	4.2	23	4			
FAS	163	8	4.2	17	0			
FAS	162	8	4.2	48	6	2		
FAS	161	8	4.2	20	6			
FAS	160	8	4.2	32	1			
FAS	159	8	4.2	38	10			
FAS	158	8	4.2	72	8			
FAS	157	8	4.2	61	8			
FAS	156	8	4.2	277	35	3		
FAS	155	8	4.2	73	5			
FAS	154	9 cont.	4.3	46	9			
FAS	153 or 155	9	4.3		14			
FAS	153	9	4.3	69	2			
FAS	152	Cleaning	Cleaning	43	9			
FAS	151	9	4.3	25	9			
FAS	151 or 150	9	4.3	7				
FAS	150	9	4.3	19	7			

Table A1.7: List of Mesolithic ornaments and ornamental shells from trench FAN.

Trench	Unit	FGP	FOP	*Cyclope. sp.*	*Antalis. sp.*	*Colombella rustica*	Perforated pebbles	Perforated *Conus mediterraneus*
FAN	231	Cleaning	Cleaning					
FAN	230	7	4.1	84	22			
FAN	229	7	4.1	na	2	na		
FAN	228	7	4.1	na	1	na		
FAN	227	7	4.1	na	5	na		
FAN	226	7	4.1	na	6	na		
FAN	225	7	4.1	na	2	na	1 FS 798	
FAN	224	7	4.1	na	5	na		
FAN	223	7	4.1	na	na	na		
FAN	222	7	4.1	na	3	na		
FAN	221	7	4.1	na	3	na		
FAN	220	7	4.1	na	na	na		
FAN	219	7	4.1	198		4	1 FS 799	
FAN	218	7	4.1	157	1	4		
FAN	217	7	4.1	3				
FAN	216	7	4.1	63	1	2		
FAN	215	7	4.1	12		1		
FAN	214	7	4.1	na	1	na		
FAN	213	7	4.1	na	na	na		
FAN	212	7	4.1	27	4	4		
FAN	211	7	4.1	13				
FAN	210	7	4.1	34		1		
FAN	209	7	4.1	na	1	na		
FAN	208	7	4.1	22	2	4		
FAN	207	7	4.1	41	1			
FAN	206	7	4.1	na	na	na		
FAN	205	7	4.1	2				
FAN	204	7	4.1	17		1		
FAN	203	7	4.1	na	na	na		
FAN	202	7	4.1	2	1	1		

Trench	Unit	FGP	FOP	*Cyclope. sp.*	*Antalis. sp.*	*Colombella rustica*	Perforated pebbles	*Perforated Conus mediterraneus*
FAN	201	7	4.1	31	2	1		
FAN	200	7	4.1	12		1		
FAN	199	7	4.1	na	na	na		
FAN	198	7	4.1	na	7	na		
FAN	197	7	4.1	na	na	na		
FAN	196	7x8	4.1x4.2	22				
FAN	195	7x8	4.1x4.2	na	na	na		
FAN	194	7x8	4.1x4.2	39		2		
FAN	193	7x8	4.1x4.2	3				
FAN	192	Cleaning	Cleaning	29		8		
FAN	191	8	4.2	2				
FAN	190	8	4.2	4				
FAN	189	8	4.2	54		8		
FAN	188	8	4.2	112		2		
FAN	187	8	4.2	13		16		
FAN	186	8	4.2	4	1 FV 186	5		
FAN	185	Cleaning	Cleaning	48	1 FV 387	4		
FAN	184	8	4.2	16		2		
FAN	183	8	4.2	62		2		
FAN	182	8	4.2	35		5		
FAN	182	8	4.2	35		5		
FAN	181	8	4.2	4				
FAN	180	8	4.2	21		2		
FAN	179	8	4.2	57	1 FV 38	7		
FAN	178	8	4.2	na	na	na		
FAN	177	8	4.2	41		5		
FAN	176	8	4.2	46		4		
FAN	175	8	4.2	47		5		
FAN	174	9	4.3	4		4		
FAN	173	9	4.3			0		

Trench	Unit	FGP	FOP	*Cyclope. sp.*	*Antalis. sp.*	*Colombella rustica*	Perforated pebbles	*Perforated Conus mediterraneus*
FAN	172	9	4.3	42		7		
FAN	171	9	4.3	2				
FAN	170	9	4.3	1		5		1
FAN	169	9	4.3	12		3		
FAN	168	Cleaning	Cleaning	4		6		
FAN	167	9	4.3	7		6		
FAN	166	9	4.3	3		3		
FAN	165	9	4.3	3		1		
FAN	164	9	4.3	3		1		

APPENDIX 2

Molluscan Remains from a Subsample of < 5 mm Residues

By André C. Colonese

Note 1: *Antalis* sp. fragments had been removed from the samples and are listed under their original unit in Appendix 1.

Note 2: Some larger fractions of residues were included with the smallest fractions and are also listed here.

Table A2.1: Identification of the micromolluscs from the small residues of trench FAS.

Trench	Unit	Species	N	Sieve (mm) and fraction sorted	Notes
FAS	227	*Bittium* sp.	2	-2.8, 1/32	3 of 3
FAS	227	*Bittium* sp.	4	-2.8, 1/32	1 of 3
FAS	227	*Bittium* sp.	2	2.8 - 5, 1/4	2 of 2
FAS	227	*Chondrina* sp.	1	2.8 - 5, 1/4	2 of 2
FAS	227	Condrinidae	2	2.8 - 5, 1/8	1 of 2
FAS	227	*Conus mediterraneus*	1	-2.8, 1/32	1 of 3
FAS	227	coral	1	2.8 - 5, 1/4	2 of 2
FAS	227	*Cyclope* sp.	1	2.8 - 5, 1/4	2 of 2
FAS	227	Higromiidae.	8	2.8 - 5, 1/8	1 of 2
FAS	227	Higromiidae	9	2.8 - 5, 1/4	2 of 2
FAS	227	*Pavicardium* sp.	1	2.8 - 5, 1/8	1 of 2
FAS	227	*Pavicardium* sp.	1	2.8 - 5, 1/4	2 of 2
FAS	227	Rissoidae	1	2.8 - 5, 1/8	1 of 2
FAS	227	Veneridae	1	2.8 - 5, 1/4	2 of 2
FAS	227	Vermetidae	1	-2.8, 1/32	2 of 3
FAS	226	*Bittium* sp.	1	-2.8, 1/32	1 of 2
FAS	226	*Bittium* sp.	1	-2.8, 1/32	2 of 2
FAS	226	Higromiidae	5	2.8 - 5, 1/16	
FAS	225	*Bittium* latreillii	5	2.8 - 5, 1/4	
FAS	225	*Bittium reticulatum*	4	2.8 - 5, 1/4	
FAS	225	*Bittium* sp.	4	2.8 - 5, 1/8	
FAS	225	*Bittium* sp.	3	-2.8, 1/16	1 of 2
FAS	225	*Bittium* sp.	4	-2.8, 1/16	2 of 2
FAS	225	*Bittium* sp.	1	2.8 - 5, 1/4	
FAS	225	*Bittium* sp.	23	2.8 - 5, 1/4	
FAS	225	*Calliostoma* sp.	1	2.8 - 5, 1/4	
FAS	225	Cerithidea	2	2.8 - 5, 1/4	
FAS	225	Cerithidea	1	2.8 - 5, 1/4	
FAS	225	*Cerithium* cf. *vulgatum*	1	2.8 - 5, 1/8	
FAS	225	*Cerithium* cf. *vulgatum*	1	2.8 - 5, 1/4	
FAS	225	*Chauvetia* sp.	1	2.8 - 5, 1/4	
FAS	225	*Columbella rustica*	1	2.8 - 5, 1/4	
FAS	225	Condrinidae	6	2.8 - 5, 1/4	
FAS	225	*Conus mediterraneus*	1	2.8 - 5, 1/4	
FAS	225	coral	1	2.8 - 5, 1/4	
FAS	225	*Cyclope* sp.	1	2.8 - 5, 1/8	

Trench	Unit	Species	N	Sieve (mm) and fraction sorted	Notes
FAS	225	*Cyclope* sp.	1	2.8 - 5, 1/4	
FAS	225	*Euspira* cf. *pulchella*	3	2.8 - 5, 1/4	
FAS	225	*Gibbula* sp.	2	2.8 - 5, 1/4	
FAS	225	Higromiidae	10	2.8 - 5, 1/8	
FAS	225	Higromiidae	58	2.8 - 5, 1/4	
FAS	225	*Ovatella* sp	1	2.8 - 5, 1/4	
FAS	225	*Pavicardium* sp.	1	2.8 - 5, 1/8	
FAS	225	*Pavicardium* sp.	3	2.8 - 5, 1/4	
FAS	225	*Pirenella conica*	1	2.8 - 5, 1/4	
FAS	225	Rissoidae	2	2.8 - 5, 1/4	
FAS	225	*Turritella* sp.	1	2.8 - 5, 1/4	
FAS	225	*Turritella* sp.	1	2.8 - 5, 1/4	
FAS	225	Veneridae	2	2.8 - 5, 1/4	
FAS	224	*Bittium latreillii*	1	2.8 - 5, 1/4	2 of 2
FAS	224	*Bittium reticulatum*	4	-2.8, 1/16	1 of 2
FAS	224	*Bittium reticulatum*	1	2.8 - 5, 1/4	2 of 2
FAS	224	*Bittium* sp.	7	2.8 - 5, 1/4	1 of 2
FAS	224	*Bittium* sp.	2	-2.8, 1/16	1 of 2
FAS	224	*Bittium* sp.	11	2.8 - 5, 1/4	2 of 2
FAS	224	*Bittium* sp.	12	-2.8, 1/16	2 of 2
FAS	224	*Chondrina* sp.	1	2.8 - 5, 1/4	1 of 2
FAS	224	Condrinidae	4	2.8 - 5, 1/4	2 of 2
FAS	224	coral	1	2.8 - 5, 1/4	1 of 2
FAS	224	Higromiidae	1	2.8 - 5, 1/4	1 of 2
FAS	224	Higromiidae	34	2.8 - 5, 1/4	2 of 2
FAS	224	*Pavicardium* sp.	1	-2.8, 1/16	1 of 2
FAS	224	*Pavicardium* sp.	1	2.8 - 5, 1/4	2 of 2
FAS	224	Rissoidae	1	-2.8, 1/16	1 of 2
FAS	224	Rissoidae	1	2.8 - 5, 1/4	2 of 2
FAS	224	*Turritella* sp.	1	-2.8, 1/16	2 of 2
FAS	224	Veneridae	1	-2.8, 1/16	1 of 2
FAS	224	Veneridae	1	2.8 - 5, 1/4	2 of 2
FAS	223	*Alvania* cf. *cimex*	1	-2.8, 1/32	2 of 2
FAS	223	*Bittium* cf. *reticulatum*	2	-2.8, 1/32	2 of 2
FAS	223	*Bittium* cf. *reticulatum*	2	-2.8, 1/32	2 of 2
FAS	223	*Bittium latreillii*	3	2.8 - 5, 1/4	2 of 2
FAS	223	*Bittium reticulatum*	5	2.8 - 5, 1/4	2 of 2

Trench	Unit	Species	N	Sieve (mm) and fraction sorted	Notes
FAS	223	*Bittium reticulatum*	3	2.8 - 5, 1/4	1 of 2
FAS	223	*Bittium* sp.	6	-2.8, 1/32	2 of 2
FAS	223	*Bittium* sp.	20	-2.8, 1/32	2 of 2
FAS	223	*Bittium* sp.	15	2.8 - 5, 1/4	2 of 2
FAS	223	*Bittium* sp.	18	2.8 - 5, 1/4	1 of 2
FAS	223	Cerithidea	1	2.8 - 5, 1/4	2 of 2
FAS	223	Condrinidae	2	2.8 - 5, 1/4	2 of 2
FAS	223	Condrinidae	1	2.8 - 5, 1/4	1 of 2
FAS	223	*Conus mediterraneus*	1	2.8 - 5, 1/4	2 of 2
FAS	223	*Conus mediterraneus*	1	2.8 - 5, 1/4	1 of 2
FAS	223	*Cyclope* sp.	1	2.8 - 5, 1/4	2 of 2
FAS	223	*Gibbula* sp.	1	2.8 - 5, 1/4	1 of 2
FAS	223	Higromiidae	34	2.8 - 5, 1/4	2 of 2
FAS	223	Higromiidae	31	2.8 - 5, 1/4	1 of 2
FAS	223	*Mangelia* sp.	1	-2.8, 1/32	2 of 2
FAS	223	Nassaridade	1	2.8 - 5, 1/4	2 of 2
FAS	223	*Nucula* sp.	2	2.8 - 5, 1/4	2 of 2
FAS	223	*Nucula* sp.	2	2.8 - 5, 1/4	1 of 2
FAS	223	Rissoidae	4	-2.8, 1/32	2 of 2
FAS	223	Rissoidae	1	-2.8, 1/32	2 of 2
FAS	223	Rissoidae	3	2.8 - 5, 1/4	1 of 2
FAS	223	*Turritella* sp.	2	-2.8, 1/32	2 of 2
FAS	222	*Bittium* cf. *reticulatum*	2	-2.8, 1/16	1 of 2
FAS	222	*Bittium* cf. *reticulatum*	3	-2.8, 1/16	2 of 2
FAS	222	*Bittium* sp.	16	-2.8, 1/16	1 of 2
FAS	222	*Bittium* sp.	30	-2.8, 1/16	2 of 2
FAS	222	Buccinidae	1		
FAS	222	*Cerithium* cf. *vulgatum*	1	-2.8, 1/16	2 of 2
FAS	222	*Mangelia* sp.	1	-2.8, 1/16	2 of 2
FAS	222	*Pavicardium* sp.	1	-2.8, 1/16	2 of 2
FAS	222	*Rissoa ventricosa*	2	-2.8, 1/16	1 of 2
FAS	222	*Rissoa ventricosa*	1	-2.8, 1/16	2 of 2
FAS	222	Rissoidae	1	-2.8, 1/16	2 of 2
FAS	221	*Bittium* sp.	3	-2.8, 1/8	2 of 2
FAS	221	*Bittium* sp.	1	-2.8, 1/8	
FAS	221	*Chondrina* sp.	2	2.8 - 5, 1/4	
FAS	221	Condrinidae	3	-2.8, 1/8	2 of 2
FAS	221	*Cyclope* sp.	2	2.8 - 5, 1/4	

Trench	Unit	Species	N	Sieve (mm) and fraction sorted	Notes
FAS	221	*Euspira* cf. *pulchella*	4	2.8 - 5, 1/4	
FAS	221	*Euspira* cf. *pulchella*	1	-2.8, 1/8	
FAS	221	Higromiidae	2	-2.8, 1/8	2 of 2
FAS	221	Higromiidae	32	2.8 - 5, 1/4	
FAS	221	Higromiidae	7	-2.8, 1/8	
FAS	221	*Hydrobia* sp.	1	2.8 - 5, 1/4	
FAS	220	*Alvania* cf. *cimex*	1	-2.8, 1/8	
FAS	220	*Bittium reticulatum*	2	2.8 - 5, 1/4	
FAS	220	*Bittium* sp.	10	-2.8, 1/8	
FAS	220	*Bittium* sp.	8	2.8 - 5, 1/4	
FAS	220	Bittium sp.	15	-2.8, 1/8	1 of 2
FAS	220	*Cardita calyculata*	1	2.8 - 5, 1/4	
FAS	220	Cerithidea	1	2.8 - 5, 1/4	
FAS	220	*Columbella rustica*	1	2.8 - 5, 1/4	
FAS	220	*Chondrina* sp.	2	-2.8, 1/8	
FAS	220	*Chondrina* sp.	5	2.8 - 5, 1/4	
FAS	220	*Conus mediterraneus*	2	2.8 - 5, 1/4	
FAS	220	Helicidae	2	-2.8, 1/8	
FAS	220	Higromiidae	3	-2.8, 1/8	
FAS	220	Higromiidae	16	2.8 - 5, 1/4	
FAS	220	*Nassarius* sp.	1	2.8 - 5, 1/4	
FAS	220	*Nucula* sp.	1	-2.8, 1/8	
FAS	220	*Pavicardium* sp.	1	-2.8, 1/8	
FAS	220	*Pirenella conica*	1	2.8 - 5, 1/4	
FAS	220	*Rissoa* sp.	2	-2.8, 1/8	1 of 2
FAS	220	*Rissoa ventricosa*	1	-2.8, 1/8	
FAS	220	*Rissoa ventricosa*	1	2.8 - 5, 1/4	
FAS	220	*Rissoa ventricosa*	1	-2.8, 1/8	1 of 2
FAS	220	Rissoidae	8	-2.8, 1/8	
FAS	220	Rissoidae	3	-2.8, 1/8	1 of 2
FAS	220	*Turritella* sp.	1	-2.8, 1/8	1 of 2
FAS	219	*Alvania* cf. *cimex*	1	-2.8, 1/8	
FAS	219	*Bittium* sp.	2	2.8 - 5, 1/8	
FAS	219	*Bittium* sp.	4	-2.8, 1/8	

Trench	Unit	Species	N	Sieve (mm) and fraction sorted	Notes
FAS	219	*Cyclope* sp.	1	2.8 - 5, 1/8	
FAS	219	Higromiidae	2	2.8 - 5, 1/8	
FAS	219	Higromiidae	2	-2.8, 1/8	
FAS	219	*Mitra* sp.	1	-2.8, 1/8	
FAS	219	Muricidae	1	-2.8, 1/8	
FAS	219	*Pirenella conica*	2	2.8 - 5, 1/8	
FAS	219	*Pirenella conica*	1	-2.8, 1/8	
FAS	219	Rissoidae	8	-2.8, 1/8	
FAS	218	*Bittium* sp.	1	2.8 - 5, 1/8	
FAS	218	*Cyclope* sp.	2	2.8 - 5, 1/8	
FAS	218	Higromiidae	2	2.8 - 5, 1/8	
FAS	218	Rissoidae	1	2.8 - 5, 1/8	
FAS	217	*Bittium* sp.	1	2.8 - 5, 1/32	
FAS	217	*Bittium* sp.	31	-2.8, 1/32	
FAS	217	Condrinidae	3	2.8 - 5, 1/32	
FAS	217	*Cyclope* sp.	2	2.8 - 5, 1/32	
FAS	217	*Cyclope* sp.	1	-2.8, 1/32	
FAS	217	*Euspira* cf. *pulchella*	1	-2.8, 1/32	
FAS	217	Higromiidae	5	2.8 - 5, 1/32	
FAS	217	*Pisana striata*	1		
FAS	217	*Rissoa ventricosa*	3	-2.8, 1/32	
FAS	217	Rissoidae	5	-2.8, 1/32	
FAS	216	Condrinidae	1	2.8 - 5, 1/16	
FAS	216	*Euspira* cf. *pulchella*	1	2.8 - 5, 1/16	
FAS	216	*Euspira* cf. *pulchella*	1	-2.8, 1/16	
FAS	216	Helicidae	1	-2.8, 1/16	
FAS	216	Higromiidae	2	2.8 - 5, 1/16	
FAS	216	Higromiidae	3	-2.8, 1/16	
FAS	215	*Bittium reticulatum*	6	-2.8 - 5, 1/16	
FAS	215	*Bittium reticulatum*	1	-2.8, 1/16	
FAS	215	*Bittium* sp.	36	-2.8, 1/16	
FAS	215	*Bittium* sp.	1	+5	
FAS	215	*Cerithium vulgatum*	1	-2.8 - 5, 1/16	
FAS	215	*Chondrina* sp.	2	-2.8 - 5, 1/16	
FAS	215	*Chondrina* sp.	1	-2.8, 1/16	
FAS	215	*Cyclope* sp.	5	-2.8 - 5, 1/16	
FAS	215	*Euspira* cf. *pulchella*	1	-2.8 - 5, 1/16	

Trench	Unit	Species	N	Sieve (mm) and fraction sorted	Notes
FAS	215	*Euspira* cf. *pulchella*	1	-2.8, 1/16	
FAS	215	*Gibbula* sp.	4	-2.8, 1/16	
FAS	215	*Gibbula* sp.	1	+5	
FAS	215	Helicidae	1	-2.8, 1/16	
FAS	215	Higromiidae	10	-2.8 - 5, 1/16	
FAS	215	Higromiidae	6	-2.8, 1/16	
FAS	215	Higromiidae	1	+5	
FAS	215	*Pavicardium* sp.	1	-2.8, 1/16	
FAS	215	*Rissoa* cf. *ventricosa*	2	-2.8, 1/16	
FAS	215	*Rissoa* sp.	1	-2.8, 1/16	
FAS	215	*Rissoa ventricosa*	1	-2.8 - 5, 1/16	
FAS	215	Rissoidae	6	-2.8, 1/16	
FAS	215	Veneridae	1	-2.8, 1/16	
FAS	214	*Alvania* cf. *cimex*	1	-2.8, 1/16	2 of 2
FAS	214	*Alvania* cf. *lineata*	2	-2.8, 1/16	2 of 2
FAS	214	*Bittium reticulatum*	1	2.8 - 5, 1/16	
FAS	214	*Bittium reticulatum*	1	+5	
FAS	214	*Bittium* sp.	7	2.8 - 5, 1/16	
FAS	214	*Bittium* sp.	20	-2.8, 1/16	
FAS	214	*Bittium* sp.	15	-2.8, 1/16	2 of 2
FAS	214	*Alvania* cf. *cimex*	1	-2.8, 1/16	
FAS	214	*Alvania* cf. *lineata*	2	-2.8, 1/16	
FAS	214	*Bittium reticulatum*	1	2.8 - 5, 1/16	
FAS	214	*Bittium reticulatum*	1	+5	
FAS	214	*Bittium* sp.	7	2.8 - 5, 1/16	
FAS	214	*Bittium* sp.	20	-2.8, 1/16	
FAS	214	*Bittium* sp.	15	-2.8, 1/16	2 of 2
FAS	214	Cerithidea	2	-2.8, 1/16	
FAS	214	*Columbella rustica*	1	2.8 - 5, 1/16	
FAS	214	Condrinidae	2	2.8 - 5, 1/16	
FAS	214	*Conus mediterraneus*	1	+5	
FAS	214	*Cyclope* sp.	2	2.8 - 5, 1/16	
FAS	214	*Euspira* cf. *pulchella*	1	2.8 - 5, 1/16	
FAS	214	*Euspira* cf. *pulchella*	1	-2.8, 1/16	
FAS	214	*Gibbula* sp.	1	-2.8, 1/16	2 of 2
FAS	214	*Gibbula* sp.	1	+5	
FAS	214	*Glans* cf. *trapezia*	1	+5	

Trench	Unit	Species	N	Sieve (mm) and fraction sorted	Notes
FAS	214	Higromiidae	12	2.8 - 5, 1/16	
FAS	214	*Hydrobia* sp.	2	-2.8, 1/16	
FAS	214	*Mangelia* sp.	1	-2.8, 1/16	
FAS	214	*Mangelia* sp.	1	-2.8, 1/16	2 of 2
FAS	214	*Rissoa ventricosa*	1	-2.8, 1/16	
FAS	214	Rissoidae	1	-2.8, 1/16	
FAS	213	*Bittium* sp.	4	2.8 - 5, 1/32	
FAS	214	*Striarca lactea*	1	+5	
FAS	213	*Bittium* sp.	18	-2.8, 1/32	
FAS	213	*Bittium* sp.	1	+5	
FAS	213	*Cyclope* sp.	2	2.8 - 5, 1/32	
FAS	213	*Euspira* cf. *pulchella*	2	-2.8, 1/32	
FAS	213	Higromiidae	2	2.8 - 5, 1/32	
FAS	213	Higromiidae	3	+5	
FAS	213	Hydrobidae	2	-2.8, 1/32	
FAS	213	*Rissoa ventricosa*	1	-2.8, 1/32	
FAS	213	Rissoidae	5	-2.8, 1/32	
FAS	212	*Bittium* sp.	1	2.8 - 5, 1/32	
FAS	212	*Bittium* sp.	10	-2.8, 1/32	
FAS	212	*Cerithium* cf. *vulgatum*	1	2.8 - 5, 1/32	
FAS	212	*Cerithium* cf. *vulgatum*	1	+5	
FAS	212	Higromiidae	2	2.8 - 5, 1/32	
FAS	212	*Mangelia* sp.	1	-2.8, 1/32	
FAS	212	*Nucula* sp.	1	-2.8, 1/32	
FAS	212	*Rissoa ventricosa*	1	-2.8, 1/32	
FAS	212	Rissoidae	4	-2.8, 1/32	
FAS	211	*Bittium reticulatum*	1	+5	
FAS	210	*Bittium latreillii*	1	2.8 - 5, 1/2	
FAS	210	*Bittium reticulatum*	2	+5	
FAS	210	*Bittium* sp.	1	2.8 - 5, 1/2	
FAS	210	*Bittium* sp.	3	-2.8, 1/16	
FAS	210	*Gibbula* cf. *turbinoide*	1	+5	
FAS	210	Higromiidae	3	2.8 - 5, 1/2	

Trench	Unit	Species	N	Sieve (mm) and fraction sorted	Notes
FAS	210	*Nassarius* cf. *unifasciatus*	1	+5	
FAS	210	*Pirenella conica*	1	+5	
FAS	210	Rissoidae	1	-2.8, 1/16	
FAS	210	*Turritella* sp.	1	2.8 - 5, 1/2	
FAS	210	Veneridae	1	-2.8, 1/16	
FAS	209	*Bittium latreillii*	1	2.8 - 5, 1/8	
FAS	209	*Bittium reticulatum*	3	2.8 - 5, 1/4	
FAS	209	*Bittium reticulatum*	1	+5	
FAS	209	*Bittium* sp.	2	2.8 - 5, 1/8	
FAS	209	*Bittium* sp.	10	-2.8, 1/32	2 of 2
FAS	209	*Bittium* sp.	8	2.8 - 5, 1/4	
FAS	209	*Bittium* sp.	2	-2.8, 1/32	1 of 2
FAS	209	*Columbella rustica*	1	2.8 - 5, 1/4	
FAS	209	*Chondrina* sp.	1	2.8 - 5, 1/4	
FAS	209	*Cyclope* sp.	1	2.8 - 5, 1/8	
FAS	209	*Cyclope* sp.	2	2.8 - 5, 1/4	
FAS	209	Higromiidae	3	2.8 - 5, 1/8	
FAS	209	Higromiidae	3	2.8 - 5, 1/4	
FAS	209	Nassaridade	2	2.8 - 5, 1/4	
FAS	209	*Pavicardium* sp.	2	2.8 - 5, 1/4	
FAS	209	*Pirenella conica*	1	+5	
FAS	209	*Rissoa* sp.	1	2.8 - 5, 1/4	
FAS	209	*Rissoa* sp.	1	-2.8, 1/32	1 of 2
FAS	209	Rissoidae	1	-2.8, 1/32	1 of 2
FAS	209	Veneridae	1	2.8 - 5, 1/8	
FAS	208	*Alvania* cf. *cimex*	1	-2.8, 1/16	
FAS	208	*Bittium latreillii*	1	-2.8, 1/16	
FAS	208	*Bittium reticulatum*	1	2.8 - 5, 1/16	
FAS	208	*Bittium* sp.	7	-2.8, 1/16	
FAS	208	Condrinidae	1	-2.8, 1/16	
FAS	208	*Cyclope* sp.	1	2.8 - 5, 1/16	
FAS	208	Helicidae	4	-2.8, 1/16	
FAS	208	Higromiidae	1	2.8 - 5, 1/16	
FAS	208	Higromiidae	1	-2.8, 1/16	

Trench	Unit	Species	N	Sieve (mm) and fraction sorted	Notes
FAS	208	Rissoidae	1	-2.8, 1/16	
FAS	207	*Alvania* cf. *cimex*	1	-2.8, 1/32	2 of 2
FAS	207	*Bittium reticulatum*	1	2.8 - 5, 1/32	
FAS	207	*Bittium* sp.	1	2.8 - 5, 1/32	2 of 2
FAS	207	*Bittium* sp.	15	-2.8, 1/32	1 of 2
FAS	207	*Bittium* sp.	6	-2.8, 1/32	2 of 2
FAS	207	*Bittium* sp.	3	+5	
FAS	207	*Cerithium vulgatum*	2	-2.8, 1/32	1 of 2
FAS	207	*Conus mediterraneus*	1	+5	
FAS	207	*Cyclope* sp.	1	2.8 - 5, 1/32	2 of 2
FAS	207	Helicidae	9	2.8 - 5, 1/32	
FAS	207	Helicidae	2	2.8 - 5, 1/32	2 of 2
FAS	207	Helicidae	17	-2.8, 1/32	2 of 2
FAS	207	Higromiidae	2	2.8 - 5, 1/32	
FAS	207	Higromiidae	1	2.8 - 5, 1/32	2 of 2
FAS	207	Higromiidae	2	-2.8, 1/32	2 of 2
FAS	207	Higromiidae	2	+5	
FAS	207	Nassaridade	2	-2.8, 1/32	1 of 2
FAS	207	*Pirenella conica*	1	2.8 - 5, 1/32	2 of 2
FAS	207	*Pirenella conica*	1	+5	
FAS	207	*Turritella* sp.	1	+5	
FAS	206	*Bittium reticulatum*	1	residue	
FAS	206	*Bittium* sp.	1	-2.8, 1/16	
FAS	206	Helicidae	1	2.8 - 5, 1/16	
FAS	206	Helicidae	15	-2.8, 1/16	
FAS	206	Higromiidae	11	2.8 - 5, 1/16	
FAS	206	Veneridae	1		
FAS	205	*Bittium* sp.	6	-2.8, 1/32	1 of 2
FAS	205	*Bittium* sp.	4	-2.8, 1/32	2 of 2
FAS	205	*Cerithium vulgatum*	1	2.8 - 5, 1/32	2 of 2
FAS	205	*Cerithium vulgatum*	1	-2.8, 1/32	2 of 2
FAS	205	Helicidae	4	-2.8, 1/32	1 of 2
FAS	205	Higromiidae	1	-2.8, 1/32	1 of 2
FAS	205	Muricidae	1	residue	
FAS	205	*Paracentrotus* sp.	1	-2.8, 1/32	1 of 2
FAS	205	*Paracentrotus* sp.	1	-2.8, 1/32	2 of 2

Trench	Unit	Species	N	Sieve (mm) and fraction sorted	Notes
FAS	205	*Pavicardium* sp.	2	-2.8, 1/32	1 of 2
FAS	204	*Alvania* cf. *cimex*	1	-2.8, 1/32	1 of 2
FAS	204	*Bittium* cf. *reticulatum*	1	+5	
FAS	204	*Bittium reticulatum*	3	2.8 - 5, 1/8	
FAS	204	*Bittium reticulatum*	3	+5	
FAS	204	*Bittium* sp.	3	-2.8, 1/32	2 of 2
FAS	204	*Bittium* sp.	1	2.8 - 5, 1/32	
FAS	204	*Bittium* sp.	4	-2.8, 1/32	1 of 2
FAS	204	*Bittium* sp.	3	+5	
FAS	204	*Cerithium* cf. *vulgatum*	2	+5	
FAS	204	*Cerithium vulgatum*	2	2.8 - 5, 1/8	
FAS	204	*Gibbula* sp.	1	2.8 - 5, 1/32	
FAS	204	Helicidae	9	-2.8, 1/32	2 of 2
FAS	204	Helicidae	2	2.8 - 5, 1/32	
FAS	204	*Pavicardium* sp.	1	-2.8, 1/32	1 of 2
FAS	204	*Turritella* sp.	1	+5	
FAS	203	*Bittium latreillii*	1	2.8 - 5, 1/32	2 of 2
FAS	203	*Bittium reticulatum*	2	-2.8, 1/32	2 of 2
FAS	203	*Bittium reticulatum*	4	+5	
FAS	203	*Bittium* sp.	36	-2.8, 1/32	2 of 2
FAS	203	*Bittium* sp.	3	-2.8, 1/32	3 of 3
FAS	203	*Bittium* sp.	1	-2.8, 1/32	2 of 3
FAS	203	*Bittium* sp.	8	2.8 - 5, 1/32	1 of 3
FAS	203	*Bittium* sp.	4	residue	
FAS	203	*Bittium* sp.	9	+5	
FAS	203	*Cecilioides acicula*	1	-2.8, 1/32	2 of 2
FAS	203	*Cerithium* cf. *vulgatum*	8	+5	
FAS	203	*Cerithium vulgatum*	1	2.8 - 5, 1/32	2 of 2
FAS	203	*Cerithium vulgatum*	1	residue	
FAS	203	*Chondrinidae*	1	-2.8, 1/32	3 of 3
FAS	203	coral	1	residue	
FAS	203	*Cyclope* sp.	1	-2.8, 1/32	2 of 2
FAS	203	*Cyclope* sp.	2	2.8 - 5, 1/32	1 of 2
FAS	203	*Cyclope* sp.	1	-2.8, 1/32	2 of 3
FAS	203	*Gibbula* sp.	9	+5	
FAS	203	Helicidae	3	-2.8, 1/32	2 of 2

FAS	203	Helicidae	15	-2.8, 1/32	3 of 3
FAS	203	Helicidae	6	2.8 - 5, 1/32	1 of 2
FAS	203	Helicidae	4	-2.8, 1/32	2 of 3
FAS	203	Helicidae	1	2.8 - 5, 1/32	2 of 2
FAS	203	Helicidae	13	2.8 - 5, 1/32	1 of 3
FAS	203	Higromiidae	1	2.8 - 5, 1/32	1 of 2
FAS	203	*Muricopsis* sp.	1	residue	
FAS	203	*Nassarius unifasciatus*	1	+5	
FAS	203	*Paracentrotus* sp.	2	2.8 - 5, 1/32	1 of 3
FAS	203	*Pavicardium* sp.	1	-2.8, 1/32	2 of 2
FAS	203	*Pavicardium* sp.	1	2.8 - 5, 1/32	1 of 2
FAS	203	*Pavicardium* sp.	1	+5	
FAS	203	*Pirenella conica*	2	residue	
FAS	203	*Rissoa* sp.	2	-2.8, 1/32	2 of 2
FAS	203	Rissoidae	1	-2.8, 1/32	3 of 3
FAS	203	Veneridae	1	+5	
FAS	202	*Bittium reticulatum*	2	+5	
FAS	202	*Cerithium vulgatum*	2	+5	
FAS	202	*Gibbula* sp.	2	+5	
FAS	202	*Pavicardium* sp.	1	+5	
FAS	202	*Turritella* sp.	1	+5	
FAS	202	Veneridae	1	+5	
FAS	201	*Bittium* sp.	1	residue	
FAS	200	*Bittium reticulatum*	1	residue 5 - 10	
FAS	200	*Cerithium* cf. *vulgatum*	1	residue 5 - 10	
FAS	199	Bittium sp.	2	residue	
FAS	199	*Cerithium vulgatum*	1	residue	
FAS	199	*Columbella rustica*	1	residue	

Table A2.2: Identification of the micromolluscs from the small residues of trench H1B

Trench	Unit	Species	N	Sieve (mm) and fraction sorted	Notes
H1B	215	*Bittium* sp.	1	-2.8, 1/32	
H1B	215	*Bittium* sp.	5	-2.8	
H1B	215	*Bittium* sp.	1	-2.8, 1/32	
H1B	215	*Bittium* sp.	2	-2.8, 1/32	
H1B	215	*Bittium* sp.	2	-2.8, 1/32	
H1B	214	*Antalis* cf. *inaequicostatum*	1	-2.8, 1/32	
H1B	214	*Bittium* sp.	2	-2.8, 1/32	
H1B	214	*Bittium* sp.	3	-2.8, 1/32	
H1B	214	Cardiidae	1	2.8 - 5, 1/32	eroded
H1B	214	*Cyclope* sp.	1	2.8 - 5, 1/32	eroded
H1B	214	Higromiidae	1	-2.8, 1/32	
H1B	214	*Jujubinus exasperatus*	1	-2.8, 1/32	
H1B	214	*Mitra* sp.	1	2.8 - 5, 1/32	eroded
H1B	214	Muricidae	1	-2.8, 1/32	
H1B	213	*Bittium* cf. *reticulatum*	7	-2.8, 1/16	non eroded
H1B	213	*Bittium reticulatum*	1	2.8 - 5	
H1B	213	*Bittium* sp.	2	-2.8, 1/4	
H1B	213	Rissoidae	2	-2.8, 1/16	eroded
H1B	213	*Tricolia* sp.	1	2.8 - 5	
H1B	212	*Bittium reticulatum*	1	-2.8, 1/4	eroded
H1B	212	*Bittium reticulatum*	2	-2.8, 1/4	
H1B	212	*Bittium* sp.	8	-2.8, 1/4	eroded
H1B	212	*Bittium* sp.	2	-2.8, 1/4	
H1B	212	*Chlamys* sp.	1	-2.8, 1/4	
H1B	212	*Chondrula tridens*	1	-2.8, 1/4	
H1B	212	*Cyclope* sp.	1	-2.8, 1/4	eroded
H1B	212	Higromiidae	4	-2.8, 1/4	eroded
H1B	212	*Mangelia* sp.	1	-2.8, 1/4	eroded
H1B	212	*Nuculidae*	1	-2.8, 1/4	eroded
H1B	212	*Rissoa* sp.	1	-2.8, 1/4	
H1B	212	Turridae	1	-2.8, 1/4	eroded
H1B	212	Vermetidae	2	-2.8, 1/4	eroded
H1B	211	*Bittium* cf. *reticulatum*	12	-2.8, 1/4	

Trench	Unit	Species	N	Sieve (mm) and fraction sorted	Notes
H1B	211	coral	1	-2.8, 1/4	
H1B	211	Higromiidae	3	-2.8, 1/4	
H1B	211	*Pitar rudis*	1	-2.8, 1/4	
H1B	211	*Rissoa* sp.	1	-2.8, 1/4	
H1B	211	*Tricolia* sp.	1	-2.8, 1/4	
H1B	211	*Truncatella* cf. *subcylrica*	1	-2.8, 1/4	
H1B	211	*Turritella* cf. *turbona*	1	-2.8, 1/4	
H1B	210	*Alvania* sp.	2	-2.8, 1/4	
H1B	210	*Antalis* cf. *inaequicostatum*	1	-2.8, 1/4	
H1B	210	*Bittium* sp.	1	-2.8, 1/4	
H1B	210	*Bittium* sp.	4	-2.8, 1/4	
H1B	210	*Cerithium* sp.	1	-2.8, 1/32	eroded
H1B	210	Rissoidae sp.	1	-2.8, 1/4	
H1B	209	*Alvania* sp.	5	-2.8, 1/4	
H1B	209	*Bittium* sp.	1	-2.8, 1/4	
H1B	209	*Bittium* sp.	60	-2.8, 1/4	
H1B	209	*Cerithium* sp.	2	-2.8, 1/4	
H1B	209	*Conus mediterraneus*	1	-2.8, 1/4	
H1B	209	*Fusinus* sp.	1	-2.8, 1/4	
H1B	209	Higromiidae	2	-2.8, 1/4	
H1B	209	*Rissoa* cf. *ventricosa*	1	-2.8, 1/4	
H1B	209	*Rissoa ventricosa*	1	-2.8, 1/4	
H1B	208	*Antalis* sp.	1	-2.8, 1/32	
H1B	208	*Bittium* cf. *reticulatum*	2	-2.8, 1/32	
H1B	208	*Bittium* cf. *reticulatum*	1	2.8 - 5, 1/32	
H1B	208	*Bittium* sp.	3	-2.8, 1/32	
H1B	207	*Bittium* cf. *reticulatum*	4	-2.8, 1/16	
H1B	207	*Bittium* sp.	18	-2.8, 1/16	
H1B	207	Cerithidea	1	-2.8, 1/16	
H1B	207	*Fusinus* sp.	1	-2.8, 1/16	
H1B	207	*Meloraphe neritoides*	1	-2.8, 1/16	
H1B	207	*Ocinebrina* cf. *aciculata*	1	-2.8, 1/16	
H1B	206	*Bittium reticulatum*	2	2.8 - 5, 1/16	

Trench	Unit	Species	N	Sieve (mm) and fraction sorted	Notes
H1B	206	*Bittium* sp.	47	-2.8, 1/16	eroded
H1B	206	*Bittium* sp.	2	2.8 - 5, 1/16	
H1B	206	Muricidae	1	2.8 - 5, 1/16	
H1B	206	*Ocenebrina aciculata*	1	2.8 - 5, 1/16	
H1B	206	Rissoidae	4	-2.8, 1/16	eroded
H1B	206	*Vexillum* sp.	1	-2.8, 1/16	eroded
H1B	205	*Bittium* cf. *reticulatum*	21	-2.8, 1/4	eroded
H1B	205	*Bittium reticulatum*	3	2.8 - 5, 1/4	
H1B	205	*Bittium* sp.	22	-2.8, 1/4	eroded
H1B	205	*Cerithium* cf. *rupestre*	1		eroded
H1B	205	*Chauvetia* sp.	2	-2.8, 1/4	eroded
H1B	205	*Columbella rustica*	1	-2.8, 1/4	eroded
H1B	205	Condrinidae	2		
H1B	205	*Euspira* cf. *pulchella*	1	2.8 - 5, 1/4	
H1B	205	Fusinus sp.	1	-2.8, 1/4	eroded
H1B	205	Higromiidae	2	2.8 - 5, 1/4	
H1B	205	*Mangelia* sp.	1	-2.8, 1/4	eroded
H1B	205	*Paracentrotus* sp.	1		
H1B	205	*Pavicardium* sp.	1	-2.8, 1/4	eroded
H1B	205	*Pirenella conica*	1		
H1B	205	Rissoidae	13	-2.8, 1/4	eroded
H1B	205	*Tricolia* sp.	1		
H1B	205	*Turritella* sp.	1	-2.8, 1/4	eroded
H1B	204	*Alvania* cf. *cimex*	1	-2.8, 1/16	
H1B	204	*Alvania* sp.	2	-2.8, 1/16	
H1B	204	*Bittium* cf. *reticulatum*	21	-2.8, 1/16	
H1B	204	*Bittium reticulatum*	5		eroded
H1B	204	*Bittium* sp.	46	-2.8, 1/16	
H1B	204	*Bittium* sp.	12	-2.8, 1/16	
H1B	204	Cerithidea	2		eroded
H1B	204	*Cerithium* cf. *vulgatum*	1		eroded
H1B	204	*Columbella rustica*	1		eroded
H1B	204	*Gibbula sp.*	1	-2.8, 1/16	

Trench	Unit	Species	N	Sieve (mm) and fraction sorted	Notes
H1B	204	Higromiidae	4		eroded
H1B	204	*Rissoa* cf. *ventricosa*	3	-2.8, 1/16	
H1B	204	*Rissoa* sp.	1	-2.8, 1/16	
H1B	204	*Rissoa ventricosa*	1		eroded
H1B	204	Rissoidae	2	-2.8, 1/16	
H1B	204	Trochidae	1	-2.8, 1/16	
H1B	204	*Turritella* sp.	1	-2.8, 1/16	
H1B	204	Veneridae	2	-2.8, 1/16	
H1B	204	*Vexillum* sp.	1	-2.8, 1/16	
H1B	203	*Alvania* cf. *cimex*	2	-2.8, 1/32	non eroded
H1B	203	*Alvania* cf. *discors*	1	-2.8, 1/32	non eroded
H1B	203	*Alvania* cf. *lactea*	1	-2.8, 1/32	non eroded
H1B	203	*Alvania* sp.	3	-2.8, 1/32	non eroded
H1B	203	*Bittium reticulatum*	27	-2.8, 1/32	non eroded
H1B	203	*Bittium reticulatum*	6	2.8 - 5, 1/32	
H1B	203	*Bittium* sp.	20	-2.8, 1/32	non eroded
H1B	203	*Chamelea striata*	1	2.8 - 5, 1/32	
H1B	203	*Fusinus* sp.	1	-2.8, 1/32	non eroded
H1B	203	*Fusinus* sp.	1	-2.8, 1/32	non eroded
H1B	203	*Fusinus* sp.	1	2.8 - 5, 1/32	
H1B	203	*Gibbula* sp.	1	-2.8, 1/32	non eroded
H1B	203	Higromiidae	2	-2.8, 1/32	non eroded
H1B	203	*Paracentrotus* sp.	1	-2.8, 1/32	non eroded
H1B	203	*Rissoa* cf. *auriscalnium*	1	-2.8, 1/32	non eroded
H1B	203	*Rissoa ventricosa*	3	-2.8, 1/32	non eroded
H1B	203	Rissoidae	2	-2.8, 1/32	non eroded
H1B	203	*Turritella* sp.	1	-2.8, 1/32	non eroded
H1B	202	*Alvania* cf. *cimex*	1	-2.8, 1/16	non eroded
H1B	202	*Alvania* sp.	3	-2.8, 1/16	non eroded
H1B	202	*Bittium* cf. *reticulatum*	18	-2.8, 1/16	non eroded
H1B	202	*Bittium* sp.	1	-2.8, 1/16	
H1B	202	*Bittium* sp.	23	-2.8, 1/16	non eroded
H1B	202	*Euspira* cf. *pulchella*	2	-2.8, 1/16	non eroded

Trench	Unit	Species	N	Sieve (mm) and fraction sorted	Notes
H1B	202	*Gibbula* sp.	1	-2.8, 1/16	non eroded
H1B	202	*Rissoa ventricosa*	1	-2.8, 1/16	non eroded
H1B	202	Rissoidae	2	-2.8, 1/16	non eroded
H1B	202	*Turritella* sp.	1	-2.8, 1/16	non eroded
H1B	202	Vermetidae	1	-2.8, 1/16	
H1B	198	*Canculus cruciatus*	1	na	
H1B	198	Cardiidae	1	na	
H1B	198	*Cerithium* sp.	2	na	
H1B	198	*Gibbula* cf. *adriatica*	1	na	
H1B	198	*Jujubinus exasperatus*	1	na	
H1B	198	Lucinidae	1	na	
H1B	198	*Nassarius* cf. *incrassatus*	1	na	
H1B	198	*Ocinebrina* cf. *aciculata*	1	na	
H1B	198	*Pavicardium* sp.	2	na	
H1B	198	*Ruditapes decussatus*	1	na	
H1B	198	Veneridae	1	na	
H1B	197	*Bittium* cf. *reticulatum*	1	na	
H1B	197	*Bittium* cf. *reticulatum*	1	na	
H1B	197	*Cerithium* sp.	1	na	
H1B	197	*Conus mediterraneus*	1	na	
H1B	197	*Mytilus* sp.	1	na	
H1B	195	*Bittium* cf. *reticulatum*	1	na	
H1B	195	*Cerithium* sp.	1	na	
H1B	194	*Ruditapes decussatus*	1	na	
H1B	193	Cardiidae	1	na	
H1B	192	*Cerithium* sp.	1	na	
H1B	192	coral	1	na	
H1B	192	Veneridae	1	na	
H1B	192	Vermetidae	1	na	
H1B	190	*Ostrea edulis*	1	na	
H1B	189	Cardiidae	1	na	
H1B	188	Cardiidae	1	na	
H1B	188	*Cerithium alucastrum*	1	na	

Trench	Unit	Species	N	Sieve (mm) and fraction sorted	Notes
H1B	188	*Mitra cornicula*	1	na	
H1B	188	Veneridae	1	na	
H1B	186	*Cerithium* sp.	1	na	
H1B	185	*Talochlamys* cf. *multistriata*	1	na	
H1B	185	*Nassarius* cf. *incrassatus*	1	na	
H1B	183	*Canculus cruciatus*	1	na	
H1B	183	Cardiidae	1	na	
H1B	183	*Cerithium* sp.	1	na	
H1B	183	*Columbella rustica*	1	na	
H1B	183	*Ocinebrina* sp.	1	na	
H1B	183	*Pavicardium* sp.	1	na	
H1B	182	*Bittium* sp.	1	na	
H1B	182	*Canculus* sp.	1	na	
H1B	182	Cardiidae	1	na	
H1B	182	*Cerithium*	1	na	
H1B	182	*Patella* sp.	1	na	
H1B	181	Cardiidae	1	na	eroded
H1B	181	*Turritella* sp.	1	na	eroded
H1B	180	*Bittium* sp.	1	na	eroded
H1B	180	Pectinidae	1	na	non eroded
H1B	178	*Bittium* cf. *reticulatum*	2	na	
H1B	178	*Cerithium* sp.	1	na	
H1B	178	*Conus mediterraneus*	1	na	
H1B	178	*Pavicardium* sp.	1	na	
H1B	178	Veneridae	1	na	
H1B	176	*Cerithium* cf. *vulgatum*	1	na	
H1B	175	*Bittium reticulatum*	2	na	
H1B	175	*Bittium* sp.	3	na	
H1B	175	Cardiidae	2	na	
H1B	175	Cerithidea	1	na	
H1B	175	*Ocinebrina* sp.	2	na	
H1B	175	*Patella* cf. *caerulea*	1	+10	non eroded
H1B	175	*Patella* sp	1	na	

Trench	Unit	Species	N	Sieve (mm) and fraction sorted	Notes
H1B	175	*Pavicardium* sp.	1	na	
H1B	175	Veneridae	1	na	
H1B	175	Vermetidae	1	na	
H1B	174	*Bittium* cf. *reticulatum*	2	na	
H1B	174	*Bittium* sp.	2	na	
H1B	174	*Cerithium* cf. *vulgatum*	1	na	
H1B	174	*Cerithium* sp.	1	na	
H1B	174	coral	1	na	
H1B	174	*Phorcus turbinatus*	1	na	
H1B	174	*Pavicardium* sp.	1	na	
H1B	174	*Ruditapes decussatus*		+10	eroded
H1B	173	Cerithidea	1	na	
H1B	173	*Ruditapes decussatus*	1	na	non eroded
H1B	172	Cardiidae	1	na	
H1B	172	Cerithidea	1	na	
H1B	172	*Pirenella conica*	1	na	
H1B	172	*Ruditapes decussatus*	1	na	
H1B	171	*Cerithium vulgatum*	1	+10	non eroded
H1B	171	*Patella* sp.	1	na	
H1B	171	*Ruditapes decussatus*	1	+10	non eroded
H1B	171	Veneridae	1	+10	eroded
H1B	164	*Cerithium* sp.	1	na	non eroded
H1B	164	*Patella* sp.	1	na	non eroded
H1B	164	*Pirenella conica*	1	na	
H1B	162	Cardiidae	1	na	
H1B	162	*Cerithium* sp.	1	na	
H1B	162	*Patella caerulea*	1	na	
H1B	162	*Patella caerulea*	1	na	
H1B	162	*Patella* sp.	1	na	
H1B	161	*Patella* cf. *caerulea*	3	na	non eroded
H1B	161	*Patella* sp.	1	na	
H1B	160	*Bittium reticulatum*	1	na	
H1B	160	*Gibbula* cf. *umbilicalis*	2	na	

Trench	Unit	Species	N	Sieve (mm) and fraction sorted	Notes
H1B	159	*Cerithium* sp.	1	residue 5-10	
H1B	159	*Mangelia* sp.	1	residue 5-10	
H1B	159	*Pavicardium* sp.	1	residue 5-10	
H1B	158	*Bittium* cf. *reticulatum*	3	-2.8, 1/32	
H1B	158	*Bittium* sp.	1	2.8 - 5	
H1B	158	*Cerithium* cf. *vulgatum*	3	-2.8, 1/32	
H1B	158	*Glans* cf. *trapezia*	1	-2.8, 1/32	
H1B	157	*Bittium* sp.	4	-2.8, 1/8	
H1B	157	*Bittium* sp.	1	-2.8, 1/8	
H1B	157	*Gibbula* cf. *adriatica*	1	5 - 10	
H1B	157	Helicidae gen. sp. undeind.	181	-2.8, 1/8	
H1B	157	Helicidae	36	-2.8, 1/8	
H1B	156	*Alvania* sp.	1	-2.8, 1/32	
H1B	156	*Bittium* sp.	1	-2.8, 1/32	
H1B	156	*Bittium* sp.	2	-2.8, 1/32	
H1B	156	*Bittium* sp.	2	2.8 - 5	
H1B	156	Helicidae	22	-2.8, 1/32	
H1B	156	Helicidae	104	-2.8, 1/32	
H1B	156	Helicidae	2	2.8 - 5	
H1B	155	*Bittium* sp.	1		
H1B	155	*Bittium* sp.	2	residue 5-10	
H1B	155	*Bittium* sp.	1	-2.8, 1/32	
H1B	155	*Bittium* sp.	3	-2.8, 1/32	
H1B	155	*Cerithium* cf. *vulgatum*	1	residue 5-10	
H1B	155	Helicidae	32	-2.8, 1/32	
H1B	155	Helicidae	144	-2.8, 1/32	
H1B	155	*Pavicardium* sp.	1	residue 5-10	
H1B	154	*Alvania* cf. *cimex*	1	2.8 - 5	
H1B	154	*Bittium* cf. *reticulatum*	1		
H1B	154	*Bittium* cf. *reticulatum*	2	2.8 - 5	
H1B	154	*Bittium* cf. *reticulatum*	1	5 - 10	
H1B	154	*Bittium* sp.	2	2.8 - 5	
H1B	154	*Bittium* sp.	2	-2.8, 1/32	

Trench	Unit	Species	N	Sieve (mm) and fraction sorted	Notes
H1B	154	*Cerithium* sp.	1	5 - 10	
H1B	154	Helicidae	165	2.8 - 5	
H1B	154	Helicidae	115	-2.8, 1/32	
H1B	154	*Ocinebrina* cf. *aciculata*	1	2.8 - 5	
H1B	154	*Paracentrotus* sp.	1	2.8 - 5	
H1B	154	*Paracentrotus* sp.	1	-2.8, 1/32	
H1B	154	Rissoidae	1	-2.8, 1/32	
H1B	153	*Bittium reticulatum*	1	2.8 - 5	
H1B	153	*Bittium* sp.	2	-2.8, 1/8	
H1B	153	*Fusinus* sp.	1	2.8 - 5	
H1B	153	Helicidae	49	-2.8, 1/8	
H1B	153	*Paracentrotus* sp.	1	-2.8, 1/8	
H1B	152	*Bittium* sp.	1	-2.8, 1/4	
H1B	152	Helicidae	20	-2.8, 1/4	
H1B	151	*Alvania* cf. *discors*	1	-2.8, 1/8	
H1B	151	*Bittium* sp.	4	-2.8, 1/8	
H1B	151	*Cerithium* cf. *vulgatum*	1	-2.8, 1/16	
H1B	151	*Chama gryphoides*	1	-2.8, 1/4	
H1B	151	Helicidae	67	2.8 - 5	
H1B	151	Helicidae	42	-2.8, 1/8	
H1B	151	Higromiidae	1	2.8 - 5	
H1B	151	*Paracentrotus* sp.		2.8 - 5	
H1B	151	*Pavicardium* sp.	1	-2.8, 1/8	
H1B	150	*Bittium* cf. *reticulatum*	2	2.8 - 5	burnt
H1B	150	*Bittium* sp.	4	1/16	
H1B	150	*Euspira* cf. *pulchella*	1	2.8 - 5	
H1B	150	Helicidae	60	1/16	
H1B	150	Helicidae	5	2.8 - 5	
H1B	149	*Bittium reticulatum*	4	-2.8	
H1B	149	*Bittium* sp.	5	2.8 - 5	
H1B	149	*Cyclope* sp.	1	-2.8	
H1B	149	*Ferussacia folliculus*	1	-2.8	
H1B	149	Helicidae	53	-2.8	

Trench	Unit	Species	N	Sieve (mm) and fraction sorted	Notes
H1B	149	Helicidae	3		
H1B	149	Helicidae	143	2.8 - 5	
H1B	149	*Paracentrotus* sp.		-2.8	
H1B	148	*Alvania* sp.	1	-2.8, 1/4	
H1B	148	*Alvania* sp.	1	1/4	
H1B	148	*Bittium reticulatum*	1	1/4	
H1B	148	*Bittium* sp.	3	-2.8, 1/4	
H1B	148	*Bittium* sp.	6	1/4	
H1B	148	*Cecilioides acicula*	2	1/4	
H1B	148	*Fusinus* sp.	1	1/4	
H1B	148	Helicidae gen. sp. unde.	73	1/4	
H1B	147	*Alvania* cf. *cimex*	1	-2.8, 1/32	
H1B	147	*Alvania* cf. *discors*	2	-2.8, 1/32	
H1B	147	*Alvania* sp.	3	-2.8, 1/32	
H1B	147	*Alvania* sp.	1	-2.8, 1/32	
H1B	147	*Bittium* cf. *reticulatum*	3	2.8 - 5, 1/32	
H1B	147	*Bittium reticulatum*	2	-2.8, 1/32	
H1B	147	*Bittium* sp.	8	-2.8, 1/32	
H1B	147	*Bittium* sp.	2	-2.8, 1/32	
H1B	147	*Bittium* sp.	5	-2.8, 1/32	
H1B	147	*Bittium* sp.	3	-2.8, 1/32	
H1B	147	*Cyclope* sp.	1	-2.8, 1/32	
H1B	147	Helicidae	117	-2.8, 1/32	8 burnt
H1B	147	Helicidae	16	-2.8, 1/32	3 burnt
H1B	147	Helicidae	25	-2.8, 1/32	
H1B	147	Helicidae	179	-2.8, 1/32	7 burnt
H1B	147	Helicidae	88	2.8 - 5, 1/32	1 burnt
H1B	145	*Bittium* sp.	1	-2.8, 1/32	
H1B	145	*Bittium* sp.	2	-2.8, 1/32	
H1B	145	Cerithidea	1	-2.8, 1/32	
H1B	145	Helicidae	73	-2.8, 1/32	1 burnt
H1B	145	Helicidae	53	-2.8, 1/32	4 burnt
H1B	145	Helicidae	35	-2.8, 1/32	

Trench	Unit	Species	N	Sieve (mm) and fraction sorted	Notes
H1B	143	*Bittium* sp.	1	-2.8, 1/16	
H1B	143	Cerithidea	1	-2.8, 1/16	
H1B	143	Helicidae	102	-2.8, 1/16	5 burnt
H1B	143	Helicidae	53	2.8 - 5, 1/16	
H1B	143	*Turbonilla* sp.	1	-2.8, 1/16	
H1B	141	*Bittium* sp.	1	-2.8, 1/32	
H1B	141	*Bittium* sp.	3	-2.8, 1/32	
H1B	141	*Cecilioides acicula*	1	-2.8, 1/32	
H1B	141	Cerithidea	2	-2.8, 1/32	
H1B	141	Helicidae	63	-2.8, 1/32	
H1B	141	Helicidae	100	-2.8, 1/32	4 burnt
H1B	141	Helicidae	57	2.8 - 5, 1/32	1 burnt
H1B	139	*Alvania* cf. *discors*	1	-2.8, 1/16	
H1B	139	*Bittium* sp.	4	-2.8, 1/16	
H1B	139	*Cecilioides acicula*	1	-2.8, 1/16	
H1B	139	Helicidae	132	-2.8, 1/16	17 burnt
H1B	139	Helicidae	58	2.8 - 5, 1/16	1 burnt
H1B	137	*Bittium* sp.	4	-2.8, 1/8	
H1B	137	Helicidae	146	-2.8, 1/8	7 burnt
H1B	137	Helicidae	62	2.8 - 5, 1/8	
H1B	137	Higromiidae	1	2.8 - 5, 1/8	
H1B	137	*Paracentrotus* sp.	1	-2.8, 1/8	
H1B	135	*Alvania* sp.	1	-2.8, 1/32	
H1B	135	*Bittium* sp.	4	-2.8, 1/32	
H1B	135	*Bittium* sp.	5	-2.8, 1/32	
H1B	135	*Chlamys* sp.	1	2.8 - 5, 1/32	
H1B	135	Helicidae	111	-2.8, 1/32	3 burnt
H1B	135	Helicidae	44	-2.8, 1/32	8 burnt
H1B	135	Helicidae	48	2.8 - 5, 1/32	2 burnt
H1B	135	*Paracentrotus* sp.	1	-2.8, 1/32	
H1B	135	Veneridae	1	2.8 - 5, 1/32	
H1B	133	*Cerithium* cf. *vulgatum*	1	2.8 - 5, 1/16	
H1B	133	*Cyclope* sp.	1	2.8 - 5, 1/16	burnt

Trench	Unit	Species	N	Sieve (mm) and fraction sorted	Notes
H1B	133	Helicidae	74	-2.8, 1/16	1 burnt
H1B	133	Helicidae	24	2.8 - 5, 1/16	
H1B	133	*Paracentrotus* sp.	1	-2.8, 1/16	
H1B	133	*Pavicardium* sp.	4	-2.8, 1/16	
H1B	131	*Cyclope* sp.	1	2.8 - 5, 1/1	burnt
H1B	131	Helicidae	3	2.8 - 5, 1/1	
H1B	131	Helicidae	10	-2.8, 1/1	
H1B	131	*Paracentrotus* sp.	1	-2.8, 1/1	
H1B	127	*Bittium* sp.	1	2.8 - 5, 1/16	
H1B	127	*Cerithium vulgatum*	1	2.8 - 5, 1/16	
H1B	127	*Cyclope* sp.	1	2.8 - 5, 1/16	burnt
H1B	127	Helicidae	98	-2.8, 1/16	21 burnt
H1B	127	Helicidae	35	2.8 - 5, 1/16	3 burnt
H1B	127	*Ovatella mysotis*	1	-2.8, 1/16	
H1B	125	*Alvania* sp.	1	-2.8, 1/1	
H1B	125	*Bittium* sp.	6	-2.8, 1/1	
H1B	125	Helicidae	148	-2.8, 1/1	15 burnt
H1B	125	*Paracentrotus* sp.	1	2.8 - 5, 1/1	
H1B	125	*Paracentrotus* sp.	1	-2.8, 1/1	
H1B	125	*Pavicardium* sp.	1	-2.8, 1/1	
H1B	123	*Alvania* sp.	2	-2.8, 1/16	
H1B	123	*Bittium* sp.	4	-2.8, 1/16	
H1B	123	*Cyclope* sp.	1	2.8 - 5, 1/4	burnt
H1B	123	Helicidae	36	2.8 - 5, 1/4	
H1B	123	Helicidae	116	-2.8, 1/16	8 burnt
H1B	123	Helicidae	78	2.8 - 5, 1/16	
H1B	123	Helicidae	41	2.8 - 5, 1/16	
H1B	123	*Paracentrotus* sp.	1	-2.8, 1/16	
H1B	123	*Paracentrotus* sp.	1	-2.8, 1/4	
H1B	123	*Paracentrotus* sp.	1	2.8 - 5, 1/16	
H1B	123	*Pavicardium* sp.	1	-2.8, 1/16	
H1B	121	*Alvania* sp.	1	-2.8, 1/16	
H1B	121	Cardiidae	1	-2.8 - 5, 1/16	

Trench	Unit	Species	N	Sieve (mm) and fraction sorted	Notes
H1B	121	Helicidae	60	-2.8, 1/16	
H1B	121	Helicidae	35	-2.8 - 5, 1/16	
H1B	121	*Paracentrotus* sp.	1	-2.8, 1/16	
H1B	121	*Paracentrotus* sp.	1	-2.8 - 5, 1/16	
H1B	119	*Alvania* sp.	2	-2.8, 1/8	
H1B	119	*Bittium* sp.	4	-2.8, 1/8	
H1B	119	*Bittium* sp.	2	-2.8, 1/8	
H1B	119	*Cyclope* sp.	1	2.8 - 5, 1/8	burnt
H1B	119	Helicidae	81	2.8 - 5, 1/8	
H1B	119	Helicidae	124	-2.8, 1/8	1 burnt
H1B	119	Helicidae	16	-2.8, 1/8	
H1B	119	*Paracentrotus* sp.	3	2.8 - 5, 1/8	
H1B	119	*Paracentrotus* sp.	1	-2.8, 1/8	
H1B	119	*Paracentrotus* sp.	1	2.8 - 5, 1/8	
H1B	119	*Paracentrotus* sp.	1	-2.8, 1/8	
H1B	117	*Bittium* sp.	1	-2.8, 1/16	
H1B	117	Helicidae	130	-2.8, 1/16	3 burnt
H1B	117	Helicidae	44	2.8 - 5, 1/16	
H1B	117	*Paracentrotus* sp.	1	-2.8, 1/16	
H1B	115	*Bittium* cf. *reticulatum*	1	-2.8, 1/16	
H1B	115	*Bittium* sp.	9	-2.8, 1/16	
H1B	115	*Cerithium vulgatum*	1	-2.8, 1/16	
H1B	115	Helicidae	127	-2.8, 1/16	
H1B	115	*Paracentrotus* sp.	1	-2.8, 1/16	
H1B	115	*Rissoa* sp.	1	-2.8, 1/16	
H1B	113	*Alvania* cf. *cimex*	1	-2.8, 1/8	
H1B	113	*Bittium* sp.	2	-2.8, 1/8	
H1B	113	Helicidae	30	2.8 - 5, 1/8	
H1B	113	Helicidae	40	-2.8, 1/8	
H1B	113	*Paracentrotus* sp.	1	2.8 - 5, 1/8	
H1B	113	*Paracentrotus* sp.	1	-2.8, 1/8	
H1B	111	*Alvania* sp.	2	-2.8, 1/8	
H1B	111	*Bittium* cf. *reticulatum*	2	-2.8, 1/8	

Trench	Unit	Species	N	Sieve (mm) and fraction sorted	Notes
H1B	111	*Bittium* sp.	9	-2.8, 1/8	
H1B	111	Helicidae	129	-2.8, 1/8	
H1B	111	*Mangelia* sp.	1	-2.8, 1/8	
H1B	111	*Paracentrotus* sp.	1	-2.8, 1/8	
H1B	111	*Timoclea ovata*	1	-2.8, 1/8	
H1B	109	*Alvania* cf. *discors*	1	-2.8, 1/16	
H1B	109	*Bittium reticulatum*	1	-2.8, 1/16	
H1B	109	*Bittium* sp.	8	-2.8, 1/16	
H1B	109	*Cyclope* sp.	1	-2.8, 1/16	
H1B	109	Helicidae	105	-2.8, 1/16	5 burnt
H1B	109	*Paracentrotus* sp.	1	-2.8, 1/16	
H1B	105	*Bittium reticulatum*	3	-2.8, 1/4	
H1B	105	*Bittium* sp.	3	-2.8, 1/4	
H1B	105	*Cerithium vulgatum*	1	-2.8, 1/4	
H1B	105	Helicidae	57	-2.8, 1/4	
H1B	105	*Paracentrotus* sp.	1	-2.8, 1/4	
H1B	105	*Rissoa ventricosa*	1	-2.8, 1/4	
H1B	105	Vermetidae	1	-2.8, 1/4	

APPENDIX 3

Modern Shell Reference Collections

Large modern reference collections were hand-collected for the three main ornamental taxa in the Franchthi Palaeolithic and Mesolithic assemblages, *Cyclope neritea/pellucida*, *Columbella rustica* and *Antalis* sp. Our aim was to collect specimens for experimental reproduction of the beads, and to monitor variation in dimensions, colour and state of preservation. We also recorded the ease of the collection, the number of specimens collected per hour and the variation from collector to collector. All taxa were collected on beaches from the Argolid, including the (recent) Paralia below Franchthi Cave and the close-by Fourni[1] beach (Fig. A3.1).

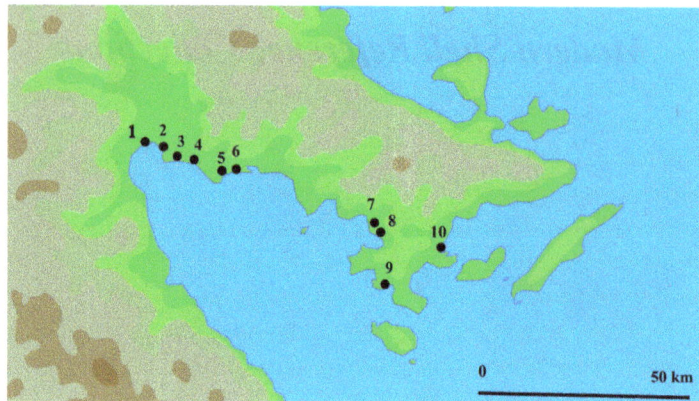

Fig. A3.1: Location of collection areas. 1: Nea Kios; 2: Nafplion (Beach 1); 3: Arvanitia (Nafplion); 4: Karathona; 5: Kastraki (Tolo); 6: Asini beach; 7: Fourni; 8: Franchthi; 9: Portocheli; 10: Kouverta.

Cyclope neritea were mostly collected alive, which enabled us to test for size variation from year to year, beach to beach and collector to collector. *Columbella rustica* were initially collected dead on beaches, from thanatocoenoses. Their dimensions and state of preservations were compared from beach to beach. No attempt was made to test for yearly variation since thanatocoenoses may include shells that died years, decades or even centuries ago (Sivan *et al.* 2006). *Columbella rustica* were later also collected under water, and their state of preservation and dimensions were compared with samples from thanatocoenoses. *Antalis* sp. were collected on various beaches from thanatocoenoses, allowing comparisons of dimensions according to the sedimentology of the beach.

In addition to these collections of several hundred specimens each, we collected smaller samples of *Conus mediterraneus*, *Phorcus (Osilinus) turbinatus*, *Cerithium vulgatum*, *Glycymeris* sp. and *Spondylus gaedoporus* to study natural perforations and to implement some experiments. We were unsuccessful in our search for *Homalopoma sanguineum,* but for one specimen.

Taxonomic identifications relied on the reference collection assembled by J. Shackleton and deposited at the Archaeological Museum of Nafplion and on several shell reference publications (Delamotte & Vardala-Theodorou 2001; Donnedu & Trainito 2005; Lindner 2000). The nomenclature follows the recommendations of the CLEMAM marine seashell data base (Check List of European Marine Molluscan Database: http://www.somali.asso.fr/clemam/index.clemam.html. Search performed January and February 2014).

NOTES

1   The proper name is Lambayana beach.

APPENDIX 3.1

Cyclope neritea *and* Cyclope pellucida

Family: Nassariidae

Subfamily: Nassariinae

Genus: *Cyclope* (Risso 1826)

Species: - *Cyclope neritea* Linnaeus 1758 (main synonyms: *Buccinum neriteum* L. 1758, *Cyclonassa neritea* Pallary 1919, *Cyclope neritoidea* Risso 1826).

- *Cyclope pellucida* Risso 1826 (= *Cyclope donavania* Risso 1826, *Cyclope donovani* auct.).

- Fossil species: *Cyclope migliorinii* Bevilaqua 1928.

Cyclope neritea is small marine gastropod that lives on sandy or muddy bottoms, in the brackish, quiet waters of coastal lagoons and salt marshes that belong to the infralittoral zone. The shell is very characteristic, slightly oval in shape, with a diameter of ca. 1.1 to 1.2 cm. The section is lenticular and markedly asymmetrical. The spire is short and convex, with a total height of 0.85 to 1.1 cm in our samples. Its summit is flat or even depressed, since the apex and first whorls are naturally sectioned on adults. On the ventral face, an extended columellar callus forms a flat and shiny base (Gili & Martinell 1999). Adults develop a well-marked curved lip, without denticulation. The dorsal surface of *Cyclope neritea*, when scraped of concretions and microalgae, shows a dull yellowish to brown colour, with variable and rather inconspicuous reticular ornamentations (Fig. A3.2). The lustrous base varies from ivory to brown (Delamotte & Vardala-Theodorou 2001; Poppe & Goto 1993).

Cyclope pellucida lives in the same environment as *C. neritea* and both species can be found together (Simon-Bouhet 2006). It is described as smaller (ca. 0.8 cm in diameter), with a lighter, more uniform dorsal colour and a white base (Delamotte & Vardala-Theodorou 2001; Doneddu & Trainito 2005). However, according to Simon-Bouhet (2006: 44), neither the size nor the colour is a reliable characteristic and DNA analyses alone can effectively discriminate *C. neritea* and *C. pellucida*. We regularly found a small proportion (about 10 %) of very small adults, ca. 9 mm in maximum diameter, with lighter dorsal colour and a white base (Fig. A3.2). They appear to correspond to *C. pellucida*, but this attribution has not been confirmed by genetic analyses.

Cyclope migliorinii is a widely distributed fossil Pliocene species, present in Greece (Gili & Martinell 1999, 2000). It can only be distinguished from *C. neritea* on juvenile specimens. Its size varies widely according to the localities, but reaches 1.8 cm in maximum diameter, a value unknown in *C. neritea.* The presence of some unusually large specimens in the early Upper Palaeolithic levels at Franchthi suggests that a few fossil specimens were also collected and used as beads.

Fig. A3.2: Cyclope neritea *and* C. pellucida *(?) collected in Nafplion, dorsal face (left) and ventral face (right). Top row: washed but unscraped specimens. 2nd and 3rd rows: adults, scraped. 4th row: juvenile. 5th row: small adults (*C. pellucida?*). Photograph C. P.*

Habitat and Conditions of Collection of *Cyclope neritea*

Along the Argolic Gulf, *Cyclope* sp. collected in thanatocoenoses are extremely poorly preserved. During a systematic search for *Cyclope* along Beach 1 (Fig. A3.1 and A3.5), where we collected hundreds of live snails, we found 38 specimens in 15 minutes. All but two (Fig. A3.3, top left and bottom left) were too poorly preserved to be used as beads. This might be specific to thanatocoenoses that build up in areas with low tidal amplitude and few storms, and where the shells remains exposed for long. On the Atlantic coast, new shells are deposited at each daily tide and specimens in good conditions can easily be collected in thanatocoenoses (Rigaud, *in litt.* 16/8/16).

Given the low tidal amplitude of the Mediterranean sea it is likely that such conditions were not met either in prehistoric times, and that *Cyclope neritea* were collected live at Franchthi. Some data on their habitat and life cycle are thus useful. *Cyclope neritea* and *pellucida* are heuryhalin species, which can tolerate wide variation in salinity and temperature but like an influx of fresh water. Both species are scavengers that feed on bacteria and dead fish or crustaceans (Southward *et al.* 1997). *Cyclope neritea* often forms large colonies, and densities up to 1600 snails per square metre are reported in favourable environments (Southward *et al.* 1997: 757; Tardy *et al.* 1985).

During daytime, only dead *Cyclope* shells, inhabited by hermit crabs, can be seen moving around on the surface of the mud under 20 to 40 cm of water. Live Cyclopes bury themselves a few centimetres deep, often in small nests of several individuals (pers. obs.), and one has to poke blindly into the mud to find them. Cyclopes are active during the night (Southward *et al.* 1997) and come out at sunset, when they become easily recognisable as little 'bumps' on the flat bottom. When missed, they are surprisingly quick to escape (Morton 1960), and Simon-Bouhet qualifies them as "especially swift gastropods" (Simon-Bouhet 2006: 20). Because of their well-developed olfactory organs (Lindner 2000; Simon-Bouhet 2006: 20), they smell dead flesh from several metres away. Another efficient way to collect them by the hundreds thus consists in simply leaving a dead fish in the water (Fig. A3.4): Southward and his colleagues report having found 371 *C. neritea* in a fish carcass (Southward *et al.* 1997: 753).

Fig. A3.3: Complete sample of C. neritea *and* C. pellucida *(?) collected in 15 minutes on Beach 1, Nafplion (see Fig. A3.5). Photograph C. P.*

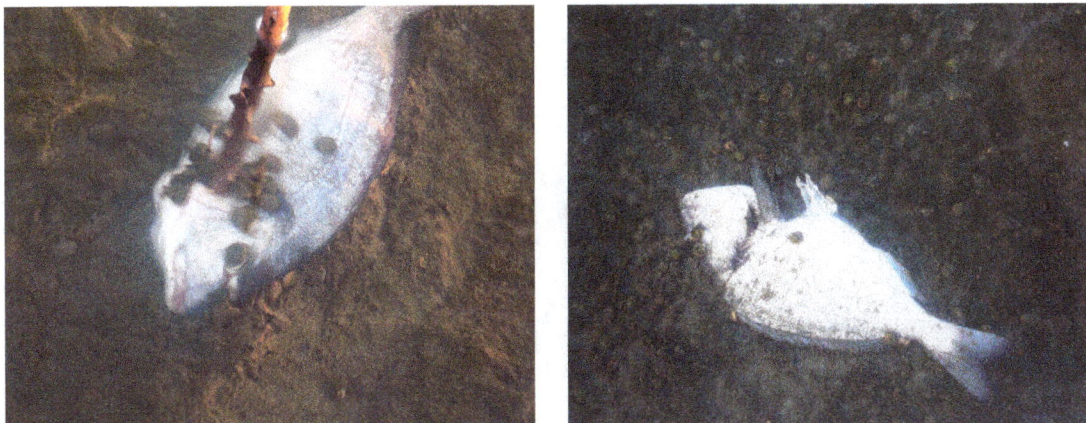

Fig. A3.4: Cyclope neritea *gathering around a dead sea-bream. The first photograph was taken 10 minutes after the fish was deposited, the second 11 hours later. The fish was seemingly too fresh for* C. neritea *to penetrate through the scales. Photograph C. P.*

Both males and females reach their maturity around one year and live for more than two years (Simon-Bouhet 2006: 20). The females lay their eggs almost all year-round with a spring peak and an autumn low, usually on the shells of *Cerastoderma (Cerastoderma glaucum* at our collection spots); juveniles emerge a month later (Boulhic & Tardy 1986). Until they reach adulthood, juveniles have no outer lip. The brittle edge of their shell, the peristome, renders them unsuitable for ornaments and, at Franchthi, prehistoric bead-makers systematically rejected by them.

Cyclope neritea is not known to be eaten by man (Reese 1990). It is difficult to extract the meat out of a live or cooked snail since the flesh breaks easily, and the yield is low: the dried meat of 130 *Cyclope neritea* collected near Nafplion weighed only 1.8 gram. On the other hand, *Cyclope neritea* and *Cyclope pellucida* are well known for their use as prehistoric ornaments all around the Mediterranean (Taborin 2004).

Reference Collections

We first collected *Cyclope neritea* in 2004 at two locations at the head of the Argolic Gulf, just outside the town of Nafplion in the direction of Nea Kios (Fig. A3.5). The locations were selected because of the shallow topography, quiet water and influx of fresh water from small perennial streams. At both locations, dead specimens on the beach were rare and badly preserved, which led us to look for the *Cyclope* in the water, either live or inhabited by hermit crabs. In the following years (2005-2008, 2010), we decided to sample only Beach 1, in order to ensure optimal comparability in the results.

The aims of the collecting trips were five-fold:

(a) To estimate the difficulty and time required to collect and process *Cyclope neritea.*

(b) To document the size range within a single population and potential yearly variation.

(c) To document the potential variability in the proportion of adults and juveniles.

(d) To document the potential influence of the collector on the rate of collection, the dimensional parameters and the age structure of the sample (collections in 2005, 2007).

(e) To obtain specimens for experiments in perforation.

Fig. A3.5: Location of the beaches where we collected C. neritea, *between Nafplion and Nea Kios. Copyright Google Earth.*

Analyses of the Reference Collections

Rates of Collection

Table A3.1 presents the basic data on our different collections. The specimens collected comprised live *Cyclope neritea,* a few probable *C. pellucida,* and *Cyclope* shells inhabited by hermit crabs. We always collected between 18.30 and 19.00 - 19.15, mostly by poking into the mud.

The collection rate varies from collector to collector and from collection to collection for the same collector. Three factors can explain this variability: the presence or absence of wind, which stirs the mud and limits visibility. The experience[1], and, finally, the motivation of the collector, itself highly variable! We would undoubtedly have picked up many more specimens if we had shifted the schedule to 19.15 – 20.00 pm, i.e. at sunset, when *Cyclope* sp. emerge from the mud to feed and become clearly visible. However, even under less than optimal conditions, one fairly quickly acquires the trick of poking through the mud for 'nests'. A single collector can gather between 200 and 300 snails an hour, or even more. This requires no special skill and could be done by children as well as adults.

Location	Date	Technique	Collector	Time	Nb. of specimens	Rate Cycl/pers./hours
Beach 1	4/07/2004	By hand	CP	nd	86	na
Beach 2	4/07/2004	By hand	CP	nd	187	na
Beach 1	7/7/2005	By hand	CP, MV, GM	30'	453	300
Beach 1	12/07/2005	By hand	CP	45'	290	386
Beach 1	12/07/2005	By hand	MV	45'	237	310
Beach 1	12/07/2005	By hand	GM	45'	211	281
Beach 1	30/06/2006	By hand	CP, MV	45'	425	283
Beach 1	29/06/2007	By hand	AC	30'	93	186
Beach 1	29/06/2007	By hand	PP	30'	107	214
Beach 1	29/06/2007	By hand	CP	30'	179	358
Beach 1	6/07/2007	Dead sea bream as a bait	CP, PP	Left 12 hours	303	
Beach 1	1/07/2008	By hand	CP	45'	392	522
Beach 1	05/07/2010	By hand	CP, PP, MM	45'	432	192
Total					3395	

Table A3.1: Summary of the data on the successive collections of Cyclope neritea *near Nafplion. Collectors: CP: C. Perlès; MM: Marian Vanhaeren; GM: Gérard Monthel; AC: André Colonese; PP: Patrick Pion; MMP: Mercedes Maya-Pion.*

State of Preservation

Except for quasi-systematic chipping on the fragile peristome of juveniles, all specimens were in a good state of preservation. We observed no drill holes from carnivorous predators, and only rare instances of characteristic breakage by crabs (Rigaud *et al.* 2014b). Some dead specimens showed evidence of demineralization of the shell.

Fig. A3.6: Cyclope neritea *with characteristic breaks made by crabs.*

Ratio of Juveniles to Adults

Since *Cyclope neritea* reproduce almost all year-round (*supra*), the ratio of juveniles to adults appeared as a potentially interesting parameter, which we had hoped would be rather stable from year to year. Indeed, as indicated above, prehistoric bead-makers systematically discarded juveniles. Thus, assuming that the snails were brought back to the cave to be washed and sorted, the number of juveniles could have given an indication of the number of adults that were initially collected (see Rigaud *et al.* 2014b). A deficit of adults in the archaeological assemblages would then have provided an estimate of the number of specimens that left the site as finished beads.

Unfortunately, the ratio of juveniles/adults fluctuates widely (table A3.2). It shows a statistically significant difference between Beaches 1 and 2 on the same day with the same collector[2]. At Beach 1, one observes a marked drop in the proportion of juveniles between 2006 and 2007[3] and this low ratio persists in 2008 and 2010. This does not appear to be due to population stress linked with our collections: we had purposely left one year out (2009) to 'let the population recover' and the hourly rate of collections remained high the following year. On the other hand, the maximal length of juveniles varies significantly from year to year[4], which suggests variation in the period(s) of birth or in the growth rate. A larger proportion of juveniles had perhaps reached adulthood by July in the last years of collection. Whichever the factors underlying these variations, they preclude the use of the ratio juveniles/adults as a reliable basis of inferences in archaeological assemblages.

Location	Year	Adults	Juveniles	% Adults	% Juveniles	Total
Beach 2	2004	137	50	73,3	26,7	187
Beach 1	2004	74	12	86	14	86
Beach 1	2005	394	59	87	13	453
Beach 1 CP	2005	257	33	88.6	11.3	290
Beach 1 MV	2005	189	48	79.74	20.25	237
Beach 1 GM	2005	169	42	80.09	19.9	211
Beach 1	2006	332	93	78.11	21.88	425
Beach 1 CP	2007	177	11	94.14	5.85	188
Beach 1 AC	2007	90	4	95.7	4.25	94
Beach 1 PP	2007	97	10	90.65	9.3	107
Beach 1 bait	2007	295	9	97.03	2.96	304
Beach 1 CP - 2	2008	377	14	96.4	3.5	391
Beach 1	2010	327	9	97.3	2,7	336

Table A3.2: Variation of the proportion of juveniles and adults in the different collections from Beaches 1 and 2 in Nafplion.

Variation in the Size Distribution of Adult Cyclope neritea

Dimensional variation among marine molluscs is often attributed to long-term climatic variation or to human (over-)exploitation (Álvarez-Fernández *et al.* 2011; Bailey & Craighead 2003; d'Errico *et al.* 2005; Gutiérrez-Zugasti 2011 and refs. therein). However, before attributing variation among archaeological samples to one or the other of these factors, terms, we wanted to evaluate potential natural year-to-year variation, and verify whether the collector influenced the range of sizes. Accordingly, we recorded with a digital calliper the maximum diameter, width and height (Fig. A3.7) of all specimens, with indication of the collector in the case of individual collections. All three dimensions on adult *Cyclope neritea* present a relatively large range and a Gaussian distribution (Fig. A3.8).

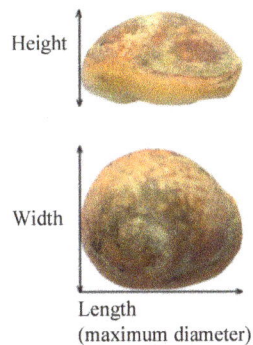

Height

Width

Length
(maximum diameter)

Fig. A3.7: Measurements on a C. neritea.

The maximum length (or maximal diameter) is strongly correlated to the maximum width[5,] while the height shows a weaker but also statistically significant correlation to the maximum length[6]. Given these results (Fig. A3.9), we can consider that the maximum length provides by itself a good estimate of the overall dimensional variation[7]. The mode is located between 1.1 and 1.2 cm (Fig. A3.8), i.e. slightly under the values published by Vanhaeren (2010: 52) for her Mediterranean sample (1.19 cm, s.d. = 0.17).

To evaluate the influence of the collector on the dimensional parameters of the samples, we used Student's tests to compare the means and standard-deviations, and χ^2 for the distribution of dimensional classes. Despite what appeared to be important variation in the mode and/or the distribution of dimensional class from one collector to another, no statistically significant variation could be established. The collector does not appear to be a source of significant variation of the dimensions, at least amongst adult collectors. We can thus group together the samples collected by different collectors to estimate inter-annual dimensional variability. The latter is limited to a few tenths of millimetres in mean and class distribution, and is usually not statistically significant (e.g. between Beaches 1 and 2 in 2004, between 2004 and 2005 for Beach 1, or between 2008 and 2010 for Beach 1). Statistically significant differences in the mean and distribution of dimensional classes do not occur every year, but were observed for Beach 1 between the samples collected in 2005 and 2006[8]. In both years the percentage of juveniles is very stable, which precludes an artifact of misidentification between adults and juveniles.

Whichever the biological or environmental factor underlying these differences in size[9], they demonstrate that small (mean ca. 0.035 cm) but significant differences can occur naturally from year to year in the same environment. Small dimensional variation should not be systematically attributed to long-term climatic fluctuations or to human pressure on natural populations.

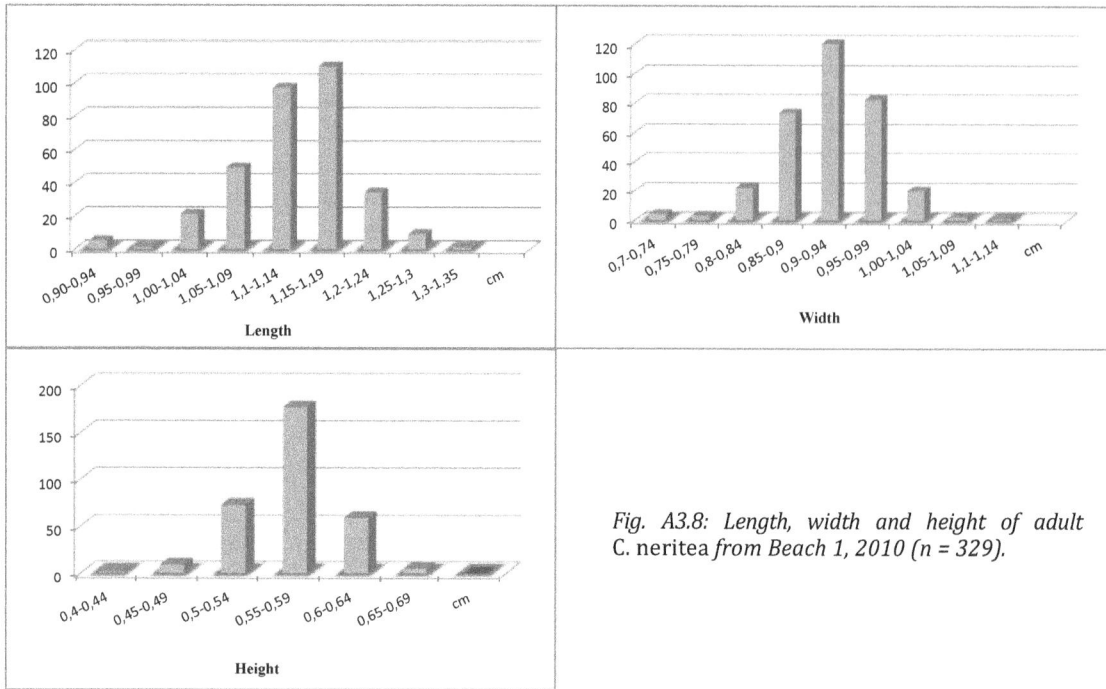

Fig. A3.8: Length, width and height of adult C. neritea *from Beach 1, 2010 (n = 329).*

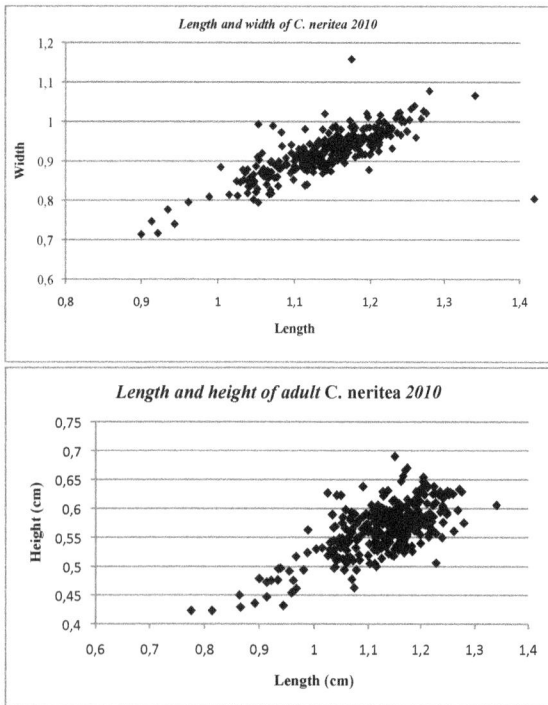

Fig. A3.9: Correlations between the length, the width and height of adult C. neritea *(Beach 1, 2010, n = 326).*

Location of collection	Year	Collector	m (cm)	σ	υ	N	Notes
Beach 1	2004	CP	1.117	0.094	0.0088	76	
Beach 1	2005	CP	1.154	0.065	0.0043	396	
Beach 1	2005	CP	1.15			257	m calculated from dimensional classes
Beach 1	2005	MV	1.14			189	m calculated from dimensional classes
Beach 1	2005	GM	1.145			169	m calculated from dimensional classes
Beach 1	2006	CP, PP	1.116	0.071	0.005	332	
Beach 1	2007	AC	1.134	0.063	0.004	90	
Beach 1	2007	PP	1.139	0.063	0.004	95	
Beach 1	2007	CP	1.12	0.067	0.004	165	
Beach 1	2007	Sea-bream	1.14	0.058	0.0034	295	
Beach 1	2008	CP, MM	1.141	0.062	0.004	377	
Beach 1	2010	CP, PP	1.14	0.064	0.0042	327	

Table A3.3: Variations in mean maximum diameter of C. neritea *from different collections and different collectors.*

Experiments in Perforation

The reference collection also served to test the perforation of the *Cyclope neritea.* We observed three main types of perforations on the archaeological specimens: initial, simple and enlarged. More rarely, the entire dorsal whorls are removed and the shell is more or less sliced in half.

It is easy to perforate the brittle shell of *Cyclope neritea* by pressure, with a small pointed wooden stick or bone awl, either on an anvil or in the hand. A stone drill can be used, but is not necessary. The perforation is initiated from the inside of the shell to the outside, through the aperture; characteristic micro-chipping can be observed on the dorsal surface. 'Simple perforations' are obtained by pressing the tool around the edge of the initial perforation to enlarge it. In case of 'enlarged perforations' or when dorsal whorls are removed, the perforation is enlarged by shifting the tool to the outside and exerting pressure from the outside towards the inside (Cristiani & Borić 2012).

Perforating *Cyclope neritea* requires no particular skill or practice, but some attention is preferable to avoid breaking the lip. The shells are also easily lost if accidentally dropped on the ground.

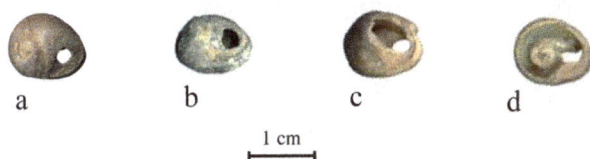

a   b   c   d

1 cm

Fig. A3.10: Different types of perforation on archaeological specimens. a: initial; b: simple; c: enlarged; d: dorsal whorls removed.

Heat Treatment

Physical and chemical analyses of blackened archaeological *Cyclope neritea* were performed at the C2RMF (*Centre de recherches et de restauration des musées de France*) by K. Lange and I. Reiche, to investigate the origin of the discoloration. The analyses demonstrated that the dark-coloured *Cyclope neritea* had been altered by heat under a reducing atmosphere (Lange *et al.* 2007, 2008). Since the shells would quickly disintegrate if not well protected from the flames and ambers, we concluded that the anomalously high proportion of blackened *Cyclope* resulted from intentional heat-treatment. We thus undertook several series of experiment to replicate they dark, homogeneous colour (Perlès & Vanhaeren 2010).

We first tested small 'polynesian pit-hearths'. The shells were wrapped in leaves and placed over and under hot embers in a small pit, protected by a layer of earth of about 1 cm thick, and left to cook for several hours after the pit was sealed with earth. None of the experiments proved successful: we observed no colour change. Placing the shells directly in a hearth was also unsuccessful: when in direct contact with embers, the shell disintegrates. When placed in the ash, it may be superficially stained but there is no colour transformation of the walls of the shell in cross-section.

We obtained satisfactory results by putting the shells, wrapped in leaves and protected by a small heap of earth about 3 cm thick, on the base of a hearth and by lighting a strong fire over them that was kept going for about 3 hours. After the hearth had slowly cooled down, the ashes were sifted to retrieve the *Cyclope neritea*. The intensity of the coloration varied slightly from experiment to experiment. In the best cases, the shells displayed a deep, lustrous black colour. Equally successful results were obtained by S. Ménard by putting in a fire some *Cyclope neritea* protected by a larger shell, in this case the shell of a whelk, *Buccinum undatum*. However, only three or four *Cyclope* can be heat-treated in each shell and we did not find in the Franchthi marine molluscan assemblage shells that would have been large enough to serve this purpose.

Fig. A3.11: Experimentally heat-treated Cyclope neritea. *Photograph C. P.*

NOTES

1   AC, for instance, was collecting for the first time, which resulted in a low hourly rate.

2    $\chi^2 = 5.28$; df= 1, p < 0.02.

3    $\chi^2 = 39.13$; df = 1, p < 0.01.

4    $\chi^2 = 26.8$; df = 4, p < 0.01 for 5 dimensional classes between 2005 and 2006.

5   r = 0.84, p < 0.01, n = 328 for the 2010 sample.

6   r = 0.625, p < 0.01, n = 262 in 2007, r = 0.663, p < 0.01, n = 391 in 2008, r = 0.53, p < 0.01, n = 326 for 2010.

7   See Álvarez-Fernández *et al.* 2011 for similar results on other shell taxa.

8   t = 4.389, p < 0.01.

9   Variations in salinity is probably not the most important factor, since *Cyclope neritea* can withstand important fluctuations (Mars 1966) and because « ... salinity is definitely not an important factor in lagoons » (Nicolaidou *et al.* 1988: 347).

APPENDIX 3.2

Columbella rustica

Family: Columbellidae

Genus: *Columbella*

Species: *Columbella rustica* (Linné 1758: Voluta).

Columbella rustica, or dove shell, is a small Mediterranean gastropod characterised by an biconical shape, a pointed apex, and 5 whorls, the last one very large and constituting almost 2/3 of the shell. The aperture is narrow, oblong, with a small posterior sinus and anterior siphonal canal. The outer lip is denticulated and presents a characteristic thickening in the middle (Delamotte & Vardala-Theodorou 2001). We noted that on the smaller specimens the lip was not formed and not closed in. These are probably juveniles, but we have not found confirmation of that assessment.

Fig. A3.12: Columbella rustica. *Dorsal and aperture sides.*

1 cm

The maximum height is variable but never exceeds 2 cm, for a maximum diameter of 1.1 cm (Cartonnet 1991). The colour is extremely variable, from almost white to beige, orange or brown with patterns of dots and zigzag lines.

Columbella rustica is a sedentary benthic snail that lives on rocks, at depths between 0.10 and 30 m. It belongs to the infralittoral algae biocenosis and is variously claimed to be omnivorous (Delamotte & Vardala-Theodorou 2001), carnivorous (Milišić 1991, 2007 quoted in Komšo & Vukosavljević 2011) or herbivorous (http://mglebrusc.free.fr/textes/la%20mer/Faune/columbella.html). We found no data on the biology of this species: season of reproduction, growth rate, life-span, etc.

Fig. A3.13: Range of colours in a sample of Columbella rustica *collected at Asini in 2011. Photograph C. P.*

Columbella rustica is not known to be eaten by man, but it was a prized prehistoric ornament, traded hundreds of kilometres inland (Álvarez-Fernández 2010; Bonnardin 2009; Cristiani *et al.* 2014b; Taborin 1993). Few data have been published concerning the dimensional variation, state of preservation and rates of collection (Cartonnet 1991; Komšo & Vukosavljević 2011; Pauc & Pauc 2006; Stiner *et al.* 2013), which is why we decided to build up our own reference collection.

Collecting *Columbella rustica*

We systematically collected dove shells to define as precisely as possible the characteristics of the populations that could be gathered in thanatocoenoses and under water. The aim was: (a) to estimate the time needed to collect dove shells, (b) to distinguish between anthropic actions (perforations, use-wear) and natural alterations, (c) to establish whether prehistoric assemblages could be constituted exclusively of naturally perforated specimens and, (d) to document a potential selection of specimens used as beads in the Franchthi prehistoric assemblages. The collections were conducted under three different conditions: dead specimens were picked up in thanatocoenoses along beaches, shells taken over by hermit-crabs were collected by sight under water, and live dove shells were gathered by touch in waist-deep water (Table A3.4).

Collecting in Thanatocoenoses along Beaches

We collected specimens from thanatocoenoses on various beaches in the Argolid, constituted of sand and/or gravels. We found them on every beach where rocks were present below the surface of the water and repeatedly collected at Asini beach, Kastraki and Arvanitia near Nafplion, at Fourni beach near Franchthi, and on the present-day Franchthi beach itself. No dove shell, on the contrary, could be found on the shallow sandy beach of Karathona, near Nafplion. Unlike other collectors (e.g. Cartonnet 1991; Pauc & Pauc 2006), we did not solely collect specimens visible on the surface, but searched through the sand or gravels. During some sessions, all intact *Columbella* and fragments were recovered in order to document the full range of size and alterations (Asini 2006, Asini 2007-2, Kastraki 2011). In other cases we specifically searched for well-preserved specimens, large enough to be used for producing beads (Asini 2009, 2011).

Collecting by Sight under Water

Other samples were collected under water by sight, with a diving mask, at depths between 0.20 and 0.80 cm. Under water, *Columbella rustica* is often covered by concretions and micro-algae, and it took us some time to realise they had to be spotted by their shape and not by their colour. Although we recovered some live specimens in these collections, most were in fact dead specimens inhabited by hermit-crabs (Fig. A3.14).

Fig. A3.14: Columbella rustica *collected under water by sight, and inhabited by hermit-crabs (near Arvanitia beach, 2011). Photograph C. P.*

Collecting by Touch in Waist-Deep Water

We only discovered how to systematically find live *Columbella rustica* several years after our first collections, on Arvanitia beach (Nafplion). *Columbella rustica* lives—possibly during the season of reproduction—in 'nests' of 5 or more than 20 individuals (Figs. A3.15, 16), in small, nutshell-sized holes in the rock. They are usually completely hidden by the surrounding (short) seaweeds and cannot be spotted by sight. To find them, one must blindly poke the rocks with a finger. Many such nests were discovered very near the surface, on flat eroded rocks at depths of sometimes less than 20 cm, making the use of a mask unnecessary. Interestingly, one or two live *Pisania striata* were sometimes found together with *Columbella rustica*. Like the dove shells inhabited by hermit-crabs, many *Columbella* found alive were partially or completely covered by concretions (Fig. A3.15). At Kastraki, near Tolo, the situation was slightly different since the rocks close to the beach were mostly bare of seaweed. The dove shells were found again in groups, usually in small crevices, which made them easier to spot by sight but they were also well protected by sea urchins!

Fig. A3.15: Live Columbella rustica *found in a single nest on rocks near Arvanitia beach (Nafplion), together with two Pisania striata (bottom right). CAD C. P.*

Fig. A3.16: Live Columbella rustica *collected under water by poking through seaweed, near Arvanitia beach, 2012. Photograph C. P.*

	Year	Recording	Collectors	Time	Nb. of C.r	Fragments
Thanatocoenose						
Argolid	2006-1	Described and measured	na		65	34
Argolid	2006-5	Described and measured	na		20	0
Asini	2007-1	Described and measured	CP+PP		41	
Asini	2007-3	Described and measured	CP + PP	35'	18	
Asini	2008	Described and measured	CP + JB		58	
Asini	2011-2	Described and measured	CP + PP+ SB	1h 10	248	
Fourni	2006	Described and measured	MV+CP+BW		71	
Franchthi	2007-1	Described and measured	CP		12	
Kastraki	2011-1	Described and measured	CP + PP + SB	1h 30	216	59
Kastratki 2012		Described and measured	CP + SB	40'	51	
Arvanitia	2006	Described and measured	BW (+AC)		114	
				Total	914	
Thanatocoenose						
Asini	2007-2	Counts by broad categories		1h 15'	123	
Asini	2009-1	Counts by broad categories			22	
Asini	2009-2	Counts by broad categories			81	
				Total	226	
Under water, by sight						
Asini and Arvanitia	2009	Described and measured	CP + SM		74	0
Arvanitia	2011-1	Described and measured	CP	45'	90	0
Andros	2011	Described and measured	CP		16	0
Arvanitia	2012-4	Described and measured	CP	45'	92	0
				Total	272	
Under water, by touch						
Arvanitia nest	2012-1	Described and measured	CP	5'	22	
Arvanitia	2012-2	Described and measured	CP	45'	92	
				Total	114	
Underwater, mixed (pred. by touch)						
Arvanitia	2012-3	Described and measured	CP	1h	203	

Table A3.4: Summary of the data on the successive collections of Columbella rustica.

Dimensional Variation

Where and how dove shells are collected is an important factor that determines the mean size of the shells and the proportion of specimens usable for the production of beads. Size differences depending on the location of collection had previously been exemplified for live *Patella vulgata* (Bailey & Craighead 2003) but not, to our knowledge, for *Columbella rustica*.

Fig. A3.17: Measurements on C. rustica.

The correlation between the height and maximum diameter of the shell is very high (Pearson's R comprised between 0.83 and 0.93 depending on the assemblage, p < 0.01, Table A3.5, fig. A3.18). The height is thus sufficient to characterise the size distribution of the reference collections and to compare it with archaeological assemblages.

Location of collect	Year	Pearson'r	n	Type of collect
Arvanitia	2006	0.88 (p < 0.01)	72	Thanatocoenose
Arvanitia	2012-4	0.83 (p < 0.01)	80	Underwater, by sight
Arvanitia and Asini	2009	0.89 (p < 0.01)	74	Underwater, by sight
Arvanitia	2012-1 and 2012-2	0.91 (p < 0.01)	112	Underwater, by touch
Asini	2007-2008	0.83 (p < 0.01)	80	Thanatocoenose
Argolid	2006-1	0.93 (p < 0.01)	67	Thanatocoenose
Fourni	2006	0.89 (p < 0.01)	81	Thanatocoenose

Table A3.5: Coefficient of correlation between the height and maximum diameter of intact Columbella rustica.

Height Distribution on Beach Samples (Thanatocoenoses)

The height distribution of *Columbella rustica* shells from large beach samples (thanatocoenoses) collected at Kastraki (2011-2012), Fourni (2006) or Asini (2007-2011) is fairly Gaussian, with a mode between 1.1 cm and 1.19 cm and a mean of 1.14 cm at Kastraki (σ = 0.12), 1.14 cm at Asini (σ = 0.16) and 1.17 cm at Fourni (σ = 0,18). However, the smaller size classes are poorly represented in these last two series (Fig. A3.19), probably because the collection was less systematic than at Kastraki. These values are much lower than the values given by Komšo & Vukosavljević (2011) for a sample of 104 specimens collected in the eastern Adriatic (mean height: 1.45 cm). We found no data on the factors influencing the growth-rate of dove shells, but the difference may be due to the cooler temperature of the Adriatic.

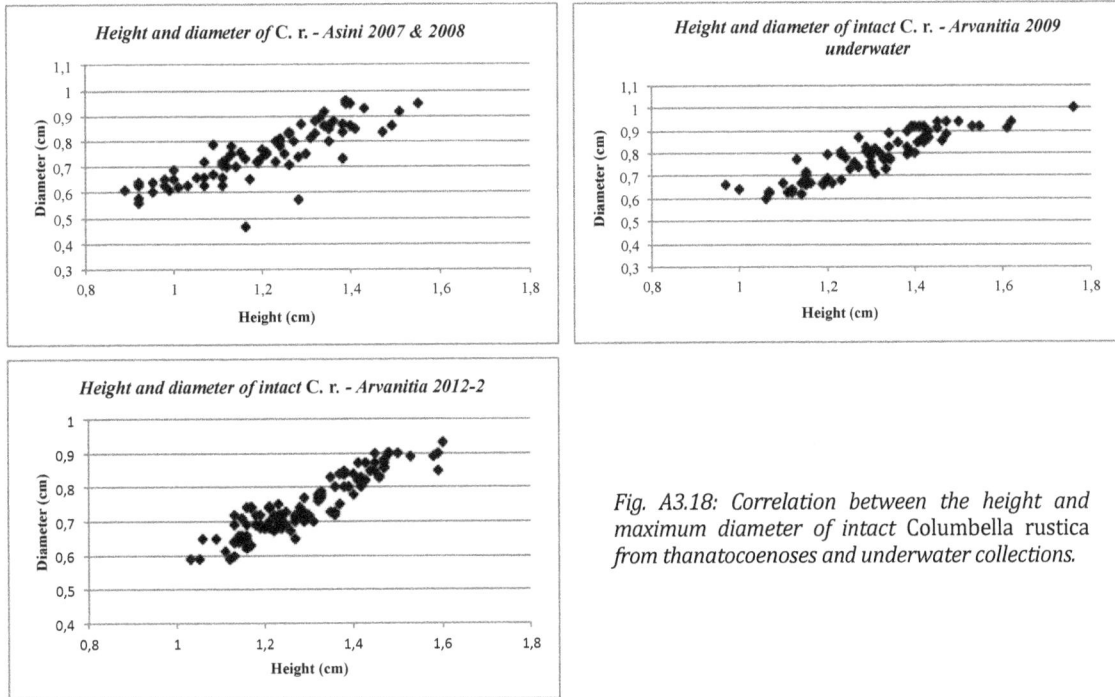

Fig. A3.18: Correlation between the height and maximum diameter of intact Columbella rustica from thanatocoenoses and underwater collections.

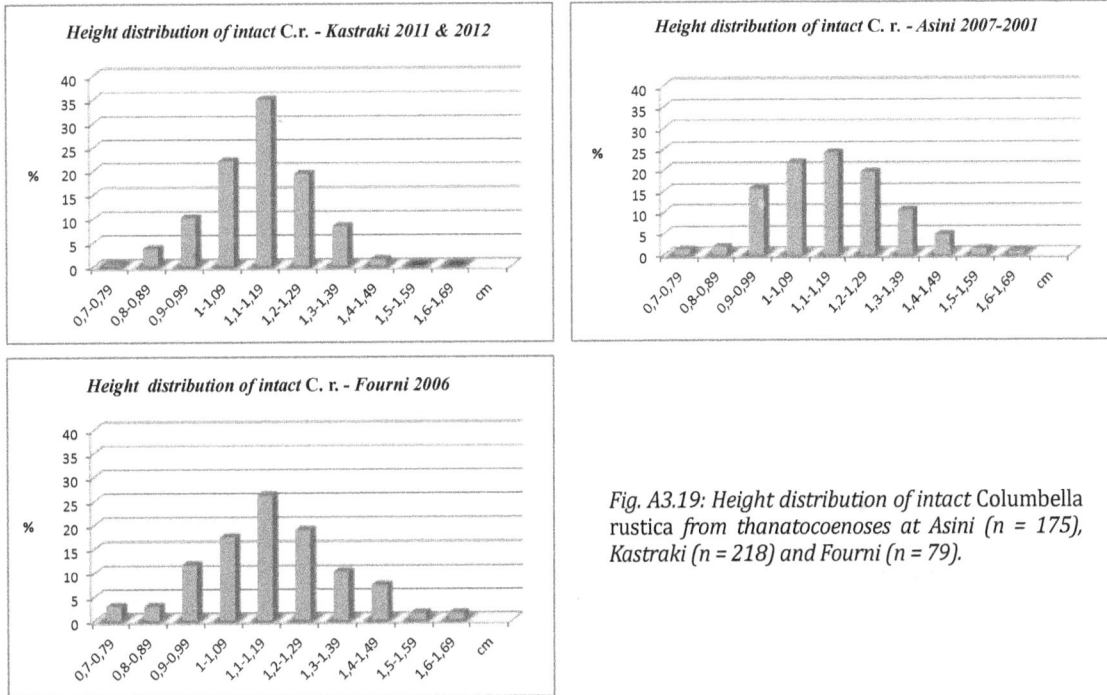

Fig. A3.19: Height distribution of intact Columbella rustica from thanatocoenoses at Asini (n = 175), Kastraki (n = 218) and Fourni (n = 79).

Height Distribution in Underwater Samples Collected by Sight

Samples collected by sight under water show a markedly different distribution (Fig. A3.20), with a smaller range and a much higher mode: 1.3 to 1.6 cm (m = 1.35; σ = 0.11; n = 79 for Arvanitia 2012-4; m = 1.37; σ = 0.13; n = 83 for Arvanitia 2011). Student's tests show that all differences between thanacoenoses samples and underwater samples are statistically significant. This is certainly due in part to the poorer conditions of visibility under water, but also, or possibly even more so, to the fact that most *Columbella rustica* were inhabited by hermit-crabs that tend to select large available vacant shells (http://en.wikipedia.org/wiki/Hermit_crab). In addition, local women collected dove shells for the touristic shop industry on Arvanitia beach, at least in 2006 and 2007. This may have biased the distribution for this beach, although it probably did not affect the later samples or the other beaches.

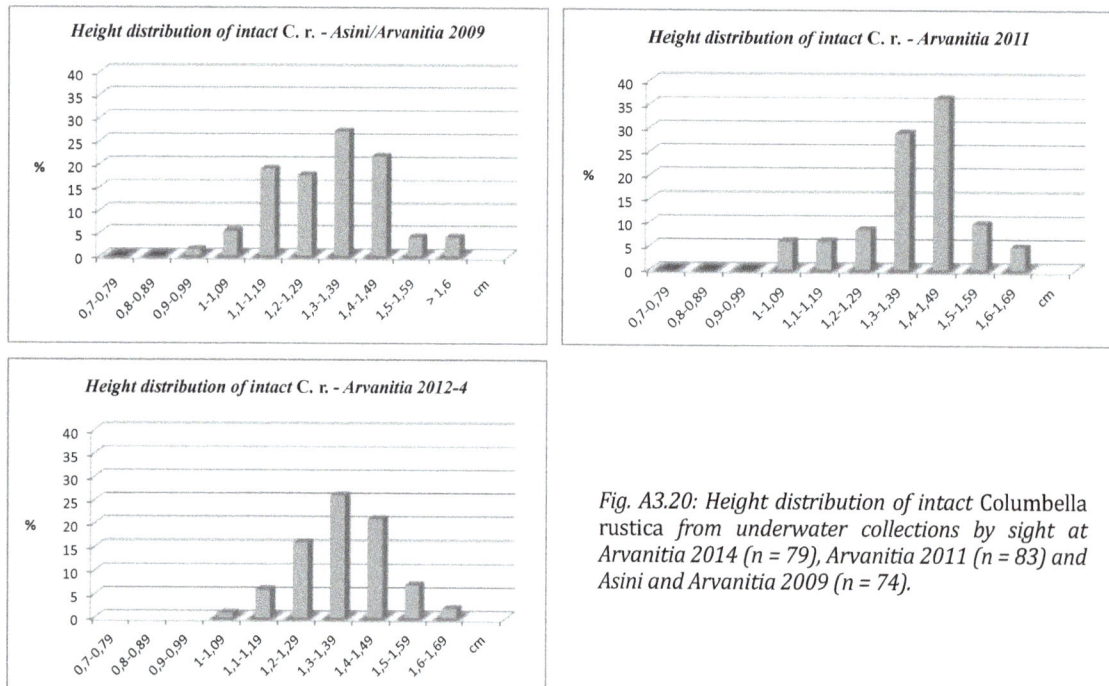

Fig. A3.20: Height distribution of intact Columbella rustica *from underwater collections by sight at Arvanitia 2014 (n = 79), Arvanitia 2011 (n = 83) and Asini and Arvanitia 2009 (n = 74).*

Height Distribution in Underwater 'Nests'

Finally, samples collected live in underwater 'nests' show intermediate values between the first two samples (Fig. 10). We grouped the samples exclusively collected in nests (Arvanitia 2012-1 and 2012-2) with the 'mixed ' collecting at Arvanitia 2012-3, since the latter was done predominantly by touch and presented no statistically significant difference with the others (Student's test : t = 0.0088). Here again, the smaller heights are poorly represented, although we systematically collected all specimens in each nest. We may thus consider that the mode, between 1.2 and 1.3 cm, and the mean (1.31 cm; σ = 0,15; n = 313) represent the actual mode and mean of live present-day populations around Arvanitia beach. This indicates that the smaller specimens tend to be over-represented in thanatocoenoses while, conversely, large specimens are over-represented in samples inhabited by hermit-crabs. The proportion of specimens that can be transformed into beads will thus differ significantly depending on where the shells were collected. This proportion, however, will also depend on the state of preservation, itself again influenced by the location of the collection.

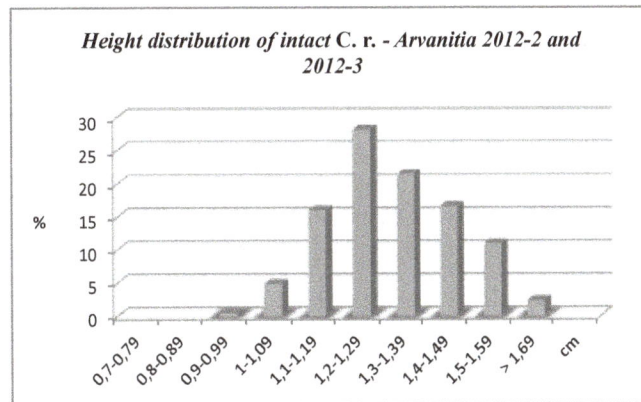

Fig. A3.21 : *Height distribution of intact* Columbella rustica *collected under water by touch at Arvanitia (n = 313).*

State of Preservation

The state of preservation of the collected shells is an important variable to assess the proportion of specimens in a good enough state to be perforated, as well as the proportion of naturally perforated shells that can directly be used as beads. To document the state of preservation, we followed, with some modification, Cartonnet's classification (Cartonnet 1991).

Fig. A3.22 : *From left to right : intact* Columbella rustica *(class 1), spire broken on the 1st, 2nd and 3rd whorl (class 2) and, right, broken on the 4th whorl (class 3). Ph. C.P.*

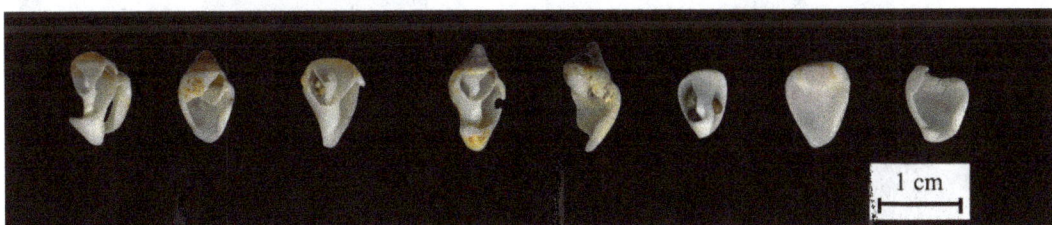

Fig. A3.23: *Broken* Columbella rustica *(class 4) and fragments. Ph. CP.*

Class 1 corresponds to complete specimens, from the base to the apex. A slight deterioration of the apex is admitted, provided it does not create a hole.

Class 2 corresponds to specimens that have lost one to three whorls on the spire.

Class 3 corresponds to specimens that have lost all whorls but the last one, with a break at the level of the last suture.

Class 4 corresponds to broken specimens and fragments unusable as ornaments.

One or several other alterations can affect each class: large and small perforations, broken bases and broken lips. We found few if any reference to the factors causing these alterations. Cartonnet (1991) attributes the perforations to the attack of predatory Muricidae on the last whorl, as well as to abrasion by sand and shocks against rocks. Given the lack of precise criteria for diagnoses, we simply distinguished the smaller holes (1 to 2 mm in diameter), probably mostly due to predators and smaller than archaeological perforations, and the larger holes, compatible with a direct use as beads and in large part certainly due to a violent impact on a rock. We noted the position of the hole for each specimen, as well as eventual breakage on the lip or the base.

The various alterations that affect the shells lead us to distinguish several subclasses within each class. Thus, 'class 1a large' corresponds to complete specimens with a perforation large enough to be used for a bead (though the position of the hole is not always compatible with this use), 'class 1a small' comprises specimens with a perforation smaller than archaeological examples, 'class 1 bl' specimens with a broken or missing lip, and 'class 1 bb' the rare specimens with a broken base. The same subdivisions apply to the other classes. Fragments (class 4) are not included in the counts since they were not systematically collected.

As shown by Table A3.5, the state of preservation varies widely depending on the mode of collection—live or dead—and, in the case of specimens collected in thanatocoenoses, depending on the beach. Broken or perforated specimens are extremely rare in underwater samples, while they can be frequent in thanatocoenoses. Within thanatocoenoses, the shells are better preserved on the sandy beach of Fourni than at Asini, where a range of low rocks separates the open water from the beach itself. The proportion of perforated specimens also varies, but, with a maximum of about 10%, it is always lower in our samples than in the sample collected below Üçağızlı I Cave in Turkey, where they reach 20% (Stiner *et al.* 2013 : 384), and than in the sample collected by Cartonnet in southern France (Cartonnet 1991), where they reached 45 %. However, if one only considers the specimens with a large dorsal perforation, as found on archaeological shell beads, the proportion barely reaches 4 to 6% in our collections (10% at Üçağızlı I). For instance, on Asini beach (2009) we collected 6 *Columbella rustica* with a dorsal perforation comparable to Palaeolithic and Mesolithic examples, out of a total of 152. Consequently, we cannot concur with Cartonnet (1991: 304) in considering that prehistoric bead-makers could rely *only* on naturally perforated specimens for their ornaments. In large assemblages such as found at Franchthi, the majority of the *C. rustica* beads had to be intentionally perforated.

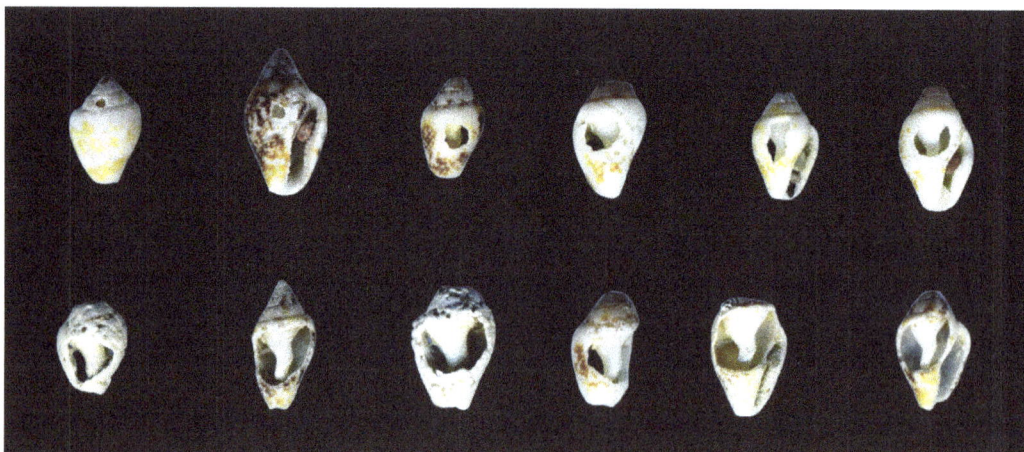

Fig. A3.24 : Small (top two left) and large dorsal, lateral and ventral perforations on Columbella rustica *collected on Kastraki beach (2012). Ph. C. P.*

| Class | | | 1 | | | | 2 | | | | 3 | | | |
Sub-class	1	1a large	1a small	1 bl	1bb	2	2a large	2a small	2 bl	3	3a large	3a small	3 bl	Total
Thanatocoenoses														
Asini 2009	53.2	8.5		3.9	0.6	13.1	2.6			9.2	0.6			152
Asini 2011-a	40.9	1.2	0.8	4.5		38.1	2.4	1.6	0.8	8.1	0.8	0.4		244
Fourni 2006	61.4	5.7	4.2	15.7	2.8	5.7	1.4	1.4						70
Kastraki 2011 and 2012	52.4	4.8	2	6		20	2.8	2	1.6	3.6	3.2	0.4	0.4	250
Underwater collections														
Arvanitia 2011	96.7					2.1	1.1							91
Arvanitia 2012-2	99.1					0.9								112
Arvanitia 2012-4	91.3	1.1	1.1			5.4	1.1							92
Arvanitia 2012-3	97.5	0.4		0.4		1.4								202

Table A3.6: State of preservation of Columbella rustica *in the largest collections, in percentages. The very rare specimens with a broken base have not been recorded in the table.*

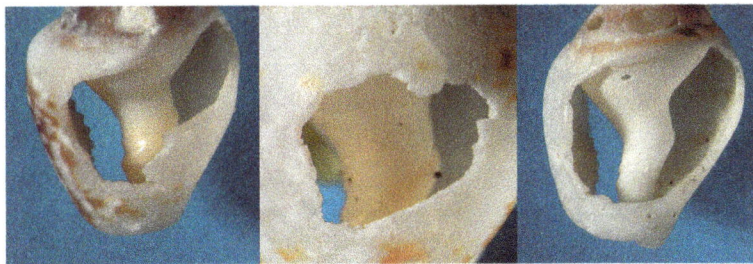

Fig. A3.25: Details of natural perforations (Asini 2006). Photographs M. Vanhaeren.

Rates of Collection

The hourly rate of collection in thanatocoenoses was highly variable. On the same beach (Asini), it ranged from 11 to 80 shells per hour and per collector, fragments excluded. This variation is independent from the aim of the collection: intact specimens only or all specimens. We did not systematically record individual variation among collectors, but is it clear that one of us (S. B.) was far more efficient than all others. Collecting by sight under water, and especially by poking for dove shell nests, is far more productive, reaching 200 specimens per hour and collector, all intact.

These relatively high figures do not mean, however, that it is easy to find *Columbella rustica* appropriate for making beads: shells collected in the sea are often covered with concretions, while many shells collected in thanatocoenoses are either too small or broken. In all archaeological periods at Franchthi (Upper Palaeolithic, Mesolithic and Neolithic), 75% or more of the *Columbella* have a height ≥ 1.2 cm (Fig. 15). This figure can thus be considered the basic minimal standard for shells to be used as beads. It corresponds well to our empirical standards for perforating the shells by direct or indirect percussion without hitting one's fingers rather than the shell. The mean height of the small Upper Palaeolithic sample of perforated dove shells actually reaches 1.42 cm ($\sigma = 0.11$, n = 10), while the larger Mesolithic sample has a mean of 1.34 cm ($\sigma = 0.15$, n = 58). Collecting from thanatocoenoses on beaches, searching through the sand or gravels, produced only 4 to 12 *Columbella rustica* of a height equal to or larger than 1.2 cm per hour and per collector (Table A3.7).

Collection	Collectors	Time	Nb. of complete specimens	Nb. of specimens ≥ 1.2 cm	% of specimens ≥ 1.2 cm	Nb. of specimens ≥ 1.2 cm per hour and per collector
Thanatocoenoses						
Asini 2011-2	CP + PP + SB	1h10	248	27	15.7	7
Kastraki 2011-1	CP + PP + SB	1h 30	216	56	29.7	12
Kastraki 2012	CP + SB	40'	51	7	13.7	4
Asini 2007-2	CP + MV + PP	1h 15'	123	25	21.1	6
Underwater collects						
Arvanitia 2011-1	CP	45'	90	73	87.9	97
Arvanitia 2012-4	CP	45'	92	72	91.1	96
Arvanitia 2012-2	CP	45'	92	84	72.3	112
Arvanitia 2012.3	CP	1h	203	164	82.6	164

Table A3.7: Rate of collection of Columbella rustica *of a standard archaeological height.*

From Reference Collections to Archaeological Inference

Seasonal variation in the dimensions of gastropod populations are often attributed to differences in environmental conditions or to the intensity of human exploitation (e.g. Álvarez-Fernández *et al.* 2011; Bailey & Craighead 2003; Gutiérrez-Zugasti 2011). Our data show that, at least for *Columbella rustica*, the mode of collection is another potential factor of variation. Since the different modes of collection each induce specific constraints and advantages, various collection strategies may have been implemented in prehistoric times according, in particular, to time constraints and aesthetic preferences.

Collecting in the sea, which, in optimal conditions, can be done without swimming, is by far the most efficient method, both by the number of specimens that can be collected per hour and by the proportion of specimens large enough to be transformed into beads. This holds true even when one discards the specimens covered with heavy concretions. On the other hand, the presence of the periosteum, the organic outer layer of the shell, renders them much duller than beach-worn specimens. In addition, naturally perforated shells that could be used directly as beads are almost non-existent, and all perforations have to be manufactured. It is difficult to prove however, that this type of collection was practiced in prehistoric times, since it presents few diagnostic features besides the large mean height and the excellent state of preservation of the apex. At Franchthi, large specimens with intact apex are only abundant in the Neolithic, but some extremely well-preserved Palaeolithic and Mesolithic dove shells may have been collected under water.

Alternately, when collected on beaches, a small percentage of the shells bears a natural dorsal perforation compatible with the perforations observed on Palaeolithic and Mesolithic specimens. The proportion is too low, however, to constitute the sole source of beads and most shells had to be artificially perforated. Yet, finding specimens sufficiently well preserved and large enough to be turned into beads is a time-consuming undertaking, at least on present-day beaches in the Argolid. On the other hand, dove shells picked up in thanatocoenoses have been washed up on the beach after having been rolled by the waves. This abrasive process removes the concretions, micro-algae and periosteum found on underwater specimens, and reveals their lustrous, vividly coloured surface.

At Franchthi, most Palaeolithic and Mesolithic specimens display the characteristics of beach-worn shells—pitting, broken spire, abrasion. It can thus be concluded that during the Upper Palaeolithic and the Mesolithic at Franchthi, preference was been given to the aesthetic quality of the shell rather than to the efficiency of the collection. Though not intrinsically rare, large and well-preserved specimens of dove shells can still be considered as valuable finds.

Experiments in the Production of Dove Shell Beads

Four different types of perforations have been observed on the Franchthi archaeological specimens. The majority of Palaeolithic and Mesolithic perforations is large and polygonal. They are associated with smaller perforations of oval shape (Fig. A3.26). Neolithic perforations tend, on the contrary, to be smaller, circular in shape, and sometimes located at the centre of a clearly abraded surface.

We undertook several series of experimentations to discriminate natural perforations from anthropic and to identify manufacturing techniques. Reproducing Neolithic perforations was easy: the first technique consists in lightly abrading the most prominent part of the dorsal surface on a pebble or a grinding stone, so that the perforator does not slip. The shell is then placed on an anvil, preferably made of wood with a small socket. A light indirect percussion on a stone awl or borer creates an initial perforation, which can then be enlarged by pressure with the same tool. The second technique consists in abrading the dorsal surface until the abrasion creates a perforation. (Figs A3.27 - 28). Neither of these techniques entails a severe risk of breaking the shell.

Conversely, we observed no trace of abrasion—or incision—on any of the hundreds of Palaeolithic and Mesolithic specimens. Even if a large perforation would have removed them, it seems unlikely that no evidence would have survived in the whole archaeological assemblage. In addition, we found it almost impossible to enlarge the perforation by pressure towards the base of the shell, where the wall is thicker. We thus experimented with perforating by direct and indirect percussion, but reproducing Palaeolithic and Mesolithic perforations has proved to be far more difficult and hazardous than Neolithic ones.

Since dove shells are too small to be hold between the fingers when hit by the hammer, we experimented with different types of anvils of stone and wood, with or without a socket to hold the shell, and with or without leather under the shell to absorb the shock. We also experimented with different hammers: stone pebbles, flint awls and a red deer antler hammer. All were tested both by direct and by indirect percussion. Overall, we implemented about 20 different combinations.

Our results were both encouraging and discouraging. We were able to reproduce the large Palaeolithic and Mesolithic perforations with all of the above-mentioned combinations, provided that the shell was secured in a small socket. When successful, a single blow is enough to produce a perforation identical to the archaeological examples. Yet, our rate of breakage was very high: often more than 50% of the attempts. Two different factors probably explain this: first, our lack of practice; and, second, the small size and greater fragility of the shells we used. Indeed, as noted above, modern dove shells found nowadays on Argolid beaches are, on the whole, smaller than archaeological ones. A second disappointment was that we did not find diagnostic criteria that would allow one to discriminate among these different operational modes. We can nevertheless conclude that Palaeolithic and Mesolithic *Columbella rustica* beads were indeed perforated by percussion, and that both direct and indirect percussion are efficient, even if we always felt more at ease with indirect percussion (Fig. A3.29).

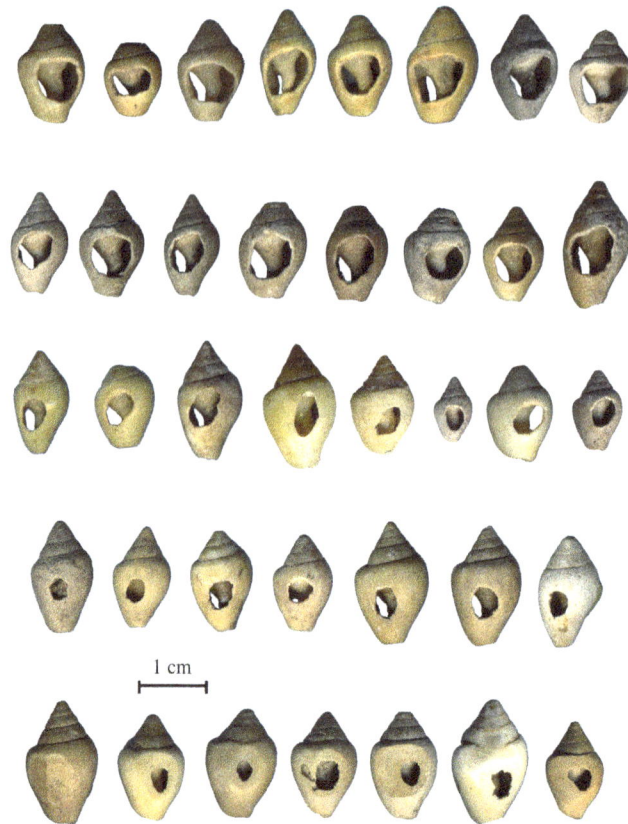

Fig. A3.26: Different types of perforations on archaeological specimens. Large angular (top two rows), oval (middle row), small circular (4th row), by abrasion (bottom row).

Fig. A3.27 : Perforations produced by light abrasion on a grinding stone and pressure with a stone borer.

Fig. A3.28 : Prolonged abrasion of the dorsal face of the shell to produce a perforation.

Fig. A3.29 : Perforations by indirect percussion with a stone pebble and a flint borer, on a wooden anvil.

Fig. A3.30 : Perforations by indirect percussion with an antler hammer (to the left) on a stone pebble.

APPENDIX 3.3

Antalis *sp.*

Family: Dentaliidae

Genus: *Antalis* (H. Adams & A. Adams 1854) (synonym: *Dentalium* Linnaeus 1758)

Species living in the Greek seas (after Delamotte & Vardala-Theodorou 2001):

- *Antalis vulgaris* da Costa 1778 (synonyms *Antalis vulgare, Dentalium vulgare* Da Costa 1778)

- *Antalis inaequicostata* Dautzenberg 1891 (synonyms *Dentalium inaequicostatum* Dautzenberg 1891, *Dentalium mutabile inaequicostatum* Dautzenberg 1891)

- *Fustaria rubescens* Deshayes 1825 (synonym *Dentalium rubescens* Deshayes 1825)

- *Antalis agile* M. Sars in G. O. Sars 1872 (synonym *Dentalium agile* M. Sars in G. O. Sars 1872)

- *Antalis dentalis* Linnaeus 1758 (synonym *Dentalium dentalis* Linnaeus 1758)

- *Antalis entalis* Linnaeus 1758 (synonym *Dentalium entalis* Linnaeus 1758)

- *Antalis panormum* Chenu 1842 (synonym *Dentalium panormum* Chenu 1842)

- *Antalis rossati* Caprotti 1966 (synonym *Dentalium rossati* Caprotti 1966)

- Fossil species: present in Pliocene deposits in Greece.

The different species of *Antalis,* better known as *Dentalium* or tusk shells, are scaphopods that live buried in the mud or the sand in both shallow and deep waters (4 to 50 m), where they feed on small molluscan larvae, foraminifera and other invertebrates (Delamotte & Vardala-Theodorou 2001: 241). Their shell is acuminate, tubular, curved. The apical, or posterior opening, is very narrow, 1 mm or less, and must be broken off if the shell is to be strung. The lower or anterior opening is larger and necessitates no modification for use as a bead. The colour is usually white, but *Fustaria rubescens*, as its name indicates, is pink to orange or brown.

The different *Antalis* species are difficult to differentiate (Kurzawska *et al.* 2013). Our archaeological series comprise smooth and very finely ribbed specimens, comparable to *A. vulgaris*, and specimens sculpted with large thick ribs, similar to *A. inaequicostata*. However, the taxonomic identification has not been verified, and we will simply differentiate the smooth (or finely ridged) *Antalis* sp. and the thick-ridged *Antalis sp.* One exceptionally large Neolithic specimen has been identified as a fossil[1]. Other fossil tusk shells may have been present and unrecognised since some fossil *Antalis* are very close to sub-recent and recent species (Rigaud 2014).

Reference Collections

We collected tusk shells to provide specimens for experiments, to discriminate anthropic use-wear from natural alterations, to estimate potential selection criteria in the archaeological assemblages and to estimate the ease and rates of collection. We never found live *Antalis*, as they are often found at depths where dredging equipment is needed (Koukouras & Kevrekidis 1986), but the shells are frequently thrown up on beaches. We thus collected all tusk shells in thanatocoenoses, either on the surface of the beach or by sifting the sand and gravels. Surprisingly, all the specimens collected were smooth or finely ribbed. We never found thick-ribbed specimens, the most abundant type in the archaeological collections, a failure that limited the validity of our bead-manufacturing experiments.

Our collections took place on four beaches (Fig. A3.1): Fourni, a beach north of Franchthi cave constituted of fine gravel (n = 202); Karathona, a large sandy beach near Nafplion (n = 41); Portocheli, in the southern Argolid, again a sandy beach (n = 17); Kouverta, in south-eastern Argolid, constituted of fine gravels (n = 75). Interestingly, we found no *Antalis* at Asini, Kastraki or Arvanitia, three beaches where we collected hundreds of *Columbella rustica* by systematic sorting through the sand and gravels. Since *Cyclope neritea* also live in an environment different from that of *Columbella rustica*, this suggest that each of the three main ornamental taxa at Franchthi had to be collected separately.

We did not record the rate of collection of tusk shells per collector and per hour, but is was low. The length, maximum and minimum diameters of the segments were recorded, as well as predators' holes and the presence of small pebbles in the apertures. Macrophotographs of natural alterations were taken on a number of specimens.

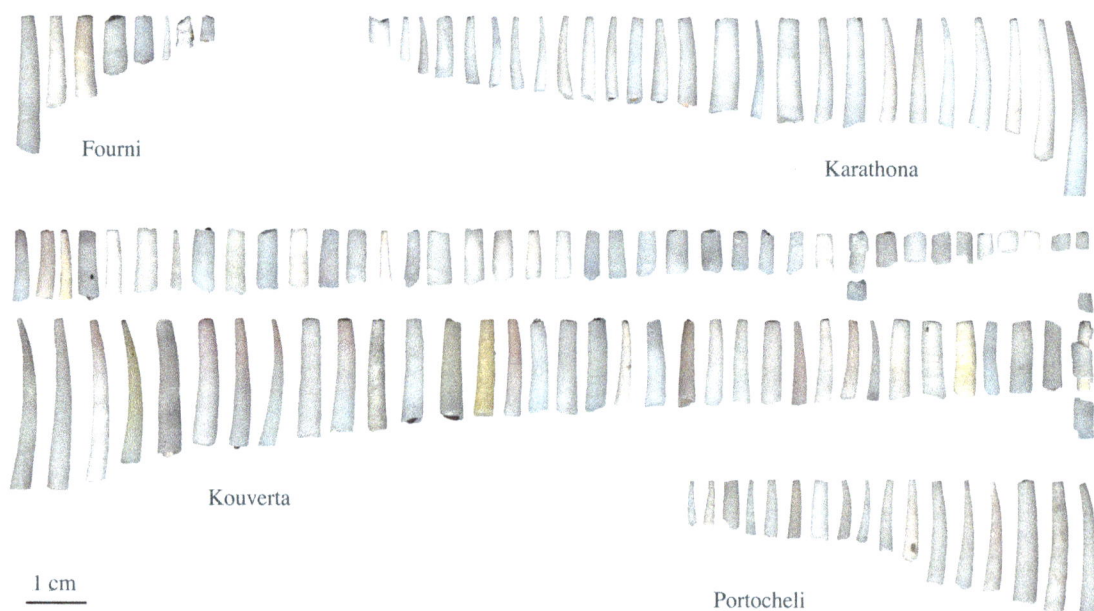

Fig. A3.31: Sample of Antalis *sp. collected on various beaches in the Argolid. CAD M. Vanhaeren*

Dimensions

All the *Antalis* sp. collected were fragmented, but the size of the segments varied according to the location of the collection and the granulometry of the beach. The distribution of the length is highly variable, but never Gaussian (Fig. A3.32). The proportion of 'long' segments (> 1.5 cm) is higher on sandy beaches, where the length is correlated to the maximum diameter. This corresponds to the recovery of proportionally numerous long segments, with a preserved apical extremity. By contrast, the assemblages from gravel beaches comprise many more small segments (< 1.5 cm); there is no correlation between the length and maximum diameter, due to the presence of many short anterior fragments, where the maximum diameter varies little. The granulometry of the beach is thus an important factor in the size distribution of *Antalis* sp. segments. Besides human preferences or scarcity of *Antalis* shells (cf. Bar-Yosef Mayer 2008), changes in the locations of collection may thus induce changes in size distribution of tusk shell beads.

Beach	Granulometry	Length mode(s)	Median length	Median max. diameter	Correlation length/max. diameter	n
Fourni	Fine gravel and sand	0.9 cm	0.86 cm	0.33 cm	-0.007	204
Kouverta	Fine gravel	0.6, 0.9 and 1.3 cm	1.04 cm	0.26 cm	0.19	74
Portocheli	Sand	0.9 cm	0.96 cm	0.31 cm	0.78	17
Karathona	Sand	1.4 and 1.8 cm	1.4 cm	0.24 cm	0.62	40

Table A3.8: Variation in the main dimensional parameters of Antalis *sp. segments according to the location of collection.*

State of Preservation

Compared to collections from French Atlantic beaches, our tusk shell segments are very small (see Vanhaeren 2009: table 10, and pers. obs.). This small initial size was further reduced by the frequent presence of a stone granule, a shell fragment or an tusk shell segment in one or the two apertures, which must then be broken off if the shell is to be threaded. In Fourni for instance, more than a third of the tusk shells presented one or both extremities blocked by a granule (n = 77). Even on the sandy beach of Karathona, 6 of the 40 *Antalis* sp. were plugged by a granule in one extremity. Predators' holes, on the other hand, were very rare (two specimens altogether).

The extremities of the segments, both intact and broken, are usually heavily abraded, rounded and polished by the action of the waves and sand (Fig. A3. 33-34). I consider this high degree of wear and polishing as characteristic of natural alterations, by contrast with a more matte surface produced by use-wear on beads. Another important feature of the naturally worn tusk shells is the presence of small indentations or notches on the extremities, which could easily be mistaken for thread use-wear.

Experiments

We broke intact *Antalis* sp. or long apical segments by flexion on the edge of a stone in order to obtain segments wide enough to be threaded and of a size comparable to the archaeological specimens. With the smooth *Antalis* sp. we used, the process was easy and required no particular strength, skill or tool (Fig. A3 35). However the situation could have been different if we had been able to experiment with the thicker ribbed *Antalis inaequicostata* or *novemcostata*: a flint tool might have been necessary to cut off the segments.

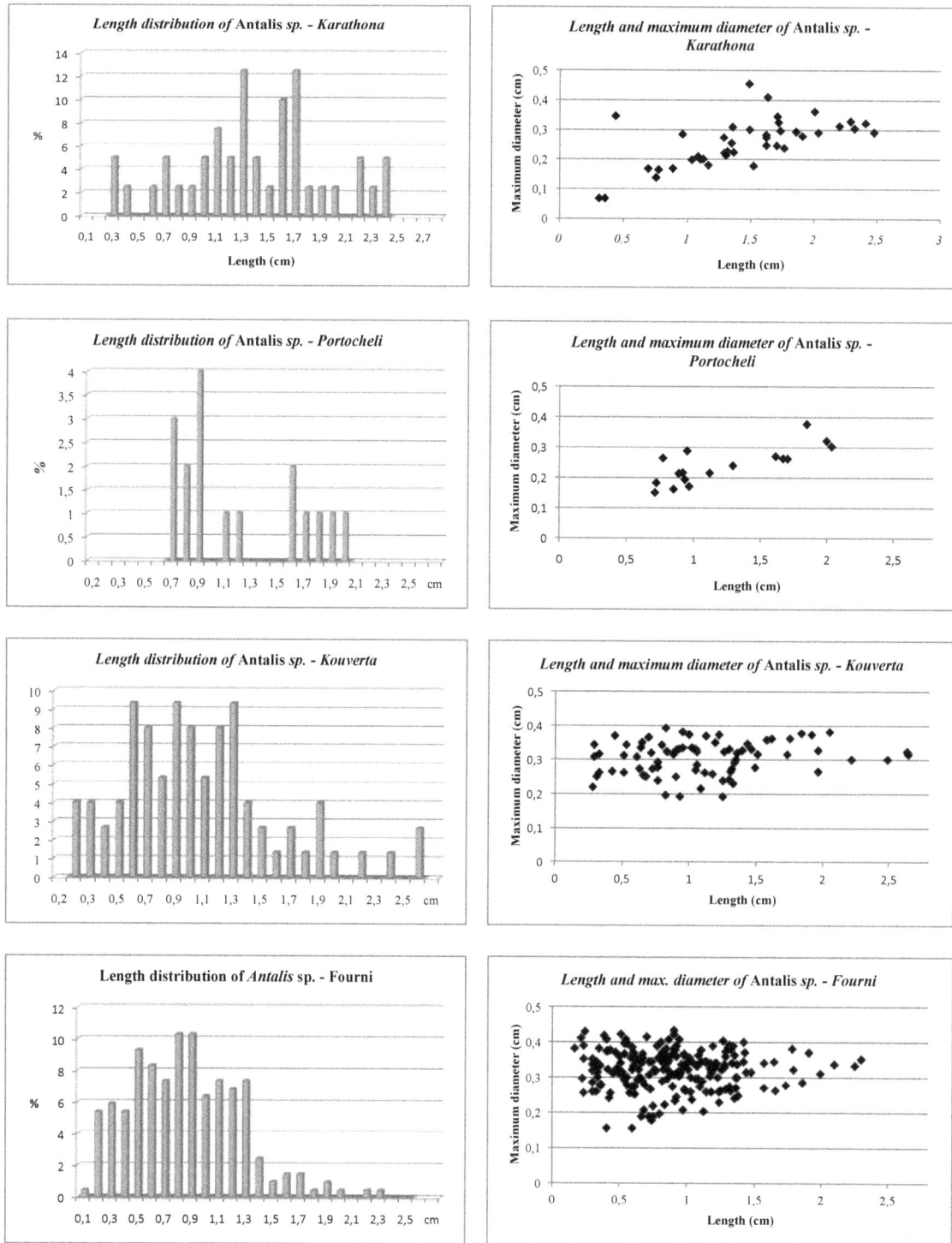

Fig. A3.32 : Length distribution of Antalis sp. segments collected on different beaches, and scattergrams of the length and maximum diameter.

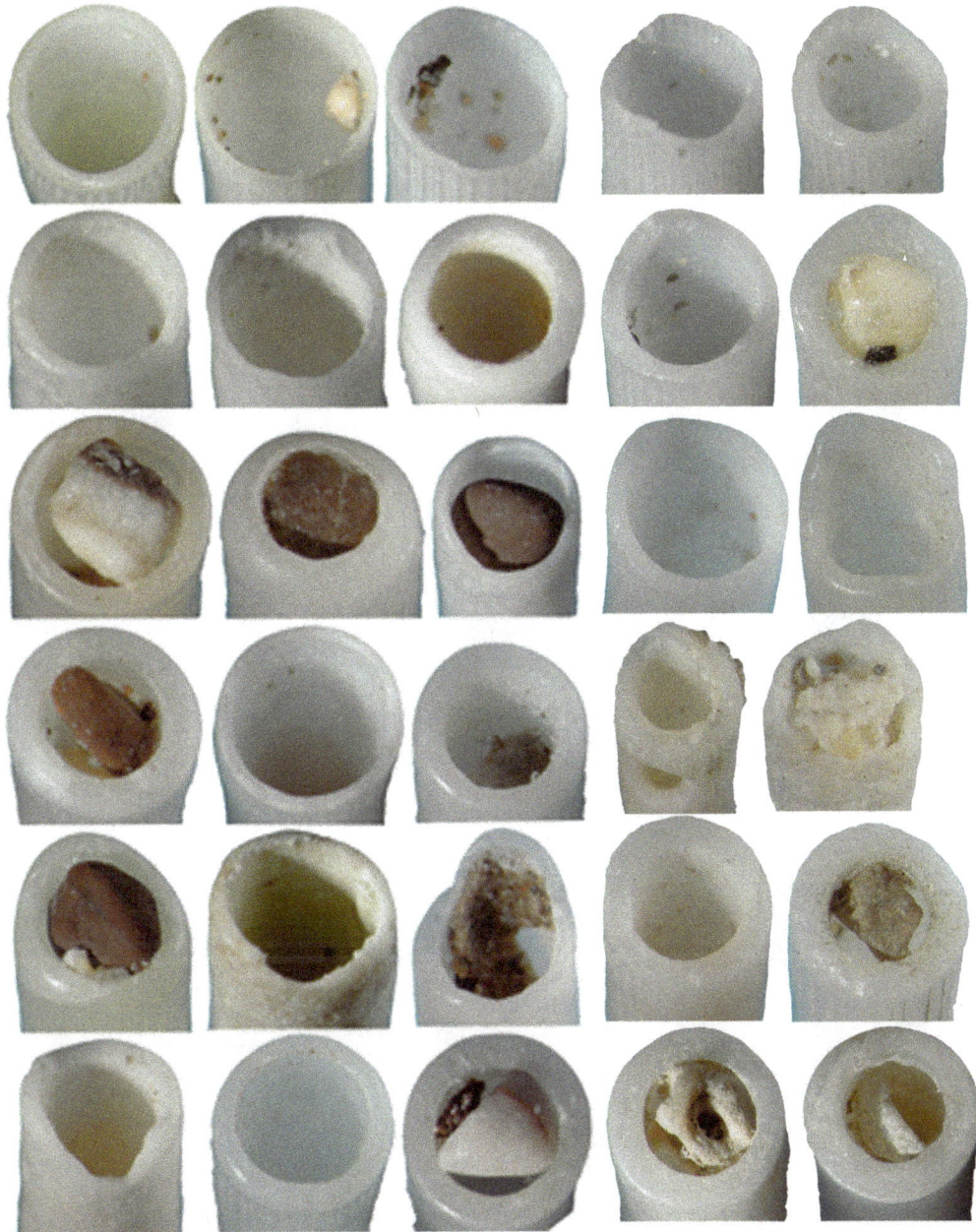

Fig. A3.33: Various degrees of abrasion of the anterior extremity of Antalis *sp. collected on Kouverta beach (first 3 columns to the left) and Karathona (4ʳᵈ and 5ᵗʰ columns). Note natural notches mimicking thread use-wear. Photographs and CAD M. Vanhaeren.*

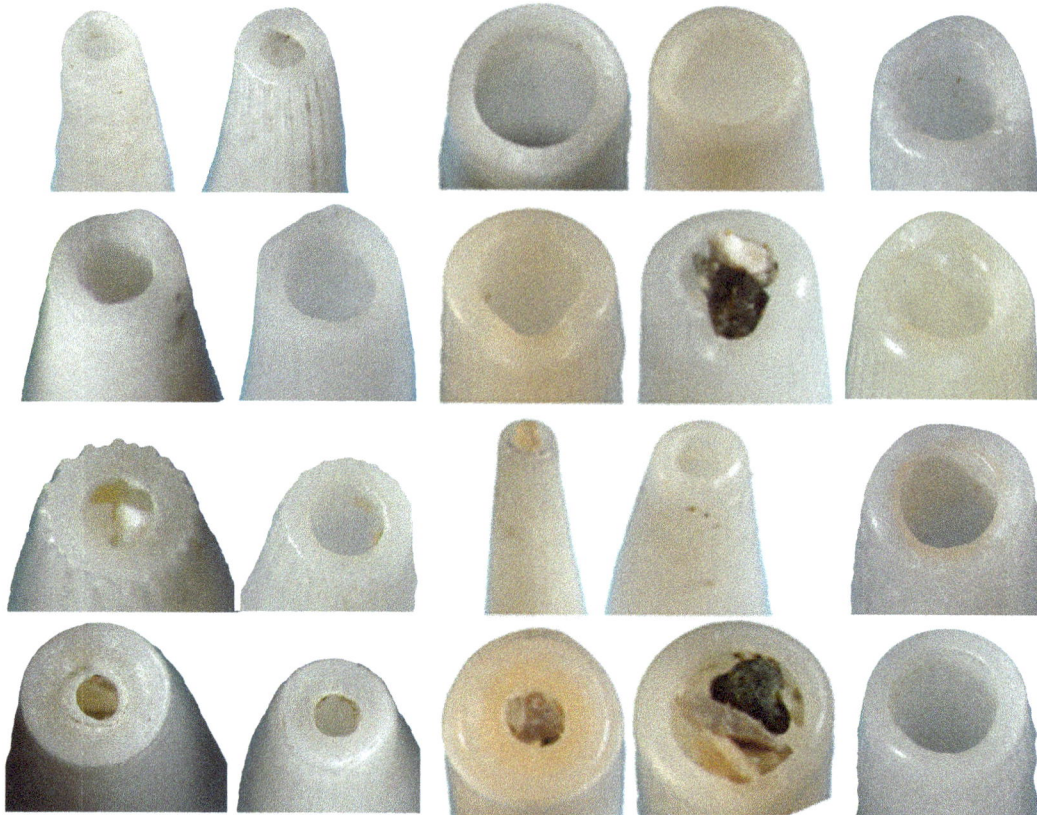

Fig. A3. 34: Various degrees of abrasion of the posterior extremity of Antalis *sp. from Portocheli (left two columns), Karathona (third and fourth columns) and Kouverta (fifth column). Note abraded and polished notches mimicking thread use-wear. Photographs and CAD M. Vanhaeren.*

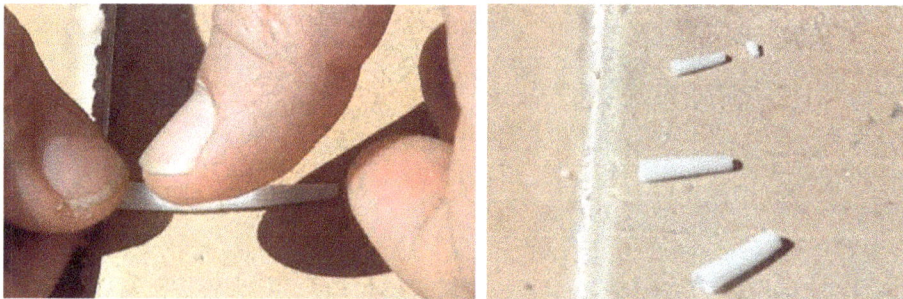

Fig. A3.35: Segmentation of an Antalis *sp. by flexion and resulting segments. Photograph C. P.*

NOTES

1   We thank E. Vardala-Theodorou for the identification.

APPENDIX 3.4

Conus mediterraneus

Family: Conidae

Genus: *Conus*

Species: *Conus mediterraneus* (Hwass in Bruguière 1792)

Conus mediterraneus is a small carnivorous Mediterranean gastropod. It lives on rocky bottoms among seaweeds and mud in the infralittoral zone, a habitat that it shares with *Columbella rustica*. The shell is biconical with a low spire. The first whorls are flat with very thin ribs, the last whorl is large and angular (Delamotte & Vardala-Theodorou 2001: 237). The overall shape is very similar to *Columbella rustica*, especially when they have one or several broken whorls, but the straight aperture and sharp-edged outer lip allows a clear distinction. The decoration alternates brown and light-coloured zigzagging lines, but this superficial pattern disappears when the shell is water-worn, to be replaced by successive horizontal brown and white bands.

Conus mediterraneus is not eaten (Katsanevakis *et al.* 2008) but it was frequently used as an ornament, a gaming piece or even a garment weight (Reese 1983). The upper whorls are often naturally broken, leaving a hole through which a thread can be directly inserted. Since *C. mediterraneus* and *C. rustica* have a similar morphology and are found in the same locations, both underwater and in thanatocoenoses, their absence in the Palaeolithic and Mesolithic ornament assemblages at Franchthi may at first appear surprising. Conversely, a few specimens are undoubtedly worked in the Neolithic, either sawn transversally or incised on the last whorl, while others show an apical perforation whose origin, anthropic or natural, remains uncertain.

Reference Collections

The reference collections comprise the specimens from the Franchthi shell reference collection assembled by J. Shackleton, and the ca. 60 specimens we collected at Asini beach. We paid special attention to broken individuals, in order to discriminate natural apical perforations[1] from man-made perforations, and to eliminate the possibility that the '*Conus* beads' of the Late Neolithic were natural. *Conus mediterraneus* being a very minor component of the Franchthi assemblages, we did not record individual specimens or rates of collect. As we were mostly interested in broken or altered specimens, we did not collect under water.

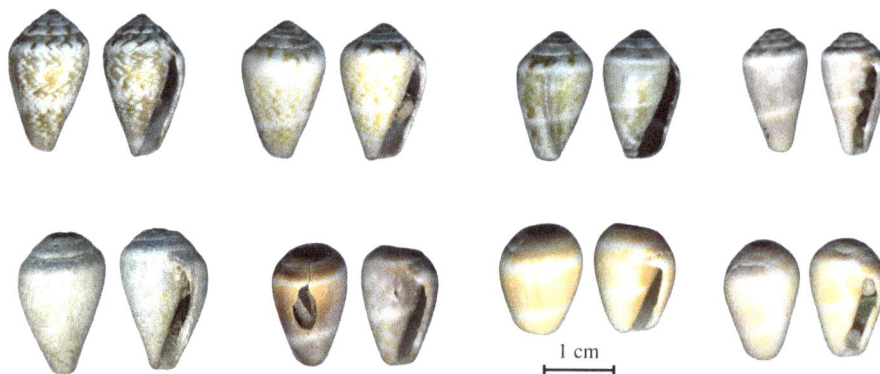

Fig. A3.36: *Different states of preservation of* Conus mediterraneus *from thanatocoenoses. CAD Fotis Ifantidis*

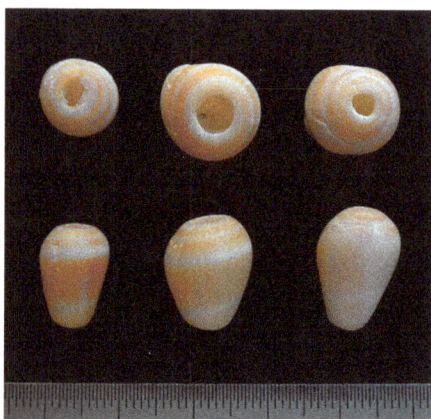

Fig. A3.37: Conus mediterraneus *with natural apical perforation (Asini beach 2010). Photograph C. P.*

Apical breaks on the first or second whorl of *C. mediterraneus* produce neat and directly usable perforations. The absence of striations is the only element that differentiates them from intentional perforation by abrasion. If the striations have been obliterated by use-wear, it becomes impossible to differentiate natural and anthropic perforations.

When the shell breaks between the spire and the last whorl, the broken spire forms cup-like pseudo-beads (Fig. A3.38). Several were found in the Neolithic deposits at Franchthi. We have no proof they were used as beads, but it is possible. These 'pseudo-beads' differ markedly from the 'Conus beads' found in Neolithic levels, manufactured by sawing off the spire and/or the base, which have no equivalent in thanatocoenoses.

Fig. A3.38: Natural Conus mediterraneus *pseudo-beads from broken and worn spires. Photograph C. P.*

Experiments

To reproduce Neolithic 'Conus beads', we selected two *shells* with a broken apex (Fig. A3.39). We cut the base off with a flint blade in about 5 minutes, and regularized the two extremities by abrasion with water on a grinding stone for a few minutes. The whole process was easy and did not requite particular skill or know-how. This experiment also showed that it was easy to reproduce the perforations by incision observed on a few Neolithic specimens.

All our attempts to perforate *C. Mediterraneus* by percussion, with the techniques used on *Columbella rustica (supra*, Appendix 3.2) failed: the shells either cracked or completely exploded under the blow. The brittleness of *C. mediterraneus* may explain why it was not exploited as an ornamental species at Franchthi during the Palaeolithic and Mesolithic: the range of techniques employed at the time—percussion and pressure—was not adapted to the nature of the shell.

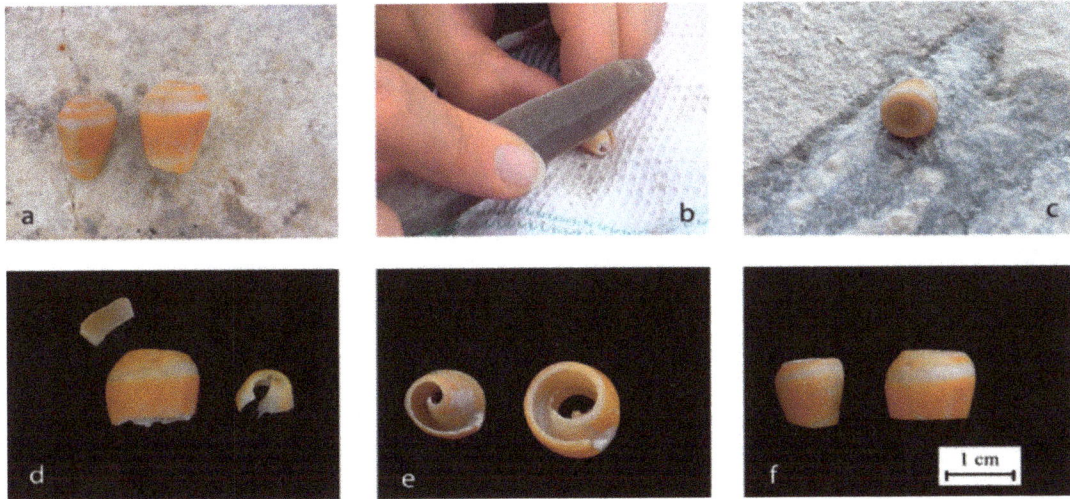

Fig. A3.39: Experimental production of 'Conus beads'. a: the two Conus. b: sawing of the base with a flint blade. c: regularisation of the base on a grinding stone. d: removal of the base of the second Conus. e – f: Basal and lateral view of the two 'Conus beads' after regularisation by abrasion. Photographs C. P.

NOTES

1   There is only one *Conus mediterraneus* with a dorsal perforation in the Franchthi assemblages.

REFERENCES

Adam, E. & Kotjabopoulou, E. 1997
The organic artefacts from Klithi. In G. N. Bailey (ed.), *Klithi: Palaeolithic settlement and Quaternary landscapes in northwest Greece*. Vol. 1: *Excavations and intra-site analysis at Klithi*, McDonald Institute for Archaeological Research, Cambridge, pp. 245-259 ("McDonald Institute Monographs").

Alarashi, H. 2014
La parure épipaléolithique et néolithique de la Syrie (12° au 7° millénaire avant J.-C.); techniques et usages, échanges et identités. Thèse de Doctorat, Université Lumière-Lyon 2, École doctorale Sciences Sociales.

Álvarez-Fernández, E, 2001
L'axe Rhin-Rhône au Paléolithique supérieur récent: l'exemple des mollusques utilisés comme objets de parure. *L'Anthropologie* 105: 547-564.

Álvarez Fernández, E. 2005
"Eloignés mais pas isolés": la parure hors de la "frontière française" pendant le Magdalénien. In V. Dujardin (dir.), *Industrie osseuse et parures du Solutréen au Magdalénien en Europe*, Société préhistorique française, Paris, pp. 25-38.

Álvarez-Fernández, E, 2010
Shell beads of the last hunter-gatherers and earliest farmers in South-Western Europe. *Munibe* 61: 129-138.

Álvarez-Fernández, E. & Jöris, O. 2008
Personal ornaments in the early Upper Paleolithic of Western Eurasia: an evaluation of the record. *Eurasian Prehistory* 5(2): 31-44.

Álvarez-Fernández, E., Chauvin, A., Cubas, M., Arias, P. & Ontañón, R. 2011
Mollusc shell sizes in archaeological contexts in Northern Spain (13 200 to 2600 Cal BC): new data from La Garma A and Los Gitanos (Cantabria). *Archaeometry* 53(5): 963-985.

Bailey, G. N. (ed.) 1997a
Klithi: Palaeolithic settlement and Quaternary environments in northwest Greece. Vol. 1: *Excavations and intra-site analysis at Klithi*, McDonald Institute for Archaeological Research, Cambridge ("McDonald Institute Monographs").

Bailey, G. N. (ed.) 1997b
Klithi: Palaeolithic settlement and Quaternary environments in Northwest Greece. Vol. 2: *Klithi in its local and regional setting*, McDonald Institute for Archaeological Research, Cambridge, ("McDonald Institute Monographs").

Bailey, G. N. & Craighead, A. S. 2003
Late Pleistocene and Holocene coastal paleoeconomies: a reconsideration of the molluscan evidence from Northern Spain. *Geoarchaeology* 18(2): 175-204.

Bailey, G. N., Carter, P. L., Gamble, C. S. & Higgs, H. P. 1983a
Asprochaliko and Kastritsa: further investigations of Palaeolithic settlement and economy in Epirus (North-west Greece). *Proceedings of the Prehistoric Society* 49: 15-42.

Bailey, G. N., Carter, P. L., Gamble, C. S. & Higgs, H. P. 1983b
Epirus revisited: seasonality and inter-site variation in the Upper Palaeolithic of North-West Greece. In G. N. Bailey (ed.), *Hunter-gatherer economy in Prehistory: A European perspective*, Cambridge University Press, Cambridge, pp. 64-78.

Bar-Yosef Mayer, D. 1989
Late Palaeolithic and Neolithic marine shells in the southern Levant as cultural markers. In C. F. Hayes III (ed.), *Proceedings of the 1986 Shell Bead conference*, Rochester Museum and Science Center, Rochester, pp. 169-174. ("Research Records 20")

Bar-Yosef Mayer, D. 1997
Neolithic shell bead production in Sinai. *Journal of Archaeological Science* 24: 97-111.

Bar-Yosef Mayer, D. 2008
Dentalium shells used by hunter-gatherers and pastoralists in the Levant. *Archaeofauna* 17: 103-110.

Bar-Yosef Mayer, D. 2010
The lessons of *Dentalium* shells in the Levant. *Journal of the Israel Prehistoric Society* 40: 219-228.

Bar-Yosef Mayer, D. 2013
Towards a typology of stone beads in the Neolithic Levant. *Journal of Field Archaeology* 38(2): 129-142.

Bar-Yosef Mayer, D. 2014
Marine resources in the Early Neolithic of the Levant: their relevance to early seafaring. *Eurasian Prehistory* 10(1-2): 83-98.

Bar-Yosef Mayer, D. & Zohar, I. 2010
The role of aquatic resources in the Natufian culture. *Eurasian Prehistory* 7(1): 29-43.

Bar-Yosef Mayer, D., Vandermeersch, B. & Bar-Yosef, O. 2009
Shells and ochre in Middle Palaeolithic Qafzeh cave, Israel: indications for modern behavior. *Journal of Human Evolution* 56: 307-314.

Barrière, J. 1969
Les coquilles marines découvertes sur le sol de la cabane acheuléeenne du Lazaret. In H. de Lumley

(dir), *Une cabane acheuléenne dans la grotte du Lazaret (Nice)*, Société préhistorique française, Paris, pp. 117-118 ("Mémoire n° 7").

Bedulli, D. 1977
Possible alterations caused by temperature on exploration rhythms in *Cyclope neritea* (L) (Gastropoda: Prosobranchia). *Bolletino di Zoologia* 44: 43-50.

Benghiat, S., Komšo, D. & Miracle, P. 2009
An experimental analysis of perforated shells from the site of Šebrn Abri (Istria), Croatia. In S. McCartan, R. Schulting, G. Warren & P. Woodman, P. (eds), *Mesolithic Horizons. Papers presented at the Seventh International Conference on the Mesolithic in Europe*, Belfast 2005, Oxbow Books, Oxford, pp. 730-736.

Besançon, M., Cassard, M. Chanut, M. & Colbachini, Fl. 2013
*L'exploitation des invertébrés de l'étang de Thau: étude bibliographique et enquêtes concernant les zones et les quantités pêchées. Réflexions sur un réensemencement en palourde (*Ruditapes decussatus*).* Projet d'élèves ingénieurs n°6, Montpellier SupAgro, 50 p.

Binford, L. R. 1980
Willow smoke and dog's tail: hunter-gatherer settlement systems and archaeological site formation. *American Antiquity* 45: 4-20.

Bon, F. 2002
L' Aurignacien entre mer et océan. Réflexion sur l'unité des phases anciennes de l'Aurignacien en France, Société préhistorique française, Paris ("Mémoire XXIX").

Bon, F. 2009
Préhistoire. La fabrique de l'Homme, Le Seuil, Paris ("L'Univers historique").

Bon, F., Costamagno, S. & Valdeyron, N. 2011
Hunting camps in Prehistory. Current archaeological approaches. *P@lethnologie* 2011: 3. www.palethnologie.org

Bonnardin, S. 2009
La parure funéraire au Néolithique ancien dans les Bassins parisien et rhénan au Rubané, Hinkelstein et Villeneuve-Saint-Germain, Société préhistorique française, Paris ("Mémoire XLIX").

Borić, D., French, Ch. A. I., Stefanovic, S., Dimitrievič, V., Cristiani, E., Gurova, M., Antonović, D., Allué, E. & Filipović, D. 2014
Late Mesolithic lifeways and deathways at Vlasac (Serbia). *Journal of Field Archaeology* 39(1): 4-31.

Borja, A. 1986
La alimentacion y distribution del espacio en tres moluscos gasteropodos: *Rissoa parva* (Da Costa), *Barleeia unifasciata* (Montagu) y *Bittium reticulatum* (Da Costa). *Cahiers de biologie marine* XXVII: 69-75.

Boulhic, M. & Tardy, J. 1986
Ponte, développement et éthologie des juvéniles de *Cyclope neritea* (Linné, 1758). *Haliotis* 15: 51-58.

Broglio, A., & Gurioli, F. 2004
The symbolic behaviour of the first modern humans: The Fumane cave evidence (Venetian pre-Alps). In M. Otte (ed.), *La Spiritualité. Actes du colloque de la commission 8 de l'UISPP (Paléolithique supérieur), Liège, 10–12 décembre 2003*, Études et Recherches Archéologiques de l'Université de Liège [ERAUL] 106, Liège, pp. 97–102.

Cameron, D., White, P., Lampert, R. & Florek, St. 1990
Blowing with the wind. Site destruction and site creation at Hawker Lagoon, South Australia. *Australian Archaeology* 30: 58-69.

Cartonnet, M. 1991
Réflexion sur la conservation différentielle des coquilles de colombelles utilisées comme parures préhistoriques. *Revue archéologique de l'Est* 42: 299-404.

Casanova, M. 2013
Le lapis-lazuli dans l'Orient ancien. Production et circulation du Néolithique au IIe millénaire av. J. C., Éditions du CTHS, Paris.

Cilli, C. & Gurioli, F. 2007
Oggetti ornemantali. In F. Martini (ed.), *L'Italia tra 15.000 e 10.000 anni fa. Cosmopolitismo e regionalita nel Tardoglaciale*, Museo Fiorentino di Preistoria "Paolo Graziosi", Firenze, pp. 79-82.

Claassen, C. 1998
Shells, Cambridge University Press, Cambridge ("Cambridge manuals in archaeology").

Clark, J. 1991
Pearl shell symbolism in Highlands Papua New Guinea, with particular reference to the Wiru people of Southern Highlands Province. *Oceania* 61: 309-339.

Colonese, A. & Wilkens, B. 2005
The malacofauna of the Upper Paleolithic levels at Grotta della Serratura (Salerno, southern Italy). In D. Bar-Yosef Mayer (ed.) *Archaeomalacoly: molluscs in former environments of human behaviour. 9th ICAZ Conference, Durham 2002*, Oxbow Books, Oxford.

Colonese, A. C., Mannino, M. A., Bar-Yosef Mayer, D. E., Fa, D. A., Finlayson, J. C., Lubell, D. & Stiner, M. C. 2010
Marine mollusc exploitation in Mediterranean prehistory: an overview. *Quaternary International* 239: 86-103.

Conard, N. J. & Bolus, M. 2003
Radiocarbon dating the appearance of modern humans and timing of cultural innovations in Europe: new results and new challenges. *Journal of Human Evolution* 44: 331-371.

Cristiani, E. 2009
Osseous artefacts from the Mesolithic levels of Pradestel rock-shelter (north-eastern Italy): a morphological and techno-functional analysis. *Preistoria Alpina* 44: 181-205.

Cristiani, E. & Borić , D. 2012
8500-year-old Late Mesolithic garment embroidery from Vlasac (Serbia): technological, use-wear and residue analyses. *Journal of Archaeological Science* 39(11): 3450-3469.

Cristiani, E., Živaljević , I. & Borić , D. 2014a
Residue analysis and ornament suspension techniques in prehistory: cyprinid pharyngeal teeth beads from Late Mesolithic burials at Vlasac (Serbia). *Journal of Archaeological Science* 292-310.

Cristiani, E., Farbstein, R. & Miracle, P. 2014b
Ornamental traditions in the Eastern Adriatic: the Upper Palaeolithic and Mesolithic personal adornments from Vela Spila (Croatia). *Journal of Anthropological Archaeology* 36: 21-31.

Cullen, T. 1995
Mesolithic mortuary ritual at Franchthi Cave, Greece. *Antiquity* 69(263): 270-289.

Cullen, T. with the coll. A. Papathanasiou, in prep.
Funerary rituals and human biology at Franchthi Cave, Greece. Excavations at Franchthi Cave, Indiana University Press, Bloomington & Indianapolis.

d'Errico, F. & Vanhaeren, M. 2000
Mes morts et les morts de mes voisins. Le mobilier funéraire de l' Aven des Iboussières et l'identification de marqueurs culturels à l'Epipaléolithique. In *Les derniers chasseurs-cueilleurs d'Europe occidentale, actes du colloque international de Besançon, Besançon octobre 1998,* Presses Universitaires Franc-Comtoises, Besançon, pp. 325-342 ("Annales littéraires 699; Série "Environnement, sociétés et archéologie", 1).

d'Errico, F. & Vanhaeren, M. 2002
Criteria for identifying Red Deer (*Cervus elaphus*) age and sex from their canines. Application to the study of Upper Palaeolithic and Mesolithic ornaments. *Journal of Archaeological Science* 29: 211-232.

d'Errico, F. & Vanhaeren, M. 2009
Earliest personal ornaments and their significance for the origin of language debate. In R. Botha & C. Knight (eds), *The Cradle of language,* Oxford University Press, Oxford, pp. 16-40.

d'Errico, F., Jardón-Giner & Soler-Mayor, B. 1993
Critères à base expérimentale pour l'étude des perforations naturelles et intentionnelles sur coquillages. In P. C. Anderson, S. Beyries, M. Otte, M. & H. Plisson (dir.), *Traces et fonction. Les gestes retrouvés. Colloque international de Liège,* CRA et Université de Liège, Liège, pp. 243-254 ("ERAUL 50").

d'Errico, F., Henshilwood, Ch., Vanhaeren, M. & van Niekerk, K. 2005
Nassarius kraussianus shell beads from Blombos Cave: evidence for symbolic behaviour in the Middle Stone Age. *Journal of Human evolution* 48: 3-24.

Davidson, A. 1972
Mediterranean Seafood, London, Penguin Books.

De Vivo, B., Rolandi, G., Gans, P. B., Cakvert, A., Bohrson, W. A., Spera, F. J. & Belkin, H. E. 2001
New constraints on the pyroclastic eruptive history of the Campanian volcanic Plain (Italy). *Mineralogy and Petrology* 73: 47-67.

Deith, M. R. & Shackleton, N. J. 1988
Oxygen isotope analysis of marine molluscs from Franchthi Cave. In J. C. Shackleton, *Marine Molluscan Remains from Franchthi Cave,* Excavations at Franchthi Cave, Greece, fasc. 4, Indiana University Press, Bloomington & Indianapolis, pp. 133-156.

Delamotte, M. & Vardala-Theodorou, E. 2001
Shells from the Greek seas, The Goulandris Natural History Museum, Kifissia.

Diamant, S. 1979
A short history of archaeological sieving at Franchthi cave, Greece. *Journal of Field Archaeology* 6(2): 203-217.

Djindjian, F., Kozłowski, J. K. & Otte, M. 1999
Le Paléolithique supérieur en Europe, Armand Colin, Paris.

Doneddu, M. & Trainito, E. 2005
Conchiglie del Mediterraneo, Il Castello, Trezzano sul Naviglio.

Douka, K., Hedges, R. E. M. & Higham, T. F. G. 2010
Improved AMS 14C dating of shell carbonates using high-precision X-ray diffraction and a novel density separation protocol(CarDS). *Radiocarbon* 52(2): 735-751.

Douka K., Perlès C., Valladas H., Vanhaeren M. & Higham T. 2011
Franchthi Cave revisited: the age of the Aurignacian in south-eastern Europe. *Antiquity* 85(330): 1131-1150.

Dubin, L. S. 1987
The History of Beads from 30,000 B.C. to the Present, Thames and Hudson, London.

Duday, H. & Courtaud, P. 1998
La nécropole mésolithique de la Vergne (Charente-Maritime). In J. Guilaine (dir.), *Sépultures d'Occident et genèses des mégalithismes (9 000- 3 500 avant notre ère),* Éditions Errance, Paris, pp. 27-37.

Duday, H., Courtaud, P., Robin, K., Dujardin, V. Gruet, Y., Gouraud, G., Martin, H. & San Juan-Foucher, C. 1998
La Vergne: La Grande Pièce (Déviation de Saint-Jean d'Angely, Charente-Maritime). *Bulletin de la Société préhistorique française* 95(3): 433-435.

Facorellis, Y. 2013
Radiocarbon dates from archaeological sites in caves and rockshelters in Greece. In F. Mavridis & J. T. Jensen, *Stable places and changing perceptions: cave archaeology in Greece,* BAR Int. Series 2558, Archaeopress, Oxford, pp 19-72.

Fairbanks, R. G. 1989
A 17,000-year-old glacio-eustatic sea level record: influence of glacial melting rates on the Younger Dryas event and deep ocean circulation. *Nature* 342: 637-642.

Farrand, W. R. 2000
Depositional history of Franchthi Cave, sediments, stratigraphy and chronology. With a report on the background of the Franchthi project by T. W. Jacobsen. Excavations at Franchthi Cave, Greece, fasc. 12, Indiana University Press, Bloomington & Indianapolis.

Floss, H. 2000
La fin du Paléolithique en Rhénanie (Magdalénien, groupes à Federmesser, Ahrensbourgien): l'évolution du choix des matières premières lithiques, reflet d'un profond changement du climat et du comportement humain In B. Valentin, P. Bodu et M. Christensen (dir.), *L'Europe centrale et septentrionale au Tardiglaciaire: confrontation des modèles régionaux de peuplement. Table ronde internationale de Nemours,* 14-15-16 mai 1997, Association pour la promotion de la recherche archéologique en Île-de-France, Nemours, pp. 87-96.

Formoso, B. 2013
Costumes du Yunnan, Société d'Ethnologie, Nanterre.

Galanidou, N. 2003
Reassessing the Greek Mesolithic: the pertinence of the Markovits collections. In N. Galanidou, & C. Perlès (eds), *The Greek Mesolithic. Problems and perspectives,* British School at Athens, Athens, pp. 99-112. ("Studies 10").

Galanidou, N. 2011
Mesolithic cave use in Greece and the mosaic of human communities. *Journal of Mediterranean Archaeology* 24(2): 219-242.

Galanidou, N. & Tzedakis, P. C. 2001
New AMS dates from Upper Palaeolithic Kastritsa. *Proceedings of the Prehistoric Society* 67: 271-278.

Gili, C. & Martinell, J. 1999
Revisión del género *Cyclope* Risso, 1826 (Gastropoda: Nassariidae) en el Plioceno mediterráneo. *Revista española de paleontologia* 14(1): 147-156.

Gili, C. & Martinell, J. 2000
Phylogeny, speciation and species turnover. The case of the Mediterranean gastropods of the genus *Cyclope* Risso, 1826. *Lethaia* 33: 236-246.

Godelier, M. 1996
L'énigme du don, Fayard, Paris.

Gowlett, J. A. J., Hedges, R. E. M. & Housley, R. A. 1997
Klithi: the AMS radiocarbon dating programme for the site and environment. In G. N. Bailey, (ed.), *Klithi: Palaeolithic settlement and Quaternary landscapes in northwest Greece. Vol. 1: Excavations and intra-site analysis at Klithi,* McDonald Institute for Archaeological Research, Cambridge, pp. 27-40.

Guillomet-Malmassari, V. 2012
D'une révolution à l'autre. Pour une épistémologie de la problématique de transition en Préhistoire, Société préhistorique française, Paris ("Mémoire LIV").

Gutiérrez-Zugasti, I. 2011
Coastal resource intensification across the Pleistocene-Holocene transition in Northern Spain: evidence from shell size and age distribution of marine gastropods. *Quaternary International* 244: 54-66.

Hansen, J. M. 1991
The Palaeoethnobotany of Franchthi Cave, Excavations at Franchthi Cave, Greece, fasc. 7, Indiana University Press, Bloomington & Indianapolis.

Higgs, E. S., Vita-Finzi, C., Harris, D. R. & Fagg, A. E. 1967
The climate, environment and industries of Stone Age Greece, part III. *Proceedings of the Prehistoric Society* 33: 1-29.

Honea, K. 1975
Prehistoric remains on the island of Kythnos. *American Journal of Archaeology* 79: 277-279.

Hunt, C. O., Reynolds, T. G., El-Rishi, H. A., Buzaian, A., Hill, E. & Barker, G. W. 2011
Resource pressure and environmental change on the North African littoral: Epipalaeolithic to Roman gastropods from Cyrenaica, Lybia. *Quaternary International* 244: 15-26.

Inizan, M.-L. & Gaillard, J. M. 1978
Coquillages de Ksar-'Akil: éléments de parure ? *Paléorient* 4: 295-306.

Jacobsen, T. W. 1969
Excavations at Porto Cheli and vicinity, preliminary report, II: The Franchthi Cave. *Hesperia* 38: 343-381.

Jacobsen, T. W. & Farrand, W. R. 1987
Franchthi Cave and Paralia. maps, plans and sections. Excavations at Franchthi Cave, fasc. 1, Indiana University Press, Bloomington & Indianapolis.

Kaczanowska, M., Kozłowski, J. K. & Sobczyk, K. 2010
Upper Palaeolithic human occupations and material culture at Klissoura Cave 1. In J. K. Kozłowski and M. C. Stiner (eds), Klissoura Cave 1, Argolid, Greece: the Upper Palaeolithic sequence. *Eurasian Prehistory* 7(2): 133-285.

Karali, L. 2010
The seashells of Maroulas, Kythnos. In A. Sampson, M. Kaczanowska, J. Kozłowski, (eds), *The Prehistory of the island of Kythnos (Cyclades, Greece) and the Mesolithic settlement at Maroulas,* Polish Academy of Arts and Sciences, Kraków, pp. 147-149.

Karali, L. 2011
Malacological material. In A. Sampson, (ed.) *The Cave of the Cyclops. Mesolithic and Neolithic networks in the Northern Aegean, Greece,* Instap Academic Press, Philadelphia, pp. 267-287 ("Prehistory Monographs 31").

Katsanevakis, S., Lefkaditou, E., Galinou-Mitsoudi, S., Koutsoubas, D. & Zenetos, A. 2008
Molluscan species of minor commercial interest in hellenic seas: distribution, exploitation and conservation status. *Mediterranean Marine Science* 9/1: 77-118.

Klaric, L. 2007
Regional groups in the European Middle Gravettian: a reconsideration of the Rayssian technology. *Antiquity* 81: 176-190.

Komšo, D. & Vukosavljecić, N. 2011
Connecting coast and inland: perforated marine and freshwater snail shells in the Croatian Mesolithic. *Quaternary International* 244: 117-125.

Kotjabopoulou, E. & Adam, E. 2004
People, mobility and ornaments in Upper Palaeolithic Epirus, Greece. In M. Otte (ed.), *La spiritualité. U.I.S.P.P. - VIIIe Commission - Paléolithique supérieur*, Études et Recherches Archéologiques de l'Université de Liège (ERAUL), 106, pp. 37-53.

Kotjabopoulou, E., Panagopoulou, E. & Adam, E. 1997
The Boïla Rockshelter: further evidence of human activity in the Voïdomatis gorge. In G. N. Bailey *et al.* (eds), *The Palaeolithic archaeology of Greece and adjacent areas: Proceedings of the ICOPAG Conference, Ioannina, September 1994*, London, British School at Athens Studies 3, pp. 197-210.

Koukouras, A. & Kevrekidis, T. 1986
Benthic fauna of the North Aegean sea III. Dentaliidae (Mollusca: Scaphopoda). *Oebalia* XIII, N. S.: 185-194.

Koumouzelis, M. 2010
Introduction: history of the excavations. In J. K. Kozłowski and M. C. Stiner (eds), Klissoura Cave 1, Argolid, Greece: the Upper Palaeolithic sequence. *Eurasian Prehistory* 7(2): 5-14.

Kozłowski, J. K. 2004
Éléments stylistiques dans la culture matérielle et symbolique comme indicateurs de l'identité ethnique: l'exemple du complexe gravettien. In M. Otte (ed.) *La spiritualité. U.I.S.P.P. - VIIIe Commission - Paléolithique supérieur*, Études et Recherches Archéologiques de l'Université de Liège (ERAUL), 106, pp. 21-35.

Kozłowski, J. K. 2015
The origin of the Gravettian. *Quaternary International* 359-360: 3-18.

Kozłowski, J. K. & Stiner, M. C. (eds) 2010
Klissoura Cave 1, Argolid, Greece: the Upper Palaeolithic sequence. *Eurasian Prehistory* 7(2): 1-321.

Kuhn, S. L. 2014
Signaling theory and technologies of communication in the Palaeolithic. *Biological Theory* 9(1): 42-50.

Kuhn, S. L. & Stiner, M. C. 1998
The Earliest Aurignacian of Riparo Mochi (Liguria, Italy). *Current Anthropology* 39 (suppl. 3): 175-189.

Kuhn, S. L. & Stiner, M. C. 2006
Les parures au Paléolithique. Enjeux cognitifs, démographiques et identitaires. *Diogène* 214(2): 47-58.

Kuhn, S. L. & Stiner, M. C. 2007
Body ornamentation as information technology: towards an uderstanding of the significance of early beads. In P. Mellars, K. Boyle, O. Bar-Yosef & C. Stringer (eds), *Rethinking the Human revolution*, McDonald Institute for Archaeological Research, Cambridge, pp. 45-54.

Kuhn, S. L., Stiner, M. C., Reese, D. & Güleç, E. 2001
Ornaments of the earliest Upper Palaeolithic: new insights from the Levant. *PNAS* 98(13): 7641-7646.

Kuhn, S. L., Pigati, J., Karkanas, P., Koumouzelis, M., Kozłowski, J., Ntinou, M. & Stiner, M. C. 2010
Radiocarbon dating results for the Early Upper Palaeolithic of Klissoura Cave. In J. K. Kozłowski and M. Stiner (eds), Klissoura Cave 1: Argolid, Greece: the Upper Palaeolithic sequence. *Eurasian Prehistory* 7(2): 37-46.

Kurzawska, A., Bar-Yosef Mayer, D. & Mienis, H. K. 2013
Scaphopod shells in the Natufian culture. In O. Bar-Yosef & F. Valla (eds), *Natufian foragers in the Levant*, International Monographs in Prehistory, Archaeological Series 19, Ann Arbor, pp. 611-621.

Kyparissi-Apostolika, N. 2003
The Mesolithic in Theopetra Cave: new data on a debated period of Greek Prehistory. In N. Galanidou & C. Perlès (eds), *The Greek Mesolithic*, London, British School at Athens Studies, pp. 189-198 ("BSA series, n°10).

Lambeck, K. 1996
Sea-level change and shoreline evolution in Aegean Greece since Upper Palaeolithic time. *Antiquity* 70: 588-611.

Lange, K., Perlès, C. & Reiche, I. 2007
Untersuchungen geschwärzter Schmuckmuschelschalen aus der prähistorichen Ausgrabungsstätte Franchthi, Griechenland. In S. Klein & S. Laue (eds), *Archäeometrie und Denkmalpflege - Kuzberichte 2007, Postdam, 19-22 sept. 2007*, pp. 148-150 ISSN 0949-4957.

Lange, K., Perlès, C., Vanhaeren, M. & Reiche, I. 2008
Heat-induced modification of marine shells used as personal ornaments at the prehistoric site of Franchthi cave, Greece: First Results of a multianalytical approach. *9th International Conference on non-destructive investigations and microanalysis for the diagnostics and conservation of cultural and environmental heritage -art 2008, mai–juin 2008, Israël*, www.ndt.net/search/docs.php3?MainSource=65

Langlais, M. 2010
Les sociétés magdaléniennes de l'isthme pyrénéen, Éditions du CTHS, Paris.

Laporte, L. 1994
Parures et centres de production dans le Centre Ouest de la France au Néolithique final, Thèse de doctorat, Université Paris I.

Laporte, L. 2009
La parure. Introduction. In L. Laporte (dir.), *Des premiers paysans aux premiers métallurgistes sur la façade atlantique de la France (3500-2000 av. J.-C.)*, Association des publications chauvinoises, Chauvigny, pp. 449-453.

Lévi-Strauss, C. 1962
Le totémisme aujourd'hui, Presses Universitaires de France, Paris ("Mythes et religions").

Lindner, G. 2000
Guide des coquillages marins, Delachaux et Niestlé, Paris.

Malinowski, B. 1922
Argonauts of the Western Pacific: an account of native entreprise and adventure in the archipelagoes of Melanesia New Guinea, Routledge & Sons, London.

Marchand, G. 2014
   Préhistoire atlantique. Fonctionnement et évolution des sociétés du Paléolithique au Néolithique, Éditions Errance, Paris.

Marino, G., Rohling, E. J., Sangiorgi, F., Hayes, A., Casford, J. L., Lotter, A. F., Kucera, M. & Brinkhuis H., 2009
   Early and middle Holocene in the Aegean Sea: interplay between high and low latitude climate variability. *Quaternary Science Reviews* 28: 3246-3262.

Mars, P. 1966
   Recherches sur quelques étangs du littoral méditerranéen français et leurs faunes malacologiques. *Vie et milieu,* Suppl. 20: 1-359.

Marshall, L. 1998
   Sharing, talking and giving: relief of social tensions among the !Kung San and their neighbors. In R. B. Lee and I. de Vore (eds), *Kalahari hunter-gatherers: studies of the !Kung San and their Neighbors,* Harvard University Press, Cambridge, pp. 349-371.

Martini, F. (ed.) 1993
   Grotta della Serratura a Marina di Camerata. Garlatti & Razzai.

Martini, F. (ed.) 2007
   L'Italia tra 15.000 e 10.000 anni fa. Cosmopolitismo e regionalita nel Tardoglaciale. Museo Fiorentino di Preistoria "Paolo Graziosi", 262p. ("Milleni. Studi di Archeologia Preistorica" 5).

Miller, M. A . 1997
   Jewels of shell and stone, clay and bone: the production, function, and distribution of Aegean Stone Age ornaments, Ph. D. dissertation, Boston University, 2 vols.

Moreau, L. 2011
   La fin de l' Aurignacien et le début du Gravettien en Europe centrale: continuité ou rupture ? Étude comparative des ensembles lithiques de Breitenbach (Sachsen-An Halt, D) et Geissenklösterle (AH I) (Bade-Wurtemberg, D). *Notae Praehistoricae* 31: 21-290.

Morton, J. E. 1960
   The habits of *Cyclope neritea,* a style-bearing stenoglossan gastropod. The habits of Cyclope neritea, a style-bearing stenoglossan gastropod. *Proceedings of the Malacological Society of London* 34: 96-105.

Munro, N. D. & Stiner, M. C. 2015
   Zooarchaelogical evidence for Early Neolithic colonization at Franchthi Cave (Peloponnese, Greece). *Current Anthropology* 56(4): 596-603.

Munro, N. D. & Stiner, M. C., in prep.
   30,000 years of human foraging and farming at Franchthi Cave, Peloponnese, Greece, Excavations at Franchthi Cave, Indiana University Press, Bloomington & Indianapolis.

Newell, R. R., Kielman, D., Constandse-Westermann, T. S., van der Sanden, W. A. & van Gijn, A. 1990
   An inquiry into the ethnic resolution of Mesolithic regional groups, University of Leiden, Leiden.

Nicolaidou, A., Bourgoutzani, F., Zenetos, A., Guerloguet, O. & Perthuisot, J.-P. 1988
   Distribution of molluscs and polychaetes in coastal lagoons in Greece. *Estuarine, Coastal and Shelf Science* 26: 337-350.

O'Shea, J. & Zvelebil, M. 1984
   Oleneostrovski mogilnik: reconstructing the social and economic organization of prehistoric foragers in northern Russia. *Journal of Anthropological Archaeology* 3: 1-40.

Orton, J. 2008
   Later Stone Age ostrich eggshell bead manufacture in the Northern Cape, *South African Journal of Archaeological Science* 35: 1765-1775.

Palma di Cesnola, A. 1993
   Il Paleolitico superiore in Italia. Garlati e Razzai, Firenze.

Pauc, C. & Pauc, A. 2006
   Enfilage de coquilles de *Columbella rustica* et de *Trivia europea. euroREA* 3: 25-29.

Payne, S. 1975
   Faunal change at the Franchthi Cave from 20.000 B.C. to 3.000 B.C. In A.T. Clason (ed.), *Archaeozoological Studies,* Elsevier, The Hague, pp. 120-131.

Payne, S. 1982
   Faunal evidence for environmental/climatic change at Franchthi Cave, 25,000 B.P. to 5,000 B.P. In J. L. Bintliff & W. van Zeist (eds), *Palaeoclimates, palaeoenvironments and human communities in the Eastern Mediterranean region in later Prehistory,* British Archaeological Reports, S. 133, Oxford, pp. 133-136.

Payne, S. 1983
   Sieving at Franchthi: an outline reconstructed history. Ms on file, Bloomington, 13p.

Pelegrin, J. 1995
   Technologie lithique: le Châtelperronien de Roc-de-Combe (Lot) et de la Côte (Lot), CNRS Éditions, Paris («Cahiers du Quaternaire n°20»).

Pelegrin, J. 2005
   Remarks about archaeological techniques and methods of knapping: elements of a cognitive approach to stone knapping. In V. Roux & B. Bril (eds) *Stone knapping. The necessary conditions for a uniquely hominin behavior,* McDonald Institute Monographs, Cambridge, pp. 23-33.

Péquart, M. & Saint-Just Péquart, M. 1954
   *Hoëdic : deuxième station nécropole du m*ésolithique côtier armoricain, De Sikkel, Anvers.

Péquart, M., Saint-Just Péquart, M., Boule, M. & Vallois, H. 1937
   Téviec, station nécropole mésolithique du Morbihan, Archives de l'Institut de Paléontologie Humaine, Paris ("Mémoire 18").

Perlès, C. 1987
   Les industries lithiques taillées de Franchthi (Argolide, Grèce). Tome I: *Présentation générale et industries*

paléolithiques, Excavations at Franchthi Cave, fasc. 3, Indiana University Press, Bloomington & Indianapolis.

Perlès, C. 1990
Les industries lithiques taillées de Franchthi (Argolide, Grèce). Tome II: *Les industries du Mésolithique et du Néolithique initial,* Excavations at Franchthi Cave, fasc. 5, Indiana University Press, Bloomington & Indianapolis.

Perlès, C. 1999
Long-term perspective on the occupation of the Franchthi Cave: continuity and discontinuity. In G. N. Bailey *et al.* (eds) *The Palaeolithic archaeology of Greece and adjacent areas: Proceedings of the ICOPAG Conference, Ioannina, September 1994,* London, British School at Athens Studies 3, pp. 311-318.

Perlès, C. 2001
The Early Neolithic in Greece. The first farming communities in Europe, Cambridge University Press, Cambridge ("Cambridge World Archaeology").

Perlès, C. 2003
The Mesolithic at Franchthi: an overview of the data and problems. In N. Galanidou & C. Perlès (eds), *The Greek Mesolithic,* British School at Athens, pp. 79-89 ("BSA series, n°10).

Perlès, C. 2010
Is the Dryas the culprit? Socio-economic changes during the Final Pleistocene and Early Holocene at Franchthi Cave (Greece). *Journal of the Israel Prehistoric Society* 40: 113-129.

Perlès, C. 2013
Tempi of change: when soloists don't play together. Arrythmia in 'continuous' change. *Journal of Archaeological Method and Theory* 20(2): 281-299.

Perlès, C. 2016a
Food and ornaments: diachronic changes in the exploitation of littoral resources at Franchthi Cave (Greece) during the Upper Palaeolithic and the Mesolithic (39,000-7,000 cal BC). *Quaternary International* 407, part B: 45-58.

Perlès, C. 2016b
Early Holocene climatic fluctuations and human responses in Greece. In P. F. Biehl & O. Nieuwenhuise (eds), *Climate and cultural change in Prehistoric Europe and the Near East,* SUNY Press, New York, pp. 169-194 ("Distinguished Monograph Series of the Institute for European and Mediterranean Archaeology").

Perlès, C. & Vanhaeren, M. 2010
Black *Cyclope neritea* marine shell ornaments in the Upper Palaeolithic and Mesolithic of Franchthi (Argolid, Greece): arguments for an intentional heat treatment. *Journal of Field Archaeology* 35(3): 298-309.

Perlès, C., Quilès, A. & Valladas, H. 2013
Early 7th millennium AMS dates on domestic seeds for the Initial Neolithic at Franchthi Cave (Argolid, Greece). *Antiquity* 87: 1001-1015.

Pesesse, D. 2013
Les premières sociétés gravettiennes. Analyse comparée des systèmes techniques lithiques, Éditions du CTHS, Paris.

Pétrequin, A.-M. & Pétrequin, P. 2006
Objets de pouvoir en Nouvelle-Guinée. Approche ethnoarchéologique d'un système de signes sociaux, Réunion des Musées Nationaux, Paris.

Pettitt, P. B., Richards, M., Magi, R. & Formicola, V. 2003
The Gravettian burial known as the Prince ("Il Principe"): new evidence for his age and diet. *Antiquity* 77(295): 15-19.

Peyron, O., Goring, S., Dormoy, I., Kotthoff, U., Pross, J., de Beaulieu, J.-L., Drescher-Schneider, R., Vannière, B. & Magny, M. 2011
Holocene seasonality changes in the central Mediterranean region reconstructed from the pollen sequences of Lake Accesa (Italy) and Tenaghi Philippon (Greece). *The Holocene* 21(1): 131-146.

Pigeot, N. 2004
Le débitage laminaire et lamellaire: options techniques et finalités. In Pigeot, N. (dir.), *Les derniers magdaléniens d'Étiolles. Perspectives culturelles et paléohistoriques,* CNRS Éditions, Paris, pp. 65-105.

Poppe, G. T. & Goto, Y. 1993
European Seashells, Verlag Christa Hemmen, Wiesbaden, 2 vols.

Radovanović, I. 1996
The Iron Gates Mesolithic, International Monographs in Prehistory, Ann Arbor (Archaeological Series 11").

Rähle, W. 1978
Schmuckschnecken aus mesolitischen Kulturschichten Stiddeutschlands une ihre Herkunft (Probstfeld, Falkensteinhohle, Burghohle Dietfurt, Zigeunerfels, Große Ofnet). In W. Taute (ed.), *Das Mesolithikum in Suddeutschland Teil 2: Naturwissenchaftliche Untersuchungen,* Tubinger Monographien zur Urgeschichte, pp. 163-168.

Reese, D. 1983
The use of cone shells in the Neolithic and Bronze Age Greece. *Bulletin of the British School at Athens* 78: 353-357.

Reese, D. 1990
Review of: Shackleton, J. C., Marine Molluscan Remains from Franchthi Cave, Excavations at Franchthi Cave, fasc. 4, Indiana University Press, Bloomington & Indianapolis, 194p. *American Journal of Archaeology* 94(4): 682-683.

Reimer, P. J. *et al.* 2009
IntCal09 and Marine09 radiocarbon age calibration curves, 0-50,000 years cal. BP. *Radiocarbon* 51: 1111-1150

Reisch, L. 1980
Pleistozän und Urgeschichte der Peloponnes, Ph. D. Diss., Friedrich-Alexander Universität.

Rick, T. C. 2002
Eolian processes, ground cover, and the archaeology of coastal dunes: a taphonomic case study from San Miguel island, California, U.S.A. *Goearchaeology* 17 (8): 811-833.

Rigaud, S. 2011
La parure: traceur de la géographie culturelle et des dynamiques de peuplement au passage Mésolithique-Néolithique en Europe, Thèse de Doctorat, Université Bordeaux 1.

Rigaud, S. 2014
Pratiques ornementales des premières communautés agro-pastorales de Bavière: intégration? Acculturation? Convergence? Nouveaux apports de la nécropole de Essenbachh-Ammerbreite. *Anthropologie* L(2): 207-227.

Rigaud, S., Vanhaeren, M., Queffelec, A., Le Bourdon G. & d'Errico, F. 2014a
The way we wear makes the difference: residue analysis applied to Mesolithic personal ornaments from Hohlenstein-Stadel (Germany). *Archaeological and Anthropological Sciences* DOI 10.1007/s12520-013-0169.

Rigaud, S., d'Errico, F., Vanhaeren, M. & Peñalber, X. 2014b
A short-term, task-specific site: Epipaleolithic settlement patterns inferred from marine shells found at Praileaitz (Basque Country, Spain). *Journal of Archaeological Science* 41: 666-678.

Rigaud, S., d'Errico, F. & Vanhaeren, M. 2015
Ornaments reveal resistance of North European cultures to the spread of farming. *PLOS One* 10(4): e0121166. doi:10.1371/journal.pone.0121166.

Roberts, N., Brayshaw, D., Kuzucuoğlu, C., Perez, R. & Sadori, L. 2011
The mid-Holocene climatic transition in the Mediterranean: causes and consequences. *The Holocene* 21(1): 3-13.

Rose, M. in prep.
Franchthi fish remains. The Aegean and Mediterranean context. Excavations at Franchthi Cave, Indiana University Press, Bloomington & Indianapolis.

Runnels, C. N. 1995
Review of Aegean Prehistory IV: The Stone Age of Greece from the Palaeolithic to the advent of the Neolithic. *American Journal of Archaeology* 99: 699-728.

Runnels, C. N. 2003
The origins of the Greek Neolithic. A personal view. In A. J. Ammerman & P. Biagi, (eds), *The widening harvest: looking back, looking forward*, Archaeological Institute of America, Boston, pp. 121-132.

Sampson, A., Kaczanowska, M. & Kozłowski, J. 2010
The Prehistory of the island of Kythnos (Cyclades, Greece) and the Mesolithic settlement at Maroulas. Polish Academy of Arts and Sciences, Kraków.

Schaeffer, P. 1977
An attribute analysis and formal typology of the ornaments from Franchthi Cave, M.A. thesis, Department of Anthropology, Indiana University, Bloomington.

Schmiedl, G. Kuhnt, T., Ehrmann, W., Ameis, K.-C., Hamann, Y., Kotthof, U., Dulski, P. & Pross, J. 2010
Climatic forcing of eastern Mediterranean deep-water formation and benthic ecosystems during the past 22 000 years. *Quaternary Science Reviews* 29: 3006-3020.

Sciama, L. D. & Eicher, J. B. (eds) 1998
Beads and beadmakers: Gender, material culture and meaning, Berg, Oxford.

Shackleton, J. C. 1988
Marine molluscan remains from Franchthi Cave, Excavations at Franchthi Cave, fasc. 4, Indiana University Press, Bloomington & Indianapolis.

Shackleton, J. C. & van Andel, Tj. H. 1986
Prehistoric shore environments, shellfish availability, and shellfish gathering at Franchthi, Greece. *Geoarchaeology* 1(2): 127-143.

Shackleton, N. J. 1969
Appendix I: Preliminary observations on the marine shells. In T. W. Jacobsen, Excavations at Porto Cheli and vicinity, preliminary report, II: the Franchthi Cave, 1967-1968. *Hesperia* XXXVIII(3): 379-380.

Siddall, M., Rohling, E. J., Almogi-Labin, A., Hemleben, Ch., Meischner, D., Schmeizer, I. & Smeed, D. A. 2003
Sea-level fluctuations during the last glacial cycle. *Nature* 423: 853-858.

Simon-Bouhet, B. 2006
Expansion d'aire et processus d'introductions biologiques en milieu marin: le cas de Cyclope neritea *(Nassariidae) sur les côtes françaises*, Thèse de Doctorat, Université de la Rochelle.

Sivan, D., Potasman, M., Almogi-Labion, A., Bar-Yosef Mayer, D. E., Spanier, E. & Boaretto, E. 2006
The *Glycymeris* query along the coast and shallow shelf of Israel, southeast Mediterranean. *Palaeogeography, Palaeoclimatology, Palaeoecology* 233: 134-148.

Sordinas, A. 1969
Investigations of the prehistory of Corfu during 1964-1966. *Balkan Studies* 10(2): 393-424.

Southward, A. J., Southward, E. C., Dando, P. R., Hughes, J. A., Kennicutt, M. C., Alcala-Herrera, J. & Leahy, Y. 1997
Behaviour and feeding of the Nassariiid gastropod *Cyclope neritea*, abundant at hydrothermal brine seeps off Milos (Aegean Sea). *Journal of the marine biological association of the United Kingdom* 77 (3): 753-771.

Stiner, M. C. 1999
Palaeolithic mollusc exploitation at Riparo Mochi (Balzi Rossi, Italy): food and ornaments from the Aurignacien through Epigravettian. *Antiquity* 73: 735-754.

Stiner, M. C. 2003
"Standardization" in Upper Paleolithic ornaments at the coastal sites of Riparo Mochi and Üçaglizli Cave. In F. d'Errico & J. Zilhão (eds), *The chronology of the Aurignacian and of the transitional complexes. Dating, stratigraphies, cultural implications*, Trabalhos de Arqueologia 33, Lisbon, pp. 49-59.

Stiner, M. C. 2010
Shell ornaments from the Upper Palaeolithic through Mesolithic layers of Klissoura Cave 1 by Prosymna, Greece. In J. Kozłowski & M. Stiner (eds), Klissoura Cave 1: Argolid, Greece: the Upper Palaeolithic sequence. *Eurasian Prehistory* 7(2): 287-308.

Stiner, M. C. 2014
Finding a common bandwidth: causes of convergence and diversity in Palaeolithic beads. *Biological Theory* 9: 51-64.

Stiner, M. C., Kuhn, S. L. 2003
Early Upper Palaeolithic ornaments from Üçağızlı Cave, Turkey. *Beads* 15: 65-74.

Stiner, M. C. & Munro, N. D. 2011
On the evolution of diet and landscape during the Upper Palaeolithic through Mesolithic at Franchthi Cave (Peloponnese, Greece). *Journal of Human Evolution*, 60: 618-636.

Stiner, M. C., Kuhn, S. L.. & Güleç, E. 2013
Early Upper Paleolithic shell beads at Üçağızlı Cave I (Turkey): technology and the socio-economic context of ornaments life-histories. *Journal of Archaeological Science* 64: 380-398.

Stuiver, M. & Grootes, P. M. 2000
GISP2 Oxygen isotope ratios. *Quaternary Research* 53: 277-284.

Taborin, Y. 1974
La parure en coquillage de l'Epipaléolithique au Bronze ancien en France. *Gallia Préhistoire* 17(1): 101-179 and 17(2): 307-417.

Taborin, Y. 1993
La parure en coquillage au Paléolithique, CNRS Éditions, Paris.

Taborin, Y. 2003
La mer et les premiers hommes modernes. In B. Vandermeersch (dir.*), Échanges et diffusion dans la préhistoire méditerranéenne*, Éditions du CTHS, Paris, pp. 113-121.

Taborin, Y. 2004
Langage sans parole. La parure aux temps préhistoriques, La Maison des Roches, Paris.

Tardy, J., Gaillard, J. & Portères, G. 1985
Cyclope neritea (Linné, 1788), une espèce de gastéropode nassaridé nouvelle pour les côtes du centre-ouest Atlantique de France. *Annales de la Société des Sciences Naturelles de Charente-Maritime*, 7(3): 391-396.

Teske, P. R., Papadopoulos, I., McQuaid, C. D., Newman, B. K. & Barker, N. P. 2007
Climate change, genetics or human choice: Why were the shells of mankind's earliest ornaments larger in the Pleistocene than in the Holocene? *Plos One* 2(7), e614. doi:10.1371/journal.pone.0000614.

Thomas, K. D. 1987
Prehistoric coastal ecology: a view from outside Franchthi Cave, Greece. *Geoarchaeology* 2(3): 231-240.

Trubitt, M. B. D. 2003
The production and exchange of marine shell prestige goods. *Journal of Archaeological Research* 11(3): 243-277.

Turgeon, L. 2004
Beads, bodies and regimes of value: from France to North America. In T. Murray (ed.), *The archaeology of contact in settler societies*, Cambridge University Press, Cambridge.

Valentin, B. 2008
Jalons pour une paléohistoire des derniers chasseurs, Publications de la Sorbonne, Paris ("Cahiers Archéologiques de Paris 1, n°1").

Valentin, F., Cottiaux, R., Buquet-Marcon, C., Cofalioneri, J. Delattre, V., Lang, L., Le Goff, O., Lawrence-Dubovac, P. & Verjux, C. 2008
Découvertes récentes d'inhumations et d'incinérations datées du Mésolithique en Île-de-France, *Revue archéologique d'Île-de-France* 1: 21-42.

van Andel, Tj. H. 1987
Part I, The Landscape. In Tj. van Andel & S. B. Sutton, *Landscape and people of the Franchthi region*, Excavations at Franchthi Cave, Greece, fasc. 2, Indiana University Press, Bloomington & Indianapolis, pp. 3-62.

van Andel, Tj. 1990
Addendum to 'Late Quaternary sea-level changes and archaeology'. *Antiquity* 64(242): 151-152.

van Andel, Tj. & Lianos, N. 1983
Prehistoric and historic shorelines of the Southern Argolid Peninsula: a subbottom profile study. *The International Journal of Nautical Archaeology and Underwater Exploration* 12(4): 303-324.

van Andel, Tj. & Lianos, N. 1984
High-resolution seismic reflection profiles for the reconstruction of Postglacial transgressive shorelines: an example from Greece. *Quaternary Research* 22: 31-45.

Vanhaeren, M. 2005
Speaking with beads: the evolutionary significance of bead making and use. In F. d'Errico & L. Blackwell (eds), *From tools to symbols. From early Hominids to Modern Humans. International round table, Johannesburg 2003*, Johannesburg, Wits University Press, pp. 525-553.

Vanhaeren, M. 2010
Les fonctions de la parure au Paléolithique supérieur: de l'individu à l'unité culturelle, Éditions Universitaires Européennes, Sarrebrück.

Vanhaeren, M. & d'Errico, F. 2001
La parure de l'enfant de la Madeleine (fouilles Peyrony). Un nouveau regard sur l'enfance au Paléolithique supérieur. *Paléo* 13: 201-237.

Vanhaeren, M. & d'Errico, F. 2003
Le mobilier funéraire de la Dame de Saint-Germain-la-Rivière et l'origine paléolithique des inégalités sociales. *Paléo* 15: 195-238.

Vanhaeren, M. & d'Errico, F. 2005
  Grave goods from the Saint-Germain-la-Rivière burial: evidence for social inequality in the Upper Palaeolithic. *Journal of Anthropological Archaeology* 24: 117-134.

Vanhaeren, M. & d'Errico, F. 2006
  Aurignacian ethno-linguistic geography of Europe revealed by personal ornaments. *Journal of Archaeological Science* 33(8): 1105-1128.

Vanhaeren, M. & d'Errico, F. 2011
  L'émergence du corps paré. Objets corporels paléolithiques. *Civilisations* 59(2): 59-86.

Vanhaeren, M., d'Errico, F., Stringer C., James, S. L., Todd, J. A., & Mienis, H. K. 2006
  Middle Paleolithic shell beads in Israel and Algeria. *Science* 312: 1785-1787.

Vanhaeren, M., d'Errico, F., van Niekerk, K. L., Henshilwood, C. S. & Erasmus, M. E. 2013
  Thinking strings: additional evidence for personal ornament use in the Middle Stone Age at Blombos Cave, South Africa. *Journal of Human Evolution* 64: 500-517.

Verjux, C. 2007
  Les pratiques funéraires mésolithiques en Europe. Diversité dans l'espace et dans le temps. In L. Baray, A. Testard & P. Brun (dir.), *Pratiques funéraires et sociétés: nouvelles approches en archéologie et en anthropologie sociale. Actes du colloque interdisciplinaire de Sens (12-14 juin 2003)*, Éditions universitaires de Dijon, Dijon, pp. 15-35 ("Art, archéologie et patrimoine").

Vialou, D. 1981
  La parure. In N. Lambert (dir.), *La grotte préhistorique de Kitsos (Attique). Missions 1968-1978. Tome I: L'occupation néolithique. Les vestiges des temps paléolithiques, de l'antiquité et de l'histoire récente*, Éditions A.D.P.F. - École Française d'Athènes, Paris, pp. 391-419.

Walter, P. 2003
  Caractérisation des traces rouges et noires sur les coquillages perforés de Qafzeh. In B. Vandermeersch (dir.), *Échanges et diffusion dans la préhistoire méditerranéenne*, Éditions du CTSH, Paris, p. 122.

Whallon, R. 2006
  Social networks and information: non-"utilitarian" mobility among hunter-gatherers. *Journal of Anthropological Archaeology* 25: 259-270.

White, R. 1989
  Production complexity and standardization in Early Aurignacian bead and pendant manufacture: evolutionary implications. In P. Mellars & C. Stringer (eds), *The human revolution: behavioral and biological perspectives on the origins of modern humans,* Edinburgh University Press, Edinburgh, pp. 366-390.

White, R. 1993
  Technological and social dimensions of Aurignacian age body ornaments across Europe. In H. Knecht, A. Pike-Tay, A. & R. White (eds), *Before Lascaux: the complex record of early Upper Palaeolithic*, CRC Press, Boca Raton, Fla., pp. 277-299.

White, R. 1999
  Intégrer la complexité sociale et opérationnelle: la construction matérielle de l'identité à Sungir. In M. Julien, A. Averbough, D. Ramseyer, C. Bellier, D. Buisson, P. Cattelain, M. Patou-Mathis & N. Provenzano (dir.), *Préhistoire d'os. Recueil d'études sur l'industrie osseuse préhistorique offert à Henriette Camps-Fabrer*, Publications de l'Université de Provence, Aix-en-Provence, pp. 319-331.

White, R. 2004
  La parure en ivoire des hommes de Cro-Magnon. *Pour la Science* Dossier n°43, pp. 98-103.

White, R. 2007
  Systems of personal ornamentation in the Early Upper Palaeolithic: methodological challenges and new observations. In P. Mellars, K. Boyle, O. Bar-Yosef & Ch. Stringer (eds), *Rethinking the Human Revolution: new behavioral and biological perspectives on the origin and dispersal of Modern Humans,* McDonald Institute for Archaeological Research, Cambridge, pp. 287-302.

Whitney-Desautels, N. A. with contributions by W. Farrand, in prep.
  Franchthi Cave Riverine and Terrestrial Molluscs, Excavations at Franchthi Cave, Indiana University Press, Bloomington & Indianapolis.

Wiessner, P. 1982
  Risk, reciprocity and social influences on !Kung San economics. In E. Leacock & E. Lee (eds), *Politics and history in band societies*, Cambridge University Press, Cambridge, pp. 61-84.

Wiessner, P. 1984
  Considering the behavioral basis for style: a case study among the Kalahari San. *Journal of Anthropological Archaeology 3*: 190-234.

Zilhão, J. 2006
  Aurignacian, behavior, modern: issues of definition in the emergence of the European Upper Palaeolithic. In O. Bar-Yosef, O. & J. Zilhão (eds), *Towards a definition of the Aurignacian*, Instituto Portugues de Arqueologia, Lisbon, pp. 53-69.

Zilhão, J. 2007
  The emergence of ornaments and art: an archaeological perspective on the origins of "behavioral modernity". *Journal of Archaeological Research* 15: 1-54.

Zilhão, J. et al. 2010
  Symbolic use of marine shells and mineral pigments by Iberian Neandertals. *PNAS* 107(3): 1023-1028.

INDEX

This index is intended to aid the reader by providing access to themes, references and discussions in the text that are not readily apparent from the Table of Contents and the List of Figures. Consequently, the ornament types at Franchthi, their characteristics and the main topics of discussions are not indexed. For references by more than two authors, only the first author is indexed.